SECOND EDITION

Mr. Cheap's®
Washington D.C.

The Mr. Cheap's® Series:

Mr. Cheap's® Atlanta, 2nd Edition
Mr. Cheap's® Boston, 2nd Edition
Mr. Cheap's® Chicago, 2nd Edition
Mr. Cheap's® New York, 2nd Edition
Mr. Cheap's® San Francisco
Mr. Cheap's® Seattle
Mr. Cheap's® Washington D.C., 2nd Edition

SECOND EDITION

Mr. Cheap's®
Washington D.C.

Bargains, factory outlets,
deep discount stores, cheap
places to stay, cheap eats,
and cheap fun things to do

Corey Sandler
with Michael Lawrence

previous edition written by Mark Waldstein

Adams Media Corporation
Avon, Massachusetts

Published by
Adams Media Corporation
57 Littlefield Street, Avon, MA 02322 U.S.A.
www.adamsmedia.com

ISBN: 1-58062-693-9

Printed in Canada.

J I H G F E D C B A

This publication is designed to provide accurate and authoritative information with regard to the subject matter covered. It is sold with the understanding that the publisher is not engaged in rendering legal, accounting,
or other professional advice. If legal advice or other expert assistance is
required, the services of a competent professional person should be sought.
—From a *Declaration of Principles* jointly adopted
by a Committee of the American Bar Association
and a Committee of Publishers and Associations.

Many of the designations used by manufacturers and sellers to distinguish
their products are claimed as trademarks. Where those designations appear
in this book and Adams Media was aware of a trademark claim, the designations have been printed in initial capital letters.

This book is available at quantity discounts for bulk purchases.
For information, call 1-800-872-5627.

Contents

Entertainment / 151

Restaurants / 241

Lodging / 313

Index / 322

An Economical Introduction to the Wit and Wisdom of Mr. Cheap

L et's get something straight right at the top: Being cheap doesn't mean wearing rags, eating leftovers, and living in a cardboard box.

Instead, I prefer to think of being "cheap" as being very smart about how I spend my money. Put another way, my goal in life is to live a lot better than the next guy on the same annual income . . . or less.

Henry David Thoreau, who knew quite a lot about living well on less, put it well: "That man is the richest whose pleasures are the cheapest." I like to eat well, but pay a reasonable grocery bill. I love to travel almost as much as I love knowing that my family is paying thousands of dollars less than the folks in front and in back of me. We dress well, but spend less.

Writing these books is a natural extension of my interests. For the past dozen years or so, I've written the *Econoguide Travel Book* series, now published by the Globe Pequot Press. In those books I've helped hundreds of thousands of readers travel around the world in high style and at a reasonable price. Another one of my books, *Buy More Pay Less*, from Prentice Hall Direct, explains how to buy just about anything anywhere.

I've traveled to Washington D.C. dozens of times as a travel writer and a newspaper reporter. I've come to realize that many visitors and residents see the trees but not the forest in the District of Columbia; this city, and its surrounding suburbs, is one of the cultural and shopping capitals of the world because of the rich mix of government employees, politicians, diplomats, journalists, and students who come from every corner of the globe.

My gold medal relay shopping team, led by Michael Lawrence with co-captains Janice Keefe and Maureen Moriarty; and long-distance runners Carol J. Bryant, Matt Zorivitch, Art Murray, and Barbara Parker, joined me in walking the streets of Washington D.C., working the telephones, and trawling the Internet in search of tens of thousands of deals and details. We built our book on the foundation laid by the original Mr. Cheap, Mark Waldstein, and his team.

We're proud of what we've uncovered, but it is important to issue a few important user's advisories: Things change: Stores close, or move, or change their philosophy. Prices go up and down and menus can be transformed overnight.

Consider the write-ups of stores, restaurants, hotels, and attractions in this book as guideposts. When we discuss a specific product, it's to give you an idea of the type of item we found on the shelves when we did our research; you may or may not find the same thing when you visit.

Make a phone call or check out a Web site when listed in the book before you make a major expedition to one of the places we write about. Tell them you read about their business in *Mr. Cheap's Washington D.C.*, and please tell us how they treat you and about your shopping experience. We'll share your comments the next time we gather in these pages.

To contact Mr. Cheap, write to:

Econoguide
P.O. Box 2779
Nantucket, MA 02584

Please enclose a stamped, self-addressed envelope if you'd like a response.

You can also send us e-mail, at info@econoguide.com

Now go forth and shop.

Shopping

You can buy it new. You can buy it used. You can buy it imperfect. And you can buy it marked down. But please, don't buy it for full price. You wouldn't want to disappoint Mr. Cheap, would you?

The hundreds of stores in this section are all places that will save you money in one way or another. They cover a broad spectrum of discount shopping, from the latest designer clothing to thrift shops, new furniture and used, major brands and second-rate imitations.

Think of the listings in this chapter as a roadmap for shopping, not as a catalog.

The prices quoted are based upon items Mr. C found at the time of his research. You shouldn't expect to find the same items, at the same prices, when you shop; these are just examples of sales philosophies and strategies. Even though prices and products change over time, this book will help you chart your course.

Many stores that sell several kinds of merchandise have been cross-referenced for you, appearing in each appropriate chapter; but remember to consult "Discount Department Stores" and "Flea Markets and Emporia" for many of the same items which have their own chapters. Similarly, the "General Markets" portion of the "Food Shops" chapter gives you more places to look for individual kinds of foods.

Okay, enough talking—go to it!

APPLIANCES

There are lots of places to save money on appliances and electronics in Washington, D.C. Some, unfortunately, are as far below repute as they are below retail. When it comes to high tech, including cameras, camcorders, and computers, be especially careful to understand the difference between authorized products and those on the gray market or the black market.

An authorized product comes with a warranty and repair policy from an importer in the United States (or Canada, or wherever you reside). Read the warranty and be sure it is of value to you.

A gray market product is a device that has been imported by someone other than an authorized reseller. The product *may* be the same as the device sold by the authorized importer, or it may have some different features; watch out for devices that are not set up to work with electrical voltage or television standards in your home. If there is a warranty at all, it may require you to ship the product to another country, which may not be a realistic option.

Another form of gray market involves something that used to be called "railroad salvage." These are devices that were scratched, dented, or otherwise damaged in shipping. The importer may allow them to be resold but without a warranty.

A black market product is either a device not meant to be sold in this country, or not meant to be sold to consumers. It may also be something that "fell off the back of the truck," which is a somewhat-nice version of "this is stolen property."

Should you buy a gray market device if it is sold at a tremendous savings? Maybe. I would never recommend buying an expensive device (more than $500, let's say) that doesn't come without a real guarantee of a reasonable service life. But if we're talking about inexpensive devices, it may be a worthwhile gamble. Just be sure to inform yourself about all of the details before you make a purchase.

Remember, you are perfectly within your rights to inquire about the warranty and to explore the provenance of any product in a store before you make a purchase.

Appliance Distributors, Inc.

- 7406-A Lockport Place, Lorton, VA; ✎ (703) 550-8585, ✎ (800) 841-0271

- 300 D Street S.W., Washington, D.C. 20024; ✎ (800) 841-0271, ✎ (202) 488-1000.

- 364 Victory Drive, Herndon, VA 20170; ✎ (703) 787-8400 Fax ✎ (703) 787-8452.

- ✐ www.abdappliancedistrib.com

This distributor's large selection of brands and models, combined with very competitive prices and great customer service, makes it a Cheap-certified one-stop source for all of your appliance needs.

Prices here tend to run 5 to 7 percent below retail. For example, you can buy an ASKO dryer for $748, compared with $849 retail, or an Amana washing machine for $425, compared with $549 retail. Extended warranties are available on all appliances for $99, and ABD provides installation and service for everything it sells for a modest fee.

Owned by Bill Deterline, who has been in the appliance business for more than two decades. ABD has been an NARI (National Area Remodeling Industry) member since its founding, as well as a member of NKBA (National Kitchen & Bath Association).

When you shop here, you'll find the ABD staff competent and, just as important, not pushy. These folks are salaried, not commissioned, which means that you'll get honest, balanced advice on the more than over 70 manufactures the store carries.

Showroom hours are Monday through Thursday from 8 a.m. to 6 p.m., Friday from 8 a.m. to 5 p.m., Saturday from 9 a.m. to 4 p.m., and Sunday from 11 a.m. to 4 p.m. The D.C. store is open Monday through Friday from 9 a.m. to 5 p.m., and Saturday from 10 a.m. to 3 p.m.

Allstate Refrigeration

- 8111 Piney Branch Road, Silver Spring, MD; ✆ (301) 589-0555; ✆ (301) 589-8056

Allstate Refrigeration is a family business that has been selling new and reconditioned major appliances since 1984. There is a large selection; at any given time, you're likely to find a couple dozen each of refrigerators, gas and electric stoves, washers, and dryers. All repairs are done on the premises

Prices vary depending on the model, features, age, and condition of the appliance. Washer-and-dryer sets begin as low as $350 for the pair (compared with $300 just for a washing machine in a regular retail store) and include such brands as GE, Kenmore, and Whirlpool. Refrigerators begin at a cheap $100. The store also boasts a scratch-and-dent department displaying both new and used appliances at discounted prices.

Reconditioned units carry a 90-day, money-back warranty. Delivery and hook-up are available for a small fee, and Allstate also offers repair services at the customer's site.

Store hours are from 9 a.m. to 6 p.m. Monday through Saturday, and from 11 a.m. to 4 p.m. on Sunday.

Best Buy

- 1201 South Hayes Street, Arlington, VA; ✆ (703) 414-7090

- 6201 Arlington Boulevard, Falls Church, VA; ✆ (703) 538-1190

- 6555 Frontier Drive, Springfield, VA; ✆ (703) 922-4980

- 1200 Rockville Pike, Rockville, MD; ✆ (301) 984-1479

- 14160 Baltimore Avenue, Laurel, MD; ✆ (301) 497-1890

- 15750 Shady Grove Road, Gaithersburg, MD; ✆ (301) 990-8839

- 1861 Fountain Drive, Reston, VA; ✆ (703) 787-3760

- 13058 Fair Lakes Parkway, Fairfax, VA; ✆ (703) 631-3332

- 9031 Snowden River Parkway, Columbia, MD; ✆ (410) 312-4900

And other suburban locations

- ✍ www.bestbuy.com

The Cheapster thought Best Buy was just for home electronics and tech gear until the day he got lost searching for the store's men's room and stumbled into the appliance section. And what a section it was! The gleaming high-tech ambiance of the rest of the store carries over here, where major brands of refrigerators, dishwashers, washer-dryers, ranges, and other home essentials are displayed three deep and available for great prices. Frigidaire, Maytag, and Kenmore are all here, and they're always "on sale." Mr. C spotted a side-by-side refrigerator for $999, a built-in dishwasher for $189.50, an upright freezer for $279, an electric range for $299, and an electric dryer for $269.

Best Buy also offers no-interest financing, so there's a way to save even more money!

Best Buy is generally open Monday through Saturday from 10 a.m. to 9 p.m., and Sunday from 11 a.m. to 6 p.m.

Bray & Scarff

- 5601-D Gen. Washington Drive, Alexandria, VA, ✆ (703) 941-7320.

- ✍ www.brayandscarff. homeappliances.com

For over 60 years, Bray & Scarff—currently located in an industrial park near the junction of Routes 395 and 495—has specialized in everything for the kitchen. They sell brand-new, first-quality appliances by Maytag, Amana, Whirlpool, JennAir, and many other top brands, all at very competitive prices. In fact, 60 is also the number of days for which they offer price protection on most models; if you see the same item somewhere else for less, they'll refund you the difference. That's longer than most department stores give you, if they do at all.

Ah, but there's something Mr. C likes even better here. The back room is filled with "scratch 'n dent" appliances, floor models, and assorted closeouts. Here, you may save $300 on a large Maytag refrigerator/freezer, replete with all the latest in-door gizmos. Or, perhaps you'll happen across a Tappan gas range, reduced from its original B & S price of $630 to a final price of $550. Not to mention air conditioners, dishwashers, and just about every kind of appliance you can wave an electrical cord at.

Generally speaking, the damages, if any, are purely cosmetic. If you're going to stick a washer and dryer into your nice, dark basement anyway, you'll never know the difference. And in a month or so, even a perfect model will look all beat up after you've put the family wash through it a few dozen times. In any case, all of these closeouts do carry the full manufacturer's warranties. C'mon, fellow Cheapsters, isn't a little "ding" worth a hundred bucks off?

Needless to say, clearance models do not get the 60-day price protection, but you're unlikely to find better deals anyway. Bray & Scarff also does cabinetry and installations, as well as its own factory-authorized repairs.

Store hours are Monday through Saturday from 9 a.m. to 8 p.m., and Sundays from noon to 6 p.m.

Brother's Sew & Vac Centers

• 3317 Connecticut Avenue N.W., Washington, D.C.; ℡ (202) 686-9500

• 4912 Hampden Lane., Bethesda, MD; ℡ (301) 657-8227

• 878 Muddy Branch Square, Gaithersburg, MD; ℡ (301) 977-1100

• 5268 Nicholson Lane, Rockville, MD; ℡ (301) 881-3470

• 10153 New Hampshire Avenue, Silver Spring, MD; ℡ (301) 445-5505

Founded in 1956, this family-run chain (not related to the sewing machine maker of the same name) sells new and used Brothers and other sewing machines along with vacuum cleaners by Miele and Venta, and a host of lesser-known brands. The stores also serve as a repair center.

The selection of new machinery is limited; the prices, however, are significantly discounted. You can buy top-grade, last-you-a-lifetime models that retail elsewhere for three times as much. Miele Hepa Vacs go for $549, with a free Hepa filter valued at $69.95 thrown in. The centers also take trade-ins, which can certainly save you some money from list.

Better yet, you can buy someone else's used model, and get a

vacuum cleaner, well . . . dirt-cheap. Used machines have been refurbished in the store, and carry a one-year warranty. Of course, if you just want to keep your old baby rolling, Brother's has tons of hard-to-find parts.

All stores are open Monday through Saturday from 9:30 a.m. to 6 p.m.

Sears

• 6211 Leesburg Pike, Falls Church, VA; ℡ (703) 237-4293

• 5901 Duke Street, Alexandria, VA ℡ (703) 914-2229

• 6001 Duke Street, Alexandria, VA ℡ (703) 914-2358

• 7702 Marlboro Pike, Forestville, MD; ℡ (301) 420-2830

• 2101 Brightseat Road, Landover, MD; ℡ (301) 322-6200

• 11255 New Hampshire Avenue, Silver Spring, MD; ℡ (301) 681-1700

• 9513 Key West Avenue, Rockville, MD ℡ (301) 417-9550

• 15528 Annapolis Road, Bowie, MD; ℡ (301) 805-2055

• 9513 Key West Avenue, Rockville, MD; ℡ (301) 417-9550

• 109 Main Street, Laurel, MD; ℡ (301) 816-6050

• 11781 Lee Jackson Highway, Fairfax, VA; ℡ (703) 385-2240

• ✐ www.sears.com

Sears has appliances? You don't say!! Well, this may be stating the obvious, but no self-respecting Cheapster could shop for washers, dryers, refrigerators, lawnmowers, and other homeowner necessities without at least taking a gander at that icon of American retail history!

Sears used to carry only the "house" labels, Kenmore and Craftsman, but they now offer many of the leading brands.

Many of the best prices are still found under the Kenmore label: On a recent visit Mr. C spotted a built-in dishwasher for just $188, a top-load washer for $277, a food disposer for a measly $39.99, a self-cleaning range and oven for $359, and a canister vacuum cleaner for $179. Craftsman lawn mowers could be had for about $220, while gas grills started at $149.

Mr. C has gotten into Cajun cooking (his specialty is blackened toast), and maybe you have too. If that's the case, you should know that Sears is offering those charcoal smokers for as little as $39.99!

Store hours can vary by location and season, but you'll usually find Sears open Monday through Saturday from 10 a.m. to 9 p.m., and Sunday from noon to 6 p.m.

Universal Appliance Recycling

- 8500 Ardwick Ardmore Road, Landover, MD; ✆ (301) 773-3400

- ✐ www.universalappliance.com

Universal Appliance Recycling, Inc., which has been in business for 50 years, sells quality-reconditioned appliances at a fraction of the cost of new ones. Here you can find reconditioned appliances for as low as $89. To add icing to that cake, you get a special 90-day warranty with every appliance purchased. The company prides itself on using environmentally sound appliance recycling practices; for example, it will pick up your used appliance when delivering your new purchase and dispose of it in environmentally safe disposal sites.

Store hours are 8 a.m. to 5 p.m. Monday through Friday, and 10 a.m. to 4 p.m. Saturday.

BOOKS

You can save extra money by shopping for used books. The D.C. area is blessed with enough stores for used books to give the hungriest bookworm indigestion; several are mixed into the listings below. Save even more by bringing in books that you no longer want. Most stores will give you a choice of cash or in-store credit; you'll usually get a higher figure by choosing the credit. It's a good, cheap way to check out new authors, and a way to clear out the deadwood from your personal library. Be sure to maintain your lifetime collection of Mr. Cheap's books, though; they're priceless.

Barnes & Noble Booksellers

- 555 12th Street N.W., Washington, D.C.; ✆ (202) 347-0176

- 3040 M Street N.W., Washington, D.C.; ✆ (202) 965-9880

- 3651 Jefferson Davis Highway, Alexandria, VA; ✆ (703) 299-9124

- 4801 Bethesda Avenue, Bethesda, MD; ✆ (301) 986-1761

- 6260 Arlington Boulevard, Falls Church, VA; ✆ (703) 536-0774

- 4720 Boston Way, Lanham Seabrook, MD; ✆ (301) 306-0400

- 6646 Loisdale Road, Springfield, VA; ✆ (703) 971-5383

- 12089 Rockville Pike, Rockville, MD; ✆ (301) 881-0237

- 21 Grand Corner Avenue, Gaithersburg, MD; ✆ (301) 721-0860

- 1851 Fountain Drive, Reston, VA; ✆ (703) 437-9490

- 2193 Fair Lakes Promenade Drive, Fairfax, VA; ✆ (703) 278-0300

- ✍ www.bn.com

Mr. C may not, uh, look the part, but he is somewhat of a bookworm. That said, he firmly believes that despite all of the wonderful charms of independent bookshops, sometime you just can't beat a national chain for great buys *and* selection. Hey, they have cozy lounge chairs for on-the-spot reading (and Mr. C admits, napping), poetry readings, story times for children, author and book signings, creative writing workshops, book groups tailored to individual perspectives (African American, gay/lesbian, and others). Books on the *New York Times* bestseller list are sold at 30 to 40 percent off the cover price. And some stores even have cafes or an adjacent Starbucks.

All in all, B&N provides a relaxed and refined setting. You can make it an evening out, especially if there is a music event. Some stores have their events listed on the B&N Web site, and of course you can always call for schedules.

You can join Barnes & Noble Readers' Advantage for $25 a year; it offers members a 10 percent discount on everything in-store and a 5 percent discount on merchandise purchased online (✍ www.bn.com) and that's on top of already discounted prices. It may seem paradoxical to pay to save money, but if you're an avid reader, you'll more than make up for your investment once you spend more than $250 in the store or $500 on the Web. Did someone say something about sharing a card among several buyers? Thought you did; sounds like a fine idea to the Cheaperoonie.

Special ordering at B&N is a breeze, and B&N's own publishing house offers classic hardcovers in easily readable print at super savings. Their edition of Thoreau's *Walden*, for example, is only $4.98; same deal for titles like *Jane Eyre*, and many other great works of literature. And any art lover will appreciate B&N's *The History of Art*, an oversized, glossy edition bargain-priced at $24.98.

B&N also usually has a bargain section where you can get more super deals than in most other bookstores in town. The Cheapster recently picked up some new hardcovers at great prices: Stephen King's *The Girl Who Loved Tom Gordon* was only $5.98; Anne Rice's *The Vampire Armand* was just $7.99, and Michael Crichton's *Timeline* was tagged at $7.99. P.J. O'Rourke's *Eat the Rich* was on sale for an amazing $4.98, and Deepak Chopra's *The Wisdom Within* was priced at a cheap $6.98.

Store hours are generally Monday through Saturday 9 a.m. to 11 p.m., and Sundays 9 a.m. to 9 p.m.

B. Dalton Booksellers

- 1331 Pennsylvania Avenue, N.W., Washington, D.C.; ✆ (202) 289-1750

- 50 Massachusetts Avenue, N.E., Washington, D.C.; ✆ (202) 289-1724

- 1671 Crystal Square Arc Arlington, VA; ✆ (703) 413-0558

- 2117 Crystal Plaza Arc
  Arlington, VA;
  ✆ (703) 415-0333

- 4238 Wilson Boulevard,
  Arlington, VA;
  ✆ (703) 522-8822

- 5345 Wisconsin Avenue, N.W.,
  Washington, D.C.;
  ✆ (202) 686-6542

- 3500 E West Highway,
  Hyattsville, MD;
  ✆ (301) 559-9779

- 7101 Democracy Boulevard,
  Bethesda, MD;
  ✆ (301) 365-6209

- 7932 Tysons Corner Center,
  McLean, VA;
  ✆ (703) 821-5706

- 6712 Franconia Road, Springfield, VA; ✆ (703) 971-7010

- 14764 Baltimore Avenue,
  Laurel, MD; ✆ (301) 490-7400

- 10300 Little Patuxent Parkway,
  Columbia, MD;
  ✆ (410) 997-7744

And other suburban locations

B. Dalton is now part of the Barnes
& Noble company, basically
offering a reduced inventory in
shops that are mostly located in
malls. Each mall location store tai-
lors their stock to fit their customers' needs. However, you get
the same discounts here as you do
at the Barnes & Noble superstores

Be sure to check out the bargain
table. Among the remainders and
closeouts scoped out by El
Cheaperio is the *Rodale Illustrated
Encyclopedia*, brought to you by
the people who publish *Prevention*
magazine, at the reduced price of
just $14.98. He also spotted *The
American Heritage Picture History
of World War II* for $19.99.

Store hours at B. Dalton generally coincide with those of the

malls, which tend to be 10 a.m. to
9 p.m. Monday through Saturday,
and noon to 6 p.m. on Sunday.
However, hours may vary
according to location, and hours are
usually extended later during the
holiday shopping season in
November and December.

The Book Alcove

- 15976 Shady Grove Road
  Gaithersburg, MD;
  ✆ (301) 977-9166

- ✐ www.bookalcove.com

Need a book? Need an alcove?
This store can provide you with
both. It's not only a great source
for secondhand books and magazines, but this family-run operation
also makes bookcases and shelves
to order, in all shapes and sizes.

Mr. C found a dizzying array of
secondhand tomes (the owners say
they have over 250,000 titles!) of
every shape, size, and value,
including signed first editions, rare
books, and limited editions. It's
almost like a small library. Find
subjects as big as art, religion, and
self-help; or as narrow as "Corporation Biography," "Dolls," and
"UFOs." They also carry children's titles, and old magazines
(mostly *Life* and *National
Geographic*).

One portion of the store displays
a sampling of pre-designed or
made-to-order bookcases constructed using solid woods like pine
and oak, stained or unfinished, at
prices starting as low as about $90
for a five-foot-tall bookcase.
They're manufactured in a factory
right in the store, where you can
watch them being made.

The Book Alcove is open
Monday through Friday from
10 a.m. to 8 p.m., Saturday from
10 a.m. to 7 p.m., and Sunday
from noon to 6 p.m.

Borders Books & Music

- 600 14th Street N.W., Washington, D.C.; ✆ (202) 737-1385

- 1800 L Street N.W., Washington, D.C.; ✆ (202) 466-4999

- 1201 S Hayes Street, Arlington, VA; ✆ (703) 418-0166

- 5333 Wisconsin Avenue N.W., Washington, D.C.; ✆ (202) 686-8270

- 5871 Crossroads Center Way Falls Church, VA; ✆ (703) 998-0404

- 11301 Rockville Pike Kensington, MD; ✆ (301) 816-1067

- 8230 Old Courthouse Road, Vienna, VA; ✆ (703) 827-4128

- 8311 Leesburg Pike, Vienna, VA; ✆ (703) 556-7766

- 6701 Frontier Drive, Springfield, VA; ✆ (703) 924-4894

- 11054 Lee Highway, Fairfax, VA; ✆ (703) 359-8420

- 4420 Mitchellville Road, Bowie, MD; ✆ (301) 352-5560

- 534 N Frederick Avenue, Gaithersburg, MD; ✆ (301) 921-0990

- 3304 Crain Highway, Waldorf, MD; ✆ (301) 705-6672

- 2904 Prince William Parkway, Woodbridge, VA; ✆ (703) 897-8100

- 21031 Tripleseven Road, Sterling, VA; ✆ (703) 430-4675

- 6151 Columbia Crossing Circle, Columbia, MD; ✆ (410) 290-0062

- 20926 Frederick Road, Germantown, MD; ✆ (301) 528-0862

And other suburban locations

- ✍ www.borders.com

Another major book chain that needs no introduction, Borders regularly offers sales on hundreds of the typical 80,000-plus titles on hand at each location, ranging from poetry to medieval history to "Esoteric Studies." They also offer a large selection of music CDs, videos, kids books, author events, and an extensive collection of foreign language magazines and out-of-town newspapers. (Just for the record: The Borders Group is the parent company of Waldenbooks.)

There are plenty of deals to be had here, including 30 percent off the current bestseller list, all the time. In addition to that nice little perk, your head will spin from the other specials, which rotate from day to day. The last time Mr. C strolled into the store, selected recently published computer books were marked down 30 percent, and a large selection of music CDs were available for just $8.99. VHS movies were offered at 50 percent off with the purchase of two others at regular prices, and they were offering a "three for two" sale on Dr. Seuss titles.

While you're almost always guaranteed good savings at Borders, the bargain books section is definitely a bonus. On a recent visit, pictorials on Claude Monet and Frank Lloyd Wright were available in the $4 to $9 range; historical picture books from *Life* magazine were priced at $5.99; and beautiful hardcover cookbooks that sold for about $50 when first published were priced $5 to $7. A Wayne Gretzky biography was only $4, and a number of formerly bestselling hardcover novels could be had for $5 each. Lots of children's titles were priced at $2 to $5.

And speaking of kids, Borders has plenty of additional deals for them, such as $5 off the next purchase after buying 10 children's

books. Also, remember that Borders' in-store events, which
include author readings and book
signings, cater to the younger set
as well: Children's book characters, such as Barney the Dinosaur,
Peter Rabbit, and even Harry
Potter, make occasional appearances for book readings.

Borders has a number of membership programs that can save you
even more money: All teachers can
get 20 percent off any book, and
corporate accounts can get big discounts on bulk purchases.

Most Borders locations are open
Monday through Saturday from 9
a.m. to 11 p.m., and Sunday from 9
a.m. until 10 p.m., though specific
store hours may vary.

Idle Time Books

- 2410 18th Street. N.W., Washington, D.C.; ✆ (202) 232-4774

You certainly won't be wasting
your time here. Located in a three-
floor Adams Morgan townhouse,
Idle Time's labyrinth of tiny rooms
is just loaded with used books, representing nearly every category
under the sun (and even beyond the
sun, in the vast sci-fi section).
You'll also find stacks of *Life* magazines from the '40s and '50s.

Most books sell for about half
the cover price (with a $2 min-
imum), but Mr. C even saw many
hardcovers priced as low as $1.50.

The first floor carries a lot of
newer titles, photography and children's books. One flight up you'll
find fiction and poetry, while the
third floor holds the nonfiction
stuff, including self-help, biography, history, cooking, gardening,
and much more.

In the unusually large (for a
used bookstore) children/young
adult's section, Mr. C found a copy
of William H. Armstrong's *Sounder*
for $1.25. Among the novels

detected in the mystery section
were several Agatha Christie who-
dunits from $1.50 each. Wander
upstairs to the humor room where
you can peruse Doonesbury and
Bloom County favorites. And no
sports buff's library would be complete without the comprehensive
Book of Duckpin Bowling for $3

Doors are open every day
between 11 a.m. and 10 p.m., and
Saturday until midnight.

Olsson's

- 1200 F Street N.W., Washington, D.C.; ✆ (202) 393-1853

- 418 Seventh Street N.W., Washington, D.C.; ✆ (202) 638-7613

- 1239 Wisconsin Avenue
  N.W., Washington, D.C.;
  ✆ (202) 338-6712

- 1307 19th Street N.W., Washington, D.C.; ✆ (202) 785-2662

- 7647 Old Georgetown
  Road, Bethesda, MD;
  ✆ (301) 652-6399

- 106 South Union Street, Alexandria, VA; ✆ (703) 684-0030

- Reagan Washington National
  Airport, Arlington, VA;
  ✆ (703) 417-1087

- 1735 North Lynn Street,
  Arlington, VA;
  ✆ (703) 812-2103

- 2111 Wilson Boulevard,
  Arlington, VA; Books:
  ✆ (703) 525-3507

- 106 South Union Street, Alexandria, VA; ✆ (703) 684-0030

- ⌖ www.olssons.com

Yes, you can find bargains at this
full-price book and music emporium. The day Mr. C visited, their
top bestsellers were on sale for 20
percent off, and Olsson's frequently
offers its own 20 percent discounts

on all books within a particular category. *Washington Post* bestsellers are always 25 percent off, as are Olsson's "Buyer's Choice" titles. For even bigger savings, remainders we discounted up to 80 percent. You can also get an Olsson's customer card that lets you earn a $5 store certificate for every $100 spent up to $200, and then a $10 certificate for each additional $100 spent.

The music deals work similarly: Recent top sellers, distributor specials, and specific selections are discounted. When Mr. C stopped in, all music on the Decca label was marked down 15 percent, as were soundtracks. New releases were also significantly reduced.

Hours vary, but all Olsson's are open seven days, generally from 8 a.m. to 7 p.m. Monday through Friday, and noon to 6 p.m. on Sunday.

Second Story Books

- 2000 P Street N.W., Washington, D.C.; ✆ (202) 659-8884

- 4836 Bethesda Avenue, Bethesda, MD; ✆ (301) 656-0170

- 12160 Parklawn Drive, Rockville, MD; ✆ (301) 770-0477

- ✍ www.secondstorybooks.com

For sheer size, Second Story's Rockville warehouse looks like a competitor to the Library of Congress. Hundreds of thousands of books are sold here at half their original prices and less—coming from individual trade-ins, estate sales, and other dealers around the country.

The downtown and Bethesda stores stock decent selections of newer titles, along with reviewers' copies and recent remainders, but Mr. C thinks the warehouse is the real find for bookworms. Here,

---

MR. CHEAP'S PICKS

Books

The Book Alcove—Here, they'll not only sell you the books, they'll sell you a bookcase to keep 'em in. Great prices on both.

Idle Time—You'll have a fine time meandering through this shop's three floors, picking up bargains along the way.

Vertigo—Savings of 10 to 30 percent on new hardcovers, plus really low prices on remainders.

---

tons and tons of older titles—in every subject you've ever heard of, and many you haven't—sell for a couple of bucks apiece. Many hardbacks, already reduced from their cover prices, are sold for half of the marked amount.

Not to mention similarly vast selections of CDs, records, tapes, posters, and prints. Hey, ya just gotta see it!

Second Story opens every day of the week at 10 a.m. The downtown and Bethesda stores close at 10 p.m., while the Rockville store closes at 8 p.m.

Vertigo Books

- 7346 Baltimore Avenue, College Park, MD; ✆ (301) 779-9300

The savings at Vertigo are enough to make Mr. C's head spin. The place is not as large as those huge bookstore chains, but it has all the super-size discounts. The staff is friendly and, better still, visible.

Store hours are Monday through Friday 10 a.m. to 8 p.m., Saturday 10 a.m. to 7 p.m., and Sunday from noon to 5 p.m.

Waldenbooks

• Washington National Airport, Washington, D.C.; ✆ (703) 416-2716

• 3222 M Street N.W., Washington, D.C.; ✆ (202) 333-8033

• 5801 Duke Street, Alexandria, VA; ✆ (703) 658-9576

• 3325 Donnell Drive, Forestville, MD; ✆ (301) 568-6911

• 2223 Brightseat Road, Landover, MD; ✆ (301) 322-9220

• 11160 Veirs Mill Road, Wheaton, MD; ✆ (301) 946-0202

• 7101 Democracy Boulevard, Bethesda, MD; ✆ (301) 469-8810

• 2001 International Drive, McLean, VA; ✆ (703) 893-2849

• 6701 Loisdale Road, Springfield, VA; ✆ (703) 971-9443

• 11781 Lee Jackson Highway, Fairfax, VA; ✆ (703) 591-8985

• 5000 Highway 301 S., Waldorf, MD; ✆ (301)645-0770

• 21100 Dulles Town Circle, Sterling, VA; ✆ (703) 430-0053

• 10300 Little Patuxent Parkway, Columbia, MD; ✆ (410) 730-6990

And other suburban locations

As B. Dalton is to Barnes & Noble, Waldenbooks is to Borders, which is to say that in most locations this chain is the "mall version" of Borders Books & Music. Here you'll find the same kinds of deals available at the mother store (see the Borders description), but with a much smaller selection of titles.

In addition to discounting bestsellers by 25 percent in recent years, Waldenbooks offers its customers a "Preferred Reader" discount card. Show it at the cash register wherever you buy something in any branch, nationwide. You'll get 10 percent off your purchase; and, for every $100 you spend during the course of a year, you'll get a $5 credit toward purchases. This credit can likewise be redeemed at any Waldenbooks store, on anything except newspapers, magazines, and cards. Membership costs $10; sign up in any store. The deal makes sense once you spend more than $100 in a year. Waldenbooks also displays a good selection of publishers' overstocks and remainder books, at significant discounts. Hours vary with each location.

Kramer Book Stores

• 1517 Connecticut Avenue N.W. Washington, D.C.; ✆ (202) 387-1400

This hip, Washington landmark just above Dupont Circle isn't really a discount bookstore, has no used books, and doesn't even have sales on new releases. So why list it? The Cheapsmeister might have elected to skip this entry if it were not for three important factors: First, Kramer has super book buyers who really know their clientele. Therefore, some of the most interesting and unusual titles you'll ever see can be found in these aisles, with diversity possibly exceeding what you would find in the big chain stores. The second factor is that Kramer is not just a very good book shop, but also a restaurant that serves delicious seafood, pasta, and American fare. The third is that Kramer is open from 7 a.m. until 1 a.m. most nights, and 24 hours on Friday and Saturday.

So . . . if you're hankering for a waffle smothered with strawberries and syrup along with a good read at, say, 3 a.m. on a Saturday, you'll know where to head! You might even ask that guy sitting across the way if his last name is "Cheap." You never know!

CAMERAS

Cameras and photographic supplies can present a real shopping challenge for the savvy shopper seeking the absolute best deal on a specific piece of equipment. Not only can the technology itself be complicated, but prices shift constantly due to advances in technology, the relative strength of the dollar against the Japanese yen (since most cameras are made in Japan), a very healthy and constantly changing market in quality used equipment, and just the plethora of stores competing for your business. All that makes locking down a "guaranteed best" price very difficult indeed!

Heck, you don't even have to go to an actual camera store anymore to find your dream unit at a great price! Cameras are increasingly available in a wide range of mass merchandisers such as Best Buy and Target, and at major pharmacy chains such as Eckerd and CVS.

The good news is that the many factors affecting the camera and photo supply market makes it possible for you to find a good deal, especially on high-quality used equipment, at just about any reputable camera store, the best of which Mr. C has included in this section. He's shied away from listing too many specific prices here, since the range of choice and price even from one day to the next can make your head spin! By all means, take any prices listed here as proverbial "snapshots in time," provided only to give you a sense of what's possible.

Word of warning: Greater Washington boasts numerous places where you can get good deals on photographic equipment. Read the section on appliances in this book for Mr. Cheap's thoughts about authorized, gray market, and black market products.

One of the best ways to protect yourself, if you have doubts as to any store's reliability, is to ask about their guarantee policy; make sure the item you want carries an American warranty. Since some stores deal directly with manufacturers in the Far East, their merchandise many carry a foreign warranty instead. Even for identical products, a foreign warranty can make repairs a hassle—unless you don't mind paying the postage to Japan. Remember, you are perfectly within your rights to inquire about this in the store.

Abbey Camera

- 8040 Georgia Avenue, Silver Spring, MD; ✆ (301) 587-3600

- 1100 Blair Mill Road, Silver Spring, MD; ✆ (301) 587-3600

- 47010 Community Plaza #150, Sterling, VA; ✆ (703) 421-3600

- 320 North Charles Street, Baltimore, MD; ✆ (410) 752-4475

- ✍ www.abbeycamera.com

Here's another long-time independent camera dealer (formerly known as Industrial Photo), with full service for the amateur and professional photographer alike. Along with competitive prices on the entire range of new equipment and supplies, Abbey boasts a large selection of used cameras. Minolta, Nikon, Canon, and many of the other name brands can usually be found here at a fraction of their original prices—and don't forget, some of these babies were really made to last.

Of course, used prices can vary widely, depending on the item's condition. But they work just fine, and you'll always get a 90-day store warranty on used cameras to boot. The store also has used accessories, and they even get second-hand enlargers and other professional gear from time to time.

Be sure to also check out Abbey Camera's Web site. Their Internet deals are great, with generous discounts and special rebate offers often applied to a range of products including digital and manual cameras, filters, darkroom paper, chemicals, power packs, flash heads and binoculars. Now, that's what Mr. Cheap calls retail therapy!

Regular store hours are Monday through Friday from 8:30 a.m. to 6 p.m., and Saturday from 9:30 a.m. to 5 p.m.

CompUSA Superstore

- 5901 Stevenson Avenue, Alexandria, VA; ✆ (703) 212-6610

- 8357 Leesburg Pike, Vienna, VA; ✆ (703) 821-7700

- 1776 E Jefferson Street, Rockville, MD; ✆ (301) 816-8963

- 12189 Fair Lakes Promenade Drive, Fairfax, VA; ✆ (703) 359-1401

- 500 Perry Pkwy Gaithersburg, MD; ✆ (301) 947-0001

- 14427 Potomac Mills Road, Woodbridge, VA; ✆ (703) 492-6262

- 6625 Ritchie Highway, Glen Burnie, MD; ✆ (410) 768-1612

- 1015 York Road, Baltimore, MD; ✆ (410) 494-4200

- 10931 W Broad Street, Glen Allen, VA; ✆ (804) 217-6888

- 🖮 www.compusa.com

One doesn't usually think of this computer superstore in regard to cameras, but when it comes to the latest digital models, this is a great resource. In fact, most CompUSA stores feature a great selection of digital cameras and camcorders at competitive prices. Here Mr. Cheap found a Nikon 2.1 megapixel camera for $399, a Kodak 2.1 megapixel model for $299, an Olympus 2.1 megapixel unit for $399, and a SiPix 1.3 megapixel model for just $80. There are plenty of other models available as well.

The stores are open weekdays and Saturdays from 9 a.m. to 9 p.m., and Sundays 11 a.m. to 6 p.m.

Embassy Camera

- 1735 Connecticut Avenue N.W., Washington, D.C.; ✆ (202) 483-7448

Embassy sells new equipment at deep discounts off list prices, and sometimes offers used equipment as well. An Olympus Super Zoom 3000, with red-eye reduction, night-scene mode, and fill-in flash was selling for about $200 less than retail rates. Canon's Z85 Sure Shot with zoom lens has a caption feature; you can imprint messages like "Season's Greetings" or "Happy Birthday" on your pictures. The list price for this camera was up to $150 less than the going list price.

Film is also reasonable here, especially for camera hounds who buy in bulk. Set discounts are on a sliding scale in that Embassy will take 10 percent off if you buy three rolls of film or more, 15 percent off if you buy 10 rolls of film or more and 20 percent off if you buy 20 rolls or more. This makes buying in volume worth your while. Otherwise, it tends to add up!

Store hours are Monday through Saturday from 9 a.m. to 6 p.m., and Saturday from 10 a.m. to 2 p.m.

Penn Camera

- 11716 Baltimore Avenue, Beltsville, MD; ✆ (301) 210-7366

- 12266 Rockville Pike, Rockville, MD; ✆ (301) 231-7366

- 352 Domer Avenue, Laurel, MD; ✆ (301) 497-0001

- 6699 Frontier Drive #D, Springfield, VA; ✆ (703) 924-2425

- 8357 Leesburg Pike #E, Vienna, VA; ✆ (703) 893-7366

- 1015 18th Street N.W., Washington, D.C.; ✆ (202) 785-7366

- 840 East Street N.W., Washington, D.C.; ✆ (202) 347-5777

And other suburban locations

- ✍ www.penncamera.com

Penn is your basic camera chain, offering high-volume discounts and frequent special sales. Here, it's possible to purchase complete kits for the same price you would pay for the camera body alone elsewhere. Case in point: Penn offered a Canon Sure Shot Classic kit with a 38-120 mm built-in zoom lens, selling for $199. In some stores, that only gets you the camera; here it came with a neck strap, soft compact carrying case, two 3V lithium batteries (which ain't cheap themselves, by the way), automatic calendar and clock programmed up to 2029, war-

ranty card, instruction manual, and a roll of film. Plus, on a periodic basis, Penn offers in-store rebates on camera purchases, sometimes up to $500 off the more high-end models.

Unlike most chain stores, though, Penn takes trade-ins and sells secondhand cameras; this means extra savings for photographers of all levels. Used cameras also carry a 90-day store warranty, and Penn offers a four-year extended warranty (which is uncommon and convenient, though Mr. C seldom finds such plans to be cost savers).

This is a full-service store, with film, developing, and those nifty Kodak "Create A Print" self-service enlargers in a number of locations. Penn also sells digital cameras, mini video camcorders and accessories at the E Street N.W. location.

Last but not least, this store also offers online digital classes. Yes, it's true! These virtual lessons include camera basics, composition, understanding light, digital camera specifications, using memory cards, and transferring files to tiff and jpeg formats. Instruction also includes "how to" instructions in utilizing the following camera menus: white balance, metering, contrast control, aperture, bracketing, auto focus, sharpening, etc. Seminars cost $50 per session. To register, call ✆ (800) 347-5770.

Store hours are Monday through Friday from 8:30 a.m. to 6:00 p.m., and Saturday from 10:00 a.m. to 5 p.m.

Pro Photo

- 1919 Pennsylvania Avenue N.W., Washington, D.C.; ✆ (202) 223-1292

The Federal architecture style of Pro Photo's 1902 Pennsylvania Avenue facade appears regal and posh; it doesn't quite fit the typical down-market kind-o-place where El Cheap usually shops. In spite of its upscale locale and fancy address, Pro Photo offers good deals on amateur and professional equipment, both new and used. The store keeps prices low, in part, by not accepting credit cards; make sure you have cash, a check, or a generous friend with you.

When Mr. C dropped into this swanky store, he was surprised to see a water resistant, 35mm Pentax kit, complete with battery and auto focus, marked from a list price of $302 down to $218. A Canon Digital Elf, popular with amateur photography students, was listed at $599, but was available from Pro Photo for $100 less. For more advanced photographers, a used Nikon F100, with both auto and manual focus, can be purchased at most camera shops for $1,100; Pro Photo was selling this same model brand new for $1,400! Similar bargains are a Canon Rebel 2000 kit with 28-80 mm lens with a list price of $560 on offer at Pro Photo for only $379.95. Plus, a basic SLR

Hikari camera kit, including body and lens, had been reduced down to $212. Film is also discounted. Buy 5, 10, 15, or 20 rolls and receive 10 percent, 15 percent, 20 percent, or 25 percent off, respectively.

Pro Photo is open Monday through Friday from 9 a.m. to 6 p.m., and Saturday from 9 a.m. to 3 p.m.

Ritz Camera Outlet Stores

- 1220 Baltimore Avenue, Beltsville, MD; ✆ (301) 419-3200

- Potomac Mills, Prince William,VA; ✆ (703) 494-2775

- ✑ www.ritzcamera.com

Consider yourselves lucky, you people in the D.C. area! You have the opportunity to visit two of the clearance centers for this vast national chain out of only 11 such stores in the whole country. Here, you can save anywhere from 40 to 80 percent (yow!) off of list prices on a big selection of 35mm cameras, video camcorders, and accessories.

These are discontinued lines, floor samples, factory-refurbished models, and otherwise slightly blemished items. But hey, a good camera is meant to last a long time. Mr. C liked a Minolta Freedom Zoom model, an automatic compact camera with a power zoom lens. Originally list priced at $440, and usually retailing for anywhere up to $300, the outlet had it for just $229.95 Plenty of good 35mm cameras and lenses start well under $200. And you can even find digital camcorders by Canon, Panasonic, and Nikon, starting as low as $299, $499, and $799 respectively.

Equipment sold at these closeout prices does not carry a warranty, although there is a 10-day free trial period.

Stores hours are Monday through Wednesday from 8:30 a.m. to 6 p.m., Thursday and Friday from 8:30 a.m. to 8 p.m., Saturday from 9 a.m. to 5 p.m., and Sunday from noon to 5 p.m.

Target

- 3101 Jefferson Davis Highway, Alexandria, VA; ✆ (703) 706-3840

- 10500 Campus Way S., Upper Marlboro, MD; ✆ (301) 324-7080

- 12000 Cherry Hill Road, Silver Spring, MD; ✆ (301) 586-0724

- 10301 New Guinea Road, Fairfax, VA; ✆ (703) 764-5100

- 4600 Mitchellville Road, Bowie, MD; ✆ (301) 352-3830

- 3343 Corridor Marketplace, Laurel, MD; ✆ (301) 483-0934

- 25 Grand Corner Avenue, Gaithersburg, MD; ✆ (301) 721-1830

  And other suburban locations

- ✑ www.target.com

Yes, this well-known discount department store also carries a full range of cameras and camcorders of both the conventional and digital variety. Mr. C priced a Vivitar 35mm zoom for just $79.99, an Olympus Accura View 35mm model for just $148, a FujiFilm FinePix digital model for just $179.99, and a Kodak 3.1 megapixel camera with 3x digital zoom for about $300.

Store hours are 8 a.m. to 10 p.m. seven days a week.

Wolf Camera & Video

- 4238 Wilson Boulevard, Arlington, VA; ✆ (703) 528-7426

- 3249 Donnell Drive, Forestville, MD; ✆ (301) 490-2280

- 1961 Chain Bridge Road, McLean, VA; ✆ (703) 821-0752

- 6686 Springfield Mall, Springfield, VA; ✆ (703) 971-3810

- 6686 Loisdale Road, Springfield, VA; ✆ (703) 971-3810

- 14800 Baltimore Avenue, Laurel, MD; ✆ (301) 490-2250

- 11781 Lee Jackson Highway, Fairfax, VA; ✆ (703) 821-0752

  And other suburban locations

- ✑ www.wolfcamera.com

Don't be afraid of a big, bad chain like Wolf Camera (even though they ate up the Ritz chain last year!). From serious high-end to everyday point-and-shoot cameras, to film, developing supplies, photo albums, and processing itself, you can huff and puff your way around town but will have a hard time finding better values than here.

Kodak film, for example, is nice and cheap; a three-pack of Kodak 24-exposure film sold for $13. Furthermore, when Mr. C was shopping, the store was offering a "buy three rolls, get one free" deal on 24-exposure rolls of Kodacolor, ASA 200 film. Professional-grade Leica cameras range from $300 (for the pocket-sized "Mini" automatic) to $2,600 for an M6 edition 35mm camera with near-silent operation, complete with a three-year warranty.

Featuring Canon, Minolta, Nikon, and Pentax, they carry a full selection of conventional 35mm single-lens reflex models, as well as cutting-edge digital cameras, camcorders, lenses, binoculars, and telescopes, and accessories of everything. On Mr. C's last visit he zeroed in on a Pentax ZX with a Quantray zoom for $269.95 and a

Canon EOS Rebel kit for $349.95. He also noticed a Minolta Freedom Zoom QD camera package, including free film processing for a year, for just $250.

The values go on and on. Optical and video equipment are available here at competitive prices: Bushness 10 x 50 binoculars start at just $44.95, while 7 x 35 binocs start at only $29.95. A Panasonic PV-IQ203 camcorder cost $700, and Sony camcorder packages, complete with filters, three video-tapes, a head cleaning tape and a Sunpak "Readylite 20" video light kit-start at $800.

In the digital department, C noticed a Nikon 2.1 megapixel Coolpix 775 Zoom digital model for under $400 and a FujiFilm FinePix A101 digital model for about $180.

Want to produce your own digital home movies? The Canon ZR-25MC mini DV camcorder that La Cheapito spotted could get you off on the right track. A rebate offered that day produced a final, out-of-pocket price of about $750, including free DV tape for a year. What's more, the bargains on DV camcorders will no doubt be even better by the time you read this.

Ritz regularly offers clearance sales on selected cameras, which means you can save even more. Recently their offerings included a Pentax Efina 35mm camera for under $130, a Nikon Lite Touch 110 QD zoom auto-focus for under $150, and a new Ricoh 35mm for under $100.

Wolf Camera stores are open seven days a week. The main location in Midtown (14th Street) is open weekdays from 8:30 a.m. to 6:30 p.m., Saturday from 10 a.m. to 5 p.m., and Sundays from 12:30 p.m. to 5:30 p.m.

CARPETING AND RUGS

Capital Carpet and Furniture

- 1917 14th Street N.W., Washington, D.C.; ✆ (202) 234-8882

- ✐ www.capitalcarpetfurniture.com

Near the hip, bustling U Street scene, this tiny shop takes advantage of low overhead and factory-direct purchasing to get you great prices on, yes, carpet and furniture. There's not much to see here in the store but catalogues; yet, any carpeting you order can be installed within a few days. Capital's prices include padding and installation.

These folks make up for small size with big service, and they pledge to find you the best quality for your budget. Carpeting comes directly from factories in Dalton, Georgia—itself the nation's capital of floor covering—and it's all fully treated with Scotch Guard or Stain Master. Nylon broadloom starts as low as $12.99 a square yard; Oriental rugs are sold at good rates, too.

Store hours are Monday through Saturday from 9 a.m. to 7 p.m., and Sunday from noon to 5 p.m.

Carpet Man

- 1071 East Gude Drive Rockville, MD; ✆ (301) 340-2007

Here's an out-of-the-way suburban shop that buys its carpeting directly from the mills that make Philadelphia, Stevens, Lees, and Cabin Crafts; you can save $3 to $5 a yard over fancier stores. Some wall-to-wall styles can cost you as little as $11.95 a square yard, installed. They have commercial broadloom as well, from just $7.95 installed, and glued down.

Carpet Man has a vast selection of remnants, over 500 in total— many large enough to cover a couple of rooms. Mr. C liked a 12-by-7-foot piece by Philadelphia, in a handsome deep blue, selling for $59 to $89 and up. And a huge (12-by-24-foot) Cabin Crafts remnant, which might cost as much as $600 in some stores, was seen here for $260.

Store hours are Monday through Friday from 10 a.m. to 9 p.m., Saturday 10 a.m. to 6 p.m., and on Sunday from 1 to 5 p.m.

Custom Carpet Shop

• 5414 Randolph Road, Rockville, MD; ✆ (301) 881-7322

An ideal place to stop off for quality carpeting at competitive prices. Store hours are Monday through Friday from 9 a.m. to 9 p.m., Saturday from 9 a.m. to 6 p.m., and Sunday from noon to 5 p.m.

Georgetown Carpet

• 2208 Wisconsin Avenue N.W., Washington, D.C.; ✆ (202) 342-2262

The "everyday" prices here aren't bad at all. Sure, you can find cheaper rugs elsewhere, but they won't be as high in quality. The truly thrifty, however, should keep an eye on Georgetown Carpet's weekly sales. When Mr. C dropped in, remnants, wall-to-walls, and Oriental rugs were all on special sale (doesn't leave much else, does it?).

La Cheapa scoped out a synthetic 6' x 9' green, pink, and white Oriental style rug for $199, an Italian wool rug, same size and style, for $299 (elsewhere $499), and a 5' x 8' wool rug from Belgium priced at $499 (regularly $799, and elsewhere as much as $1,100!).

As for wall-to-wall, plush Philadelphia carpeting by Shaw was a not-too-shabby $13.99 per yard. If you have got a sophisticated taste, check out the Couristan wool interloom carpeting from Tibet, ticketed at a not-so-cheap $59.99 per yard.

Store hours are Monday through Friday from 10 a.m. to 9 p.m., Saturday from 10 a.m. to 6 p.m., and Sunday from 1:00 p.m. to 5 p.m.

Persepolis Oriental Rugs

• 8453-B Tyco Road, Vienna, VA; ✆ (703) 448-1818

Persepolis has been at the same location for over 20 years, specializing in handmade rugs of wool and silk—at prices definitely worth checking out. This store operates on a wholesale basis and offers their clientele everyday sales at more-than-reasonable fixed prices. It's definitely the spot to invest in a serious rug. Just be sure to save your receipt though, because if you grow tired of your rug after a long while, say . . . four years later, someone from Persepolis will come pick it up from your home, at your request. Plus, Persepolis guarantees 80 percent cash back on what you paid in their store.

Mr. Cheap is told that overhead costs are kept low by not actively advertising in consumer or trade magazines or newspapers. This allows rugs such as 6' x 9' Indian style to drop from a list price of $450 to $300.

Store hours are Monday through Saturday from 10 a.m. to 6 p.m., and Sunday from noon to 5 p.m.

Tuesday Morning

• 3501 Carlin Springs Road, Falls Church, VA; ✆ (703) 845-3710

• 11111 Georgia Avenue, Wheaton, MD; ✆ (301) 942-1884

- 3025 Nutley Street, Fairfax, VA;
  ✆ (703) 280-2130

- 136 Maple Avenue, W Vienna,
  VA; ✆ (703) 938-6707

- 6230 Rolling Road, Springfield,
  VA; (703)866-0379

- 25 Beall Avenue, Rockville,
  MD; ✆ (301) 424-2480

- 131 Bowie Road, Laurel, MD;
  ✆ (301) 953-7907

- 353 Muddy Branch Road,
  Gaithersburg, MD;
  ✆ (301) 921-9542

- 492 Elden Street, Herndon, VA;
  ✆ (703) 471-5571

- ✐ www.tuesdaymorning.com

We all know how much better
Tuesday mornings are compared to
Mondays. TM's bargains will make
you feel that much better, since
they offer a 50 to 80 percent
"everyday" discount on upscale

merchandise found in better department stores.

Selections range from room and
area rugs to luxury linens, fine
crystal, china, decorative accessories, lawn and garden accents,
gourmet cookware and housewares,
luggage, toys, and seasonal decorations or gifts.

Tuesday Morning can save you
a lot of money on quality rugs
since they buy direct from manufacturers and artisans from all over
the world. Whether you're interested in factory-made major brands
or colorful and artistic handmade
selections, you'll find a wide selection of 100 percent wools, hand-
hooked 100 percent cottons,
acrylics, and machine-woven
polypropylenes.

Store hours are generally
Monday through Friday from
10 a.m. to 7 p.m., Saturday from
10 a.m. to 6 p.m., and Sunday
from noon to 6 p.m.

CDs, RECORDS, TAPES, AND VIDEO

You can save extra money on music by shopping for used items.
Like used book shops, many of the stores below will allow you to
trade in music you no longer want. Alas, they won't take just anything; used LPs, in particular, have become less marketable in the
age of compact discs. Most stores will give you a choice of cash or
in-store credit; you'll usually get a higher figure by choosing the
credit. It's a good, cheap way to check out artists you might not take
a chance on at full price.

Atticus

- 2308 Mount Vernon Avenue,
  Alexandria, VA;
  ✆ (703) 548-7580

This cozy little shop packed with
secondhand books and music is a
surprisingly refined oasis in the
heart of colonial Old Towne
Alexandria. Pick up a recent novel
or history tome, settle into an easy
chair, and while a little time away;

in the background, opera music
competes with the warbling of a
birdcage of pet finches.

Atticus's selection is strongest in
classical music, as well as jazz and
rhythm and blues, with most used
CDs at reasonable prices. Mr. C
noticed a Philips three-disc set of
Mozart's opera, *Così fan tutte*,
priced under $30. There are also
cassette tapes and lots of good ol'

vinyl LPs—all with more than affordable price tags.

Used (and some new) books, though, dominate this narrow shop. There's also a fun selection of T-shirts and gift items—in all, a cool hangout.

Store hours are Monday through Friday from 10 a.m. to 7 p.m., and Saturday from noon to 8 p.m.

Barnes & Noble Booksellers

- 555 12th Street N.W., Washington, D.C.; ✆ (202) 347-0176

- 3040 M Street N.W., Washington, D.C.; ✆ (202) 965-9880

- 3651 Jefferson Davis Highway, Alexandria, VA; ✆ (703) 299-9124

- 4801 Bethesda Avenue, Bethesda, MD; ✆ (301) 986-1761

- 6260 Arlington Boulevard, Falls Church, VA; ✆ (703) 536-0774

- 4720 Boston Way, Lanham Seabrook, MD; ✆ (301) 306-0400

- 6646 Loisdale Road, Springfield, VA; ✆ (703) 971-5383

- 12089 Rockville Pike, Rockville, MD; ✆ (301) 881-0237

- 21 Grand Corner Avenue, Gaithersburg, MD; ✆ (301) 721-0860

- 1851 Fountain Drive, Reston, VA; ✆ (703) 437-9490

- 2193 Fair Lakes Promenade Drive, Fairfax, VA; ✆ (703) 278-0300

- ✑ www.bn.com

Barnes & Noble isn't just for books any more. Indeed, most B&N superstores these days have entire sections devoted to music CDs (from classical to folk to show tunes to rock) and videos. You'll always save a few bucks on new releases here. You can join Barnes & Noble Readers' Advantage for $25 a year, which offers members a 10 percent discount on everything in-store and a 5 percent discount on merchandise purchased online (✑ www.bn.com), and that's on top of already discounted prices.

Store hours are Monday through Saturday 9 a.m. to 11 p.m., and Sundays 9 a.m. to 9 p.m.

Borders Books & Music

- 600 14th Street N.W., Washington, D.C.; ✆ (202) 737-1385

- 1800 L Street N.W., Washington, D.C.; ✆ (202) 466-4999

- 1201 S Hayes Street, Arlington, VA; ✆ (703) 418-0166

- 5333 Wisconsin Avenue N.W., Washington, D.C.; ✆ (202) 686-8270

- 5871 Crossroads Center Way, Falls Church, VA; ✆ (703) 998-0404

- 11301 Rockville Pike, Kensington, MD; ✆ (301) 816-1067

- 8230 Old Courthouse Road, Vienna, VA; ✆ (703) 827-4128

- 8311 Leesburg Pike, Vienna, VA; ✆ (703) 556-7766

- 6701 Frontier Drive, Springfield, VA; ✆ (703) 924-4894

- 11054 Lee Highway, Fairfax, VA; ✆ (703) 359-8420

- 4420 Mitchellville Road, Bowie, MD; ✆ (301) 352-5560

- 534 N Frederick Avenue, Gaithersburg, MD; ✆ (301) 921-0990

- 3304 Crain Highway, Waldorf, MD; ✆ (301) 705-6672

- 2904 Prince William Parkway, Woodbridge, VA; ✆ (703) 897-8100

- 21031 Tripleseven Road, Sterling, VA; ✆ (703) 430-4675

- 6151 Columbia Crossing Circle, Columbia, MD; ✆ (410) 290-0062

- 20926 Frederick Road, Germantown, MD; ✆ (301) 528-0862

And other suburban locations

- ✍ www.borders.com

Borders is another major book chain that also offers a large selection of music CDs and videos. The last time Mr. C strolled into the store, he noted that a large selection of music CDs were available for just $8.99, and VHS movies were offered at 50 percent off. It's hard to beat that.

Most Borders locations are open Monday through Saturday from 9 a.m. to 11 p.m., and Sunday from 9 a.m. until 10 p.m., but specific store hours may vary.

CD Cellar

- 709-B West Broad Street, Falls Church, VA; ✆ (703) 534-6318

Yep, it's down in the cellar, all right. But the used compact discs for sale here are no castoffs; there's a wide range of everything from classical to country to rap to alternative rock to electronica to techno, mostly priced from $3.99 to $9.99. All are guaranteed to be scratch-free (yes, even CDs can be plagued by such neglect), unless you delve into the "Slightly Scratched" discs, which go for as little as $6.99. Even this section can yield genres of music such as blues, folk, classical, dance, jazz, and country.

In any case, player machines with headphones allow you to take prospective purchases for a test spin. Another nice touch to distinguish this shop is that all of their discs have been remounted into brand-new jewel cases (that's plastic boxes to you and Mr. C). There are some new and import CDs for sale here, including local bands; imported singles sell for as low as just $8.99 each—much less than in major chains.

So if you're wondering how to spend all that saved moola, go upstairs to indulge in CD Cellar's new coffee and ice cream shop. Here you can now get food for thought while contemplating whether or not to buy another art, rock, or movie poster ($6 for regular sizes posters and $12 for the larger ones) and/or possibly a used DVD. The house specialty seems to be empanadas, which come in all flavors—steak, chicken, sausage, spinach, ricotta, and so on. As an added bonus, CD Cellar is also a Ticketmaster outlet for area live performances.

Store hours are Monday through Friday from 10 a.m. to 9 p.m., Saturday from 10 a.m. to 8 p.m., and Sunday from 11 a.m. to 6 p.m.

Circuit City

- 3551 32nd Avenue, Temple Hills, MD; ✆ (301) 630-3704

- 5710 Columbia Pike, Baileys Crossroads, VA; ✆ (703) 845-1446

- 6231 Columbia Park Road, Landover, MD; ✆ (301) 386-4444

- 2009 Brightseat Road, Landover, MD; ✆ (301) 386-5020

- 11160 Veirs Mill Road, Wheaton, MD; ✆ (301) 933-1776

- 1200 Mercantile Lane, Upper Marlboro, MD; ✆ (301) 386-6120

- 1905 Chain Bridge Road, McLean, VA; ✆ (703) 893-6112

And other suburban locations

- ✐ www.circuitcity.com

You probably don't need Mr. C to tell you about mega stores like this, but Circuit City can certainly save you some bucks on music, the equipment to play it on, and more. After all, the chain's vast product line includes TV, VCR, DVD, camcorders, car stereo, home stereo, computers and home office products, CD, tapes and cellular phones.

Circuit City's low-price guarantee insures that they'll match any lower price for the same item advertised in newspapers, radios, TV, and flyers. So if you prefer not to take the "used" route to save money on CDs, cassettes, and videos, this is a good place to consider instead.

Circuit City in recent times has offered about 40 of the top CDs for $11.99 each. They also regularly price a substantial rotating selection of older releases at just $8.99. Mr. C was able to pick up The Who's *The Millennium Collection* and Eric Clapton's *Time Pieces* with his last remaining $20. Long live rock 'n' roll!

Of course, Circuit City is also "DVD Central," with lots of popular movies usually available for less than $20. The last time the Cheapster cruised the aisles he noticed *Bridget Jones's Diary* priced at $17.99, with *The Mummy Returns* and *A Knight's Tale* both available for only $19.99.

Need something to play those DVDs on? Circuit City can save you money there as well, with a selection of name-brand players priced in the $99 range.

Store hours are 10 a.m. to 9 p.m. Monday through Saturday, and 11 a.m. to 6 p.m. Sunday.

Circuit City Express

- 3222 M Street N.W., Washington, D.C.; ✆ (202) 944-1870

- 1100 S Hayes Street, Arlington, VA; ✆ (703) 418-2290

- 7101 Democracy Boulevard, Bethesda, MD; ✆ (301) 365-3378

The Cheapmeister thinks of this establishment as a "mini-Circuit City." It has a great CD and DVD selection, as well as all of the deals and policies as Circuit City, but without a lot of additional computers and electronic equipment sold in the big stores.

Hours are 10 a.m. to 9 p.m. Monday through Saturday, and noon to 6 p.m. on Sunday.

High Tech Service and Exchange

- 7700 Old Georgetown Road, Bethesda, MD; ✆ (301) 718-2824

- 6541 Arlington Boulevard, Arlington, VA; ✆ (703) 534-1733

- ✐ www.soundimagesusa.com

High Tech carries an array of rock CDs at reasonable rates. Not only are there a large selection of competitive prices, there are also a broad range of products.

High Tech has CD accessories, too. Broke one of your CD covers? High Tech is one of the few stores that carry empty single jewel cases for 49 cents, double-density jewel cases for 99 cents, and a case that holds up to 6 CDs for just $1.49. And, to store your music collection, you can also get CD shelving units for $79. The store also offers a large selection of audiovisual equipment.

Store hours are Monday through Friday from 11 a.m. to 8 p.m. and Saturday from 10 a.m. to 6 p.m.

Kemp Mill Music

- 1900 L Street N.W., Washington, D.C.; ✆ (202) 223-5310

- 1113 F Street N.W., Washington, D.C.; ✆ (202) 638-7077

- 1619 Connecticut Avenue N.W., Washington, D.C.; ✆ (202) 986-0300

- 3801 Branch Avenue #C, Temple Hills, MD; ✆ (301) 423-6311

- 8661 Colesville Road #B153, Silver Spring, MD; ✆ (301) 562-7945

- 7415 Baltimore Avenue #B, College Park, MD; ✆ (301) 985-1213

- 6551 Springfield Mall #505, Springfield, VA; ✆ (703) 922-7708

  And other suburban locations

- ✆ www.williesmusic.com

Leave it to Mr. C to find a store that sells tapes for as low as 99 cents and CDs for as little as $1.99.

MR. CHEAP'S PICKS

CDs, Records, Tapes, and Video

CD Cellar—Used CDs are sold at bargain basement prices, and you can take a test listen to be sure you like what you're getting.

High Tech—Part music store, part audio-video, High Tech sells used rock CDs for almost half-price.

Video Movie Liquidators—Save by buying pre-viewed (read: used) videotapes. VML also discounts manufacturer's overruns of new tapes.

Okay, they may not be latest, hottest, hip tunes, but these prices give you plenty of room for musical experimentation. None of these are used; Kemp Mill has phenomenal prices because they carry overstocks, out-of-prints, and cutouts, along with current releases. So, why not broaden your horizons with a cassette of *Metaphysical Graffiti* by the Dead Milkmen, seen here for 99 cents? Take the time to look through the displays, which are eclectic to say the least, and you may find a treasure that suits you.

Even "full price" CDs aren't that expensive. The top new titles are always discounted a few bucks. For instance, the following CDs range anywhere from $13.99 to $17.99: J. Lo, Remix, State Property, Cracker, Cooly Hot Box, Oleta Adams, Jaguar White, and Sade. Who could go wrong with any of those?

Kemp Mill is part of one of the largest chains you never heard of, Willies Music. The group includes Kemp Mill, Willie's, Starship, Peppermint, and Turtles Music. Many of the stores in the chain are expected to be renamed under the Turtles Music umbrella in coming years.

Store hours are Monday through Friday from 8:30 a.m. to 9 p.m., Saturday from 10 a.m. to 7 p.m., and Sunday from noon to 5 p.m.

Melody Record Shop

- 1623 Connecticut Avenue N.W., Washington, D.C.; ✆ (202) 232-4002

Though the word "record" remains in its name, this smallish store is crammed with CDs. All the merchandise is new, ranging from current sounds to classical, with an emphasis on jazz. Indeed, in the vast jazz and blues area, Mr. C found a Citizen Cope disc for $10, marked down from $12.99, and a new Radiohead release for $13.99, reduced from $17.

Boxed sets are priced especially low. For example, a four-disc Beethoven collection featuring the Berlin Philharmonic was just $29.99 the last time The Cheapster checked out this store. And the going rate for the *Les Miserables* series includes highlights for $18.99, the 10th anniversary concert for $29.99, and $33.97 for the whole bloody thing!

Plus you'll find plenty of movie soundtracks, and good ol' rock and roll discs, many of which sell for under $20. For example, the *I Am Sam* movie soundtrack was seen for $14.99, down from the suggested retail of $18.97. Tapes are also discounted, but the best deals are on the CDs.

Store hours are from 10 a.m. to 10 p.m. daily.

Olsson's

- 1200 F Street N.W., Washington, D.C.; ✆ (202) 393-1853

- 418 Seventh Street N.W., Washington, D.C.; ✆ (202) 638-7613

- 1239 Wisconsin Avenue N.W., Washington, D.C.; ✆ (202) 338-6712

- 1307 19th Street N.W., Washington, D.C.; ✆ (202) 785-2662

- 7647 Old Georgetown Road, Bethesda, MD; ✆ (301) 652-6399

- 106 South Union Street, Alexandria, VA; ✆ (703) 684-0030

- Reagan Washington National Airport, Arlington, VA; ✆ (703) 417-1087

- 1735 North Lynn Street, Arlington, VA; ✆ (703) 812-2103

- 2111 Wilson Boulevard, Arlington, VA; Books: ✆ (703) 525-3507

- 106 South Union Street, Alexandria, VA; ✆ (703) 684-0030

- ✍ www.olssons.com

  See the listing under *Books*.

Second Story Books

- 2000 P Street N.W., Washington, D.C.; ✆ (202) 659-8884

- 4836 Bethesda Avenue, Bethesda, MD; ✆ (301) 656-0170

- 12160 Parklawn Drive, Rockville, MD; ✆ (301) 770-0477

- ✍ www.secondstorybooks.com

  See the listing under *Books*.

Video Movie Liquidators

- 763 Frederick Road, Rockville, MD; ✆ (301) 217-0570

Where do videos go after you've rented them? Eventually, many wind up here at this Rockville shop, which looks like any other video store, except that everything on these racks is for sale.

Most movies are priced at up to $15, with a good selection of recent major feature films. You'll also find some brand-new tapes of recent movies; these are manufacturers' overruns, priced mostly from $10.95 to $18.95.

Like your corner rental store, these folks also have children's tapes, exercise programs, and concert videos. Unlike many other stores, VML has a room filled with X-rated movies; the entrance to this area is clearly marked as off-limits to minors.

Store hours are from Monday through Sunday from 10 a.m. to 9 p.m.

Yesterday & Today Records

- 1327 Rockville Pike,
  Rockville, MD; ✆ (301) 279-
  7007

Originally two shopping center
storefronts, merged into one, this
place is now a gargantuan record-
hunter's haven. Tons of LPs and 45
rpm singles (remember those?) fill
the bins; there are CDs and tapes
too. Specifically, Mr. C found colored vinyl reissues of Beatles 45s
for $25 to $30 each.

Be sure to also check out the
clearance section, wherein everything is priced from as little as $1
to no more than $5. Mr. C found
titles by the Church, Paula Abdul,
the Eagles, and lots of oldies from
the 1950s and 1960s there.

Store hours are Monday through
Saturday from 11 a.m. to 7 p.m.,
and Sunday from noon to 4 p.m.

For mountains of music at melo-
dious prices, check out these
national chains:

Sam Goody

- 50 Massachusetts Avenue NE
  #105, Washington, D.C.;
  ✆ (202) 289-1405

- 1100 S Hayes Street #B-1,
  Arlington, VA;
  ✆ (703) 415-3844

- 5335 Wisconsin Avenue N.W.,
  Washington, D.C.;
  ✆ (202) 364-1957

- 3500 E West Highway,
  Hyattsville, MD;
  ✆ (301) 559-3330

- 3283 Donnell Drive, Forestville,
  MD; ✆ (301) 735-5590

- 2107 Brightseat Road, Landover,
  MD; ✆ (301) 322-3637

- 7101 Democracy Boulevard,
  Bethesda, MD;
  ✆ (301) 365-3050

- 11301 Rockville Pike, Kensington, MD; ✆ (301) 365-3050

- 6701 Loisdale Road #6780,
  Springfield, VA;
  ✆ (703) 971-3336

- 14704 Baltimore Avenue,
  Laurel, MD; ✆ (301) 776-9696

- 11781 Lee Jackson Highway,
  Fairfax, VA; ✆ (703) 273-8321

- 11923 Market Street Reston,
  VA; ✆ (703) 904-0861

- 5000 U.S. Highway 301 #1028,
  Waldorf, MD; ✆ (301) 843-4780

- ✐ www.samgoody.com

Target

- 3101 Jefferson Davis Highway,
  Alexandria, VA;
  ✆ (703) 706-3840

- 10500 Campus Way S., Upper
  Marlboro, MD;
  ✆ (301) 324-7080

- 12000 Cherry Hill Road, Silver
  Spring, MD; ✆ (301) 586-0724

- 10301 New Guinea Road,
  Fairfax, VA; ✆ (703) 764-5100

- 4600 Mitchellville Road, Bowie,
  MD; ✆ (301) 352-3830

- 3343 Corridor Marketplace,
  Laurel, MD; ✆ (301) 483-0934

- 25 Grand Corner Avenue, Gaithersburg, MD; ✆ (301) 721-1830

And other suburban locations

- ✐ www.target.com

In his never-ending quest for good
deals, Mr. C is not adverse to dipping deep into the bubbling caldron
of lowbrow Americana, even to the
extent of cruising his vintage VW
micro-bus over to that millennial
icon of budget-minded consumer-
ism: Target. Sure, the whole place
smells like popcorn and sawdust,
but don't knock their CD sales.

New releases normally priced at $14.99 are often stickered as low as $11.88 during weekly sales. Less current CDs, including such gems as self-titled albums from The Cars and Green Day, as well as B.B. King's *Greatest Hits*, were recently available for as little as $7.99.

Store hours are 8 a.m. to 10 p.m. seven days a week.

Tower Records and Video

- 2000 Pennsylvania Avenue, N.W., Washington, D.C.; ✆ (202) 331-2400

- 8389 Leesburg Pike, Vienna, VA; ✆ (703) 893-6627

- 6200 Little River Turnpike, Alexandria, VA; ✆ (703) 256-2500

- 1601 Rockville Pike #B, Rockville, MD; ✆ (301) 468-8901

- 4110 West Ox Road, Fairfax, VA; ✆ (703) 273-2555

- ✐ www.towerrecords.com

Open until midnight every single day of the year, Tower is the place to run to if the baby won't stop crying and you think that playing a Frank Sinatra song just might do the trick, or if you're simply an insomniac yourself.

Tower's top-selling CDs, (based on the top 25 in store sales) are always discounted 35 percent off list price. Newer releases, rising up the charts, also tend to be marked down—usually to about $13.99 for CDs and $11.99 for cassettes. And be sure to check the cutout bins, where overstock music is always drastically reduced. You can usually find all varieties of music represented, from Patsy Cline to Fleetwood Mac to P. Diddy. The store also stocks a bowling-alley-lane-long aisle of magazines, from *Sassy* to *Spin*. And, by the way, Tower opens at 9 a.m. for you early risers.

You may experience limited hours on Thanksgiving, Christmas, and New Year's Day holidays, when the store closes at 10 p.m. instead of midnight.

CLOTHING—NEW

A Welsh proverb says that clothes are two-thirds of beauty. In Mr. Cheap's case, they may be the whole thing. On Mrs. C, though, handsome clothing enhances her natural beauty. But what really gets Mr. and Mrs. C going, if you know what I mean, are spectacular deals on glad rags.

And speaking of two-thirds, who wouldn't get excited about the prospect of getting to save up to that much—and sometimes even more—off the top-shelf prices you might pay at major department stores or fancy boutiques for the same quality duds you'll find at the stores featured below.

You'll find bargains here to outfit yourself in from head to toe, casual to dressy, and summer to winter. To grab those really deep discounts, in fact, one important secret of savvy shoppers is to buy off-season. Look for swimsuits after Labor Day. Capital-area denizens into the joys of snow skiing should also shop for parkas and boots around Easter.

MEN'S AND WOMEN'S WEAR—GENERAL

When you see a price tag with an irresistible promise of "30 percent off" (or even more), how can you be sure you're getting the good stuff at a really good deal, and not just being sold an inferior bill of goods?

Mr. Cheap has an important piece of advice: Know what you're buying! Clothes, like anything else, are sold at discount for many reasons. Let's quickly go over some basic terms.

With new merchandise, "first-quality" means perfect clothing with no significant flaws, as you would find in any full-price store. Such items may be reduced in price as a sales promotion, because they're left over from a past season, or because too many were made (or too few were sold). Some stores are able to discount first-quality clothing simply through high-volume selling and good connections with wholesalers.

"Discontinued" styles are left-overs from past seasons, or models that have been superseded by new products; these products are usually new and still perfectly good.

"Second-quality," sometimes called "irregulars," "seconds," or "IRs," are new clothes that have some slight mistakes in their manufacture or that have been damaged in shipping. Often, these blemishes are hard to find. Still, a reputable store will call your attention to the spot, either with a sign near the items or a piece of masking tape directly on the problem area.

If you're not sure whether you're looking at a first or a second, go ahead and ask!

Dress Barn

- La Promenade, 420 L'Enfant Plaza S.W., Washington, D.C.; ℡ (202) 484-5062

- 1701 K Street N.W., Washington, D.C.; ℡ (202) 785-2487

- 900 19th Street N.W., Washington, D.C.; ℡ (202) 785-0783

- 1009 Connecticut Avenue N.W., Washington, D.C.; ℡ (202) 293-3875

- Largo Town Center, Capitol Heights, MD; ℡ (301) 350-4793

- Fair City Mall, Annandale, VA; ℡ (703) 764-0480

- Crystal Square Arcade, Arlington, VA; ℡ (703) 412-6086

- ✍ www.dressbarn.com

No, you won't look like a farm hand if you shop here; you'll just have more cash in hand to spend at the hootenanny, that's all.

Dress Barn is a well-known retailer of women's career and casual fashion offering a selection of in-season, first-quality merchandise at value prices. This national chain has some name-brand clothing, but the majority of the merchandise carries their own private Dress Barn label, providing customers with substantial cost savings. The first Dress Barn opened in Stamford, Connecticut, in 1962. Now there are over 750 stores nationwide (and 10 new ones in and around Atlanta since 1994), so they're obviously doing something right.

Mr. Cheap scoped out the place on a hunt for a last-minute Christmas gift for the always-stylish Mrs. C and was pleased to discover that merchandise was discounted 30 to 50 percent off list price. There were also some incredible deals on sweaters and blouses, including a deal to buy one and get the second at 50 percent off. The Cheapster saw a beautiful cable knit acrylic sweater for $34.99, and he could have gone home with two of those sweaters for only $52.49, with "mix and match" definitely permitted! Even better, he was able to pick up a necklace to complete the ensemble.

This national chain is a good place to stock up on basics like T-shirts and jeans. Mr. Cheap saw ribbed long sleeve tees for half price at $9.99. If you need a pair of jeans try the Gloria Vanderbilt or Westport offerings for only $24.99. For those cool days there are comfortable corduroy pants by Princeton Club for $26.99. Dress Barn has its own label stretch pants in different colors for $29.99, and casual cotton shirts were $21.99, featuring the same promotion as sweaters—buy the second for half price.

There are a great many suits to choose from, with both jackets and skirts. You could furnish your whole wardrobe for work right here and save lots of money in the process. Mr. Cheap found a lovely gold colored pant suit trimmed with earthtone beading from Collection for Le Suit, that could be dressy or casual, for only $99.99. Dress Barn label suits that are very smart are priced under $100. If you look around you'll find some dressy fashion, too. And C also discovered an Anne Charles royal blue blouse with a black velvet overlay design for $34.99.

You can really stock up on basics here; 60 percent cotton/40 percent polyester turtlenecks were only $9.99, and cotton crew and fashion socks were a bargain at four for $10. Some stores also carry cozy flannel pajamas and slippers.

La Cheaperina found shopping at Dress Barn to be very comfortable, and the service is fantastic.

Most of the stores are open Monday through Saturday from 10 a.m. to 9 p.m. and Sunday noon to 6 p.m., but call ahead because some stores have different hours.

Fashion Warehouse

- 700 H Street N.E., Washington, D.C.; ✆ (202) 546-5600

- 1422 H Street N.W., Washington, D.C.; ✆ (202) 783-2600

- 3239 Rhode Island Avenue, Mt. Ranier, MD; ✆ (301) 927-5054

- 6822 New Hampshire Avenue, Takoma Park, MD; ✆ (301) 270-8632

- 4019 Branch Avenue, Temple Hills, MD; ✆ (301) 899-2265

- 8661 Colesville Road #141, Silver Spring, MD; ✆ (301) 565-2580

- 932 Largo Center, Hyattsville, MD; ✆ (301) 350-5190

- 7851 Richmond Highway, Alexandria, VA; ✆ (703) 799-1526

- 14400 Smoketown Road, Woodbridge, VA; ✆ (703) 490-6808

And other suburban locations

Fashion Warehouse is Mr. C's pick as the area's premier "under $10" women's clothing store. The vast selection here includes styles ranging from dressy to office to casual, and just about everything in between. The Warehouse even excels in petite and plus sizes. These brands aren't exactly top-notch, and the quality isn't beyond compare, but hey, for this money, these garments are pretty nice. Consider, for instance, long- and short-sleeve dresses of silk, cotton, or rayon—in all colors and designs, lacy and sporty—for $10 to $69 each.

Going out to the clubs? Putting together an entire outfit for under $50 is easy: A pair of black stretch pants was only $29.99; a slinky "of the moment" blouse to top off the ensemble, list price $39.99, was $10. And the clearance racks are even better: Cotton sweaters and turtlenecks were on sale for a mere $9.99. Ah! the look, the life, the savings!

Fashion Warehouse is open Mondays through Saturdays from 10 a.m. until 6:30 p.m., and Sundays from 11.30 a.m. to 4:30 p.m.

Filene's Basement

- 1133 Connecticut Avenue N.W., Washington, D.C.; ✆ (202) 872-8430

- 5300 Wisconsin Avenue N.W., Washington, D.C.; ✆ (202) 966-0208

- 529 14th Street N.W., Washington, D.C.; ✆ (202) 638-4110

- 3904 Ironwood Plaza, Landover, MD; ✆ (301) 583-7493

And other suburban locations

Boston's original Filenes's Basement is the king of all bargain treasure troves. Bostonian brides-to-be flock to the Basement's semi-annual wedding gown sales, showing up in packs to breathlessly await opening of the store's main entrance. On all other days, normally sane women pounce upon tables strewn with piles of clothing closeouts, flinging wrong sizes into the air, in search of The Find. If and when they come up with their coveted prize, they clutch it tightly and head immediately for the nearest register—or, to another table. The place can be a real madhouse, which is part of its charm.

Alas, the atmosphere in Washington-area stores lacks the spirit of this crazed, shopping frenzy, but the locations here appropriately match the original's huge selection of jewelry, cosmetics, first-quality clothing, house-ware close outs, and irregulars. Mr. C noticed well-coiffed women with

Gucci bags and men with diamond cufflinks. Perhaps they could afford these fancy trinkets by saving on the rest of their wardrobe at the Basement.

Actually, the Washington-area Filene's Basement stores are no longer directly connected to the mothership in Boston. They are owned by a different company, but they maintain the philosophy.

Designer and brand names found in both the men's and women's departments include Evan Picone, Perry Ellis, Yves Saint Laurent, Levi's, Ralph Lauren, Donna Karan, and Jones New York, to name a few. For the kids, snatch up discounts on Keds sneakers, Nike inscribed logos, Esprit casual wear, and Willi Wear Sport gear. El Cheapo recently checked out a storewide clearance sale, where he saw substantial savings of up to 40 percent on a cross-section of sweaters, shirts and suits—all with coveted labels.

Filene's is also a good place to buy better-name cosmetics, which run at least 10 to 25 percent below retail. The selection includes brands such as Lancome, Estee Lauder, Origins, and Clinique. Lots of great jewelry buys, too. Take for instance, a strand of Carolee 6mm pearls for $28, a 14-kt gold American flag pen for $99.99, and an Anne Klein II Crystal watch for $95. The Cheapmeister believes these luxury item prices are unsurpassable.

Filene's Basement is open from 9.30 a.m. to 8 p.m. Monday through Friday, and Sunday from noon to 5 p.m.

Fit to a Tee

- 3222 M Street N.W., Washington, D.C.; ✆ (202) 965-3650

- 107 Main Street, Annapolis, MD; ✆ (410) 268-6596

This family-run T-shirt store has been outfitting college kids and other casual dressers for more than 20 years. They refer to their product line as "unique screen printed sportswear" and "for the literate and educated," but that's hardly an apt description. Mr. C spent a (free) half-hour laughing at the amusing, sometimes ribald quotations and silly cartoons before he even got down to shopping. Prices start at $15.

These guys literally have over a thousand designs. Among the G-rated slogans were shirts bearing such inscriptions as "Dads against Diapers," "College: The Best Five or Six Years of Your Life," and "The Top 10 Reasons Why Beer Is Great" (okay, maybe PG-13). Images from Salvador Dali, the Far Side, and Star Trek, mixed with an array of other fun, erudite themes, are among Fit to a Tee's designs. You'll also enjoy the friendly, enthusiastic, and vibrant staff.

Open Monday through Saturday from 10 a.m. to 7 p.m., and Sunday 11 a.m. to 6 p.m.

The Gap Outlet

- 102 S. Washington Street, Alexandria, VA;
  ☎ (703) 683-0181

- 100 Prime Outlets Boulevard, Hagerstown, MD;
  ☎ (301) 745-5612

- ✑ www.gap.com

Mr. Cheap says if you're going to "fall into the Gap," do it here. He highly recommends family outings to this locale, where it's possible for the entire clan to score an array of full-price dress pants, khakis, skirts, sweaters, jackets, and T-shirts at bargain basement prices.

Here denim washes range from light to dark hues, or as the Gap

---

MR. CHEAP'S PICKS

Men's and Women's Wear— General

K & G Men's Center—Contrary to popular belief, men love bargains, too. Here, they'll find over 10,000 suits—all discounted.

Nordstrom Rack—If you love Nordies, but hate high prices, come to the Rack. All that great stuff, discounted.

Syms—This well-established national chain sells manufacturer's overruns on big-name suits, coats, and more.

Talbots Outlet Store—Women take note—and save 35 to 70 percent off overstock clothing from this popular national retailer.

---

prefers to label them, "moonlight, blue stone, sulfur and blue frost." A pair of jeans can be easily matched with a variety of V-neck sweaters, blouses, and T-shirts for a weekend look, and all are available at a discount from original Gap retail rates. In fact, it's possible to stock up and save big on all clothing and accessories for men, women, children, and babies at the outlet.

Store hours are from 10 a.m. to 9 p.m. Monday through Saturday, and 11 a.m. to 7 p.m. on Sundays.

Just One Tight Outfit

- 3224 22nd Place S.E., Washington, D.C.; ☎ (202) 889-7354

Yo, yo, yo, word up! Stylin' funky, hip-hop trendsetters will surely find their thang at this urban apparel shop. Jermaine

Holliway opened this killer shopping spot, and nobody should mess around with these kinds of dealios. P. Diddy himself gave the knowing nod, smile, and big thumbs up when he saw a pair of fitted stretch jeans, originally $60, for $35; the same goes for a velour sweat suit discounted from $200 to just $140. (How can anyone not be down with that?) While J. Holliway turns out his own labels and designs, he regularly offers Phat Farm jeans and T-shirts at 30 percent off, plus sunglasses in all colors and shades anywhere from $15 to $30. As an added bonus, patrons can custom-order long sleeve cotton shirts and embroidered or silk screened tees at $40 each.

Mr. C's knows his daughter will dig her upcoming B-day present: a thick thermal long dress-n-hood in charcoal gray, reduced from $65 to $40. And if you're not hooked up with a Sprint, Nextel, or AT&T wireless cell phone, be sure to get one on your way out, it's "social suicide" to be without. Now that's a fresh concept! Check it out.

JOTO is open everyday from 10 a.m. to 9 p.m.

Group USA

- Potomac Mills Mall, 2700 Potomac Circle, Prince William, VA; ✆ (703) 490-5227

Don't miss out! This store offers beautiful clothes at deep, deep discounts. It's essentially a "one stop shop" where you can literally find things for all occasions—anything from casual weekend clothes to bridal, wedding attire and an array of other items for evening affairs (sequin bags, gloves, shawls). Among "must have" deals The Cheapster checked out included

high-end satin skirts reduced from $130 to $60; nice quality, black suede, lined trousers marked from $99 to $50; and blazers, perfect for playtime or office, originally $139, reduced to a sweet $69. Some notable store brands: Ice Cube, Donna Gray, and 2000. Hey, it's the new millennium shopping spot.

Mall operating hours are Monday to Saturday from 10 a.m. to 9:30 p.m., and Sunday from 11 a.m. to 7 p.m.

K & G Men's Center

- 5832 Columbia Pike, Falls Church, VA; ✆ (703) 931-1124

- 1713 Whitehead Road, Baltimore, MD; ✆ (410) 594-9700

- 1113 Cromwell Bridge, Townsend, MD; ✆ (410) 938-8370

Connections to a thousand other stores around the country allow K&G to get high volume rates on men's clothing—and sell it for less. This is a no-frills department store for fancy duds; they've got everything a guy could need, head to toe, for every occasion.

The stores stock some 10,000 suits, from day-to-day blends to designer tuxedos. This includes a nice selection of long pants and shorts, not to mention larger men's sizes all the way to 50XL. It's all first quality, current styling, and nicely discounted. So confident are they in their low prices, that if you find an identical item selling somewhere else for less, they pledge to give to you for free.

Here's a secret: K & G is owned by Men's Wearhouse, which is also a good place to shop.

So, if you've got an appointment with the prez and want to look your best, you may find a double-breasted suit by Albert Napon, sometimes reduced more than 50 percent off the suggested retail price. Case in point, Mr. Cheap saw an Albert Napon suit marked from $450 to $149.99. To accessorize, get a handkerchief for $2.99, or, add a dress shirt for $40, silk ties and socks from $4.99 to $14.99. Plus, designer shoes at drastic reductions. Toss in a pair of cufflinks and you'll be amongst the snappiest of dressers.

Or, if your date is for, let's say, a walk around the park, you can find Perry Ellis sweaters, reduced from $70 to $40. K & G's business is mostly word of mouth only; their ads are few and far between. From a business standpoint, this allows them to offer everyday, low bargains along the lines of champion crew-neck sweatshirts, leather jackets, and all kinds of casual separates at drastic reductions. You'll come out way ahead budget-wise here.

The sales staff does not work on commission, making them genuinely friendly with no pressure.

K & G Men's Center is a three-day operation and only open on extended weekends. Store hours are Friday from 10 a.m. to 9 p.m., Saturday 10 a.m. to 7 p.m., and Sunday noon to 6 p.m.

Last Stop

- Eighth Street & Pennsylvania Avenue S.E., Washington, D.C.; ✆ (202) 546-2391

- 924 F Street N.W., Washington, D.C.; ✆ (202) 628-4304

- 1332 G Street N.W., Washington, D.C.; ✆ (202) 347-6949

- 711 H Street N.E., Washington, D.C.; ✆ (202) 543-4005

- City Place Mall, 8661 Colesville Road, Silver Spring, MD; ✆ (301) 587-0053

- 405 8th Street S.E., Washington, D.C.; ✆ (202) 546-2391

- 3897 Branch Avenue, Temple Hills, MD; ✆ (301) 702-2856

- 8661 Colesville Road, Silver Spring, MD; ✆ (301) 587-0053

- 2300 Perkins Place, Silver Spring, MD; ✆ (301) 562-1393

- 3277 Donnell Drive, Forrestville, MD; ✆ (301) 967-6472

- 2269 Brightseat Road, Landover, MD; ✆ (301) 341-6455

- 6206 Greenbelt Road #A, Greenbelt, MD; ✆ (301) 982-0242

And other suburban locations

Last Stop is an ideal source for stocking up on all the basics. Start here to find jeans and casual wear without spending tons of money. Jeans from Levi's, Boss, Guess, and other big names sell around $35, but you can do even better here—especially on the "Half-Off" rack. That's where Mr. C found Venucci jeans for $22. On another sale rack, long winter coats of all styles and lengths were marked 30 percent off. Heavier all-season corduroy jackets were also available at reasonable prices. Classic leather motorcycle jackets that will do the job all winter ranged from $79 to $100.

Last Stop offers tempting tops, too: men's and women's turtlenecks for $9.99 and a variety of sweaters for $20–$30.

Store hours are Monday to Thursday from 10 a.m. to 7 p.m., Friday and Saturday from 10 a.m. to 8 p.m., and Sunday 11 a.m. to 5.00 p.m.

Loehmann's

- 5230 Randolph Road, Rockville, MD; ✆ (301) 770-0030

- 7241 Arlington Boulevard, Falls Church, VA; ✆ (703) 573-1510

- 120 West Ridgely Rd, Timonium, MD; ✆ (410) 252-7177

- ✍ www.loehmanns.com

Loehmann's means low prices on upscale designer names for women and men's clothing and shoes, plain and simple. Frieda Loehmann practically invented the designer closeout store. She opened the first Loehmann's store in 1921 in Brooklyn, New York. By 2002, there were 44 stores in 17 states.

Upscale designer names can be found here for 40 to 80 percent lower than in the department stores. In addition to fancy clothing, Loehmann's carries career and casual wear, swimwear, sleepwear, purses, shoes, fragrances, gifts such as crystal glasses or Mikasa vases, intimate apparel, and other accessories. You could do all of your holiday shopping in this one store.

Loehmann's is best known for its world-famous Back Room, where you will find very fancy evening wear from the top designers like Kay Unger, Adrianna Papell, Tadashi, Tahari, Harvé Bernard, Oleg Cassini, Donna Karen, Jeffrey & Donna, Cachet, and more. Mr. Cheap saw a gorgeous gold 100 percent silk pantsuit by Ice Cube by Michael, originally listed at $278, selling for a mere $99.99. That's music to C's ears!

Talk about holding the line on inflation! C was amazed to find that designer suit prices had hardly changed since the last time we wrote about this place. A beautiful vibrant color jacket and skirt suit by Kasper for A.S.L., and a

double-breasted jacket and skirt by Jones New York originally valued at $230 to $299, were $99.99 each. Long-length wool sweaters by Grace Knitwear listed for $72 were $49.99, and 100 percent cashmere sweaters listed for $140 were marked at $59.99. Finity 95 percent silk blouses were only $19.99.

The list of top designer names is endless—Leon Max, Harlow, Bisou Bisou, Albert Nipon, Bill Blass, and DKNY to name just a few. Ralph Lauren 100 percent cotton blouses were priced at only $19.99. Moa Moa turtlenecks were listed at $22.99; at that rate, give me more, more.

Loehmann's also features dressy and casual outwear for men and women.

Petites can also do very well for themselves here, with plenty of suits, dresses, and pants to choose from. A petite Larry Levine pantsuit that listed for $190 was priced here for $79.99.

In the junior department, Ralph Lauren sweaters listed at $79.90 were marked at $44.99, and corduroy pants by this designer that listed for $59.50 were priced at $29.99. They carry the XOXO brand jeans that juniors love, priced for only $19.99. Mr. Cheap saw a XOXO long tailored black jacket listed for $68, marked down to $26.99. A very pretty lacey pant by Free People that lists for $76.00 was $19.99 here.

Lots of purses by Calvin Klein, Ralph Lauren, Kenneth Cole, and more are sold at Loehmann's. Mr. C found a unique Maxx NY purse listed for $100, priced here at $29.99. Lots of sleepwear here too, luxurious August Silk pajamas priced at $49.99.

Incredible deals on upscale designer clothing can be found here, but you must have patience and persistence—you have to sift through all the merchandise yourself, since there is virtually no sales help.

For further discounts check out Loehmann's Insider Club on the Web at ✍ www.loehmanns.com or ask them about it when you visit the store. Store hours are Monday through Saturday from 10 a.m. to 9 p.m., and Sunday from noon to 6 p.m.

Marshalls

- 6200 Little River Turnpike, Alexandria, VA; ✆ (703) 354-1770

- 9640 Main Street, Fairfax, VA; ✆ (703) 323-6043

- 8353 Leesburg Pike, Vienna, VA; ✆ (703) 556-0160

- 6700 Richmond Highway, Alexandria, VA; ✆ (703) 768-8725

- 5830 Crossroads Centerway, Bailey's Crossroads, VA; ✆ (703) 820-4424

- 1201 South Hayes Street, Arlington, VA; ✆ (703) 413-1668

- 3100 Donnell Drive, District Heights, MD; ✆ (301) 967-7994

- 8661 Colesville Road, Silver Spring, MD; ✆ (301) 495-9566

- 940 Largo Center Drive, Upper Marlboro, MD; ✆ (301) 499-5301

- 6000 Greenbelt Road, Greenbelt, MD; ✆ (301) 345-0660

- 12059 Rockville Pike, Rockville, MD; ✆ (301) 984-3440

And other suburban locations

Well, you all know about Marshalls. Mr. C doubts that you need to "discover" this national chain by reading about it in these pages. Still, he could hardly write about dis-count clothing, shoes, and home furnishings without at least acknowledging the place, right?

Marshalls truly excels in low prices, thanks to its well-executed discount store philosophy of keeping overhead down while buying in very large quantities. Here you'll find top-notch designer brands for women, men, and children—names like Liz Claiborne, Calvin Klein, Kasper, Jones New York, and Polo by Ralph Lauren—almost always at 20 to 60 percent off standard retail prices!

Marshalls has also expanded beyond its clothing store roots to offer a serious selection of bath and body products, cosmetics and fragrances, tool sets, CDs, travel and camping gear, picture frames, candles, and much more. So, what's not to love?

Marshalls is usually open Monday to Saturday from 9:30 a.m. to 9:30 p.m., and Sunday from 11 a.m. to 6 p.m.

Men's Wearhouse

- 1024 Connecticut Avenue, N.W., Washington, D.C.; ✆ (202) 463-3015

- 3825 Jefferson Davis Highway, Alexandria, VA; ✆ (703) 683-9542

- 3539 South Jefferson Street, Falls Church, VA; ✆ (703) 820-6288

- 6686 Fleet Drive, Alexandria, VA; ✆ (703) 924-5925

- 8342 Leesburg Pike Vienna, VA; ✆ (703) 748-0826

- 6500 Frontier Drive, Springfield, VA; ✆ (703) 313-9475

- 12218 Rockville Pike Rockville, MD; ✆ (301) 770-6922

- 15770 Shady Grove Road, Gaithersburg, MD; ✆ (301) 990-9029

- 3353 Corridor Marketplace Laurel, MD; ✆ (301) 725-9417

- 11842 Spectrum Center, Reston, VA; ✆ (703) 318-0420

- 12227 Fair Lakes Parkway, Fairfax, VA; ✆ (703) 273-4993

- 11110 Mall Circle, Waldorf, MD; ✆ (301) 705-8134

- 2784 Prince William Parkway, Woodbridge, VA; ✆ (703) 491-5606

- 9021 Snowden Square Drive, Columbia, MD; ✆ (410) 872-0434

And other suburban locations

- ✍ www.menswearhouse.com

As important as clothing is to Mr. C's global image, he's certainly not going to waste any money on the effort. That's why Men's Wearhouse is one of his favorite places. Buying in *big* lots lets these guys sell top names like Yves Saint Laurent, Ralph Lauren, Oscar de la Renta, and Givenchy at 15 to 20 percent off the regular prices. This place was known as a suit store for the last 25 years, but has in recent years diversified its product line, and is offering more selection in the "business casual" category.

Here you'll find first-quality, current fashions at 15 to 20 percent off retail. There's not a heck of a lot here for smaller-sized or really big guys; but it you're an "average size," the stock is plentiful. The suits lean toward conservative, classic styles.

For shirts, Mr. C found out that the lesser-known Vito Rufolo brand sold here, made by the same company that makes Perry Ellis dress shirts, with retail list prices

of $55, is just $35 here. Shirts from brands like Damon, Adolfo, John Clarendon, and Pattinni are priced in the $20 to $30 range.

The vast selection of ties is worth a trip all by itself. They're offered in 100 percent silk from County by the Sea starting at $22.99. Lizard-skin belts were about $29, and Kenneth Cole socks are always $5 off retail.

Men's Wearhouse is open Monday through Friday from 10 a.m. to 9 p.m., Saturday from 9:30 a.m. to 6 p.m., and Sunday from noon to 6 p.m.

Motherhood

- 15731 Columbia Pike, Burtonsville, MD; ✆ (301) 881-1090

And other suburban locations

- ✍ www.motherhood.com

Motherhood has met the Internet age at this chain of stores that offers good selection and prices. Believe it or not, the Cheapster himself is not an expert in maternity wear, but Mrs. C was duly impressed with the scope of maternity clothing, both career and casual wear, available here at 30 percent off.

Motherhood uses top-quality fabrics in expanding families of colors, which allows you to mix and match separates flawlessly. The up-to-date garb is good quality, excellent value, and considerably less expensive than similar goods available at comparable retail department and specialty stores.

Not wanting to get left behind in cyberspace, the Motherhood folks have put together a spiffy Web site. Well, at least expectant mothers can now purchase stylish "mothertime" garments from the comforts of home. Mr. Cheap logged onto this Web site and got absorbed in the "baby names" section.

Motherhood store hours are from 10 a.m. to 9 p.m. on Mondays and Thursdays; 10 a.m. to 6 p.m. on Tuesday, Wednesday, and Friday; and Sunday from noon to 5 p.m.

Nordstrom Rack

- 2700 Potomac Mills Circle, Woodbridge, VA;
  ℰ (703) 490-1440

- 45575 Eastern Plaza, Dulles Town Crossing, Sterling, VA;
  ℰ (703) 948-0100

- ℰ www.nordstrom.com

In medieval times, "send him to the rack" implied a gruesome torture. When it comes to Nordstrom's clothing, going to this Rack is a delight since it means relief from this otherwise-expensive store's prices. Men, women, and kids alike can find fantastic closeout bargains on designer clothing and accessories. And when the Rack holds extra-special sales, advertised in the papers, look out.

The Rack's sales are also listed on the Web but you won't find them easily on the home page. To unearth these bargains online, it's necessary to look in the secondary page of Nordstrom's Web site with a "Nordstrom Rack" advanced search entry. This just takes a few seconds and is definitely worth your while. As Nordstrom Rack maintains, "It's all about savings, what could be simpler?" With markdowns representing savings of up to 30 to 70 percent off retail value both in-store and online, uh, why not take advantage?

Women may find a wool cashmere blazer originally retailing for $118, selling here for $29.00. A ladies leather button front coat

previously $118 is now $124. Whether in the mood to dress up or down, the Rack carries just about everything from a Donna Karan li'l black dress, all-weather Calvin Klein overcoat to Bill Blass jeans, Danskin leotards, and Ryka aerobics sneakers, all at substantial savings.

For the men (c'mon, you love this stuff too), Mr. C found a Calloway Golf knit shirt reduced from $45 to $33; Halogen Toggle loafers originally $135, now 35 percent off.

Not to mention basics, underwear, outerwear, and clothing for children—like kids' Jordache jeans and OshKosh B'Gosh overalls. All sales at Nordstrom Rack stores are "as is" and final, but even if you go for something that's slightly damaged and have it tailored, you'll probably still come out ahead financially.

So, come partake in these savings. Nordstrom Rack is where all the bargains in town are at; the old "Lord of Cheap" nearly lost his head with these deals.

Open seven days a week. Store hours are from 10 a.m. to 9:30 p.m. Monday to Saturday, and Sunday from 11 a.m. to 7 p.m.

Racquet & Jog Warehouse Store

- 11910 Parklawn Drive, Rockville, MD;
  ℰ (301) 881-0021

See the listing under *Sporting Goods.*

Ranger Surplus Plus

- 2549 Ennalls Avenue, Wheaton, MD; ℰ (301) 946-5547

- 8393 Leesburg Pike, Vienna, VA; ℰ (703) 917-0711

  And other suburban locations

- ℰ www.rangersurplus.com

For any G.I. Joe, dream can turn reality at this army/navy surplus store. Commander Cheap himself says there's everything you'd expect to find—and tons of it. This place is a bargain basement boot camp, so there's no need to "lock and load" your wallet.

During C's recent reconnaissance mission to the store, genuine BDU (battle dress uniforms) were for sale at $24.88; and new U.S. Army standard issue berets were sacrificed for a mere $13.99.

The vast military collection also includes coats and field jackets ranging from $17.99 to $58.49, sage green, or khaki G.I.–style flight suits anywhere from $44.99 to $170.99. Safari cargo vests go for as low as $44.99. There's also a comprehensive collection of "men in uniform" T-shirts, available for $10 apiece, allowing anyone to pretend membership in the FBI, CIA, Army, Air Force, Navy, Marines, or even the Bureau of Tobacco and Firearms. And if you're in the market for a token gift, you can always special-order dog tags with your name, rank, and serial number (or maybe phone number) imprinted on silver, black, or faux gold for as low as $6.30. Plus, these folks carry just about every type of camping gear imaginable.

Ranger Surplus is an all-around win/win experience. The stores are highly organized and clean. Here, you'll find a helpful, knowledgeable staff—always "armed and ready," especially with self-defense tips, because . . . well, you never know.

Store hours are Monday through Friday from 9:30 a.m. to 9 p.m., and Saturday and Sunday from 11 a.m. to 6 p.m.

Ross Dress For Less

- 9230 Old Keene Mill Road, Burke, VA; ✆ (703) 440-9144

- 13065 Lee Jackson Memorial Highway, Chantilly, VA; ✆ (703) 818-2180

- 9652 Main Street, Fairfax, VA; ✆ (703) 764-9603

- 6201 Arlington Boulevard, Falls Church, VA; ✆ (703) 237-3204

Dress for Less is an off-price retailer selling all kinds of clothes—many of which are well-known brand names and designer labels—for much less than their intended prices. Brand names abound, in men's and women's departments, including Ralph Lauren Polo, Jones New York, Pierre Cardin, Liz Claiborne, and Perry Ellis. Jeans by B.U.M. Equipment and Lee will keep everyone in the family happy.

There are plenty of inexpensive trendy looks too, perfect for the teen with an insatiable clothes appetite. Ross also carries shoes, including athletic styles like Reeboks, as well as some housewares and accessories. Tags indicate whether merchandise is first quality or irregular; most of the stuff is the former. Clearance sales of up to 20 to 30 percent off on men's, women's, and children's apparel often occur on a seasonal basis.

Store hours are from 9:30 a.m. to 9:30 p.m. Monday through Saturday, and Sunday from 11 a.m. to 6 p.m.

Smash!

- 3279 M Street N.W., Washington, D.C.; ✆ (202) 337-6274

For the truly trendy, genuine punks, or those who just want to look cool, Smash! has the duds you need. While this stuff isn't exactly cheap, it beats the popular Commander Salamander in price, and is a bit more authentically grungy.

Shoe fanatics can get radical deals with reductions of up to 40 percent off. The footwear of choice is by Doc Marten; the ever-popular basic black boot was marked down from $160 (no steel or commando soles here). Sure, you could find mock-Docs for less, but whom are you fooling? This is a good source for Converse high-tops and "no-tops," too.

It's possible to find industrial, hardcore tees from anywhere between $4.99 and $16.99. These T-shirts don't sport your average logos either: Designs cover the hippest of music and movies, from Nine Inch Nails, Skinny Puppy, and Le-tigre, to Clockwork Orange and stuff you may not even recognize ("Gorilla Biscuits" . . . hmmm). Jackets galore fill the rest of the shop. The always-popular leather biker jackets start at $99.

You'll also find a wide array of postcards, 'zines, CDs, posters, jewelry, and stickers, all certain to peeve your parents.

Get Smashed! from 11 a.m. to 9 p.m. Monday through Thursday ('til 11 p.m. Fridays and Saturdays), and from noon to 6 p.m. on Sunday.

Sport Zone

- 1501 K Street N.W., Washington, D.C.; ✆ (202) 371-8810

Athletes still waiting for six-figure salaries and athletic supporters (the human kind) who want to cheer on their favorite teams can stock up on sweats, jackets, and sneakers at this outlet store. Sport Zone typically takes 40 to 50 percent off the price tag, which sure makes it easy to do the math.

Mr. Cheap spotted lots of things on first sight in this store—initially sweatshirts, both crew neck and hooded—in a rainbow of colors, with sweatpants to match. The savings here are truly amazing, especially when combined with a concurrent sale. Take, for example, recent promotions that lopped an additional 30 percent off Timberland shoes, and 30 percent off Phat Farm clothes.

In addition to being the source of a cool workout look, there's also a good selection of technical sports gear for the more hardcore, serious athletic types. That's music to Mr. C (as in couch potato).

For more footwear information, see the listing under *Shoes and Sneakers.*

Drop into the Zone Monday through Saturday from 10 a.m. to 10 p.m., and Sunday from 11 a.m. to 7 p.m.

Sunny's

- 912 F Street, N.W., Washington, D.C.; ✆ (202) 737-2032

- 1416 H Street N.W., Washington, D.C.; ✆ (202) 347-2774

- 3342 M Street N.W., Washington, D.C.; ✆ (202) 333-8550

- 2090 Veirs Mill Road, Rockville, MD; ✆ (301) 279-0777

- 4513-A Duke Street, Alexandria, VA; ✆ (703) 461-0088

And other suburban locations

Here's another well-priced, well-stocked surplus store, though Sunny's adds much more retail clothing, too. Find jeans by Levi's and Lee from about $34.99 to $49.50; or consider Sunny's private label, Basix, with jeans in a range of colors and styles from $25.95. Fleece pullovers were also

on sale during C's last visit. Originally $39, they were marked down
to $19.99 and $14.99. Camouflage
and ski jackets were discounted
from $80 to $59, and $50 to
$34.99 respectively; Work boots
and jungle boots were going for
$39.99 and $29.99, respectively.
You can also pick up heavy socks,
long johns, rain gear, backpacks,
camping air mattresses, and
pumps.

Some irregulars are mixed right
in on these racks and shelves, at
further discounts. Mr. C found
some denim shirts for a cool
$14.99, $12.99, and $9.99. There
is a fairly good selection of big &
tall sizes, too. Meanwhile,
Sunny's also excels in secondhand
military surplus clothing and
accessories.

Store hours are Monday through
Saturday from 9 a.m. to 6:30 p.m.,
and Sunday from 11 a.m. to 5 p.m.

Syms

- 11840 Rockville Pike, Rockville,
  MD; ✆ (301) 984-3335

- 1000 E. Broad Street, Falls
  Church, VA; ✆ (703) 241-8500

- 2700 Potomac Mills Prince
  William, VA; ✆ (703) 497-7332

- ✍ www.syms.com

You've probably heard the ads for
this national men's and women's
clothing chain: "An educated consumer is our best customer."
That's very much the way Mr. C
thinks of his readers, too; an educated bibliophile gets the best
bargains.

The folks at Syms were buying
up manufacturers' overruns, and
selling them at discount way before
it caught on as a retail craze.

That's mainly what you're
looking at here: When Yves St.

Laurent makes a coupla thousand
suits too many in some particular
design, the overrun is too small a
quantity for their major department
store clients. The suits may instead
wind up at a place like this. And,
having gotten them at a reduced
price, Syms can charge, say, 20 to
30 percent less.

On an impromptu shopping
spree, Mr. C also noticed women's
alpaca topcoats by Harvé Bernard,
petite sized blazers by Anne Klein,
men's leather loafers by Cole Haan,
and Perry Ellis "America" jeans—
all considerably marked down at a
recent Syms "bash" sale. Plus a full
range of accessories, ranging from
handbags to handkerchiefs, was
sometimes as much as 40 percent
off. Syms applies these low price
reductions to children's clothing
too: A boy's suit by Stanley
Blacker and an infant's denim
jumpsuit by Hush Puppies (complete with a pink top) were seen at
almost half off the original retail
prices.

Other big names frequently
found here include Givenchy, Bill
Blass, Jones New York, and Adri-
enne Vittadini.

Syms store hours are Monday to
Friday from 10 a.m. to 9 p.m., Sat-
urday from 10 a.m. to 6 p.m., and
Sunday from noon to 5:30 p.m.

Talbots Outlet Store

- Center Shopping Plaza, 6825
  Bland St., Springfield, VA;
  ✆ (703) 644-5115

- ✍ www.talbots.com

Okay ladies, you know what Talbots is all about. Well, here at this
outlet, everything that hasn't
moved fast enough at their regular
stores is clearance priced at 35 percent to 70 percent off, and some
in-store sales lop another 20 per-

cent off that! Thus it's possible to purchase high quality blazers for $29 and under. Classic trench-coat-style raincoats were half-price. Other special promotions include 35 percent off career clothes, 50 percent off fall dresses, and a 50 percent clearance sale on pants and shirts.

There are lots of fashions for petite and larger sizes too, as well as clothing for girls and teens. Don't pass up the "$20 and Under" rack, filled with dressy casual basics, or the "As Is" rack, where just about everything looks good at half-price.

Talbots is open weekdays from 10 a.m. to 9 p.m., Saturdays from 10 a.m. to 6 p.m., and Sundays from noon to 5 p.m.

BRIDAL AND FORMAL WEAR

Filene's Basement

- 1133 Connecticut Avenue N.W., Washington, D.C.; ✆ (202) 872-8430

- 5300 Wisconsin Avenue N.W., Washington, D.C.; ✆ (202) 966-0208

- 529 14th Street N.W., Washington, D.C.; ✆ (202) 638-4110

- 3904 Ironwood Plaza, Landover, MD; ✆ (301) 583-7493

    And other suburban locations

See the description under *Men's and Women's Wear—General.*

Champs Elysees

- 1669 Wisconsin Avenue N.W., Washington, D.C.; ✆ (202) 333-2648

Mr. C was perfectly delighted to find that the designer who runs this little discovery of a shop goes by the name of Pari. She customizes

fabric, lace, and beadwork according to your wishes, and charges as little as $200 for her creations—the price seen on an elegant crepe and chiffon sheath, for example. And a gorgeous, full-skirted satin gown, entirely covered with delicate lace, was selling for a very reasonable $1,500. Or, bring in something of your own to be lovingly reborn—an excellent cost-cutter for the budget conscious bride.

Pari doesn't make every dress in the store; she also carries gowns by Demetrios, which range in price from $400 to $1,800. Custom-made headpieces run between $100 and $300. Bridesmaids' gowns are also made and altered here.

Champs Elysees is open Mondays through Saturdays from 10 a.m. until 7 p.m.

CHILDREN'S AND JUNIOR WEAR

Jelly Beans

- 9928 Liberia Avenue, Manassas, VA; ✆ (703) 330-2326

This little shop of curiosities offers girls' general sports clothing to meet just about any need you may have, whether your little one is a star track, cross-country, basketball, volleyball, or soccer athlete. Jelly Beans also sells leotards, shorts, dance costumes, jazz pants, ballerina shoes, tutu's—you name it—to equip young damsels with every accessories as need be for dance class, recitals, and any number of other pursuits.

Plain T-shirts by Sophie go for about $9.99 and more decorative tees can be had for $19.99. Stuffed toys like Beanie Babies and doll clothes are also available.

Store hours are Monday and Thursday from 10 a.m. to 9 p.m.;

Tuesday, Wednesday, and Friday from 10 a.m. to 6 p.m.; and Saturday and Sunday from noon to 5 p.m.

Kids 'R' Us

- 3500 E West Highway, Hyattsville, MD; ✆ (301) 853-2202

- 3524 S Jefferson Street, Falls Church, VA; ✆ (703) 820-0034

- 10901 Georgia Avenue, Wheaton, MD; ✆ (301) 946-1151

- 11818 Rockville Pike, Rockville, MD; ✆ (301) 770-0660

- 8459 Leesburg Pike, Vienna, VA; ✆ (703) 356-0301

- 46301 Potomac Run Plaza, Sterling, VA; ✆ (703) 404-8145

- 20904 Frederick Road, Germantown, MD; ✆ (301) 916-5433

- ✆ www.inc.toysrus.com

This national chain has surprisingly good deals and discounts on a wide variety of children's clothing, including items tagged with its own Kids 'R' Us brand, as well those by OshKosh, Healthtex, Levis, Adidas, Nike, and others. You can almost always find a bargain here, often through unadvertised promotions in the store that feature clearance items at 20 to 50 percent off the tagged price. Deals can be especially plentiful during or just after holiday seasons.

Kids 'R' Us also carries numerous accessory items that go with the clothing, including such items as toy bowling sets, umbrellas, backpacks, and purses. And, most locations even have a little Muppet car "ride" and other amusements that tikes can enjoy during the visit.

Note that Toys 'R' Us has struck a deal with Amazon.com to sell toys through that online store, at ✆ www.toysrus.com.

Store hours are generally Monday through Saturday from 10 a.m. to 9:30 p.m., and Sunday from noon to 6 p.m.

Syms

- 11840 Rockville Pike, Rockville, MD; ✆ (301) 984-3335

- 1000 E. Broad Street, Falls Church, VA; ✆ (703) 241-8500

- 2700 Potomac Mills, Prince William, VA; ✆ (703) 497-7332

- ✆ www.syms.com

See the listing under *Men's and Women's Wear—General.*

Not enough for ya? There are a couple of other national chains worth checking out:

The Answer—Large Sizes for Less

- 1707 L Street N.W., Washington, D.C.; ✆ (202) 296-6569

- 7577 Greenbelt Road, Greenbelt, MD; ✆ (301) 982-9777

- 4009 Branch Avenue, Temple Hills, MD; ✆ (301) 423-8385

- 7300 Pearl Street, Bethesda, MD; ✆ (301) 961-6523

- 4550 Montgomery Avenue #210, Bethesda, MD; ✆ (301) 961-6500

- 1153 University Boulevard East, Hyattsville, MD; ✆ (301) 439-8234

- 7263 Arlington Boulevard, Falls Church, VA; ✆ (703) 573-0485

- 9600 Main Street #5, Fairfax, VA; ✆ (703) 250-0971

And other suburban locations

Store hours are Monday through Saturday from 10 a.m. to 6 p.m., and Sunday from noon to 5 p.m.

TJ Maxx

- 10300 Main Street, Fairfax, VA; ✆ (703) 352-0197
- 3504 South Jefferson Street, Falls Church, VA; ✆ (703) 578-3335

- 8117 Sudley Road, Manassas, VA; ✆ (703) 335-9070
- 8389 Leesburg Pike, Vienna, VA; ✆ (703) 893-2420
- ⌨ www.tjmaxx.com

Store hours are Monday to Saturday from 9:30 a.m. to 9:30 p.m., and Sunday from 9:30 a.m. to 5 p.m.

CLOTHING—USED

Recycling doesn't just mean bottles and cans, y'know. In uncertain economic times, people are taking this approach to nearly everything, and it makes a lot of sense.

Let's define a few terms: "Consignment" and "resale" shops generally sell what they call "gently used" clothing. Often, these are fancy outfits that some of the beautiful people don't want to be seen in more than once or twice. This is how you can get these high fashion clothes at super low prices. Since they still look new, your friends will never know the secret (unless, of course, you want to brag about your bargain-hunting prowess).

And used clothing—clean and well-maintained—is a natural when it comes to outfitting a baby. They grow through their ensemble so quickly, and besides, what do they care?

You can also sell things from your own closets at these shops, if they are recent and in good shape; the store owners will split the cash with you.

"Vintage" clothing is usually older and may show a bit of "character." Sometimes it can cost more than you'd expect for used clothing, depending on which "retro" period is back in style at the moment.

Finally, "thrift shops" sell used clothing that has definitely seen better days. These items have generally been donated to the stores, most of which are run by charity organizations; in such places, you can often find great bargains, and help out a worthy cause at the same time.

CONSIGNMENT AND RESALE SHOPS

Carousel Consignments

- 12168 Nebel Street, Rockville, MD; ✆ (301) 230-1300

Some of the good deals here could make your head spin. One block parallel to Rockville Pike (off Old Georgetown Road), Carousel welcomes you into a pleasant atmosphere of fashion. Like a beautiful boutique, this place offers a lovely array of high-quality clothing, featuring labels such as St. John, Escada, Dior, DKNY, Dana Buchman, and bebe with separate sections for petites, formal gowns, cocktail attire, and furs. They offer an abundant selection of high-quality, up-to-date women's clothing and accessories—offered in a fun and caring atmosphere.

Quite famous for their great selection of purses (including Louis Vuitton, Prada, Chanel, Coach, and Dooney & Bourke), Carousel also has an overflowing shoe department with labels such as Ferragamo, Bally, Prada, Joan and David, and Gucci. Their range of jewelry ranges from costume, vintage, sterling, and marcasite to fine 14- to 21-kt gold, diamonds, and gemstones. Hermes and Tiffany are among their many choices of scarves. They also have gorgeous leathers, vintage evening bags, and fragrances.

Mr. Cheap scoured the clearance rack of wearables for 50 percent off, where he found the following high-stake finds: a Dior red suit, originally $148, for $50; a Mondi jacket, originally priced at $600, for $30; Jill Sanders suits for $275; a Velda three-piece suit for $325; and an Armani tank top, originally $475, priced at just $100.

MR. CHEAP'S PICKS

Consignment and Resale Shops

Carousel Consignments—Lots of high-quality women's clothing comes around for the second time here.

Secondi—Second clothing in a first-class atmosphere, the styles and fashions are current—even though the prices are from yesteryear.

Approximately one-third of Carousel's items are new, never worn, and with original tags. Customers benefit from the gracious and fashion-knowledgeable staff, capable of outfitting anyone from head to toe. These guys have a lay-away program and accept credit cards, *and* there's free parking! Consignments are taken by appointment on a 90-day contract at a commission rate of 50 percent.

Store hours are Monday through Saturday from 10 a.m. to 6 p.m.

Classy Consignments

- 7100 Brookfield Plaza, Springfield, VA; ✆ (703) 644-4655

Set into your basic suburban strip mall, Classy Consignments comes a bit closer to thrift stores than its name implies, both in terms of condition and range of merchandise. Here you're just as likely to find a Hawaiian shirt as a Lizwear jumpsuit. There is a lot of stuff to see, though, especially for women and children, including the "Baby Room" at the back. And even if it looks like the Salvation Army from the outside, yes, it really is a resale shop.

Store hours are Monday through Friday from 10 a.m. to 7 p.m., and Saturday from 10 a.m. to 5.

Designer Too

- 3404 Connecticut Avenue N.W., Washington, D.C.; ✆ (202) 686-6303

Designer Too is too much—and Mr. C rarely means that as a compliment! He was delighted to find many better women's labels to choose from at this classy emporium. For career wardrobes, power-party formal wear, and casual stuff, you'll look like you spent a lot more than you really did. El Cheap noted a Tahari suit in perfect condition for $85, a Calvin Klein cashmere sweater ($36 to $85). The shop also has lots of accessories—shoes, hats, costume jewelry, and purses—like a Louis Vuitton handbag for approximately $75, depending on size and style. There's also an entire Chanel section featuring special discounts!

Any clothing that hangs around for more than 30 days gets marked down either further, as much as 20 percent off. After 60 days, the savings increase even more.

Store hours are Monday through Saturday from 11 a.m. to 6:00 p.m., and Sunday from noon to 5 p.m.

Good After New

- 1826 Greenplace Terrace, Rockville, MD;
  ✆ (301) 907-3448

It will be a good afternoon when you stop into this packed little store filled with clothing, jewelry, furniture, and housewares. Jewelry is their specialty, from sterling silver-and-rhinestone rings to 14-kt gold chains to watches and batteries (including service).

Clothing deals seen here recently have included a men's Pierre Cardin blazer, in great condition, a fuchsia short dress by Nicole Miller, and a pair of suede Nine West heels, all at substantial markdowns. Prices are dropped every 30 days for items that haven't sold, too.

Nor is this a bad place to check for traditional furniture: The Cheapster found an oak dining table with six upholstered chairs selling for less than $500.

Store hours are Monday through Saturday from 9 a.m. to 6 p.m.

Second Chance

- 7702 Woodmont Avenue, Bethesda, MD;
  ✆ (301) 652-6606

This is a great mother/daughter shopping spot, with a large selection of women's clothes and girls' clothing from shopping mall brands to designer labels.

On any visit, you may find Prada clothes, handbags, and shoes in current, perfect condition at 1/3 off retail price, or Diesel for 10 bucks. For the office, a pair of well-preserved Manolo Blahniks between $80 to $100 would be both impressive and comfortable.

Really fancy duds are in the back. An Armani three-piece suit in black was on sale for $400—and it would easily be worth twice that much new. Zoran cashmere sweaters and jackets were in the $300 to $400 range. While not entirely inexpensive, this still beats paying full price. Second Chance also offers Chanel and Gucci clothes, shoes, and handbags on a regular basis as well as Escada and Jill Sanders summer/wintertime suits. Stop by at the end of each season for terrific clearance sales when these prices are knocked down 20 percent to 50 percent more.

Second Chance store hours are Tuesday through Saturday from 10 a.m. to 5:30 p.m., and Sunday from noon to 4.

Second Glance

- 821 King Street, Alexandria, VA; ✆ (703) 836-0737

At first glance, this almost looks like a regular retail boutique. But no such place would sell you an Escada suit for a little over $100, now, would it? Nor, for that matter, could it part with a three-piece Nicole Miller suit—blazer, skirt, and silk chemise—in the same slightly over $100 price range. This shop gets a lot of high-fashion designer names, in pristine condition, at amazing prices. Mr. C even saw a brand new St. John black wool dress, a sales sample, priced at $245.

Plus there's plenty of tasteful costume jewelry, shoes, and other accessories at reasonable prices. And don't miss Second Glance's end-of-season clearance sales, when these snazzy items are marked down to $10 to $25, just to get them out of the store.

Store hours are Tuesday through Saturday from 10 a.m. to 6 p.m., and Sunday from noon to 4.

Secondhand Rose

- 1516 Wisconsin Avenue N.W., Washington, D.C.;
  ✆ (202) 337-3378

First of all, this small Georgetown boutique is not to be confused with the flea market-style place of the same name in Rockville (see the listing below). This Rose sports high fashion at great prices. Mr. C found high-quality designer garments on his visit, including Via Spagia boots for $78, in addition to reductions on designer footwear from designers such as Escada and Yves Saint Laurent. Grab the good stuff when you see it here; designer labels fly out of Secondhand Rose's door almost as quickly as they come in. Other clothes with lesser names are also available, and are good enough to keep company with these highly coveted labels.

In addition to casual and career basics, you can choose from all kinds of fancy dress suits. For example, Mr. C spotted Chanel suits from $250 to $395—depending on condition—in addition to Armani jackets and suits reduced from $165 for $125. Plus, the selection of purses is vast with a number of quality Gucci, Fendi bags. A red wool Kate Spade purse was on sale for $60. Other accessories, such as fur wraps, coats and vintage leather pieces are on hand to complete your new look.

Store hours are Monday through Saturday from 11 a.m. to 6 p.m.

Secondhand Rose

- 730 East Gude Drive, Rockville, MD; ✆ (301) 424-5524

Okay, this is not the fancy downtown one—not by a long shot. This is industrial eastern Rockville, and a huge warehouse turned into a bazaar of large and small vendors. The largest of these is Secondhand Rose, with several rambling rooms, five warehouse bays in length, filled to their high ceilings with decent (but hardly upscale) used clothing.

Here, you can find racks and racks of $6 to $12 jeans, $3.50 sweaters, suits for $20, and tons more for men, women, and kids. There are occasionally some samples, or closeouts; on Mr. C's visit, there was a selection of new wedding gowns from a bridal store that had gone out of business, all priced around $150 to $300.

And clothes ain't all they have here. You're just as likely to find furniture, jewelry, toys, tapes, videos, Christmas items, ice skates, or a toaster, again in varying conditions, in this part of the complex. End-of-season 10-percent-off sales are not to be missed. For more details on the other businesses under this roof, see the listing under *Flea Markets and Emporia.*

Secondhand Rose is open Monday through Saturday from 10 a.m. to 6 p.m.

Secondi

- 1611 Connecticut Avenue N.W., Washington, D.C.;
  ✆ (202) 667-1122

- ✐ www.secondi.com

When you walk upstairs and step inside Secondi, you may think you've mistakenly entered a private boutique rather than a consignment shop. Stained glass windows, silk flower arrangements, and a refined atmosphere will certainly make you feel pampered as you look through racks of previously owned designer clothes for men and women.

The styles are no more than two years old, and new fashions come in daily. When Mr. C stopped by, there were finds like a cross-section of women's trousers, blouses, skirts, and sweaters with midrange labels such as Gap and Ann Taylor to higher quality designers such as Chanel, BCBG, Anne Klein, Donna Karan, Kate Spade, Coach, and Prada.

Also in shorter supply are men's fashions with well-known brand names and—of course—reasonable deals. Anything that hasn't sold after one month is cut in price by 20 percent; if it's not sold after two months, another 20 percent is taken off. And nothing stays on the racks longer than three months.

For even more savings, be on the lookout in February and August for Secondi's storewide sales.

Store hours are Monday and Tuesday 11 a.m. to 6 p.m.; Wednesday, Thursday, Friday 11 a.m. to 7 p.m.; Saturday 11 a.m. to 6 p.m.; and Sunday 1 p.m. to 5 p.m.

Think New

• 4912 Cordell Avenue, Bethesda, MD; ✆ (301) 654-3313

Just think: "All brands" and "all styles." "Think New" looks tiny, but it actually extends waaaay back to include several rooms crammed with fantastic deals. Their objective is to sell in volume at reasonable prices. From sporty to formal dresses, men's suits, shoes, winter coats, and children's clothes—it's all mixed together within general categories. In order to save here, plan on spending some time. But then, time is money, no?

The front of the store is filled with fancy outfits—you may find a range of dresses anywhere from $30 to $40. Same price for lots of blazer/skirt sets. There aren't many big names here, but Mr. C did spot Burberry raincoats lined and unlined from $29 to $189 and a pair of Nine West loafers for $9.50 and up. There's a large selection of exotic secondhand items such as furs, too; alligator purses range from $39 to $450. Other items of interest include 1950s "I Love Lucy" style dresses, along with a few well-preserved vintage gowns dating as far back as the 1920s.

Surprisingly, there is also a large collection of men's clothing, especially suits—a rarity among resellers. The children's selection is more limited, but with some digging, you may find some nice things. Often times, prices are dropped up to 50 percent on an article that has not been sold the first 60 days. Well, that's something nice to think about!

Store hours are Monday through Saturday from 10 a.m. to 5 p.m.

CHILDREN'S RESALE

Kid to Kid

• 6039 Centreville Center Crest Lane, Centreville, VA; ✆ (703) 222-4595

This children's resale store offers everything from infant, babies, and toddlers to size 14 children's clothing. Here, it's possible to buy a wide range of children's items ranging from shoes, toys, books for kids, maternity books, portable crib packs, and Gymboree playground sets. OshKosh B'Gosh overalls range from $2 to $4, and "Sunday's best" frilly dresses range from $5 to $11.99. Their children's illustrated counting books for $1.25 each are also a tremendous find—an ideal start in teaching the rugrats about the importance of savings.

Store hours are Monday through Friday from 10 a.m. to 7 p.m., Saturday from 10 a.m. to 6 p.m., and Sunday from 1 p.m. to 5 p.m.

VINTAGE CLOTHING

Meeps & Aunt Neensie's Fashionette

- 1520 U Street N.W., Washington, D.C.; ✆ (202) 265-6546

One of the coolest stops in the cool U Street/Cardozo area, this store takes up two narrow floors of a converted townhouse—including the bathroom.

Meeps carries mostly '70s clothing. The rock music on the speakers sets the tone—perfect for browsing through bell bottoms, faux-leopard coats, and lots of basic black. Find a well-broken-in leather jacket for $40 and a newer one for $400, Levi's jeans for $30 to $50, platform shoes for $20, cowboy boots for $30, and vintage dresses for $30 to $50. Plus great retro hats, gloves, and handbags by the bin-full.

Upstairs, rooms are filled with vintage formalwear, from tuxedos and sharkskin suits to little black cocktail dresses. Almost everything Mr. C saw was in the $30 to $60 range. Up here, you'll also find the "Bargain Bathroom" of slow-sellers and really distressed clothes. Back downstairs is the corresponding "Cheap Meeps" rack of half-price items. And, twice a year, the whole store goes on a "Buy one, get one free" clearance sale. How could Mr. C not love this place?

There's no real Meeps or Aunt Neensie, though the two women who run the place are willing to speak for them. It just gives you an idea of the offbeat nature of this fun shop.

Store hours are Tuesday through Thursday from 4 p.m. to 7 p.m. and Saturday and Sunday from 12 noon to 6 p.m. They're closed on Monday.

THRIFT SHOPS

American Rescue Workers Thrift Shop

- 1107 H Street N.W., Washington, D.C.; ✆ (202) 397-6149

American Rescue Workers provide food, clothing, shelter, and social service programs for men and women, and their minor children who are in need. The ARW Thrift Shop helps raise money for these causes, and in doing so, also makes available very inexpensive used clothes and furniture—note the "prices negotiable" sign as you enter.

ARW receives shipments of clothing every week. To keep the merchandise "fresh," alphabet sales are conducted on a regular basis. Case in point, clothes that come into ARW's thrift store on a specific week are assigned specific letters for that particular week, starting with the letter "a" and eventually working thru the 12 months to "z." Each week an alphabet sale takes place and all tags marked with, say, a "c" might be 50 percent off that week. There's also a regular "95 cent rack" also known as the "gift rack." That's the sort of present-shopping that gives Mr. Cheap a dose of good cheer.

The spacious store is half-filled with baby clothes, up through men's and women's wear. The clothes are a little worn but still have lots of life left in 'em.

Women's blouses start at $1.95 and most men's jackets are under $10.

Store hours are Monday through Sunday from 9 a.m. to 4 p.m.

Amvets Thrift Stores

- 6101 Georgia Avenue N.W., Washington, D.C.;
  ✆ (202) 291-4013

- 5944 George Palmer Highway, Capitol Heights, MD;
  ✆ (301) 925-4668

- 3115 Sherwood Hall Lane, Alexandria, VA;
  ✆ (703) 799-4166

- 211 Collins Avenue South, Baltimore, MD; ✆ (410) 242-8111

One of the better thrifts around, Amvets is a national chain of stores that are big, bright, and bulging with very low-priced clothing. Long racks of suits, pants, shirts, sweaters, coats, dresses, and more—for women, men, and kids—all seem to be priced between 99 cents and $9.90. Much of the merchandise is well-worn, but there's enough clothing in good condition to make scouring the racks worth your while.

Every weeks Amvets runs a 50 percent off sale, and the Cheapster made a pretty awesome deal when he applied that offer to pants ranging in price from 99 cents to $14.96.

There is also a good amount of furniture—mostly chairs and tables—as well as books, TVs, and radios.

Store hours are Monday through Saturday 9 a.m. to 9 p.m., and Sunday from 11 a.m. to 7 p.m. Every Tuesday, senior citizens get 25 percent off clothing purchases.

Best Kept Secrets

- 12956 Middlebrook Road, Gemantown, MD;
  ✆ (301) 916-9855

- 4890 Boiling Brook Parkway, Rockville, MD;
  ✆ (301) 881-0744

- 5838-B N. Kings Highway, Alexandria, VA;
  ✆ (703) 329-8628

- 13227 Occouquan Road, Woodbridge, VA; ✆ (703) 690-6807

The secret is that when Goodwill receives donations of really fine stuff, it goes to this type of upscale thrift stores instead of to the regular ones. Here, you can find designer label (and other better-quality) clothing in great condition, gently handled, and neatly arranged by color and size.

You may find a rabbit fur short jacket for $30, dresses for $15 to $20, shoes for $10, men's blazers for $20, and children's fashions at good prices. There are clean fitting rooms to try things on. BKS gets some closeouts on new clothing as well; they also deal in housewares and gift items. Senior citizens (60 and over) get a 10 percent discount every day.

Store hours are Monday through Friday from 10 a.m. to 8 p.m., Saturday from 10 a.m to 8 p.m., and Sunday from 11 a.m. to 5 p.m.

Funk & Junk

- 106 1/2 North Columbus, Arlington, VA;
  ✆ (703) 836-0749

- ✍ www.funkandjunk.com

As the name suggests, this is a cool store with cool stuff and at very cool prices! It's a commercial thrift store specializing in vintage clothing and collectibles from all eras up to and into the '80s, so there's something for everyone. Their '60s and '70s clothes are the most popular, as they offer distinct, unique looks that individually minded people can call their very own.

The owners of Funk and Junk prefer to part from the typical stale antique collecting stereotype, envisioning their business as being about a lifestyle wherein you should always surround yourself with possessions you love and use. For example, you could purchase a vintage robe, book, and ash tray, take them home, and then put everything to use in everyday life instead of allowing dust to collect on them in a drawer or on a shelf. Hey, it's a new twist on "living history."

Funk & Junk keeps its doors open Monday through Friday from 10 a.m. to 9 p.m., Saturday from 10 a.m. to 6 p.m., and Sunday from noon to 5 p.m.

Goodwill

- 2200 South Dakota Avenue N.E., Washington, D.C.;
  ✆ (202) 636-4233

- 9200 Wisconsin Avenue, Bethesda, MD;
  ✆ (301) 530-6500 0 6471

- Marlboro Pike, District Heights; MD; ✆ (301) 568-0246

- 7702C Richmond Highway, Alexandria, VA;
  ✆ (703) 799-4885

- 4714 Columbia Pike, Arlington, VA; ✆ (703) 992-8897

- 6136A Arlington Boulevard, Falls Church, VA; ✆ (703) 533-1840

- 14041 Jefferson Davis Highway, Woodbridge, VA;
  ✆ (703) 551-4102

- 8016 New Hampshire Avenue, Hyattsville, MD;
  ✆ (301) 445-5492

- 6700 Laurel Bowie Road, Bowie, MD; ✆ (301) 352-0002

- 6814 Laurel Bowie Road, Bowie, MD; ✆ (301) 652-0565

- 619 South Frederick Avenue, Gaithersburg, MD;
  ✆ (301) 527-0970

Goodwill is another of those American institutions that needs no introduction. Here you can get lost in the large selection of clothing in good condition, and at very low prices. The funds raised through Goodwill stores help support this organization's programs, which give job training to people with disabilities.

There is always enough stock on the floor, it seems, to make sure that you never leave here emptyhanded. Women's two-piece professional outfits start as low as $6.95 and up; men's suits from $9.95; lots and lots of blue jeans from $4.95, dress shirts from $2.95; outerwear from $9.95; and much more. Often, the stores get closeout deals on new clothing as well.

Just about every day brings a different special: Tuesdays are senior citizen days, when they get 25 percent off their total purchases. On other days, all dresses become half-price, all items with green tags are reduced to $1, sleepwear and jewelry are 25 percent off, shoes go for 25 percent off the tagged price, and so on. Call before you go to find out about current specials.

Store hours are Monday through Saturday from 8 a.m. to 5:30 p.m.

Montgomery County Thrift Shop

- 7125 Wisconsin Avenue, Bethesda, MD; ✆ (301) 654-0063

This thrift boutique offers an assortment of men's, women's, and children's designer clothing at rockbottom bargains. Take for instance, the possibility in bundling up in hopes of thwarting wintertime elements for under five bucks—with a

scarf going for $1 and gloves for
50 cents!

On a daily basis, you'll find
women's blouses and men's shirts
for $2 to $3, and kids' shirts for 50
cents. Seniors get 10 percent off on
Mondays. Proceeds benefit county-
wide health, welfare, and educational programs. It's a worthy
cause—on all fronts.

Store hours are Monday through
Saturday from 9 a.m. to 4:45 p.m.

The Opportunity Shop

- 4710 Bethesda Avenue,
  Bethesda, MD;
  ✆ (301) 654-4999

Opportunity knocks at this classy
store for bargain bounty-hunters
and, as a result, for two dozen mis-
sions funded by St. John's Epis-
copal Church in Chevy Chase.
Though all of the clothing is
donated, many decorative items are
sold on consignment. In fact,
dealers and collectors browse here
on a regular basis—especially on
Tuesday mornings, when they line
up to check out new items making
their Op Shop debuts.

A special cabinet holds the finer
goodies; Mr. C noted jewelry (both
real and costume), silver, and crystal.
Among the clothing finds were a
men's Christian Dior navy pinstripe
suit and a women's Anne Klein
skirt—both for under $10. This
store is very selective with what it
takes in, limiting itself to clothing of
high quality and in good condition.

Store hours are Tuesday through
Saturday from 10 a.m. to 4 p.m.

The Opportunity Shop of
the Christ Child Society

- 1427 Wisconsin Avenue N.W.,
  Washington, D.C.;
  ✆ (202) 333-6635

For over 100 years, this society has
raised funds to help the needy.

MR. CHEAP'S PICKS

Thrift Shops

Amvets Thrift Stores—One of
the nicest thrifts around, Amvets
is bulging with clothing that all
seems to be priced between 99
cents and $9.90.

Best Kept Secrets—Not anymore; Mr. C tells all about these
upscale spots selling the cream of
Goodwill's crop.

The Opportunity Shop—Who
says it knocks but once? This selective spot attracts lots of dealers
along with us regular shoppers.

The Twig—Run by an Alexandria
hospital, it's got more deals than
you can shake a stick at.

Among the programs funded by its
shop are a summer camp for inner-
city children, and a social workers
program to provide counseling for
emotionally disturbed children.

The first floor of this spacious
shop is filled with clothing. The
styles aren't exactly up-to-the-minute,
but they are in good condition. It's
easy to find women's and men's
clothing for $15 and under.

The second floor is a consignment shop filled with lovely silver,
especially candlesticks and serving
dishes. These are good values and
they sell out fast.

Store hours are from Tuesday
through Saturday from 10 a.m. to
3:45 p.m.

Prevention of Blindness
Thrift Shops

- 2216 Rhode Island Avenue N.E.,
  Washington, D.C.;
  ✆ (202) 269-0203

- 3716 Howard Avenue, Kensington, MD; ✆ (301) 942-4707

- 942 Wayne Avenue, Silver Spring, MD; ✆ (301) 585-0331

- 900 King Street, Alexandria, VA; ✆ (703) 683-2556

For some 60 years, this society has aided people throughout the greater D.C. area. Its thrift shops are small and basic, but packed with clothing, toys, books, small appliances, and other housewares at next-to-nothing prices. Mr. C found men's suits, rumpled but salvageable, a pair of women's Levi's jeans, tons of kiddie clothes, and even some framed paintings by local artists—each item under an affordable $15.

Store hours are Tuesday through Saturday from 9 a.m. to 5 p.m.

Salvation Army Thrift Store

- 7440 Sudley Road, Manassas, VA; ✆ (703) 361-9904

- 3304 Kennelworth Avenue, Bladensburg, MD; ✆ (301) 403-1705

- 7505 New Hampshire Avenue, Takoma Park, MD; ✆ (301) 431-0042

- 2421 Centreville Road #A6, Herndon, VA; ✆ (703) 713-6691

- 14647 Jefferson Davis Highway, Woodbridge, VA; ✆ (703) 494-9346

And other suburban locations

The Salvation Army is more than Santa's shaking the bells in front of stores during the holidays. They not only accept donations from good-hearted folks, but they also pick up more than 50 truckloads of donated furniture, clothing, and household items every week, and then use those donations to provide merchandise for the thrift stores scattered about the metropolitan area.

Needless to say, these stores carry a wide variety of nearly every imaginable household and clothing item. Profits from sales support the Adult Rehabilitation Center.

Store hours are Monday through Saturday from 9:30 a.m. to 7:30 p.m. Donations are accepted Monday through Saturday from 10 a.m. to 7:30 p.m.

The Twig

- 106 North Columbus Street, Alexandria, VA; ✆ (703) 683-5544

Run by the Junior Auxiliary of Alexandria Hospital, the Twig is two floors of nice finds for everyone in the family. Mr. C found men's Harris Tweed blazers; for women, a red wool overcoat, and a pair of Capezio silver lame sandals; plus, tons of clothing and shoes for infants and kids—all for under $30 on a "per item" basis.

The Twig also carries a good selection of housewares, linens, toys, and books, everything in a clean and bright setting. Each year, the store's profits are dedicated to one particular unit of the hospital, such as the neo-natal care unit.

Store hours are Tuesday through Saturday from 9:30 a.m. to 2:30 p.m.

COSMETICS AND PERFUMES

Take it from The Cheapster: It's a sweet feeling indeed to look pretty and smell beautiful without having to drop a load of bills to do it. Mrs. C feels the same way.

The most popular cosmetics products, like alcohol, build and maintain their value through savvy branding and marketing by their manufacturers. "In cosmetics, packaging is everything," an ad exec once confided to Mr. C. Indeed, most of the price you pay for top-of-the-line designer brands goes to support all of those fancy boxes and bottles, as well as the high-gloss photo shoots with high-strung art directors and pouty international models. If you're willing to forgo the Paul Mitchells and Jheri Rheddings, and you know where to look, you can find some incredible deals on lesser-known (but nearly identical) scents, soaps, rinses, moisturizers, and what have you. Or, if you're one who demands name-brand goods, there are discount places for you, too, specializing in factory-direct and whole-sale deals With a little help from the missus, your loyal Cheapness has selected the area's best in each category for your perusal here.

Bodywares

- 2000 Pennsylvania Avenue N.W., Washington, D.C.; ✆ (202) 785-0716

- ✐ www.bodywares.com

Bodywares carries all natural, alternative hair and skin care items, along with its own line of custom-scented perfume oils. However, Bodywares manages to keep its prices within everyone's reach. They can do this by limiting advertising, using simple containers, and offering refills when you've finished a product (a 4-oz. bottle refill saves you 25 cents; 8-oz., 50 cents; and 16-oz., 75 cents). And Bodywares is very conscientious about animal cruelty: No animals are used in testing.

That said, on to the wonderful items Mr. C found. Eight-ounce bottles of chamomile shampoo and sea kelp protein conditioner were $7 each. A large variety of scented glycerin soaps, including apricot, sandalwood, cucumber, juicy peach, petals, rain, pear, coconut milk, oatmeal, and jasmine, are priced at $3.50. Other "Barbie Beauty" center options: Try Vitamin E Body mist, 8 oz. for $7.50; a 10.4 oz. bar of olive soap for $9.25; a 4.5 oz. cucumber and lime loofah for $3.50; and a Japanese

washcloth for $7.50. Remove your makeup with mineral oil-free aloe cleanser ($8 for 4 oz.); then deep clean and exfoliate your face with granola scrub ($7.70 for 2 oz.). It tastes great with milk, too—nah, just kidding.

Lotions are also quite popular here; and just about all, like the jojoba moisturizer ($8 for 8 oz.), can be custom-scented for you. Added bonus: Gift baskets are available for all occasions and can be custom-ordered to fit your personal preference and price range. There are over 75 aromas to choose from, including Egyptian musk, tea rose, grapefruit, almond, China Lily, and "Infinity" (Bodywares' version of "Eternity"). You'll probably want several. There are even scents for men. Stop by and treat yourself.

Store hours are Monday through Saturday from 11 a.m. to 8 p.m., and Sunday from noon to 7 p.m.

Classic Beauty Supply

- Hillcrest Plaza, 1080 West Patrick, Frederick, MD; ✆ (301) 698-0944

- Federal Plaza, 12226 Rockville Pike, Rockville, MD; ✆ (301) 881-5337

- Glennmont Plaza, 12335 E.
  Georgia Avenue, Wheaton, MD;
  ✆ (301) 946-2223

This small local chain offers big
discounts on a full range of hair,
skin, and nail care products, as well
as makeup. The stores specialize in
professional-grade lines at just
above wholesale prices; many items
are not usually sold at discount.

On Mrs. C's last foray into this
soft and sweet world, she noticed
that the generic versions of Aveda
and Biolage shampoos were priced
considerably less than retail. For
example, she found a bottle of
Nexxus Therappe shampoo on sale
for $14.50. (Try finding the 32-oz.
size under $20 anywhere else!)
Other goodies included a Super
Solano hair dryer, used by salons,
reduced a third off retail, and low
prices on all sorts of hair products,
from coloring kits to perm relaxers.

Classic also has poetic copies of
popular, expensive brands If you'd
rather not pay full price for a Lancome eyeliner, consider one by
Sorme instead—again for a third
off retail value.

Classic Beauty Supply is open
Monday through and Saturday from
9:30 a.m. to 7 p.m., Saturday from
9:30 a.m. to 9:30 p.m., and Sunday
from noon to 4 p.m.

The Cosmetic Center

- 12129 Rockville Pike, Rockville,
  MD; ✆ (301) 816-9701

- 2425 L Street N.W., Washington
  D.C.; ✆ (202) 293-3333

And other suburban locations

Imagine an entire department store
just for beauty products, and
you've got the idea behind the Cosmetic Center. It's enough to make
Mrs. C blush.

Everything you need, from head
to toe (or rather, shampoo to nail
polish) is available at discount here.

And, in addition to good everyday
prices, frequent sales allow you to
save as much as 70 percent off
retail.

All of the small, everyday products are here: lip gloss, toothpaste,
facial scrubs, bath oil, makeup, and
the rest. Many of the popular all
natural, hypo-allergenic, or other
specialty brands are represented; or,
further economy-size with CCs in-
house generic brand, Courtney
Brooke, which copies such makers
as Paul Mitchell, Jean Naté, and
other top lines.

Even though it's a discount
chain, these stores have a full-
service counter with perfume
testers, makeup consultants, gift
sets, and all the selection you'd
find at any downtown department
store.

Store hours are Monday through
Saturday from 10 a.m. to 9 p.m.,
and Sunday from 11 a.m. to 6 p.m.

Morton's Cosmetics and Beauty Supply

- 1055 West Broad Street, Falls
  Church, VA; ✆ (703) 534-8882

This small, out-of-the-way shop
sells top-name perfumes at 20 to
30 percent below retail prices. A
White Diamond gift set, listed at
$60, was seen here for $39.95; a
large bottle of 5th Avenue fragrance was reduced from $39.95
to $26; and a bottle of Elizabeth
Arden's "Visible Difference"
moisture lotion was on sale for
$38, a savings of $10 a bottle.
Don't forget to have a look at the
"Big Markdown" shelf, where you
may find products at 10 percent
off salon rates, and special deals
like a two-quart jug of Jheri Rhed-
ding shampoo for a generous 50
percent off.

Many of the items in here are
sold in those industrial-size containers; hey, if you use the stuff

every day, it's just as economical for you as it is for salons. Morton's also carries nail polishes, makeup, and styling tools.

Store hours are Monday through Friday from 9:30 a.m. to 7 p.m., and Saturday from 9:30 a.m. to 6 p.m.

Perfumania

- 1331 Pennsylvania Avenue N.W., Washington, D.C.; ✆ (202) 737-6220

- Montgomery Mall, 7101 Democracy Boulevard, Bethesda, MD; ✆ (301) 767-0971

- Pentagon City Mall, 1100 South Hayes Street, Arlington, VA; ✆ (703) 418-0877

This large national chain store's vast buying power enables it to sell top-name designer perfumes at cut-rate prices—20 to 60 percent off retail, and that's a proposition that smells pretty sweet to The Cheapster! Better yet, Perfumania stands by its prices: If you find the same product advertised for less they will refund 110 percent of the difference.

On a recent foray into this aromatic world, Mr. Cheap picked up a 3.3 oz. bottle of Elizabeth Taylor's "White Diamonds" for $35.99 and 6.8 oz. of "Escada for Women" by Escada for $24.99. Men's colognes by designers Tommy Hilfinger, Gucci, Nautica, and many others were available at similar savings.

Perfumania also has perfumes for children. Baby BlueJeans for Boys and Baby Rose Jeans for Girls by Gianni Versace were $14.99 a bottle, marked down from $29.00,

You can sample as many of these as you like; the staff is extremely knowledgeable and relaxed. The scents are sprayed

onto special papers, which are then labeled for you with the respective brand; this way, you don't walk out of the store wearing 10 contrasting fragrances.

The store also specializes in boxed gift sets, again, at up to half off or more. In many cases, you can get cologne set, with matching lotion, shower gel (or whatever), for the same price as the perfume alone. There are some cosmetic gift sets as well, such as eye shadow color kits. And you should try Nature's Elements aromatherapy oils, discounted here at almost half price!

Store hours are Monday through Saturday from 10 a.m. to 9:30 p.m., and Sunday from 11 a.m. to 6.

Rodman's

- 5100 Wisconsin Avenue N.W., Washington, D.C.; ✆ (202) 363-3466

- 4301 Randolph Road, Wheaton, MD; ✆ (301) 946-3100

About half of each Rodman's store is filled with inexpensive groceries, leaving the other half for health and beauty aids, which are also priced very reasonably.

When C's better half dropped by, L'Oreal's studio line of hair styling products were all on sale for 20 percent off retail price, including styling spritz, Pumping Curls, and Anti-Frizz Gel—not to mention shampoos and conditioners to wash all that styling stuff out.

Rodman's boasts the widest selection of scents in the Washington D.C. area. Over 100 fragrances are discounted weekly and the savings are transferred to the customer. Even big-name perfumes and colognes are significantly reduced here: Just try to find a 1.7-oz. bottle of Hermes Rogue cologne anywhere else for $32 (it commands about $85 in department stores), or get a daily whiff of Don or Yves Saint Laurent for the same. All kinds of cosmetics are available, too; and ethnic brands like "Shades of You" are well represented.

Store hours are Monday through Saturday from 9 a.m. to 10 p.m., and Sunday from 10 a.m. to 7 p.m.

Sally Beauty Supply

- 6213 Oxon Hill Road, Oxon Hill, MD; ✆ (301) 839-2999

- 6244 Little River Turnpike, Alexandria, VA; ✆ (703) 354-6817

- 7672 Richmond Highway, Alexandria, VA; ✆ (703) 765-7767

- 40 South Glebe Road, Arlington, VA; ✆ (703) 920 8080

- 9600-D Main Street, Fairfax, VA; ✆ (703) 764-0994

- 6112-N Arlington Boulevard, Falls Church, VA; ✆ (703) 241-7493

- 2008 Daniel Stuart Square, Woodbridge, VA; ✆ (703) 494-9055

This is a nationwide chain of 1,500 stores owned by Alberto Culver, the "VO5" folks. They have plenty of factory-direct products, many of which are for professional use only. This means high quality, large sizes, and good prices. Thus, you can get a 16-oz. can of hair spray by TRESemme, Alberto's salon brand, for about half price. Other brands sold at discount include Aussie Moist shampoos, Jheri Redding "Volumizers," Infusium, and Faberge.

Sally also carries those generic hair products made with the same ingredients as expensive name brands. Here it's possible to purchase 12 ounces of moisturizer for $1.49, and Ecco Gel, Aloe Vera, or Herbal Tea Tree for 99 cents. Aura products, which copy the Aveda line, save you about half the cost of those salon exclusives. You'll find generic versions of Paul Mitchell and Sebastian hair products too. Plus nail and skin care items, full lines of ethnic hair products, and discounted professional hair dryers priced anywhere from $9.99 to $18, as well as curling irons ranging in price from $6.99 to $29.99. Be sure to also check the "Reduced for Quick Sale" with $1 off coupons and "Cheaper by the Case" sections, too.

Store hours are Monday through Saturday from 9 a.m. to 8 p.m., and Sunday from 11:00 a.m. to 5 p.m.

DISCOUNT DEPARTMENT STORES AND WAREHOUSE CLUBS

What a combo: department stores full of all sorts of wonders . . . sold at discount. Discount department stores are some of Mr. C's favorite playgrounds. Here's the concept: these places sell goods that had their chance in retail stores. For basic necessities at good prices, and splurges you'd never buy at full price, they can be lots of fun.

You cannot count on finding everything you might expect at a full-service, full-price store. It's a lot more happenstance than that: They sell whatever they can buy at a cheap price—something that warms the cockles of the Cheapster. Sometimes you'll find a store full of stuff and nonsense that never really should have been offered for sale at any price; on other visits, you may be amazed to be offered brand-name treasures worth writing a book about.

Before we go on, a word or two about membership warehouse clubs. Be sure to consider the cost of a membership against the value you'll receive. If you expect to spend a few hundred dollars or more per year at one of the clubs, a membership probably makes sense. If you're just an occasional shopper, or if you're unsure about the value of a club, look for a one-day (or longer) "visitor's pass" to allow you to check the store out before you buy in.

Some of the warehouse clubs allow short-term passes that include a price surcharge over the price for card-carrying members. One such deal seen by the Cheaperino added 5 percent to member prices. Do the math: If a membership costs $50 and there's a 5 percent surcharge, you're still ahead of the game for the first $1,000 you spend at the store.

These mega-stores are not for all customers. You may not have the kind of storage area to take advantage of grocery deals by the case, and there are some stores listed under "General Markets" in the "Food Shops" chapter that offer similar rates on smaller quantities, without memberships.

And be careful to avoid bad shopping habits: getting a great price on a huge tub of mayonnaise may make you happy, but finding that it spoils before you get to the bottom can make you sick. So, too, there is little joy in buying a huge box of some exotic food at a great price only to find that you can't stand the stuff.

For other kinds of merchandise, the discounts can be terrific, but the selection is often limited. Many of the televisions, computers, clothing, furniture, and even jewelry items they sell are closeouts; you can only choose from whatever deals they've been able to snap up from manufacturers. If you're looking for the best price on a particular model of refrigerator, you may not find joy; they most likely stock last year's leftovers. On the other hand, if you only care about the bottom line, this may suit you fine. Again, look before you leap.

Amazing Savings

- 4816 Boiling Brook Parkway, Rockville, MD;
  ☎ (301) 770-9022

- ✐ www.amazingsavings.com

What's more amazing? That so many companies in the world make such cheap-grade wares, or that there's always a market for them?

Though it's somewhat hard to find the Randolph Hills Shopping Center that contains the Amazing Savings liquidation store, the joint was jumping the day Mr. C checked in. The place is quite large and meandering, sort of like an old

Woolworth's, with areas devoted to cookware, china, toys and games, clothing basics, party supplies, and household junk. Certainly, the price is right on many of these goods, which have been cleared out from various retail stores.

Furthermore, Amazing Savings does occasionally snap up some pretty incredible deals, for instance, on Mikasa crystal and china giftware, seen just in time for the holidays.

The best thing about this place is finding ways to fit the unusual and special-purpose products into your day-to-day usage.

Amazing Savings is open Sunday through Wednesday from 10 a.m. to 7 p.m., Thursday from 10 a.m. to 9 p.m., and Friday from 10 a.m. to 3 p.m.

Best Buy

- 1201 South Hayes Street, Arlington, VA; ✆ (703) 414-7090

- 6201 Arlington Boulevard, Falls Church, VA; ✆ (703) 538-1190

- 6555 Frontier Drive, Springfield, VA; ✆ (703) 922-4980

- 1200 Rockville Pike, Rockville, MD; ✆ (301) 984-1479

- 14160 Baltimore Avenue, Laurel, MD; ✆ (301) 497-1890

- 15750 Shady Grove Road, Gaithersburg, MD; ✆ (301) 990-8839

- 1861 Fountain Drive, Reston, VA; ✆ (703) 787-3760

- 13058 Fair Lakes Parkway, Fairfax, VA; ✆ (703) 631-3332

- 9031 Snowden River Parkway, Columbia, MD; ✆ (410) 312-4900

And other suburban locations

- ✍ www.bestbuy.com

Sure, this is just another major chain. Still, Mr. C just can't ignore the fact that on many products this store fulfills his basic needs: great deals and selection on just about any consumer device that uses batteries or a wall outlet. This is a primo place to shop for computers and peripherals, home audio and video equipment, digital photo and imaging equipment, home office supplies, major appliances, CDs, videos, and more.

Depending on the national financial conditions, Best Buy sometimes offers no-interest financing on major purchases, a nice way to save even more money. (But get the best price first; if you pay way too much for something, free financing won't make up the difference.)

You can check prices for many products on the company's Web site, which also includes a copy of weekly newspaper ads.

Store hours are 10 a.m. to 9 p.m. Monday through Saturday, and 11 a.m. to 6 p.m. on Sunday.

Big Lots

- 6419 Marlboro Pike, District Heights, MD; ✆ (301) 420-7220

- 19142 Montgomery Village Avenue, Gaithersburg, MD; ✆ (301) 947-7748

- 13969 Jefferson Davis Highway, Woodbridge, VA; ✆ (703) 492-9388

- ✍ www.cnstores.com

Go ahead—call this place cheap. They love it. They have fun with it, in signs all over the store that declare "We must be crazy . . ." and other such happy claims. More than 40 aisles are packed with closeouts, salvage from other stores, discontinued items, knock-off brands, and every other way to save money. They have a huge selection, as much as the major liquidation places Mr. C has seen in New York and other cities.

You never know what they may have here. As with any store specializing in closeouts, you can't expect them to have exactly the item or brand you want. But you'll probably find something comparable. Or, as many folks do, you can go out and just see what's there—chances are pretty good you'll find at least a few things you can really use, or at least really want, at rock-bottom prices.

You want toys? They got toys. Need some sneakers? Maybe you'll find Nike running shoes for $15.99. What about hair care? You may be able buy generic copies of salon brands like Paul Mitchell and Nexxus for $1.49 a bottle, or go for the real thing with Jhirmack and Revlon for a buck each.

And El Cheapedo could mention domestics and other home furnishings, hardware and tools, sports equipment, household products, a 15-pound sack of kitty litter for $1.99, greeting cards at 40 percent off the printed price, and several aisles of reduced-price grocery items. BL is also a good place to check out for seasonal items, like Halloween costumes and Christmas decorations—discounted before the holidays, not after.

BL also has furniture departments in most stores offering living room, dinette and bedroom sets, mattresses, home office furniture, entertainment centers, and more.

All stores are open 8 a.m. to 10 p.m. seven days a week. Since merchandise may vary from store to store, you might want to call ahead before you make the trek.

BJ's Wholesale Club

- 1000 Saint Nicholas Drive, Waldorf, MD; ✆ (301) 705-5100

MR. CHEAP'S PICKS

Discount Department Stores and Warehouse Clubs

Amazing Savings—The place is quite large and meandering, sort of like an old Woolworth's, with areas devoted to cookware, china, toys and games, clothing basics, party supplies, and household junk.

Marshalls—Marshalls has some truly low prices, thanks to its well-executed discount store philosophy of keeping overhead down while buying in very large quantities.

Tuesday Morning—TM offers a 50 to 80 percent "everyday" discount on upscale merchandise found in better department stores.

- 13053 Fair Lakes Shopping Center, Fairfax, VA; ✆ (703) 803-0200

- 14123 Noblewood Plaza, Woodbridge, VA; ✆ (703) 730-0100

- ✐ www.bjswholesale.com

Part of the nationwide wholesale club chain of warehouse stores that have all of the charm of an aircraft hangar. But there's not much you can't buy here . . . in extra large packages, as in olives by the gallon, shampoo by the tub, and cereal by the case. These stores are especially well stocked with tires from major makers like Michelin, Goodrich, and Uniroyal and other automotive merchandise; installation can be arranged. And the food court may come in handy if you work up an appetite lugging those steel radials around.

BJ's is open from 9 a.m. to 9 p.m. Monday through Saturday, and from 10 a.m. to 6 p.m. on Sunday.

Burlington Coat Factory

- 3516 S Jefferson Street, Baileys Crossroads, VA; ✆ (703) 379-7878

- 3200 Donnell Drive, Forestville, MD; ✆ (301) 736-6685

- 6200 Greenbelt Road, Greenbelt, MD; ✆ (301) 982-2386

- 11284 James Swart Circle, Fairfax, VA; ✆ (703) 267-6939

- 3286 Crain Highway, Waldorf, MD; ✆ (301) 645-6226

- 22350 South Sterling Boulevard, Sterling, VA; ✆ (703) 444-7044

- 7351 Assateague Drive, Jessup, MD; ✆ (410) 799-8802

  And other suburban locations

- ✐ www.coat.com

Don't be deceived by a name! Not content with being a popular clothing discounter for the entire family, Burlington Coat Factory stores have expanded to become something almost like actual department stores. They are quite large, and in each one you'll not only find discounted clothing for the whole family, but also shoes, linens, luggage, cosmetics, and jewelry.

Most folks know of Burlington for its clothing. They carry big names at good prices; some are very good bargains indeed. You can outfit yourself from top to toe here, inside and out, in conservative or stylish looks. True to its name, you can find all kinds of coats here; Mr. C has seen sights like a Pierre Cardin lambskin bomber jacket, list priced at $300 for just $180, or racks of simulated fur

coats for women. How about a *faux* fox, reduced from $200 to $120?

But there's more here than meets the elements. Underneath those coats, guys could be wearing a Harvé Bernard double-breasted suit of 100 percent wool, discounted from $400 to $180, or creations by Ralph Lauren, Perry Ellis, Nino Cerruti, and Christian Dior at similar savings.

For the gals, selections include a nifty black two-piece Oleg Cassini set, not for $270, but $150, a Jones New York turtleneck sweater reduced from $140 to $90, or 100 percent silk blouses for $12.95. Size selection is good here, from petite to plus sizes for women, as well as big and tall sizes for men.

Then there are all the fashions for children, from tots to teens. Boys' Jordache ski jackets were recently seen reduced from $70 to $40; girls will look smart in a dressy red coat by London Fog, marked down from $110 to $80. Both can save 10 bucks or so off Levi's jeans, Guess denim fashions, and other trendy labels.

You can also stock up on basics and accessories here, like ties, hats, and underwear (particularly Burlington hosiery, at $1 to $2 off all styles). There is also a small but serviceable jewelry counter, selling gold chains, bracelets, watches, and the like at permanent discounts of 40 to 50 percent off retail prices. And don't forget to look for the clearance racks in every clothing department!

But what about the other specialty departments? Here you can also realize savings on all kinds of basic and classy shoes for men, women, and kids. Current styles in dressy shoes and boots are mostly sold at $10–$20 off list prices; for deeper discounts, though, look over on the long self-service racks, arranged by size. These are mainly closeouts and overstocks, all perfectly good. In the women's category, you may find a pair of tailored loafers for $16.99 or Ann Marino pumps from $14.98. On the guy's side, you can ease your dogs into some dressy Dexter tasseled loafers that have been marked down from $80 to $59.98, or perhaps some Banker wing tips discounted from $55 to only $24.99. There is a more limited selection of sneakers, like ankle-high tennis shoes by Reebok for $49; plus shoes for little Cheapsters by Sesame Street, Fisher Price, and Hush Puppies.

The "Baby Depot" department sells discounted clothing, furniture, and accessories for newborns and small children. Along with good prices on infant and maternity wear, you can find things like a white crib, reduced from $200 to $144.75, or sheets sets that run from $16.95 to $29.95. There are also plenty of soft and cuddly toys and accessories to put in the crib along with the sheets (and the baby.) You'll also find such diverse items as a Little Tykes plastic table and chairs, for toddler tea parties; Glider Lite strollers priced under $80; an Accel DX convertible car seat, reduced from $100 to $79.99; and clothing for both newborns and maternity moms.

Burlington boasts a Christopher Lowell Collection featuring designer linens, rugs, towels, and other accessories for bed and bath, as well as a range of other home furnishings and accessories at very competitive prices. Mr. C found things like California King comforter sets ranging in price from $129 to $289, a Christopher Lowell King sheet set for under $50, towels beginning at $10.99, plus bed pillows (including orthopedic styles), throw pillows, shower cur-

tains, decorative baskets, and more, stacked from floor to ceiling.

Interested in picking up some luggage? How about a Luggage America three-piece set for only $69.99, or a 44-inch Peabody Brown Suede garment bag, normally retailing for about $100, on sale here for under $60.

Burlington keeps its stores open from 10 a.m. to 9 p.m. Monday through Saturday and 1 p.m. to 6 p.m. on Sunday. They're usually open a bit later during the holiday season.

Costco

- 1200 South Fern Street, Arlington, VA; ✆ (703) 413-3240

- 10925 Baltimore Avenue, Beltsville, MD; ✆ (301) 595-3400

- 4725 West Ox Road, Fairfax, VA; ✆ (703) 802-8273

- 7373 Boston Boulevard, Springfield, VA; ✆ (703) 912-1200

- 880 Russell Avenue, Gaithersburg, MD; ✆ (301) 417-1530

And other suburban locations

- ✍ www.costco.com

This is Mr. C's favorite place in the world to stock up on 10-pound jars of pickle relish; Mrs. C is partial to the bathtubs of mayonnaise. We make great tartar sauce together.

This membership warehouse club offers such great prices on name-brand merchandise, including appliances, other household accessories, books, DVDs and CDs, computers and other electronics, furniture, hardware, outdoor supplies, health and beauty products, gourmet foods, jewelry, office products, pharmaceuticals, photo supplies, and travel services.

Of course, you have to become a member to shop here, but it's well worth the annual fee, which at press time was $45. From time to time, the store offers short-term "free" memberships and discounts. Call to check.

Costco is open from 10 a.m. to 8:30 p.m. Monday through Friday, from 9 a.m. to 8 p.m. on Saturday, and from 10 a.m. to 6 p.m. on Sunday.

Hecht's Metro-Center

- 1201 G Street N.W., Washington, D.C.; ✎ (202) 628-6661

- ✐ www.maycompany.com

Not *all* the Hecht's stores have left the D.C. area. Though Mr. C dearly misses Hecht's Clearance Center in Alexandria (a loss to make any bona fide cheapster tear up), he is grateful to still have this terrific all-purpose department store right here in D.C. Yes, the great buys are fewer because this is a conventional store, but there are still so many things to look at and it's so convenient to shop here.

This is part of the May Company department store chain, so you can expect the usual overwhelming variety of items: cosmetics; jewelry; men's, women's, and children's clothes; home furnishings; a bridal registry; and more. Walk in, ask for it, and find out where it is. Of course, you'll find the greatest savings in the post-holiday period, when many items in the store are marked down by 50 percent or more!

Store hours are Monday through Friday from 10 a.m. to 8 p.m., Saturday from 9 a.m. to 10 p.m., and Sunday from noon to 6 p.m.

Kmart

- 6411 Riggs Road, Hyattsville, MD; ✎ (301) 853-3102

- 6163 Oxon Hill Road, Oxon Hill, MD; ✎ (301) 839-0550

- 3101 Donnell Drive, Forestville, MD; ✎ (301) 568-6600

- 4251 John Marr Drive, Annandale, VA; ✎ (703) 941-5100

- 8829 Greenbelt Road, Greenbelt, MD; ✎ (301) 552-4753

- 8827 Woodyard Road, Clinton, MD; ✎ (301) 868-8600

- 14200 Baltimore Avenue, Laurel, MD; ✎ (301) 448-9331

- 14014 Connecticut Avenue, Silver Spring, MD; ✎ (301) 871-6640

- 6364 Springfield Plaza, Springfield, VA: ✎ (703) 644-5230

- 4080 Germantown Road, Fairfax, VA; ✎ (703) 591-7010

- 6000 Burke Commons Road, Burke, VA; ✎ (703) 764-2095

- 1647 Crofton Center, Crofton, MD; ✎ (410) 721-7000

- 209 Kentlands Boulevard, Gaithersburg, MD; ✎ (301) 208-9091

- 494 Elden Street, Herndon, VA; ✎ (703) 437-7900

- 3297 Plaza Way, Waldorf, MD; ✎ (301) 932-8002

- 13412 Jefferson Davis Highway, Woodbridge, VA; ✎ (703) 491-7089

- 13910 Metrotech Drive, Chantilly, VA; ✎ (703) 263-0762

    And other suburban locations

- ✐ www.bluelight.com

Bigger is better, and over the years Kmart has tried to battle against the Wal-Marts and the Costcos and other megastores by getting bigger and bigger. The Big Kmart stores are super-sized versions of the familiar discount stores; many include grocery items along with clothing, small appliances, jewelry, and all sorts of other *stuff*. Along the way, it has brought its prices down to interesting levels.

In 2002, Kmart hit a financial wall; as this book goes to press the company's future was a bit clouded. We may see some of the smaller and less-successful stores turning off the blue light forever.

Kmart departments cover household accessories, electronics and CDs, clothes, shoes, hardware, camping gear, pet supplies, groceries and pharmaceuticals, gardening supplies, auto repair supplies, and more. The great thing about this place is that you can find such a large selection of products—many respected name brands—for far less money than you'll pay in the typical mall-based retailer. Whether you're picking up a six-pack of large wine goblets for $8.99, socks at 3 for $3.99, or a pair of rugged, brand-name hiking boots for $19.99, you stand an excellent chance of being quite pleased with yourself when you walk out of those big front doors. And if you're careful, you can manage to fill an entire shopping cart with items that do not include the name Martha Stewart!

Most Kmart stores are open seven days from 8 a.m. to 11 p.m., with extended hours during the holiday season.

Marshalls

- 1201 South Hayes Street, Arlington, VA; ✆ (703) 413-1668

- 5830 Crossroads Center Way, Baileys Crossroads, VA; ✆ (703) 820-4424

- 8661 Colesville Road, Silver Spring, MD; ✆ (301) 495-9566

- 3100 Donnell Drive, District Heights, MD; ✆ (301) 967-7994

- 6200 Little River Pike, Alexandria, VA; ✆ (703) 354-1770

- 6000 Greenbelt Road, Greenbelt, MD; ✆ (301) 345-0660

- 6700 Richmond Highway, Alexandria, VA; ✆ (703) 768-8725

- 940 Largo Center Drive, Upper Marlboro, MD; ✆ (301) 499-5301

- 8353 Leesburg Pike, Vienna, VA; ✆ (703) 556-0160

- 12059 Rockville Pike, Rockville, MD; ✆ (301) 984-3440

- 9640 Main Street, Fairfax, VA; ✆ (703) 323-6043

- 341 Montrose Avenue, Laurel, MD; ✆ (301) 498-8948

- 2925 Festival Way, Waldorf, MD; ✆ (301) 870-9613

- 18326 Contour Road, Gaithersburg, MD; ✆ (301) 330-4075

- 13007 Lee Jackson Memorial Highway, Fairfax, VA; ✆ (703) 222-0976

And other suburban locations

- ✐ www.marshallsonline.com

Mr. C doubts that you need to "discover" this national chain by reading about it in these pages. Still, he could hardly write about discount clothing, shoes, and home furnishings without at least acknowledging the place, right? In case you didn't know, though, Marshalls is in the same corporate family and pretty similar to TJ Maxx.

Marshalls has some truly low prices, thanks to its well-executed discount store philosophy of keeping overhead down while buying in very large quantities. Here you'll find selected top-notch designer brands for women, men, and children—names like Liz Claiborne, Calvin Klein, Kasper, Jones

New York, and Polo by Ralph Lauren—almost always at 20 to 60 percent off standard retail prices!

Marshalls has also expanded beyond its clothing store roots to offer a serious selection of bath and body products, cosmetics and fragrances, tool sets, CDs, travel and camping gear, picture frames, candles, and much more. So, what's not to love?

Marshalls is usually open from 9:30 a.m. to 9:30 p.m. Monday through Saturday, and 11 a.m. to 6 p.m. on Sundays. During the holidays, they extend their hours in both the morning and evening.

Sam's Club

- 8500 Landover Road, Landover, MD; ✆ (301) 386-5577

- 3535 Russett Green, Laurel, MD; ✆ (301) 604-2060

- 2365 Crain Highway, Waldorf, MD; ✆ (301) 645-6116

- 610 North Frederick Avenue, Gaithersburg, MD; ✆ (301) 216-2550

- 14050 Worth Avenue, Woodbridge, VA; ✆ (703) 491-2662

And other suburban locations

- ✑ www.samsclub.com

Sam's Club is another national membership discount chain, where for a mere $35 or so a year you can browse through a warehouse full of clothing, appliances, electronics, food, jewelry, office supplies, books, sports merchandise, pet supplies, outdoor gear, and more. What Sam's Club lacks in atmosphere it makes up for in pure choice. Heck, you could almost supply your whole life without ever shopping anywhere else. As with the other discount merchants, Sam's Club is able to offer great prices through volume purchasing,

thanks to hundreds of stores in major urban centers across the country and its 50 million members.

Store hours are 10 a.m. to 8:30 p.m. Monday through Friday, 9:30 a.m. to 8 p.m. on Saturday, and 11 a.m. to 6 p.m. on Sunday.

Target

- 3101 Jefferson Davis Highway, Alexandria, VA; ✆ (703) 706-3840

- 10500 Campus Way S, Upper Marlboro, MD; ✆ (301) 324-7080

- 12000 Cherry Hill Road, Silver Spring, MD; ✆ (301) 586-0724

- 10301 New Guinea Road, Fairfax, VA; ✆ (703) 764-5100

- 4600 Mitchellville Road, Bowie, MD; ✆ (301) 352-3830

- Grand Corner Avenue, Gaithersburg, MD; ✆ (301) 721-1760

- 3343 Corridor Marketplace, Laurel, MD; ✆ (301) 483-0934

- 12197 Sunset Hills Road, Reston, VA; ✆ (703) 478-0770

- 3300 Western Parkway, Waldorf, MD; ✆ (301) 645-7114

And other suburban locations

- ✑ www.target.com

This chain has positioned itself as a slightly upscale discount store, which is a fair definition. In fact, among some trendy shoppers, it is referred to with a faux-French name: "Tar-jay."

You'll find its stores full of good deals on clothes, jewelry and accessories, electronics, music and video, kitchen supplies, sports equipment, luggage, toys, and more. On top of the everyday low prices, they almost always have some kind of departmental clearance sale where you can get merchandise at up to 50 percent off the regular price.

On a recent expedition, Mrs. C was offered a women's wool sweater for a mere $16, and women's pants, jumpers, and tank tops were available for $7.99. In the other departments, a 19-inch color TV was on sale for $119, a number of just-released music CDs were priced at $12.88, and a range of popular entertainment and productivity software was available for $15 to $30.

Most Target stores are open seven days a week from 8 a.m. to 10 p.m.

Tuesday Morning

- 3501 Carlin Springs Road, Falls Church, VA; ✆ (703) 845-3710
- 11111 Georgia Avenue, Wheaton, MD; ✆ (301) 942-1884
- 136 Maple Avenue West, Vienna, VA; ✆ (703) 938-6707
- 6230 Rolling Road, Springfield, VA; ✆ (703) 866-0379
- 25 Beall Avenue, Rockville, MD; ✆ (301) 424-2480
- 131 Bowie Road #A, Laurel, MD; ✆ (301) 953-7907
- 353 Muddy Branch Road, Gaithersburg, MD; ✆ (301) 921-9542
- 750 State Route 3 South, Gambrills, MD; ✆ (410) 923-1194
- 492 Elden Street, Herndon, VA; ✆ (703) 471-5571
- 5619 Stone Road, Centreville, VA; ✆ (703) 222-7730
- 14516 Potomac Mills Road, Woodbridge, VA; ✆ (703) 494-1215

And other suburban locations

- ✐ www.tuesdaymorning.com

TM's bargains will make you feel much better any day of the week, offering a 50 to 80 percent "everyday" discount on upscale merchandise found in better department stores. Selections range from room and area rugs to luxury linens, fine crystal, china, decorative accessories, lawn and garden accents, gourmet cookware and housewares, luggage, toys, and seasonal decorations or gifts.

For more information, see the section on *Carpeting and Rugs.*

Wal-Mart

- 5800 Kingstowne Center, Alexandria, VA; ✆ (703) 924-8800
- 7910 Richmond Highway, Alexandria, VA; ✆ (703) 780-4194
- 8745 Branch Avenue, Clinton, MD; ✆ (301) 877-0502
- 3330 Crain Highway, Bowie, MD; ✆ (301) 805-8850
- 3549 Russett Green, Laurel, MD; ✆ (301) 604-0180
- 11930 Acton Lane, Waldorf, MD; ✆ (301) 705-7070
- 13059 Fair Lakes Shopping Center, Fairfax, VA; ✆ (703) 222-2953
- 14000 Worth Avenue, Woodbridge, VA; ✆ (703) 497-2593

And other suburban locations

- ✐ www.wal-mart.com

Talk about American icons! This is another of those places that needs no description; this place tries—and sometimes succeeds—at being your everyplace.

Wal-Mart is the world's largest retailer of general merchandise goods; by the way, they also operate Sam's Clubs, a warehouse club. (Sam Walton gave his first name to Sam's Clubs and part of his last name to the mother shop, Wal-Mart.)

Wal-Mart has a fine and bargain-priced selection of electronics, cameras, video games, toys, jewelry, home and garden supplies, movies, books, music, clothes, auto supplies—just about any retail category you can wrap your hands (or arms) around.

Buy a ¼-carat three-stone diamond ring for just $149 (perfect for a wedding at the Elvis Chapel in Las Vegas). How about a Mr. Coffee Pump Espresso and Cappuccino maker for under $50, a computer desk with pullout keyboard for under $60, or a Hunter 42-inch ceiling fan for under $70? In the music department, you can get a wide selection of recently released CDs in the $13 to $15 range. The list goes on and on, of course.

Most Washington area Wal-Mart stores are open 24 hours. Call to confirm hours.

ELECTRONICS

There are lots of places to save money on appliances and electronics in and around D.C. Some, unfortunately, are as far below repute as they are below retail. With merchandise that is imported from foreign countries, there is a greater possibility of shady deals, or inferior quality. Be careful out there!

If you have doubts as to any store's reliability, one of the best ways to protect yourself is to ask about their guarantee policy; make sure the item you want carries an American warranty. Since some stores deal directly with manufacturers in the Far East, their merchandise may carry a foreign warranty instead. Even for identical products, a foreign warranty can make repairs a hassle—unless you don't mind paying the postage to Japan! Remember, you are perfectly within your rights to inquire about this in the store.

AUDIO/VIDEO EQUIPMENT

Best Buy

- 1201 South Hayes Street, Arlington, VA; ✆ (703) 414-7090

- 6201 Arlington Boulevard, Falls Church, VA; ✆ (703) 538-1190

- 6555 Frontier Drive, Springfield, VA; ✆ (703) 922-4980

- 1200 Rockville Pike, Rockville, MD; ✆ (301) 984-1479

- 14160 Baltimore Avenue, Laurel, MD; ✆ (301) 497-1890

- 15750 Shady Grove Road, Gaithersburg, MD; ✆ (301) 990-8839

- 1861 Fountain Drive, Reston, VA; ✆ (703) 787-3760

- 13058 Fair Lakes Parkway, Fairfax, VA; ✆ (703) 631-3332

- 9031 Snowden River Parkway, Columbia, MD; ✆ (410) 312-4900

And other suburban locations

- ✑ www.bestbuy.com

See the listing under *Discount Department Stores.*

Belmont TV

- 4723 King Street, Arlington, VA; ✆ (703) 671-8500

- 9101 Marshall Avenue, Laurel, MD; ✆ (301) 498-5600

- 12500 Layhill Road, Silver Spring, MD; ✆ (301) 942-1300

- ✐ www.belmonttv.com

"We're very service-oriented here," the Arlington branch manager told Mr. C. "We keep our prices at or below the superstores, and you get good service." Indeed, even with competitive prices on audio and video equipment, Belmont TV offers free delivery and setup in your home, as well as a good stock of replacement parts and a repair department in the store.

The goods themselves included, on Mr. C's visit, a JVC stereo system, including a CD player, cassette recorder, and speakers, discounted from a list price of $199 to Belmont's $187. A Toshiba Flat-Screen 20-inch color TV, averaging about $329 elsewhere, was going for $287 here. And they offer similar deals on VCRs, camcorders, projection TVs, and the like.

Belmont is open Monday through Friday from 10 a.m. to 7 p.m., Saturday from 9 a.m. to 6 p.m., and Sunday from noon to 5:30 p.m.

Circuit City

- 3551 32nd Avenue, Temple Hills, MD; ✆ (301) 630-3704

- 5710 Columbia Pike, Baileys Crossroads, VA; ✆ (703) 845-1446

- 6231 Columbia Park Road, Landover, MD; ✆ (301) 386-4444

- 2009 Brightseat Road, Landover, MD; ✆ (301) 386-5020

- 11160 Veirs Mill Road, Wheaton, MD; ✆ (301) 933-1776

- 1200 Mercantile Lane, Upper Marlboro, MD; ✆ (301) 386-6120

- 1905 Chain Bridge Road, McLean, VA; ✆ (703) 893-6112

- 6640 Loisdale Road, Springfield, VA; ✆ (703) 922-0565

- 7039 Old Keene Mill Road, Springfield, VA; ✆ (703) 912-7219

- 845 Rockville Pike, Rockville, MD; ✆ (301) 881-4581

- 11220 James Swart Circle, Fairfax, VA; ✆ (703) 385-7720

- 14301 Matawoman Drive, Brandywine, MD; ✆ (301) 782-3355

- 3000 Festival Way, Waldorf, MD; ✆ (301) 932-8160

- 602 Quince Orchard Road, Gaithersburg, MD; ✆ (301) 990-3948

- 46301 Potomac Run Plaza, Sterling, VA; ✆ (703) 421-7015

And other suburban locations

- ✐ www.circuitcity.com

Here's another national chain where you can get just about any consumer electronics item you desire. Computers, cameras, home and car audio systems, wireless phones, and video gear are all here. If you're a savvy shopper and hit Circuit City on the right days, you'll also find some decent deals. This place tends to have regular weekly specials, and they usually offer bonus accessories and manufacturer's rebates with many of their products.

The last time that Mr. C shuffled down these gleaming aisles, he noticed a Sherwood 105-watt stereo receiver for only $79.99 and a

Phillips portable CD player for under $50. He could have picked up a 1.1GHz Compaq PC system, complete with a monitor, CD-ROM drive, and printer, for under $600, as well as an AA Alkaline battery 20-pack for just 99 cents (after a rebate). They also had an Olympus 2.1 megapixel camera available for under $400.

Store hours are 10 a.m. to 9 p.m. on Monday through Saturday, and noon to 6 p.m. on Sunday.

Graffiti Audio-Video

* 1214 Connecticut Avenue N.W., Washington, D.C.;
  ✆ (202) 296-8412

* 4914 Wisconsin Avenue N.W., Washington, D.C.;
  ✆ (202) 244-9643

* 7810 Old Georgetown Road, Bethesda, MD;
  ✆ (301) 907-3660

* Fair City Mall, Fairfax, VA;
  ✆ (703) 323-6900

* ✍ www.graffitiaudio.com

All kinds of new electronic equipment, including TVs, VCRs, camcorders, cordless phones, and answering machines are sold here at good prices.

There's an equally impressive lineup of brands: Sony, JVC, right on up to high-end Bose products. Mr. C liked a Denon 5-Disc CD Changer for $159. Need a visual? How about a Quasar 20-inch color TV for $189, or a Panasonic VCR with four heads and hi-fi stereo for $89. The store even sells used CDs—good and cheap!

Not only does Graffiti claim to have the lowest prices, they guarantee it. If you buy something here and within 30 days see it advertised for less, within a 100-mile radius, they'll refund you the difference.

Store hours are 10 a.m. to 7 p.m. Monday through Saturday, and noon to 6 p.m. on Sunday.

Radio Shack

* 1345 F Street N.W., Washington, D.C.; ✆ (202) 737-9480

* 1100 15th Street N.W., Washington, D.C.; ✆ (202) 296-2311

* 442 L'Enfant Plaza S.W., Washington, D.C.; ✆ (202) 484-6050

* 1150 Connecticut Avenue N.W., Washington, D.C.;
  ✆ (202) 833-3355

* 1850 K Street N.W., Washington, D.C.; ✆ (202) 467-5052

* 401 M Street S.W., Washington, D.C.; ✆ (202) 488-4544

* 717 D Street S.E., Washington, D.C.; ✆ (202) 544-9660

* 1767 Columbia Road N.W., Washington, D.C.;
  ✆ (202) 986-5008

* 1528 Benning Road N.E., Washington, D.C.; ✆ (202) 397-3090

- 1100 South Hayes Street, Arlington, VA; ℡ (703) 415-5960

- 1651 Crystal Square Arc, Arlington, VA; ℡ (703) 413-6685

- 4250 Connecticut Avenue N.W., Washington, D.C.; ℡ (202) 537-0600

- 2837 Alabama Avenue S.E., Washington, D.C.; ℡ (202) 582-3440

- 4531 Wisconsin Avenue N.W., Washington, D.C.; ℡ (202) 363-2541

- 4238 Wilson Boulevard #3062, Arlington, VA; ℡ (703) 522-2087

- 5201 Indian Head Highway, Oxon Hill, MD; ℡ (301) 749-5890

- 3500 E West Highway, Hyattsville, MD; ℡ (301) 559-2266

- 3911 Branch Avenue, Temple Hills, MD; ℡ (301) 423-7505

- 3425 King Street #A, Alexandria, VA; ℡ (703) 845-0300

- 3521 S Jefferson Street, Baileys Crossroads, VA; ℡ (703) 931-0320

And other suburban locations

- ✑ www.radioshack.com

Nerds rule! From transistors and coaxial cable to weather radios, headphones, PCs, home audio, and radio-controlled toy cars, this old, reliable redoubt of the high-water trouser and pocket protector crowd has everything electronic, of course, and always at competitive prices. What's more, Radio Shack seems to always have sales on selected items, allowing you to save 25 percent or more when your need to acquire meets their need to unload.

On a recent stealth mission of holiday shopping, Mr. C became intrigued with a cordless phone headset marked down from $49.99 to only $29.99, a long-range, cordless 2.4 GHz phone for only $59.99 (33 percent off their normal price), a full-sized MIDI keyboard fore just $149.99, and a nifty *noncontact* infrared thermometer for $49.99. (Awesome!)

My rule here is: shop when there is a sale. Luckily, that's most of the time, although not everything is reduced at once. Read the flyers, check the online Web site, and make a phone call to track the object of your electronic desire.

Depending upon financial conditions, Radio Shack also offers 12-month, no-interest financing on big-ticket items such as computers.

Store hours are generally 10 a.m. to 9 p.m. Monday through Saturday, and noon to 6 p.m. on Sunday. However, hours may vary by location, so call before you go!

Sound Images

- 7700 Old Georgetown Road, Bethesda, MD; ℡ (301) 718-2824

- 5541 Arlington Boulevard, Falls Church, VA; ℡ (703) 534-1733

- ✑ www.soundimagesusa.com

Sound Images carries used, reconditioned, and new audio and visual equipment, and it features lots of great bargains.

The Cheapster spotted a new set of PSB "Image 2B" speakers marked down from a $399 list price to $349. If you are willing to go used (and save *big* bucks), you may find a high-end VCR for $100 or so. Most of the used equipment is between five and 10 years old, but it's all in tip-top shape. Sound Images does its own repair work in-store and backs it up with a 90-day guarantee.

The Falls Church store is open 7 days a week: Monday through Friday from 11 a.m. to 8 p.m., Saturday from 10 a.m. to 6 p.m., and Sunday from noon to 5 p.m. The Bethesda store has the same hours but is not open on Sunday.

The Speaker Factory

- 15815 Frederick Road, Rockville, MD; ✆ (301) 840-0747

- ✐ www.speakerfactoryusa.com

Wayyy up near Shady Grove, this company manufactures its own lines of high-end audio speakers for your home. (It also carries, but does not make, speakers for your car). If you like space-age design, you'll love the black-lacquer pyramid-shaped tower speakers. Why shouldn't your speakers look as good as they sound?

Why is merchandise like this cheap? Because, if you're at all handy with a screwdriver, you can assemble these babies yourself in an hour or two—and save big bucks in the process. It's not terribly difficult, since the intricate electronic work is done for you. Your task is mainly that of assembling the wooden cabinets. But their 250-watt "Gemini" tower, which could cost as much as $1,500 a pair in a preassembled version, was just $500 in kit form when Mr. C dropped by. That's music to Mr. C's ears.

There are lots of models to choose from, in varying degrees of power and complexity. For true electronics buffs, the store also stocks the individual parts—woofers, tweeters, cables, etc.—suitable for home or car installations. Many of these come from outside manufacturers, but

since SF gets them directly, before the labels go on, it can sell them at as little as half the retail price. You can even upgrade your current speakers in an existing enclosure, instead of starting from scratch. The staff is friendly and helpful.

Store hours are Tuesday through Friday from 10 a.m. to 6 p.m., Thursday from 10 a.m. to 9 p.m., and Saturday from 10 a.m. to 5 p.m.

COMPUTERS

Prices and specifications on computers change daily—almost always in the consumer's favor, with capabilities going up while prices remain the same or drop. What a deal!

The best way to shop for a computer is to know more than the salesperson. Check out the online Web sites, ask your neighborhood weenie, and read the ads in newspapers and specialty magazines. Then walk into a store already knowing what you want to buy and about how much it costs; let the salesperson try to convince you of a better deal than the best you have already found.

Best Buy

- 1201 South Hayes Street, Arlington, VA; ✆ (703) 414-7090

- 6201 Arlington Boulevard, Falls Church, VA; ✆ (703) 538-1190

- 6555 Frontier Drive, Springfield, VA; ✆ (703) 922-4980

- 1200 Rockville Pike, Rockville, MD; ✆ (301) 984-1479

- 14160 Baltimore Avenue, Laurel, MD; ✆ (301) 497-1890

- 15750 Shady Grove Road, Gaithersburg, MD; ✆ (301) 990-8839

- 1861 Fountain Drive, Reston, VA; ✆ (703) 787-3760

- 13058 Fair Lakes Parkway, Fairfax, VA; ✆ (703) 631-3332

- 9031 Snowden River Parkway, Columbia, MD; ✆ (410) 312-4900

  And other suburban locations

- ✍ www.bestbuy.com

  See the listing under *Discount Department Stores.*

Circuit City

- 3551 32nd Avenue, Temple Hills, MD; ✆ (301) 630-3704

- 5710 Columbia Pike, Baileys Crossroads, VA; ✆ (703) 845-1446

- 6231 Columbia Park Road, Landover, MD; ✆ (301) 386-4444

- 2009 Brightseat Road, Landover, MD; ✆ (301) 386-5020

- 11160 Veirs Mill Road, Wheaton, MD; ✆ (301) 933-1776

- 1200 Mercantile Lane, Upper Marlboro, MD; ✆ (301) 386-6120

- 1905 Chain Bridge Road, McLean, VA; ✆ (703) 893-6112

- 6640 Loisdale Road, Springfield, VA; ✆ (703) 922-0565

- 7039 Old Keene Mill Road, Springfield, VA; ✆ (703) 912-7219

- 845 Rockville Pike, Rockville, MD; ✆ (301) 881-4581

- 11220 James Swart Circle, Fairfax, VA; ✆ (703) 385-7720

MR. CHEAP'S PICKS

Computers

CompUSA—Sure, it's another soulless superstore, but with its huge selection CompUSA is definitely a prime resource when it comes to new computers and accessories

PC Warehouse—Okay, it's a chain store, but if you're looking for pre-built, new systems, PC Warehouse's combination of great selection and good prices is hard to beat.

- 14301 Matawoman Drive, Brandywine, MD; ✆ (301) 782-3355

- 3000 Festival Way, Waldorf, MD; ✆ (301) 932-8160

- 602 Quince Orchard Road, Gaithersburg, MD; ✆ (301) 990-3948

- 46301 Potomac Run Plaza, Sterling, VA; ✆ (703) 421-7015

  And other suburban locations

- ✍ www.circuitcity.com

  See the listing under *Electronics.*

CompUSA

- 5901 Stevenson Avenue, Alexandria, VA; ✆ (703) 212-6610

- 8357 Leesburg Pike, Vienna, VA; ✆ (703) 821-7700

- 1776 E Jefferson Street, Rockville, MD; ✆ (301) 816-8963

- 12189 Fair Lakes Promenade Drive, Fairfax, VA; ✆ (703) 359-1401

- 500 Perry Pkwy Gaithersburg, MD; ✆ (301) 947-0001

- 14427 Potomac Mills Road, Woodbridge, VA; ✆ (703) 492-6262

- 6625 Ritchie Highway, Glen Burnie, MD; ✆ (410) 768-1612

- 1015 York Road, Baltimore, MD; ✆ (410) 494-4200

- 10931 W Broad Street, Glen Allen, VA; (804) 217-6888

- ✍ www.compusa.com

Yet another soulless superstore, but, with its huge selection CompUSA is definitely a prime resource when it comes to new computers and accessories, including software packages, printers, scanners, storage options, networking equipment, handhelds, digital cameras, software, computer books, and much more.

Other necessities at good prices include things like scanners, printers, cables, software, books, and more. USB scanners from UMAX and Hewlett Packard are available in the $69 to $79 range. You can buy a 50-pack of Sony CD-R discs for just $29.99, and a Microsoft optical trackball for $39.99. CompUSA's own "house brand" knockoffs are even cheaper. You can also save big on paper and printers.

A friend of Compu-Cheapo's, who is a high-tech expert, loves CompUSA because the store puts all of its hardware out on display. Most everything is up and running, from desktops to laptops to digital camcorders, so you can compare models and play with them to your heart's content.

The stores are open weekdays and Saturdays from 9 a.m. to 9 p.m., and Sundays 11 a.m. to 6 p.m.

National Computer Warehouse

- 3706 Mount Vernon Avenue, Alexandria, VA; ✆ (703) 836-4900

- ✍ www.ncwpc.com

You wouldn't expect that this quiet little storefront to sell more than 500 computers a week—but they do. Many of these sales are mail order, and this high-volume business translates into lower prices for you.

NCW puts Windows desktop systems together from component parts, so that you can get just about any configuration imaginable. This also means you can order a computer with just the features and power you need, rather than going to a department store and paying for bells and whistles you'll never use.

The company serves both home and office clientele, and has done so for nearly 15 years. Their store warranty covers parts for three years and labor for one year on everything in the system except monitors (which are covered by the manufacturer's warranty).

NCW sells component parts as well, along with printers, peripherals, and software. One warning: Another reason for the low overhead/low price is the small size of the sales staff, who know computers inside and out and take lots of time with their customers. This is a fine thing—but don't come in here if you are in a hurry.

Store hours are Monday through Friday from 9 a.m. to 6:30 p.m., and Saturday from 11 a.m. to 4 p.m.

PC Warehouse

- 11000 Baltimore Avenue #107, Beltsville, MD; ✆ (301) 937-5027

- 706 Rockville Pike #C, Rockville, MD; ✆ (301) 309-1900

- ✍ www.pcwarehouse.com

It's not your typical mile-high-ceiling "warehouse," but there's still plenty of selection, plus a knowledgeable staff at this national chain.

They've got a good selection of brand names, including Compaq, Epson, and IBM.

Of course, PC Warehouse has nearly every conceivable PC peripheral and accessory, including PC parts and miscellaneous computing supplies. They even have a selection of digital cameras.

For Macintosh enthusiasts, PC Warehouse offers a dedicated "store within a store" filled with Apple computers, monitors, printers, scanners, and other accessories at current prices.

If you're having a problem with a computer that you already own, you'll be happy to know that Mr. C found PC Warehouse's in-house repair shop to have much better rates than some of its national chain competitors.

The only real drawback with PC Warehouse is that it was not open at night or on weekends the last time the Cheapster checked: Store hours were 9 a.m. to 5:30 p.m. Monday through Friday.

FACTORY OUTLET CENTERS

Factory outlets are usually good for saving a few hard-earned bucks. Although Mr. C has not been shy about mentioning these types of stores wherever appropriate in the book, he thought you might be able to also save some hard-earned time by focusing in on retail areas or shopping centers boasting several of these stores in one spot. Some of these are a little further from central Washington—as much as an hour or two out of town—but for some shoppers they're worth the trip.

But first a word of education: just because it's called a factory outlet doesn't necessarily mean it 1) is owned by a factory, or 2) offers prices that are better than you'll find in a retail store, or 3) sells the same type and brands of products you might find in a retail store. When you think about it, *every* store is an outlet for a factory; that's what they do.

As a savvy shopper, you need to know the merchandise. Compare items in factory outlets to those you find elsewhere; don't always assume they are better deals.

Shopping at such outlet malls can save you time and money, but it does not always guarantee incredible deals that you would not be able to find anywhere else. Here are some important things to keep in mind:

- You won't clothe your entire family for $9.99.
- Not every item in these stores is sold at discount; many stores offer a mix of clearance and regular merchandise. Look for

unadvertised specials; unlike department stores, these shops tend to put these up front, to lure you in.

- Some outlet stores sell goods made specifically for them—close, but not identical, to goods in full-price stores. Some manufacturers use pseudonyms for their outlet merchandise. Escada goes by First Choice, OshKosh B'Gosh uses The Genuine Article, and the Hero Group refers to Oleg Cassini, Bill Blass, and Bob Mackie.
- It helps to do a little advance research. Go in knowing what you want, and how much it costs elsewhere, so you'll know a bargain when you see it.

Having gotten that off his chest, Mr. C certainly recommends that you check these malls out. Careful shoppers will indeed come away with some good deals, especially those who are willing to wait until late in the retail season. This makes perfect sense; only full-price retailers want you to think about winter coats in the height of summer.

Potomac Mills

- 2700 Potomac Mills Circle, Prince William, VA; ✆ (800) VA-MILLS

- ✐ www.potomacmills.com

The nearest (and best) of the outlet malls, this is just 45 minutes south of the district at exit 156 off I-95. In fact, it's become one of the biggest tourist attractions in Virginia; some 13,000 tour buses pull in here each year, making the Mills more popular than Colonial Williamsburg, Busch Gardens, Monticello, or Mount Vernon. What's the big attraction? Well, Potomac Mills is huge: 1.7 million square feet to be precise. Some 220 stores tout up to 70 percent savings on famous name clothing and shoes, housewares, toys, gifts, luggage, and more.

Here are just some of the many well-known stores found at Potomac Mills:

Anchor stores: AMC 15 Theatre, Books-A-Million, Burlington Coat Factory, Daffy's, Group USA,

JCPenney Outlet, Linens 'N Things, Marshalls, Mikasa, Nordstrom Rack, Off 5TH-Saks Fifth Avenue, Spiegel Outlet, Syms, TJ Maxx, Vans Skatepark.

Specialty stores: Ann Taylor Factory Store, Big Dog Sportswear, Brooks Brothers, Calvin Klein, Donna Karan Company Store, Eddie Bauer Outlet, Escada, ESPRIT, Fossil Outlet, Gap Outlet, Guess? Outlet, Harry & David, Jones New York, L.L. Bean Factory Store, Laura Ashley Outlet, Lenox, Nautica Clearance Center, Nine West Outlet, Oilily Outlet, Old Navy Outlet, Tahari, Tommy Hilfiger, Polo Ralph Lauren Factory Store.

The hours of operation are Monday through Saturday from 10 a.m. to 9:30 p.m., and Sunday from 11 a.m. to 7 p.m.

Chesapeake Village

- 441 Chesapeake Village Road, near the intersection of Routes 50 and 301, Queenstown, MD; ✆ (410) 827-8654

A bit further afield, but worth the drive, Chesapeake Village is home to some 60 major-name outlet stores. Roughly an hour's drive east of Washington, D.C., this center has attracted hordes of budget-conscious shoppers since its opening in 1989. Factory-direct prices are as much as 40 to 70 percent off normal retail for clothing, accessories, home furnishings, and more.

Some of the shops to check out include American Tourister Luggage, Anne Klein Designer Clothing, Chicago Cutlery, Guess?, Izod/Gant, J. Crew, Lenox, Liz Claiborne, Maidenform, Nine West, Perfumania, Rocky Mountain Chocolate Factory, Seiko, and Toys Unlimited.

Hours are 10 a.m. to 8 p.m. Mondays through Saturday, and 11 a.m. to 7 p.m. on Sunday (except from January through March, when the mall closes at 6 p.m. daily).

Blue Ridge Outlet

- 315 West Stephen Street, Martinsburg, WV; ✆ (800) 445-3993

Of course, some people are willing to drive even further for a bargain. If you fit that description, head over to the Blue Ridge Outlet Center in Martinsburg, West Virginia. Once an old textile mill, today this historic building boasts more than 50 stores with bargains of up to 70 percent off retail. It's about a 90-minute drive from either Washington or Baltimore.

Stores at this outlet include Book Warehouse, Capacity, Dooney & Bourke, Factory Brand Shoes, Hawkins Leather, L'Eggs Hanes Bali Playtex, Paper Factory, Pfaltzgraff, Robert Scott/David Brooks, Woolrich, and others.

The center is open Monday through Wednesday from 10 a.m. to 6 p.m., Thursday through Saturday from 10 a.m. to 9 p.m., and Sundays from 11 a.m. to 6 p.m. Hours are usually extended at Christmas.

Prime Outlets

- 495 Prime Outlets Boulevard, Hagerstown, MD; ✆ (888) 883-6288

- ✍ www.primeoutlets.com

Another drive worth taking is that to Prime Outlets at Hagerstown, Maryland (I-70 west to exit 29), where you'll find more than 100 (count 'em) designer and specialty outlets. Stores here include Adidas, American Outpost, Ann Taylor Factory Store, April Cornell, Banana Republic, Bass Outlet, Beauty Express, Big Dogs, Black & Decker Factory Store, Bombay Co., Book Cellar, BOSE, Britches, Brooks Brothers Factory Store, Dexter Shoes, Dockers by Design, Dress Barn/Dress Barn Woman, Eddie Bauer, Gap, Izod, KB Toy Outlet, Liz Claiborne Shoes, Motherhood Maternity Outlet, OshKosh B'Gosh, Reebok Factory Direct Store, Rockport Factory Direct Store, Samsonite, The Home Co., Timberland, Van Heusen Direct, Wilson's Leather, Woolrich, Zales the Diamond Store, and many, many others. (Check their Web site for a complete list!)

Outlet hours are Monday through Saturday from 10 a.m. to 9 p.m., and Sunday from 11 a.m. to 6 p.m.

And check out these other outlets:

Leesburg Corner Premium Outlets

- 241 Fort Evans RD N.E., Leesburg, VA; ✆ (703) 737-3071

Located at the intersection of Rt. 7 and the Rt. 15 bypass, store hours are Monday through Saturday from 10 a.m. to 9 p.m., and Sunday from 11 a.m. to 6 p.m.

Massaponax Factory Outlet Stores

- I-95 at exit 126, Fredericksburg, VA; (540) 898-3242

- ✎ www.simplyfredericksburg. com/shopping/massaponaxfactory. shtml

Hours are Monday through Thursday from 10 a.m. to 8 p.m., Friday ad Saturday from 10 a.m. to 9 p.m., and Sunday from noon to 6 p.m.

Ocean City Factory Outlets

- Intersection of Route 50 and Golf Course Road, Ocean City, MD; ✆ (410) 213-1538

- ✎ www.ocfactoryoutlets.com

From January 1 to April 30, store hours are Monday through Thursday from 10 a.m. to 6 p.m., Friday and Saturday from 10 a.m. to 9 p.m., and Sunday from 10 a.m. to 6 p.m.

From May 1 to September 30, they're open Monday through Saturday from 10 a.m. to 9:30 p.m., and Sunday from 10 a.m. to 6 p.m. Hours from October 1 to December 31 are Monday through Thursday from 10 a.m. to 8 p.m., Friday and Saturday from 10 a.m. to 9 p.m., and Sunday from 10 a.m. to 6 p.m. New Year's Day, 10 a.m. to 6 p.m. Closed Easter Sunday, Christmas Day, and Thanksgiving Day.

Prime Outlets at Queenstown

- 441 Outlet Center Drive, Queenstown, MD; ✆ (410) 827-8699

- ✎ www.primeoutlets.com

Just 10 miles east of the Chesapeake Bay Bridge, this is an excellent pit stop on the way to the Eastern Shore beaches and resorts. Store hours are Monday through Saturday from 10 a.m. to 8:00 p.m., and Sunday from 11 a.m. to 7 p.m. A great Internet resource for finding new outlets is at http://outletsonline.com. Happy bargain hunting!

FLEA MARKETS AND EMPORIA

Eastern Market Flea Market

- Seventh Street between C Street and Independence Avenue S.E., Washington, D.C.; ✆ (301) 918-9300

Management has changed here recently, but while the chef may be new, the recipe is the same: a huge, barn-like structure that houses a world-class food emporium. Mr. C. loved the food when he visited, but what was outside caught his attention, too.

Along with the historic food stalls inside, Eastern Market is also

home to a weekend flea market throughout the year. Under canopies, along sidewalks, from tables, and sometimes just spread out on a blanket, vendors hawk their wares.

An eclectic assortment of crafts, clothing, jewelry, and the ever-popular bric-a-brac appears to have the building completely surrounded. New and used, gems to junk—there's a lot to browse. Mr. C found hand-painted silk neckties for $20; same price for brand-new Levi's jeans (irregulars from a certain very well-known chain);

freshly cut roses at $5 for a small bunch; sterling silver rings for $8; and much more. For even better bargains, a little gentle haggling is always worth a try

The flea market generally runs Saturdays and Sundays from 9 a.m. to 5 p.m., closing up a little later in the summer and earlier in the winter. Saturdays lean a bit more towards arts and crafts, with one area completely dedicated to large works by local artists, who are on hand to chat about their work. Live music also accompanies the experience. And for sustenance, well, there's always Market Lunch and the whole mishmash of food stands inside the market itself. It's all fun, popular, and usually crowded.

Montgomery Farm Women's Cooperative

- 7155 Wisconsin Avenue, Bethesda, MD;
  ✆ (301) 652-2291

- ✐ www.montgomerycounty
  md.com/events/montgomery_
  market.htm

Founded in 1932 by a group of farm wives who needed to raise some Depression-era cash, this co-op lives on as a thriving link to bygone days. Inside this wooden building right in the center of town, it feels as though nothing has changed. You can walk around the large circle of counters displaying fresh produce, meats, baked goods, flowers, and handcrafted gifts. Many of the stands sell the same or similar products, so Mr. C suggests you start off with a quick loop to see the full range of prices and selections.

Like downtown's Eastern Market, these offerings don't stop at the doorway. The co-op spills out onto the grounds, with tables full of more flea-markety things,

like jewelry, scarves, leather, bags, flowers, collectibles, *objets d'art*, and even Oriental rugs. It's an especially good place to check at Christmastime, for unique and inexpensive gifts as well as freshly made gingerbread houses, wreaths, and the like.

The food market is open Wednesday and Friday from 7 a.m. to 3 p.m.; the flea market outside runs Wednesday, Saturday, and Sunday from 9 a.m. to 5 p.m. (weather permitting).

Secondhand Rose

- 730 East Gude Drive, Rockville, MD; ✆ (301) 424-5524

First of all, this is *not* the fancy downtown consignment shop—not by a long shot. SR is in industrial eastern Rockville, in a warehouse-sized building. It could best be described as a huge department store for cheapniks on the hunt.

They've got *everything* here but large appliances: hardware, jewelry, furniture, books, records and CDs, dishes, blenders, toasters, sewing goods, flowers, and more. In fact, if it's on your list of things-to-buy, and you're looking for rock-bottom prices, this is the place for you.

Here you can find racks and racks of $8 jeans, $3.50 sweaters, men's and women's suits for as little as $30, and lots more. Children's clothes? Yup, and plenty of 'em, at astonishingly low prices. SR even carries used wedding dresses. *Vintage,* we mean.

This used to be a flea-market type operation, with other vendors and businesses housed here, but no longer. It's all Secondhand Rose now! The quality of merchandise can be a bit thorny, and all sales are "as is" and final, but for cheapsters who love the thrill of the hunt, it's a fun place to prowl around for a few hours.

Secondhand Rose is open from 10 a.m. to 6 p.m. Monday through Saturday.

FLOWERS AND PLANTS

Nothing warms the heart of Mrs. C than a pretty display of flowers, especially when she can be certain Mr. C isn't frittering away the vacation fund on such frivolities.

Many of the great deals you'll find on flowers are only available for cash-and-carry purchases. If you want your flowers delivered, you'll probably wind up paying at least $10 more than the prices described below, plus an additional delivery charge. Also, be aware that while some florists advertise long-stem roses, they may not always be available in red; or if they are, they may sell out early in the day. Mr. C advises you to call ahead to find out for sure.

Eastern Market

- Seventh Street between C Street and Independence Avenue S.E., Washington, D.C.; ✆ (301) 918-9300

See the listing under *Food Stores—General Markets.*

Johnson's Flower and Garden Center

- 4200 Wisconsin Avenue N.W., Washington, D.C.; ✆ (202) 244-6100

- 10313 Kensington Parkway, Kensington, MD; ✆ (301) 946-6700

- 12201 Darnestown Road, Gaithersburg, MD; ✆ (301) 948-5650

Judging from the front of this glitzy complex, you wouldn't expect to find a large nursery on the lower level. From the rear, which is actually one of the store's entrances, you'll barely be able to see the building for the trees—and shrubs, and plants, and . . .

But should cheapsters shop here at all? You bet! For one thing, Johnson's has spectacular sales on the first Monday of every month. Basically, everything inside the store is sold at 20 percent off regular prices, while everything in the back lot outside is 10 percent off. And now credit cards are accepted on sale days, as well as checks and cash.

Johnson's carries a larger selection of cut flowers than any other store in the area, retail or wholesale, and the big walk-in refrigerator is a cheap way to cool off during the hazy days of summer. Prices fluctuate with the seasons, but recently a bunch of 25 carnations went for $12.99, while "Sweetheart" roses were $1.99 a stem and $22.99 a dozen. And there were lots of other beautiful, reasonably priced blossoms chillin' out in the 'fridge as well.

The rest of Johnson's carries seasonal favorites—rows of Christmas poinsettias in red, white, or pink were on display during one of Mr. C's recent visits for $14.95. Azalea plants, in full bloom, were $19.95, and 6-inch tall cyclamen plants were $14.99. All the plants and flowers here are fresh, healthy, and beautiful.

Along with this lovely flora are baskets of all shapes and sizes, starting at 95 cents and going *wayyyy* up from there; colorfully glazed ceramic pots, starting at $24.95, too. Seeds, ribbons, candles, crafts, and craft supplies are also available.

Johnson's is open Monday through Thursday from 8:30 a.m. to 6:30 p.m., Friday from 8:30 a.m. to 7:30 p.m., Saturday from 8:30 a.m. to 6:30 p.m., and Sunday from 9 a.m. to 5:30 p.m.

Montgomery Farm Women's Cooperative

- 7155 Wisconsin Avenue, Bethesda, MD;
  ✆ (301) 652-2291

See the listing under *Flea Markets and Emporia*.

ROSExpress

- 200 K Street NorthWest #6, Washington, D.C.;
  ✆ (202) 842-1000

- 24 hour Telephone Orders:
  ✆ (800) Long Rose (566-4767)

- ✍ www.rose-express.com

Here's a flower deal that isn't cheap but does have a lot of flair, which is why Mr. C calls it a bargain. For $49.99 you can buy a dozen three-foot long-stemmed roses, boxed and gift-wrapped. That's already a decent price, but for an additional $10 you can have them delivered anywhere (local D.C. delivery is only $6.) When you put this all together, it's a way to really impress someone without going into debt.

Part of a nationwide chain, ROSExpress specializes in high-quality gifts and services. Their roses are flown in daily, directly from growers in Central and South America. Over a dozen color varieties are available, from Royalty red to Sterling Silver lavender to Cream Ariana white.

The company is pioneering the delivery side of the business in other ways too. They offer guaranteed delivery, within 24 hours, of a dozen roses anywhere in the country for $69.99; these are shipped in special boxes, lined by hand with Styrofoam to keep the flowers fresh. Oh yes, they even have a "Frequent Flower" credit program. Gotta love it.

Though they do some walk-up business, this is primarily a telephone service that you can call 24 hours a day, 7 days a week. Store hours are Monday through Friday from 8 a.m. to 6 p.m., and Saturday from 10 a.m. to noon.

MR. CHEAP'S PICKS

Flowers and Plants

Johnson's Flower and Garden Center—Johnson's has spectacular sales on the first Monday of every month. Basically, everything inside the store is sold at 20 percent off regular prices, while everything in the back lot outside is 10 percent off.

FOOD STORES

Quoting prices on fresh foods, like meat and produce, is about as smart as quoting politicians on their promises. Neither seems to keep very long. The prices mentioned herein, like everything else in this book, are simply examples, which should give you some idea of each store's general pricing.

Many of the foods listed under individual categories can also be found at stores in the "General Markets" section.

BAKERIES

Entenmann's Bakery Outlet Store

- 1327-A Rockville Pike, Rockville, MD; ✆ (301) 762-1215

Readers with a sweet tooth will want to take advantage of the chance to get Entenmann's baked goods at tremendous savings—in many cases over half off. This clearance outlet has a large quantity of cakes, cookies, pastries, and bread, plus some non-bakery items.

Mr. Cheap wishes Entenmann's had kept up with its developing line of fat-free goodies, but apparently not every consumer of pastries is so attentive to waistline and health . . . oh well.

There are three levels of discount on boxed pastry. Fresh goods are sold at bakery-direct prices, about 30 percent off. Market returns, which haven't yet reached their expiration dates, are about 50 percent off. Finally, the markdown section includes overstocked fresh goods, all priced at $1. You may find a box of chocolate chip cookies for a buck that had been $2.39 a week earlier. Entenmann's stuff is so good, though, that it doesn't go stale very quickly.

For senior citizens, there is a further 10 percent discount off the total at the register, and if the purchase is over $20, the discount goes up to 20 percent. Schools and large organizations get a 20 percent discount as well. And how about this: As you come in the door, you pass a table full of half-priced breads. Buy one of these fresh loaves and you'll get another one free! And every month there's a drawing for a basket full of $10 worth of cakes, bread, and waffles.

Entenmann's is open Saturday through Tuesday from 9 a.m. to 5 p.m., and Wednesday through Friday from 9 a.m. to 6 p.m.

Pepperidge Farm Thrift Store

- 10350 Lee Highway, Fairfax, VA; ✆ (703) 385-6966

- 6818 Bland Street, Springfield, VA; ✆ (703) 451-6979

More than just a bakery thrift store, this is like a discount mini-supermarket. Check the tag colors: Red is for fresh items at 25 percent off retail. Black is just past the expiration date, but still good, at 50 percent off; and blue means closeouts—though never spoiled—at more than 50 percent off.

Loaves of bread and rolls are as low as 99 cents; a large chocolate layer cake reduced from $2.79 to $2.09; bags of soft-baked cookies, in the gourmet varieties, same price; and of course, good ol' Goldfish. The store has weekly specials, and senior citizen discounts on

Tuesdays and Wednesdays. And, every few months a clearance sale reduces these *discount* prices by half. Stock up!

Store hours are Monday through Friday from 9:30 a.m. to 6 p.m., Saturday from 9:30 a.m. to 5:30 p.m., and Sunday from 10 a.m. to 5 p.m.

COFFEE AND TEA

Franklyn's Coffeehouse-Café

* 2000 18th Street N.W., Washington, D.C.; ✆ (202) 319-1800

This neighborhood coffeehouse in Adams Morgan holds monthly fundraisers for local charities. The menu here includes salads, sandwiches, soups, and breakfast foods.

Store hours are Monday and Tuesday from 7 a.m. to 10 p.m.; Wednesday through Friday from 7 a.m. to 12 midnight; Saturday from 8 a.m. to 12 midnight; and Sunday from 9 a.m. to 6 p.m.

Total Beverage

* Landmark Plaza, 6240 Little River Turnpike, Alexandria, VA; ✆ (703) 941-1133

* 1451 Chain Bridge Road, McLean, VA; ✆ (703) 749-0011

* 6711 Bland Street, Springfield, VA; ✆ (703) 912-9387

* 46301 Potomac Run Plaza #110, Sterling, VA; ✆ (703) 433-0522

And other suburban locations

* ✑ www.wineaccess.com

In addition to offering great prices on wines, beers, and sodas (see the listing under "Liquor"), Total Beverage (known as "Total Wines and More" at all but its Alexandria location) makes good on its name by selling bulk coffee for, well, just

beans. Choose from among three dozen flavored roasts, from Colombian Supremo to Hawaiian Kona, all at one low price: when Mrs. C shopped for a jolt, a mere $5.99 a pound and $10.99 for 2 pounds. Kona, in particular, is hard to find anywhere for under $10 for *one* pound!

Total has equally good prices on loose teas, as well as gourmet cheeses (Imported Brie for $4.49 a half pound) and other Epicurean delights.

Store hours are Monday through Saturday from 9 a.m. to 10 p.m., and Sunday from 10 a.m. to 7 p.m.

World Imports

* 1850 K Street N.W., Washington, D.C.; ✆ (202) 296-5767

Located in the corner of International Square, World Imports sells a variety of imported goods at fairly reasonable prices. What caught Mr. Cs attention was the selection of coffee beans by the barrel-full. Now, buying a pound of coffee here isn't cheap per se; the average price is around $8.50 or so. However, for frequent customers, the store offers its own version of discount cards. For every nine pounds of coffee you buy the tenth one is free. Now that's frequent flying!

World Imports is open 7 a.m. to 6 p.m., weekdays only.

GENERAL MARKETS

Eastern Market

* Seventh Street between C Street and Independence Avenue S.E., Washington, D.C.; ✆ (301) 918-9300

This historic landmark, built in 1873, has been a focal point for meat, fish, and produce sellers ever since. Here is one of the best food sources in the District, whether you

---

MR. CHEAP'S PICKS

General Markets

Eastern Market—For over 120 years, this market has been filled with stalls selling fish, meat, produce, baked goods, and more. Low overhead means low prices.

Shoppers Food Warehouse—Tight cost controls (bring your own shopping bags) allow this grocery chain to offer discounts of 10 to 30 percent below retail.

---

pick up 10 pounds of turkey wings for $7.95, fresh swordfish for $7.50 a pound, cow's feet, coffee beans, blocks of cheese, or baked pastries.

Because they share overhead costs, these vendors can sell their wares at reasonable rates. Roaming around from stall to stall, from building to building, is a gastronomic paradise-and a just-plain-fun outing for tourists and natives alike.

An extra attraction is the flea market held outside on weekends; see the separate listing in the *Flea Markets and Emporia* section. And back inside, Market Lunch is a popular spot for a snack or a meal; see the listing under *Restaurants—Capitol Hill*.

The Eastern Market itself is open from 7 a.m. to 6 p.m. Tuesdays through Saturdays, and from 9 a.m. to 4 p.m. on Sunday.

Montgomery Farm Women's Cooperative

• 7155 Wisconsin Avenue, Bethesda, MD;
  ✆ (301) 652-2291

See the listing under *Flea Markets and Emporia*.

My Organic Market

• 1171 East Parklawn Drive, Rockville, MD;
  ✆ (301) 816-4944

This place is worth the hunt for anyone who wants to save on produce and all-natural products. Mr. C found that you can save anything from a dime to a dollar on a given item, compared to the prices at many health food and upscale grocery stores. This includes excellent prices on lots of big names in the health food biz, like Westsoy, Barbara's, Arrowhead, and Nature's Gate.

MOM (say, look at that!) also carries grains, nuts, and dried fruits in bulk; and you can save an extra 10 percent on anything you purchase by the case.

My Organic Market is open from 10 a.m. to 9 p.m. Monday through Friday, Saturday from 9 a.m. to 8 p.m., and Sunday from 10 a.m. to 7 p.m.

Rodman's

• 5100 Wisconsin Avenue N.W., Washington, D.C.;
  ✆ (202) 363-3466

• 4301 Randolph Road, Wheaton, MD; ✆ (301) 946-3100

• ✐ www.rodmans.com

Mr. C was just delighted to find Rodman's. They have a huge selection of goods, and you can save on everything from Coca-Cola to imported foods (that go for significantly less than at most gourmet specialty shops).

Speaking of Coke, how about a two-liter bottle for 88 cents? Not bad. The wine selection is enormous, with just about every country represented. Mr. C was pleased to find three-liter jugs of Gallo for $6.99 and higher-quality vinos that were also well priced.

To satisfy your upscale sweet tooth at a downscale price, Nutella chocolate-hazelnut spread ($2.99 for the 13-ounce size) and Lindt truffles ($7.99 for an 8-ounce box) are just two of the mouthwatering treats found here. And you'll also find cooking and baking ingredients, and fresh produce, at market price or better. Rodman's is also a full-service drug store.

Store hours are Monday through Saturday from 9 a.m. to 10 p.m., and Sunday from 10 a.m. to 7 p.m.

Shoppers Food Warehouse

- 2441 Chillum Road, Hyattsville, MD; ✆ (301) 864-1256

- 6881 New Hampshire Avenue, Takoma Park, MD; ✆ (301) 270-5324

- 6228 North Kings Highway, Alexandria, VA; ✆ (703) 768-8116

- 4223 John Marr Drive, Annandale, VA; ✆ (703) 750-9601

    And other suburban locations

- ✐ www.shoppersfood.com

You want no-frills shopping? This is the place for you.

By all outward appearances, Shoppers Food Warehouse, with some three dozen stores in shopping plazas throughout the 'burbs, resembles any standard supermarket chain; but by keeping overhead costs down they can afford to charge anywhere from 10 percent to 30 percent less than most competitors. In other words, this chain is a low-price leader. And, unlike warehouse clubs, you don't have to be a member to shop here.

Like the clubs, you can often purchase items in large quantities—such as toilet paper in packs of 24 for $5.99 or a 25-pound bag of Purina Dog Chow for $8.88.

Other deals recently seen here have included boneless chuck roast for $1.48 a pound; coffee beans for $5.98 a pound; a three-liter jug of Gallo Chablis for $7.98 (cheap wine, cheap); and a cellophane-packed dozen roses for $6.98.

Short on cash? There's a full-service bank on the premises. And if you get hungry, there's a hot-food bar and a salad bar to visit while you rest up before your next foray into shopping melee.

Chances are, one of these places is near you. All stores are open 24 hours, seven days a week, except on Saturday night/Sunday morning, when they're closed from 12 midnight to 6 a.m.

The Uncommon Market

- 1041 South Edgewood Street, Arlington, VA; ✆ (703) 521-COOP (2667)

- ✐ www.uncommonmarket.coop

A lesson in global economics? Not really. When this co-op talks about market forces, they're referring to the shoppers, whose memberships bring food prices down, By joining this commercial organization, and volunteering to help run it, citizens actually reduce the prices of the food they purchase.

Membership in the co-op is open to everyone, and becoming a member-owner is easy! Complete a membership request, available at the co-op. Return your request with at least one share payment (shares cost $10), plus a one-time administrative fee of $10.

If you're in "good standing" as a member, you receive discounts on purchases—currently, 5 percent off all purchases and an additional 15 percent off when buying full cases of products. There are lots of other benefits as well.

The market itself is a complete grocery store, leaning as most coops do toward healthy foods and organic produce. Bulk dispensers allow you to buy just the quantities you need (definitely a cost-cutter) for anything from rice to olive oil to cereal.

The Uncommon Market is open from 9 a.m. to 9 p.m. Monday through Saturday, and from 9 a.m. to 6 p.m. on Sunday. Stop in, call or check the Web site for member-ship information. It's one of sev-eral similar operations around the D.C. metro area, which also include:

- The Bethesda Food Co-op, 6500 Seven Locks Road, Bethesda, MD; ☎ (301) 320-2530

- The Common Market, 5813 Buckeystown Pike, Frederick, ☎ (301) 663-3416

- The Greenbelt Co-op, 121 Cen-terway, Greenbelt, MD; ☎ (301) 474-0522

- The Takoma Park/Silver Spring Co-op, 623 Sligo Avenue, Silver Spring, MD; ☎ (301) 588-6093.

- The Maryland Food Collective, College Park, MD; ☎ (301) 314-8089

MEAT AND FISH

A & H Seafood Market

- 4960 Bethesda Avenue, Bethesda, MD; ☎ (301) 986-9692

Next door to the Bethesda Crab House (well known for its all-you-can-eat crab deal), this shop is a wholesale and retail business with a full range of fish and shellfish. Market prices vary, of course, but Mr. C found good prices on sword-fish, salmon, and clams during his visit.

Store hours are Monday through Friday from 9:30 a.m. to 7:30 p.m., and Saturday from 9:30 a.m. to 6:30 p.m.

Captain White's Seafood City

- 1100 Maine Avenue S.W., Washington D.C.; ☎ (202) 484-2722

Right on the Potomac, in the shadow of the Case Bridge, sev-eral fishing companies sell their fish straight off the boat. This wharf was, in fact, decreed as a public service, by no less than Congress itself, in 1794. Captain White's is one of the largest of these businesses, specializing in crabs (fresh or cooked), spiced shrimp, and the other assorted shellfish for which these waters are known. You just can't get it any fresher than this.

Elsewhere along this small wharf are a half-dozen other similar vendors, each with its own mix of fish and shellfish, ready to sell you an order of fried clams to walk with or enough to cater that big party you're planning. And of course, each one sells at direct-to-you prices. Wander around, check 'em all out, find the best price, and dive right in.

The wharf is open all year long, with hours that vary between summer and winter; basically, though, most stands are open seven days a week, dawn to dusk.

Eastern Market

- Seventh Street between C Street and Independence Avenue S.E., Washington, D.C.; ☎ (202) 546-2698

See the listing under *General Markets*.

FURNITURE AND BEDS

This chapter combines stores selling new and used furniture, for the home as well as the office. Many of your favorite retailers operate clearance centers, where you can find leftovers and slightly damaged at drastic savings—if you're patient.

A caveat to the cash-conscious: Be very careful when you're going for any leather products. The quality of leather used in making can vary widely, and this can determine how durable your sofa will be in the long run. If you see lots of very obvious flaws in the grain of the leather, think twice before buying.

HOME FURNITURE—NEW

Belfort Furniture

- 22267 Shaw Road, Dulles, VA; ☎ (703) 406-7600

- ✐ www.belfortfurniture.com

Weave your way through Belfort's expansive showroom and view beautiful furniture from such makers as Pennsylvania House, Clayton Marcus, Broyhill, Millwood Creek, Hues Dining Collections, and the Office Collection from Stanley, to name just a few.

More than 210 room settings are displayed in 35,000 square feet of space, but the real bargains can be found at the warehouse sale away from their showroom every Saturday and Sunday at 22510 Sterling Boulevard in Sterling.

Store hours are from Monday through Friday from 10 a.m. to 9 p.m., Saturday from 10 a.m. to 6 p.m., and Sunday from noon to 5 p.m.

Capital Carpet and Furniture

- 1917 14th Street N.W., Washington, D.C.; ☎ (202) 234-8882

- 1825 14th Street N.W., Washington, D.C.; ☎ (202) 234-8828

- ✐ www.capitalcarpetinc.com

Near the hip, bustling U Street scene, these shops take advantage of low overhead (go ahead, squeeze in) and factory-direct purchasing to get you great prices on, yes, carpet and furniture. There's not much to see here in the store except for catalogs, but anything you order can be shipped within two or three days. With over 2,000 styles of flooring to choose from, you'll be able to find the perfect fit for that "whatever" room.

In addition, Capital carries current lines of furniture for every room in the house, by such manufacturers as Bassett, Lane, and all the major midgrade and even high-end brands. And the prices, at 30 to 60 percent savings, can be astonishing. You can save hundreds of dollars on a complete ensemble—all for first quality, fully warranted goods.

Service is the store's strong point. They pledge to find you the best quality for your budget.

Capital is open from 10 a.m. to 7 p.m. every day but Sunday.

CL Barnes Fine Furniture

- 8228 Richmond Highway, Alexandria, VA; ☎ (703) 780-7444

- 8349 Centreville Road, Manassas, VA; ☎ (703) 368-2417

- 3115 Golansky Blvd., Dale City/Woodbridge VA; ☎ (703) 680-0651

- Route 301 and Demarr Road,
  Waldorf, MD;
  ✆ (301) 645-8040

- 🖘 www.clbarnes.com

Don't be intimidated by the posh
selection at CL Barnes. Since 1943,
they've had something for everyone, even for Mr. C.

Barnes Rooms Express is
designed to make it easy for budget
conscious customers who may want
to buy a complete room setting,
like a sofa, loveseat, cocktail table,
end tables, lamps, etc. They have
also made the decorating process
easier by packaging rugs, accessories, and matching dining and
bedroom furniture.

Be sure to look for their yearly
tent sale for even deeper discounts
on fine furniture by Lane, American Drew, Stanley, and more.

Store hours are from Monday to
Saturday from 10 a.m. to 9 p.m.

The Market

- 3229 M SL N.W., Washington,
  D.C.; ✆ (202) 333-1234

- 13048 Fair Lakes Pkwy, Fairfax,
  VA; ✆ (703) 222-1200

- 🖘 www.markethomefurnish-
  ings.com

Did Mr. C hear someone say
futon?! With its own vast suburban
warehouse and a high-volume business, the Market is able to market
good quality home furnishings at
affordable prices. From its posh
Georgetown location, this store
sells fashionable furniture at surprisingly low prices. Futons are the
items here, in all shapes, sizes and
colors. A full-size with a frame was
recently seen for $269; other com-
plete sets start under $200. And
you can get a complete bed/sofa for
as little as $140. Brands carried
include Suder and O'Sullivan.

Along with futons are other
inexpensive furnishings for the
home, like a sturdy, four-foot-tall
chest with a cherry finish ($159), or
a metal-frame architect's desk, with
metal baskets for drawers, a swivel
lamp and matching chair for $60.
Four-shelf bookcases start at $30.
Plus dressers, coffee tables, halogen
lamps, CD racks, and other yuppie
accoutrements.

Quality is middle-grade, but if
you're willing to give up the myth
of immortality—at least when it
comes to furniture—this is your
place.

The Market is open Mondays
thru Saturdays 10:30 a.m. to 8 p.m.,
and Sundays from noon to 6 p.m.

Marlo Furniture
Clearance Center

- 5650 General Washington Drive,
  Alexandria, VA;
  ✆ (703) 941-0800

- 🖘 www.marlofurniture.com

You like Marlo? You like really
low prices? Here at their home
offices, you can get both. From this
vast warehouse, Marlo clears out
leftovers, floor models, sales samples, and slightly damaged goods at
30 to 70 percent off regular store
prices.

The moment you walk in, you'll
be dazzled by the amount of these
bargains, literally stacked up in
front of you on metal shelves.
Among these, Mr. C. found a nifty
white linen loveseat, with a Southwestern pattern; originally selling
for $459, it had been reduced to
$359 and again to just $229. Why?
It was a "last item," with no other
matching pieces from the original
set. Good deal. And a white Italian
leather sofa, a bit soiled (but not
irreparably so), was marked down
from $1,799 to $949.

Move on further into the warehouse and you'll find more traditional kinds of display areas—several rooms filled with bargains like a glass-topped dining table with a green marble base, once $799, now $298. The original chairs were AWOL, but you can easily find a substitute set in lots of complementary styles here. Not to mention recliners, bedroom ensembles, mattresses, lamps, framed art, wine racks . . . you name it.

Actually, each Marlo store has a clearance area, but this is the largest one, with the biggest selection. It's open 10 a.m. to 10 p.m. Mondays through Saturday, and noon to 7 p.m. on Sunday.

Mattress Warehouse

- Pike Center, 12127 Rockville Pike, Rockville, MD; ✆ (301) 253-5550

- Rockledge Plaza, 1046 West Patrick Street, Frederick, MD; ✆ (301) 696-9688

- 451 North Frederick Avenue, Gaithersburg, MD; ✆ (301) 869-9727

And other suburban loctions
- ✐ www.sleephappens.com

Nothing fancy here, just your basic no-frills bedding store-at no-frills pricing. MW sells mattresses, box springs, and sets by Sealy, Serta, SpringAir, and other makers. Would you believe a twin set for $58? Okay, it's hotel-grade. How 'bout a full-size Classic "Super Plush" mattress for $159? That's better. These were some recent closeout specials, which the chain gets frequently. Above certain price levels, they'll also give you free metal frames, delivery, and removal of your old bed.

Store hours at their over 50 locations vary, so it's best to call or visit their Web site.

McLean Furniture Gallery

- 2721 Merrilee Drive, Fairfax, VA; ✆ (703) 280-9174

- ✐ www.mcleanfurniture.com

Just off Lee Highway, between Falls Church and Vienna, this no-man's land of an industrial district is worth finding for quality furniture at a discount—thanks to this dealer and Stanis Furniture (see below).

McLean Furniture Gallery leases furnishings to model homes in the area, but you can walk in anytime and get the same rates as the trade. That's around 40 percent off furniture by Hickory, Broyhill, Bassett, and others, plus mattresses by King Koil and Englander. You can even order your choice of upholstery fabrics and wood finishes. Some of these are pretty fancy: A mahogany dining table by Bernhardt, with six chairs, would retail for over $6,000 but sells here for $3,950. Not everything is that ritzy; basically, you can order just about anything in these makers' catalogues. Several ensembles are on display in the crowded showroom.

Upstairs, MFG also sells the newest-looking used furniture you may ever see. That's because these pieces are barely touched; they've been sitting in those model homes, and have now outlived this purpose. So the store sells them off at 50 to 60 percent below retail. The selection is limited, and they're sold "as is," but you may find a just-like-new steal.

Delivery is available for a flat 2 percent of the purchase price.

McLean Furniture Gallery is open Monday through Friday from 10 a.m. to 7 p.m., Saturday from 10 a.m. to 6 p.m., and Sunday from noon to 5 p.m.

Skynear and Company

- 1800 Wyoming Avenue, N.W., Washington, D.C.; ✆ (202) 797-7160

- 🖰 www.skynearonline.com

Because about two-thirds of its business is done through direct ordering, Skynear can save you anywhere from 10 to 50 percent off furniture and unusual accessories for the home. But don't go thinking that this is merely a catalog showroom.

When Mr. C dropped in, a Gatsby Club chair (upholstered with grade "F" gold dust fabric) was being sold for $429—about 70 bucks off its list price. In fabric grades, by the way, "A" is the lowest quality, with each letter getting consecutively better. A luxurious, deep burgundy hatchet arm sofa (the ends fold down) was reduced from $3,295 to a "mere" $1,999. Slipcover sofas, which are growing in popularity for their ease of care, are available in a wide choice of fabrics.

Okay, so this place isn't cheap, it's just cheap-er. But you can get out of here with some tasteful items for a lot less financial outlay. Create the feel of a New York art gallery with wine glasses that are meant more for looking than drinking—they've got silver bands winding up their bases, with a partial handle dangling a big, glass droplet, and they're $15.95 each. Or, add a little gothic flair to your home with a 6-inch gargoyle figurine for $9.50. If the sky's the limit, it may be nearer than you think.

Skynear is open 11 a.m. to 7 p.m. Monday through Saturday, and noon to 6 p.m. on Sunday.

Stanis Furniture

- 2809 Merrilee Drive, Fairfax, VA; ✆ (703) 698-9500

- 🖰 www.stanisfurniture.com

Along the same road as McLean Furniture Gallery (see above), Stanis is one of the area's biggest discounters of new furniture. In fact, only in a non-retail area like this could Stanis afford to operate such a vast showroom at such prices. Once you enter, say goodbye to standard bargain hunting. The atmosphere is refined; the service is helpful and yet low-key. Specializing in Queen Anne, American Traditional, Country, and 18th Century, the place just goes on and on, packed with elegant pieces from Lexington, Thomasville, Henredon, and over 100 others.

Mr. C found an extra-long Laine sofa with a hardwood frame, originally $1,695, selling here for $1,100; a handsome grandfather clock reduced from $635 to $229; and the same price for a cherry wood rocking chair by Virginia House. Among clearance items mixed in throughout the store, he spotted a tag taking $1,600 off the price of a mahogany dining table by Thomasville.

Low prices too on lamps, mirrors, and other accent pieces, including deals on things like Noritake China to put in your new China cabinet, of course. Stanis also has a limited selection of office furniture, from plush leather chairs to computer desks. On all furniture, they offer free delivery and setup around the Fairfax area, and full refunds and exchanges (even on sale items, within two weeks). They even have Polaroid cameras on hand; in case you need to think your decision over at home, as well as a play area for kiddies while you shop. They must be doing something right—Stanis has been at it for over 25 years.

Stanis is open Monday through Friday from 10 a.m. to 9 p.m., Saturday from 10 a.m. to 6 p.m., and Sunday noon to 5 p.m.

GENERAL WASHINGTON DRIVE, ALEXANDRIA

Just inside Exit 2 (Edsall Road, eastbound) off I-395, a nondescript industrial park yields a hidden treasure of furniture bargains. Despite its impressive-sounding name, this quiet, winding road has nothing to do with the GW Memorial Parkway. These low-rent, no-frills warehouse stores can thus afford to keep prices down on furniture in a variety of styles, both new and used, for the home and office. If you're shopping you can see a lot here all in one place. The Marlo Clearance Center (listed above) is here too, on the street between GVVID and I-395. Here are some of Mr. C's highlights:

Aaron Sells Furniture Clearance Center

- 5720 Gen. Washington Drive, Alexandria, VA;
  ✆ (703) 941-7097

- ✐ www.aaronrents.com

Aaron rents, but when he gets his stuff back, he usually sells it off from this store at a discount. The showroom is vast, with separate areas for home and office pieces; you can find recliners for $99, glass-top kitchen tables for $59 and up, or perhaps a matching linen sofa and loveseat for $199. For the office: Oak-finish executive's desks from $319, leather swivel chairs, bookcases, and more. Some of these are soiled or scuffed, but at these prices, you can fix 'em and still come out ahead.

Aaron also offers special deals for students and the military.

Store hours are Monday through Friday from 9 a.m. to 6 p.m., and Saturday from 9 a.m. to 5 p.m.

The Chair Shop

- 5601-B General Washington Drive, Alexandria, VA;
  ✆ (703) 750-3351

- ✐ www.chairshop.com

Ah, we do live in an era of specialization. For over 10 years, this store has sold nothing but seats—in all sizes, shapes, and quantities—at about 40 percent below retail prices. These are high quality, solid wood, mostly traditional styles from established manufacturers, most based in New England. The pleasant folks here can show you hundreds of designs, and they can custom order any variation you want. And they also, er, stand behind their chairs: They pledge to service everything they sell, for as long as you own it. If you're looking to spruce up the dining room, and can't afford a whole new set, replacing just the chairs—at a discount—is a clever alternative.

Store hours are Monday through Thursday from 11 a.m. to 8 p.m, Friday and Saturday 10 a.m. to 6 p.m., and Sunday from noon to 4 p.m.

K. Baum & Son Office Furniture/Chair City Seating

- 6629 Iron Place, Springfield, VA; ☏ (703) 354-0037

- ✑ www.chaircityseating.com

Chair City is a division of Capitol-Baum Office Furniture, Inc., the Washington, D.C. metropolitan area's commercial and home-office specialists. This longtime family business (since 1884!) sells brand-new office furnishings by Globe, Miller, and other top names, at discounts of up to 40 percent below retail. They also rent furniture out and sell off the returns at even better reductions; you can also trade used furniture in for credit toward the purchase of new stuff.

K. Baum is open weekdays from 9 a.m. to 5 p.m., and Saturdays from 9 a.m. to 2 p.m.

Saah Unfinished Furniture

- 811 Hungerford Dr., Rockville, MD; ☏ (301) 424-6911

- 5641-F Gen. Washington Dr., Alexandria, VA; ☏ (703) 256-4315

- Columbia Pike, Arlington, VA; ☏ (703) 920-1500

- 14802 Build America Dr., Woodbridge, VA; ☏ (703) 494-4167

- ✑ www.saahfurniture.com

Saah makes most of its own furniture in solid pine, oak, birch, and, in a few instances, plywood/veneer (for you rock-bottom Cheapsters). You'll find plenty of choices at any branch, all at no-frills pricing. And with those few exceptions, everything is sturdy and well constructed. Mr. C found a terrific deal in a solid oak china cabinet, with glass doors and a dark-stained finish, for only $498.

Plus dressers, coat trees, and tons of those starving-student classics, the pine bookcase. Yes, you can have Saah do staining and lacquering in a variety of finishes, but you'll save money by doing it yourself.

Call your nearest store for hours.

Sleep Sofa Distributors

- 5641-K Gen. Washington Drive, Alexandria, VA; ☏ (703) 941-7632

One of the very first furniture discounters on this stretch, SSD specializes in convertible sofas from Sealy, Serta, Stearns & Foster, and others. Mr. C found an attractive blue floral sofa, which opens into a queen-size bed, selling here for $400 less than the same thing at a certain major retailer. You can custom order any combination of sofa, fabric, and mattress and still rest easy on the price; the store offers a lifetime low-price guarantee, and they service everything they sell. There's also a limited selection of easy chairs, tables, and other furniture to complement the sofas; or, visit their companion store, Solid Cherry & Oak Gallery (listed below).

Store hours are Monday through Thursday from 10 a.m. to 8 p.m., Friday and Saturday from 10 a.m. to 6 p.m., and Sunday from noon to 4 p.m.

Solid Cherry & Oak Gallery

- 5641-L General Washington Drive, Alexandria, VA; ☏ (703) 256-2497

- ✑ www.cherryandoakgallery. com

Okay, so it's not the most creative name in the world. But it tells no lies, as ol' General George himself would approve. Bedroom and dining rom sets are the focus here, brought in from North Carolina and Pennsylvania, at 30 to 70 percent savings. Ever think you'd find an

oak dining table, complete with
five Windsor chairs to match, all
for $699? Mr. C did.

Store hours are Monday to
Thursday from 11 a.m. to 8 p.m.,
Friday from 11 a.m. to 6 p.m., Sat-
urday from 10 a.m. to 6 p.m., and
Sunday from noon to 4 p.m.

Z Futons and Furniture

- 5620 Gen. Washington Drive.,
  Alexandria, VA;
  ✆ (703) 941-5042

- 2130 P Street N.W., Washington
  D.C.; ✆ (202) 833-3717

- ✍ www.zfurniture.com

Whether your sailing near the
waters off Alexandria or getting
funky in Dupont Circle, these stores
cover trendy Washingtonians' needs
for futons and frames, rice-paper
shoji screens, wrought-iron and
platform beds, halogen lamps,
techno-desks, and cool-looking
accessories to go with them.
Though these look like they've
sprung from the pages of *Architectural Digest,* the makers are mostly
mid-grade. But at these prices, if
the furniture only lasts as long as
the fashion, it probably maintains
some kind of household karma.

Anyway, you can find pine futon
frames as low as $79 here, dinette
sets from $125 or so, track lights,
artsy clocks, picture frames, and
more.

"Z" is open Monday to Friday
from 11 a.m. to 8 p.m., Saturday
from 10 a.m. to 8 p.m., and Sunday
from noon to 6 p.m.

HOME FURNITURE—USED

American Rescue Workers Thrift Shop

- 1107 H Street N.E., Washington,
  D.C.; ✆ (202) 397-6149

- ✍ www.arwus.com

ARW provides food, clothing,
shelter, and social service programs
for needy men, women, and their
children. Their thrift shop helps
raise money for these causes, and
for those of us who are only somewhat needy, offers very inexpensive
used clothing and furniture. Half of
this spacious store is taken with
clothes (for more details, see listing
under *Clothing—Used: Thrift
Shops*). The other half has all
manner of well-worn, still-func-
tional furniture, like a table for
$19.95 and a recliner for $49.50.
Items are brought in regularly, so
there's no telling what you may
find from week to week.

American Rescue Workers Thrift
Shop is open Mondays through Saturdays from 9 a.m. to 4 p.m.

Consignment Furniture Gallery

- 11722 Parklawn Drive, Rockville,
  MD; ✆ (301) 770-4400

- ✍ www.ybuynew.com

CFG gets a nice selection of furniture in a hodgepodge of styles.
Want a $2,500 leather couch but
you only have $999? There was
one here when Mr. C visited. A
hutch of solid teak, with glass
doors, was seen for $499. Same
price for a midgrade complete

bedroom ensemble. Most of the stuff is in good condition.

The store is open Tuesday to Saturday from 10 a.m. to 6 p.m., Sundays 12 noon to 5 p.m., and closed Mondays.

Cort Furniture Clearance Center

- 3137 Pennsylvania Drive, Landover, MD; ✆ (301) 773-3369

- 5710-A General Washington Drive, Alexandria, VA; ✆ (703) 354-2600

- 801 Hampton Park Boulevard, Capitol Heights, MD; ✆ (301) 324-8684

- ✑ www.cort1.com

Cort is a national chain that rents home and office furniture to businesses, model homes, trade show/event managers, and the general public. When these are returned, still in good shape if not sparkling new, they go into the clearance center at the rear of this large showroom. That's where you can snap up a comfy $325 designer chair for just $89. Or a huge, arc-shaped sectional sofa for $629, marked down from a retail value of $1,100. Plus lamps, dining tables, and more.

On the office side, there are plenty of desks and fancy chairs, such as a 30" x 60" oak desk, marked down from $550 to $179. There is also a "damaged" area, with further reductions on items that have been banged up (flaws are pointed out for you). Here, Mr. C saw a solid cherry dining table, reduced from $875 to $175. Stock changes all the time; most pieces are in fine shape and are good-looking contemporary fashion styles. Open Mondays through Fridays 10 a.m. to 7 p.m., and Saturdays from 10 a.m. to 5 p.m.

McLean Furniture Gallery

- 2721-A Merrilee Drive, Fairfax, VA; ✆ (703) 280-9174

See the listing under *Home Furniture—New.*

Upscale Resale

- 8100 Lee Highway, Falls Church, VA; ✆ (703) 698-8100

- ✑ www.upscaleresale.com

Washington's largest consignment shop sprawls over 28,000 square feet of merchandise at 10 to 80 percent off retail and daily markdowns. These folks truly live up to their slogan: "Where Prices Drop Until You Shop."

Okay, things here aren't necessarily cheap, just cheaper than they once were. This store gets a mix of consigned pieces and estate sale furniture, both ways to save on the otherwise pricey. So, if you've just got to have a cherry writing desk for the study, you may find one here—as Mr. C did for $400. The good people at Upscale Resale figure they could get you a hardwood dining room table and six chairs for $810 and up. There's always new stuff coming in; they say that 80 percent of their stock arrives and gets sold within 30 days.

Of course, the range is, to put it mildly, eclectic. Victorian dressers stand proudly next to bedroom sets from the 1950s. And some items are in better shape than others. But it's a fun browse.

UR also gets occasional consignments of new items directly from manufacturers; these are usually closeouts or pieces delivered in the wrong finish. On Mr. C's visit, a leather sofa by a very well-known maker was selling for $1,300— easily several hundred below retail. Ya never know!

Upscale is open Monday through Friday from 10 a.m. to 7 p.m., Saturday from 10 a.m. to 6 p.m., and Sunday from noon to 5 p.m.

OFFICE FURNITURE—NEW AND USED

Dulles Office Furniture

- South Eads Street, Crystal City, VA; (703) 486-1140

- 106-A Oak Grove Road, Sterling, VA; (703) 478-9748

- www.dullesofficefurn.com

The 40,000-square-foot Crystal City location is the largest source for office furniture in D.C., with mostly used stock. Mr. C loved roaming around the vast furniture warehouse, where he found things like a barely worn ergonomic executive's chair by United—a high backed model, originally priced at $900—going for $275 here. That'll make the boss happy.

You'll also find lesser-quality ergo chairs from $65 and up, Steelcase and Shaw-Walker file cabinets for $75, slightly scuffed (but refinishable) oak executive desks from $300, and even secondhand modular office partitions and workstations at one-third to one-half of their original prices.

The best-looking stuff is up front; the further you work your way back, the more grungy the pieces look—but then, the prices drop accordingly. Dulles will fix anything up for you, if you wish. There's even some room for a bit of wheeling and dealing, so make 'em an offer!

Dulles is open Monday through Friday from 9 a.m. to 6 p.m., and Saturdays from 9 a.m. to 5 p.m. The Sterling location is open from 9:30 a.m. to 5:30 p.m. on Monday through Saturday.

HOME FURNISHINGS

Bed Bath and Beyond

- 5810 Crossroads Center Way, Falls Church, VA; (703) 578-3374

  And other suburban locations

- www.bednbath.com

What's just beyond the bed and bath? In addition to small appliances, BBB can outfit your kitchen with just about every doodad known to man (or woman), including the popular line of Oxo "ergonomically designed" kitchen gadgets.

Mr. C. also found a brushed aluminum, good quality flip-top kitchen garbage can for $40, and knit throw rugs and runners to move you barefoot in comfort can be had for as little as $12.

Of course, the bed and bath are where this company made its name (literally). They have such a wide selection of linens at all price points for each room that you could easily adjust your decor preferences to the changing seasons.

Regular couponing for regular customers regularly includes $5 off purchases of $20 or more. So stop in often, and watch your mailbox. But beware: you'll always leave with more than you planned to buy.

BB&B is open Monday through Saturday from 9:30 a.m. to 9:30 p.m., and Sunday from 10 a.m. to 6 p.m.

Fan Fair

- 2251 Wisconsin Avenue N.W., Washington, D.C.; ✆ (202) 342-9255

Fan Fair, and its companion store, Park Place, are two separate shops in the same place; they have the same owners and salespeople, and the merchandise is mixed together. Fan Fair, as the name indicates, specializes in fans, and also lighting fixtures, while Park Place carries fine furniture (which, alas, goes a bit beyond Mr. Cheap range). Mr. C was especially impressed by Fan Fair's relatively inexpensive high-end merchandise; prices are kept down because the store deals in high volume, and carries lots of discontinued and non-current items.

Almost every item is tagged with its list price, along with the store price. A Tiffany rose-bordered glass was recently seen for $210, with a Victorian base for $75—the thing could easily cost up to $500 elsewhere. A Baldwin "James River" style brass-base lamp (originally $340, down to $270 here), and a Hunter ceiling fan with white blades (list price $400, here $249, and on clearance sale for $119) were also eye-catching.

Fan Fair is open 10 a.m. to 6 p.m. Monday to Friday, 10 a.m. to 5 p.m. Saturday, and noon to 5 p.m. Sunday.

Frame Factory Warehouse

- 5700-F Gen. Washington Drive, Alexandria, VA; ✆ (703) 941-0737

Mr. C predicts you will save you up to 30 percent over the regular prices at FF's suburban Virginia stores. Yet, this outlet has the same selection as the rest, all in stock, plus the full framing service.

Of course, if you're a do-it-yourselfer, you can save even more—as much as 50 percent off. Once you've chosen your materials, FF will do the cutting of frame, matte, and glass for you—all you have to do is assemble it. What an easy way to save on redecorating your home.

They will also sell you the raw materials—matte board, foam core, even cutting tools—at prices below many art supply retail stores. And if you really want something in a hurry, the store has ready-made frames in standard sizes. Friendly service, too.

Frame Factory is open Monday through Friday from 9 a.m. to 5 p.m., and Saturday from 9 a.m. to 3 p.m.

G Street Fabrics

- 11854 Rockville Pike, Rockville, MD; ✆ (301) 231-8998
- 5077 Westfield Boulevard, Centreville, VA; ✆ (703) 818-8090
- 6250 Seven Corners Center, Falls Church, VA; ✆ (703) 241-1700
- ✑ www.gstreetfabrics.com

Once a downtown legend, these stores have farmed out and expanded into a suburban legend. The Rockville location of GSF boasts two elegant floors of fabrics and supplies for sewing, upholstery, and even bridal wear—not to mention sewing machines, patterns, books, and everything else you could ever need.

Being such a high-volume operation, G Street is able to price all of this very reasonably, with lots of stuff at discount. Better yet is their selection of remnants, with a wide assortment in every department. You may find run-of-the-mill (excuse the pun) remnants as low as $2.97 a yard, right on up to Waverly, Kaufman, and the like, for around $5 to $6 a yard—easily half of their bolt prices, often in large pieces.

The stores are big on service, offering everything from drapery making and custom upholstering to all kinds of sewing classes for the do-it-yourselfer. It's quite the resource, often with quite the savings.

G Street Fabrics is open Monday through Saturday from 10 a.m. to 9 p.m., and Sunday from 11 a.m. to 6 p.m.

Home Depot

- 15740 Shady Grove Road, Gaithersburg, MD; ✆ (301) 330-4900

- 2815 Merrilee Drive, Fairfax, VA; ✆ (703) 205-1245

- 12275 Price Club Plaza, Fairfax, VA; ✆ (703) 266-9800

- 46261 Cranston Street, Sterling, VA; ✆ (703) 444-2900

And other suburban locations

- ✑ www.homedepot.com

They are everywhere, and they have everything. With over 25 D.C.–area locations, you're not far from this home improvement behemoth. Mr. C likes to drop in regularly to see what has changed in the seasonal departments and what's on special near the registers. He recently purchased some heavy-duty plastic storage shelving for his garage at $40 a pop . . . not bad for utility-type applications.

The Depot is also getting quite the reputation for full kitchen designs, including flooring. They'll even design your kitchen for you for a nominal fee (and reimburse you if you decide to buy). Not bad for you do-it-yourself weekend warriors.

Store hours vary by location, so call ahead. Generally they are Monday through Saturday from 5 a.m. to 10 p.m., and Sunday from 8 a.m. to 10 p.m.

MR. CHEAP'S PICKS

Home Furnishings

Fan Fair—With fans, lighting fixtures, furniture, and more, Mr. C was especially impressed by Fan Fair's relatively inexpensive high-end merchandise;

Lamps Unlimited—How illuminating! Discounted lamps, in all shapes, sizes, and styles.

Reed Electric Company—Reed offers discounted prices on everything from bathroom fixtures to Tiffany-style lamps.

Union Hardware Clearance Center—If you like the look of fancy bathroom fixtures, but not the cost, check out this clearance center where prices are up to 70 percent below retail.

Lamp Factory Outlet

- 13011 Fair Lakes Center, Fairfax, VA; ✆ (703) 818-7430

- 6396 Springfield Plaza, Springfield, VA; ✆ (703) 569-5330

For quick and easy deals, LFO is a no-frills winner. The shelves are stocked mainly with low- to midgrade brands, in a manner that reminds Mr. C of those shoe stores where everything sits out on self-serve racks. The pricing is similar to clearance outlets too: All table lamps are sold at 30 percent off retail every day, for example, while replacement shades are all 20 percent off.

So, when you can find an Emerson ceiling fan and light fixture reduced from $118 to $70, this kind of place can be worth it. Mr. C also found a Baldwin table lamp, in colonial brass with a green fabric shade, about a hundred dollars off list at $225; halogen floor lamps

from $30; and kids' novelty lamps,
in the shapes of things like footballs and globes of the Earth.

The store does offer a repair
service and a lifetime electrical
warranty on all its lamps. Also, you
can order higher-grade lights from
major catalogues at discounted
prices.

Lamp Factory is open from 10
a.m. to 9 p.m. Mondays through
Saturdays, and 11 a.m. to 5 p.m. on
Sundays.

Lamps Unlimited

- 1364 Chain Bridge Road,
  McLean, VA; ✆ (703) 827-0090

Packed from, well, floor to
ceiling, this store is a great
source for table, floor, and
ceiling lamps—at 10 to 30 percent less than many competitors.
Most of the styles here, in
keeping with the environs, are
traditional; a few modern looks
are mixed in. A solid brass and
crystal table lamp by Remington,
for example, was recently seen
for $199—about $100 below
retail. You can also find Tiffany
lamps, cloisonné from China, lots
of replacement shades, and first-
class service (including repairs).
Occasionally, the store takes
advantage of special closeouts
and keeps the prices accordingly
low. Nice stuff.

Lamps Unlimited is open
Monday through Saturday from 10
a.m. to 6 p.m.; Thursday and
Friday until 8 p.m.

Minnesota Fabrics/ Hancock Fabrics

- 7980 New Hampshire Boulevard, Langley Park, MD;
  ✆ (301) 439-3100

- 13837 Briggs Chaney Road,
  Silver Spring, MD;
  ✆ (301) 890-7277

- 6660 Richmond Highway, Alexandria, VA; ✆ (703) 765-4440

- 6343 Columbia Pike, Falls
  Church, VA; ✆ (703) 941-1994

- 9650 Main Street, Fairfax, VA;
  ✆ (703) 323-1311

- 8042 Rolling Road, Springfield,
  VA; ✆ (703) 569-3232

- 144 Branch Drive S.E., Vienna,
  VA; ✆ (703) 281-7307

And other suburban locations

For sheer selection at great prices,
Minnesota Fabrics has got the city
covered. They are a full-service
chain, with fabrics, patterns, tools,
supplies, fillings, and even sewing
classes.

They've got vinyl and burlap
for upholstery, cotton cloth for
draperies, lace for bridal gowns,
Lycra for swimwear, and supplies
for making and stuffing quilts and
pillows. You name it. Furthermore,
there are always plenty of these
items on sale—below MF's
already-low prices.

There are lots of remnants, generally selling at half of the original
bolt price, and other clearance tables
where fabrics are 20 percent to 50
percent off. Most branches also have
a monthly senior citizen's discount
day, when they'll take a further 10
percent off the total purchase.

You get the idea. This place is
like a fabric supermarket; they even
have shopping carts for the truly
industrious. The staff is extremely
courteous and helpful, guiding you
about the store or cutting lengths of
fabric for you; they can also custom
order anything you may need. They
offer sewing machine repair and
scissor sharpening services (try
saying that three times fast) at fair
rates. And, as noted above, you can
register for classes in sewing, craft-
making, creating your own
Christmas presents, and the like.

Many of these vary from store to store, so you'll want to check in with the branch nearest you.

Store hours vary slightly by location but generally are Monday through Friday from 9:30 a.m. to 9 p.m., Saturday from 9:30 a.m. to 8 p.m., and Sunday from noon to 5 p.m.

Pier 1 Imports

- 4477 Connecticut Avenue, Washington, D.C.; ✆ (202) 362-4080

- 3307 M Street N.W., Washington, D.C.; ✆ (202) 337-5522

- 6801 Wisconsin Avenue, Chevy Chase, MD; ✆ (301) 657-9196

- 5609 Baltimore Avenue, Hyattsville, MD; ✆ (301) 779-8354

- 1590 Rockville Pike, Rockville; MD; ✆ (301) 230-9028

- 4349 Duke Street, Alexandria, VA; ✆ (703) 823-9377

- 117 S. Washington Street, Alexandria, VA; ✆ (703) 548-7478

- 3045 Columbia Pike, Arlington, VA; ✆ (703) 486-8164

- 11123 Lee Highway, Fairfax, VA; ✆ (703) 352-5766

- 7253 Arlington Boulevard, Falls Church, VA; ✆ (703) 573-1931

- 7204 Old Keene Mill Road, Springfield, VA; ✆ (703) 644-4677

And other suburban locations

- ✑ www.pier1.com

Pier 1 practically invented the term "lifestyle furniture," with its rattan fan, California cool vibe. Comfortable casual is the watchword here. Pier 1's selection is constantly being updated based on the changing tastes of its funky clientele, so be on the lookout for discontinued items.

Mr. C spotted a Santa Fe dining table with four chairs for $950—about $300 off original price. But it's the accessories that really make a trip here worthwhile. A blown glass pitcher with six matching glasses came in at $90, perfect for kicking back with some iced tea and a good book. And a three-wick, bucket-sized candle was $20.

Store hours vary by location, so call ahead if you're planning to visit early or late in the day.

Reed Electric Company

- 1611 Wisconsin Avenue N.W., Washington, D.C.; ✆ (202) 338-7521

For traditional, contemporary, and decorative styles, Reed has become something of a tradition in itself—a fixture, one might say . . .? Since 1949, Reed has been offering discounted prices on everything from bathroom fixtures to Tiffany-style lamps. A three stem torchère floor lamp that normally sells for $125 can be found here for $90, for example; and a leaded crystal chandelier (there are tons to choose from, in classic and contemporary styles), list priced at $979, goes here for $588.

Not to mention all kinds of hanging lamps, starting at $100 for larger styles, and about $70 for smaller ones. You'll find bankers' desk lamps, with brass bases and green glass shades, reduced from $56 to $42. And Mr. C liked a colorful Tiffany-style glass shade, list price $308, here $231; its Victorian-style base, list priced at $84, was $63.

Reed is open Monday through Friday from 8:30 a.m. to 7 p.m., Saturday from 9:30 a.m. to 5 p.m., and Sunday from noon to 5 p.m.

Union Hardware Clearance Center

- 711 D Street N.W., Washington, D.C.; ✆ (202) 628-8663

- ✐ www.unionhardware.com

Established in 1914, this upscale home decorating center is one of the largest such dealers in the country. Downtown, near the art gallery district, you can check out their clearance store, filled with fancy fixtures at 30 to 70 percent off. A pedestal sink by the Italian maker Torena, list priced at $1,089 (that's some sink!), was recently seen here for $499—with a matching toilet for $599. Still too rich for your tastes? Porcelain vanity sink tops start at $69 (were $175). Add a brass faucet set, less than half-price at $149. Plus similar deals on mirrors, cabinets, switchplates, door knobs, and the rest. All sales are final; the sales staff will spend lots of time with you, just as they would at their regular stores in Bethesda and Falls Church.

Clearance store hours are Monday through Friday from 9 a.m. to 5 p.m., and Saturday from 9 a.m. to 12:30 p.m.

Upscale Resale

- 1456 Duke Street, Alexandria, VA; ✆ (703) 683-3333

- 810 Lee Highway, Falls Church, VA; ✆ (703) 698-8100

See the listing under *Home Furniture—Used.*

Z Futons and Furniture

- 5620 Gen. Washington Drive, Alexandria, VA; ✆ (703) 941-5042

- 101 West Broad Street, Falls Church, VA; ✆ (703) 532-9207

See the listing under *Home Furniture—New.*

JEWELRY

Shop for gold and gems very carefully! Diamonds vary greatly in quality, especially clarity and color; there is a very intricate set of official ratings, far more detailed than the A, B, and C grades some stores use. Be sure to have the jeweler explain any diamond's rating to you before you decide to buy, and don't hesitate to seek a second opinion. There are similar ratings for other gemstones, too.

If you're buying something very expensive—even if it seems to be a fabulous deal—the Cheapster recommends you protect yourself by hiring an independent appraiser to check the quality and price.

The Diamond Exchange

- Rockville, MD; ✆ (301) 770-0100

Wondering why there is no street address? In 1996, The Diamond Exchange was robbed at gunpoint of almost all its inventory—the crooks left only a few pieces of jewelry in the window, just so no one would suspect anything amiss. Before the robbery, DE priced its jewelry with little markup and now the prices are even cheaper—at bare minimum. Owner Ira Kramer has no employees to pay, no mall or shopping center rent (just private office rent), no advertising expense, and no long hours; in fact, all business is done by appointment only when it is convenient for the customer.

Though the inventory is limited, DE's contacts are vast, so that any gold, platinum, diamond, or gemstone jewelry can be ordered at the most competitive price. Of course, diamonds are the specialty as the name suggests. Quotes are gladly given over the phone.

By the way, the FBI did catch the thief, somewhere in Pennsylvania, but not before he had robbed a total of 14 jewelry stores. Mr. Kramer says he likes the new, more flexible arrangement for his store.

Direct Jewelry Outlet

- 101 East Broad Street, Falls Church, VA; ✆ (703) 534-2666

- 14111 Saint Germain Drive, Centreville, VA; ✆ (703) 266-8200

- ✑ www.djo.com

Here's a unique approach to a tricky business. What really sets Direct Jewelry Outlet apart is that gold and silver are sold by weight, not the piece.

Even shopping mall stores would find that hard to beat. Maybe that's why DJO is one of the few jewelry stores that make its prices plainly visible—all tags are right side up; their numbers are low, and they want you to know it. DJO has been cited in local magazines for more than a decade as one of the best places to buy jewelry in the area.

Another reason for the good prices is that these stores also do a lot of business through catalog. If you don't see what you want, they can order it for you from their suppliers with quick delivery.

Several exquisite pieces caught Mr. C's eye. A women's Geneve quartz watch of 14-kt gold, which

might cost up to $2,500 elsewhere, is a more reasonable $725 here. An 18-inch 14-kt gold rope chain, easily $1,500 in many boutiques, was priced at $625. DJO carries Parrisian wheat 14K gold that has a lifetime guarantee. These chains are strong enough to hold a brick (look for the brick when you visit the stores).

Prefer the simplicity of pearls? Mr. C was shown a pair of 6.5mm, AA-grade pearl studs, with backs and posts of 14K gold, selling here for $29. Elsewhere, these earrings would retail for $65.

Diamonds are also affordable here, generally priced about 30 percent less than comparable stones at most other stores. You'll find loose diamonds in all shapes ready to be placed in 14-kt, 18-kt, platinum, and even custom-made mountings, and certainly there are precious and semiprecious gemstones. Plenty of items for men, too. Goldsmiths are on staff ready to alter or repair your jewelry.

Store hours at the Falls Church location are Tuesday through Friday from 10 a.m. to 7 p.m. and Saturday 10 a.m. to 5 p.m. Centreville hours are Tuesday, Wednesday, and Friday 10 a.m. to 6 p.m., Thursday 10 a.m. to 6:30 p.m., and Saturday 10 a.m. to 5 p.m. Both stores are closed Monday and Sunday. The Falls Church location does not sell silver.

Hyde Park Jewelry

- 2401-J Columbia Pike,
  Arlington, VA;
  ✆ (703) 892-1222

Here's a good place to check out for diamonds, colored stones, gold jewelry, and Asian artifacts, many of which are imported directly from Southeast Asia. These include jade ("Not the dyed kind," as the owner proudly points out), opals, and pearls. There are also unusual ceramic pieces here, which make unique gifts.

Being a small store on the out-skirts of a shopping plaza, instead of in a glitzy mall or downtown, Hyde Park keeps its costs down, which translates to lower prices than at those kinds of stores. Legions of repeat customers attest to its success.

The store is open from 11 a.m. to 6 p.m. Tuesday through Saturday. It's closed Sunday and Monday.

Impostors

- Union Station, 50 Massachusetts
  Avenue N.E., Washington, D.C.;
  ✆ (202) 842-4462

- Georgetown Park, 3222 M Street
  N.W., Washington, D.C.;
  ✆ (202) 625-2363

- White Flint Mall, 11301
  Rockville Pike, Kensington,
  MD; ✆ (301) 816-8952

Impostors are the real deal. The majority of the jewelry is faux, but the quality is well above that of common costume jewelry. In fact, as one store manager told Mr. C, "Our standards are 50 percent higher than the industry standard for fashion jewelry." Impostors car-ries some of the same metals that fine jewelers do, such as 14K yellow and white gold and sterling silver in a wide range of prices, and they are discounted.

Believe it when Mr. Cheap says "no one will ever know." Some

jewelry is layered gold over a bronze based metal; or rhodium, which looks just like white gold; or vermeil (gold over sterling silver). Tennis bracelets are particularly popular; in sterling silver they start at $55, vermeil at $95, and solid 14-kt gold at $325. Can't afford a dia-mond ring? A one-carat total weight cubic zirconia ring set in 14-kt yellow gold will cost you only $115, and for those who prefer white gold, the price is just $125.

But wait! The deals get better: these rings in plated yellow gold or rhodium start at $25—a tiny per-centage of the price for the "real thing." Austrian crystal is one of the materials used to simulate other gems, such as rubies.

Impostors' stores glimmer with necklaces, rings, bracelets, and more, as well as a helpful staff, which lets you know what you are (or aren't) paying for. Open seven days and evenings, hours vary between branches.

National Jewel Center

- 1351 Wisconsin Avenue N.W.,
  Washington, D.C.;
  ✆ (202) 333-5555

A group of independent jewelry dealers share the space and rent at this Georgetown location, allowing them to pass low prices on to Cheapsters looking for good deals on quality bangles. These rows of counters give you a chance to bounce from one dealer to another and do some true comparison-shopping, maybe even try some haggling under one roof. Hours vary at different NJC counters. Here are a few of the jewelers that impressed Mr. C during his recent visit:

Desiree Jewelry & Gifts

Desiree is one of the few dealers here for sterling silver jewelry and gifts. Pieces are Native American, Italian, South American, Mexican, Indonesian, and domestic, in styles for women, men, and children. Some of the gifts carried are baby items such as silver spoons, cups and rattles, and key chains, money clips, and other items. Jewelry repair is also available.

Lucky CNN Corp

They sell fine jewelry, diamonds, and custom designs in gold. The jewelers were very helpful, and prices good: a 1-carat diamond tennis bracelet in 10K gold was $129 and the 14K gold price was $149. One-carat diamond rings set in 10K gold were $180 and 14K gold was $220.

Masis Jewelers

Masis carries fine jewelry, mostly 10K gold, at near-wholesale prices. Necklaces, rings, and bracelets are sold by either weight or piece, depending on how much labor was involved in making the individual item. They also repair all kinds of jewelry here, except watches.

Tuesday Morning

- 3501 Carlin Springs Road, Falls Church, VA; ✆ (703) 845-3710

- 11111 Georgia Avenue, Wheaton, MD; ✆ (301) 942-1884

- 3025 Nutley Street, Fairfax, VA; ✆ (703) 280-2130

- 136 Maple Avenue, W Vienna, VA; ✆ (703) 938-6707

- 6230 Rolling Road, Springfield, VA; ✆ (703) 866-0379

- 25 Beall Avenue, Rockville, MD; ✆ (301) 424-2480

- 131 Bowie Road, Laurel, MD; ✆ (301) 953-7907

- 353 Muddy Branch Road, Gaithersburg, MD; ✆ (301) 921-9542

- 492 Elden Street, Herndon, VA; ✆ (703) 471-5571

- 750 State Route 3 South, Gambrills, MD; ✆ (410) 923-1194

- 5619 Stone Road, Centreville, VA; ✆ (703) 222-7730

- 14516 Potomac Mills Road, Woodbridge, VA; ✆ (703) 494-1215

- ✍ www.tuesdaymorning.com

TM's bargains, covered in several previous sections, also extend to jewelry. One sale the stylish Mrs. C found offered stylishly sculpted rings in 10-carat gold set with pearls or semiprecious stones. The retail values of these rings ranged from about $200 to much more, but here they were all selling for prices under $100.

Another style, the narrow "stack" ring, meant to be worn in groups, was on sale for $29.99 each. There were several versions to choose from, decorated with rows of tiny emeralds, sapphires, gannets, amethyst, and more; they had originally retailed for as much as $89 each.

Of course, since Tuesday Morning sells closeouts on discontinued styles, the selection can be limited. Not all sizes may be available in all designs. Should you decide to gamble on something here as a gift, and it does not fit, TM does have a 30-day return policy; just remember to keep your receipt!

Store hours are Monday, Tuesday, Wednesday, and Friday from 10 a.m. to 7 p.m.; Thursday from 10 a.m. to 8 p.m.; Saturday from 10 a.m. to 6 p.m.; and Sunday from noon to 6 p.m.

LIQUOR AND BEVERAGES

Whether your taste runs from Thunderbird to Tuscany, or from Chardonnay to Cuervo, it usually doesn't take long to find a halfway decent price on your favorite beverage. After a rigorous campaign of firsthand research, Mr. Cheap has determined that there are literally hundreds of liquor and beverage stores around D.C., and most of them are very competitive in the prices they can offer. Most have regular specials on selected wines and liquors, and nearly all of them will offer customers a 10 percent discount on purchases of wine by the case. Where these stores differ most is in the size of their selection, and the personal knowledge their managers bring to their offerings (especially when it comes to wine). Here Mr. C showcases a few of the biggest, best, and most unique of the many shopping options available to the savvy but cheap connoisseur.

Calvert Woodley Wines and Liquors

- 4339 Connecticut Avenue N.W., Washington, D.C.;
  ℡ (202) 966-4400

- ✐ www.calvertwoodley.com

You can't mess with success. This longtime dealer is perhaps one of the best known in the District, not to mention its national mail-order clientele. From the humblest chardonnay (Sutter Home was seen recently for a mere $6.99 per bottle!) to the finest champagnes, CW discounts a vast selection of liquors. Few stores could have more to choose from, in every price range; there are half a dozen cognacs by Courvoisier alone. Not to mention a slew of single malt scotches, barrels of bourbons, and lots of liqueurs.

Save money on gin by going with Calvert's own private label. Save on notable French wines, or save even more by choosing from the little known, highly rated bargains in Spain, Chile, and Australia—many of which are under $10 a bottle. Everything is clearly labeled, and the sales staff is not snobby about answering questions.

Perhaps the best deal of all is the store's free parking lot, given its bustling location. Sign up for their newsletter to receive listings for wine tasting and dinners with winemakers from the major wine producing regions in the world. They also host frequent wine tastings and dinners; serious sippers sign up to receive their newsletter.

Calvert Woodley is open daily from 10 a.m. to 8:30 p.m. Liquor stores are closed on Sunday.

Giant Liquors

- 3504 Georgia Avenue N.W., Washington, D.C.;
  ✆ (202) 829-2444

This northwest D.C. institution (of the non-Smithsonian variety) is a large place with great prices on a wide range of beers, wine, and liquor.

Store hours are 9 a.m. to 9 p.m. every day of the week.

Paul's Discount Wines & Liquors

- 5205 Wisconsin Avenue. N.W., Washington, D.C.;
  ✆ (202) 537-1900

- ✍ www.paulswine.com

Whenever you drop by Paul's, expect it to be crowded. Dozens of labels, well known and not, line the aisles. Every week Paul's runs an ad in the *Post* or the *Times* listing dozens of products—fine wines included—marked down significantly from their typical retail prices. Even better: Anything not listed in the ad is marked down 20 percent, so you're guaranteed to find significant discounts on fine wines and spirits any time, all the time.

Wines are a particular specialty here, with hundreds of bottles available at discount. You may nab a deal on Louis Jadot white Burgundies (1997); Mr. C found an award-winning Jadot Chassagne-Montrachet for $19.99—seen for about $28 elsewhere. Not all the savings are as dramatic, but they're quite good, indeed.

In the hard liquor aisles you could pick up a 750 ml bottle of J & B Scotch for $27.99, Tanqueray Gin for $24.88, and Stolichnaya Vodka for $27.99—not bad, eh?

How about some after-dinner libations? A 750 ml bottle of Bailey's Irish Cream was $17.99, a bottle of Drambuie, $28.88, and Courvoisier VSOP was $32.99. Dessert wines and ports are available, too.

You'll find good prices on beer, too, from humble Bud to much more sophisticated brews.

You can also get on Paul's mailing list to receive regular e-mail newsletters covering the specials of the week. Send your request to paulswine@aol.com.

Store hours are Monday through Saturday from 9:30 a.m. to 8:45 p.m.

Pearson's Liquor and Wine Annex

- 2436 Wisconsin Avenue N.W., Washington D.C.;
  ✆ (202) 333-6666

- ✍ www.pearsonswinewebsite. com

In their weekly ads in the *Washington Post*, the smallest but tremendously busy liquor store calls itself "Plain Old Pearson's." It is old—vintage 1933—but far from plain. The bargains are extraordinary, and the selection surprisingly large.

Just about everything seems to be on sale, all the time—it can be very overwhelming if you don't know exactly want you want, but fortunately there are plenty of helpful staff people around. Here are just a few of the deals Mr. C found: Southern Comfort ($19.99 for a 1.75-liter bottle), Chivas Regal ($51.99, 1.75 liters), and Cuervo Gold ($29.99).

A large selection of California and imported wines and champagnes are also available, and the folks here are really into the grape, stocking plenty of very good stuff for sale at good prices. If you buy a case—mixing and matching 12 bottles or more—you'll get a 25 percent discount. As far as the individual bottles go, Mr. C noticed that a superb 1998 Pouilly-Fume Sauvignon Blanc could be had for just $14.99, a fruity and delicious 2000 Chateau Lauduc Bordeaux was $11.99, and a Chateau Mayne Cassan Medoc was available for a good 'n cheap $11.99. The list goes on and on, and changes all the time, but you can keep up with the bargains by subscribing to Pearson's e-mail letter. Just give them your e-mail address when you come to the store, or send an e-mail to steve@pearsonswinewebsite.com.

For beer, all the popular brews are on hand. Pearson's also carries a number of interesting microbrews priced very reasonably. On the week Mr. C darkened their doors, the folks here were offering Flying Dog Ale, brewed in Denver, for just $11.99 for a 12-pack.

Check out their ads to see what the specials are, or stop by and see for yourself. Pearson's is open Monday through Saturday, 10 a.m. to 8:45 p.m.

Total Wine and More

- Landmark Plaza, 6420 Little River Turnpike., Alexandria, VA; ✆ (703) 941-1133

- Greenbriar Town Center, 13055 Lee Jackson Memorial Highway, Chantilly, VA; ✆ (703) 817-1177

- 1451 Chain Bridge Road, McLean, VA; ✆ (703) 749-0011 PICK-UP ONLY

- 6711 Bland Street, Springfield, VA; ✆ (703) 912-9387

- 46301 Potomac Run Plaza #110, Sterling, VA; ✆ (703) 433-0522

- West Gate Plaza Shopping Center, 8099 Sudley Road, Manassas, VA; ✆ (703) 368-2580

- ✑ www.totalwineandmore.com

When they say total, this wine (and beer) giant *means* total. They offer bargain prices on everything from fine wine to the glasses you serve it in. Total claims to stock some 8,000 wines and 500 different beers (300 of which are microbrews). It's sort of the "superstore" approach, with good everyday prices. Their tremendous buying power (20 stores in five states) and the fact that they work directly with wineries, allows them to pass on the savings to their customers. Total is one of the lowest priced wine stores in the D.C. area. The staff is very knowledgeable when it comes to wine, which is very helpful when it comes to matching wine with food; Mr. Cheap always has difficulty when it comes to choosing the proper grape to accompany corned beef hash and take-out moo goo gai pan.

You'll be able to save at least a dollar or two on hundreds of low- and mid-grade wines; fancier vintages, the kind in the $50–$100 range, can be as much as $15 to $25 less than their suggested prices. You can also score case discounts on 750 ml bottled wine.

In any given week, you may find six-packs of Samuel Adams, or some similar micro, selling for a mere $5.49. And get this—Total offers free wine tastings on Saturdays from noon to 5 p.m. Hey, the Cheapster will be there, hiding a tub of takeout Chinese food in his jacket.

True to its name, Total also discounts sodas with everyday low prices, bottled waters, coffee beans (at some stores), and cheeses (at some stores). The Chantilly, Alexandria, and McLean stores are open Monday to Saturday from 9 a.m. to 10 p.m., and Sunday from 10 a.m. to 7 p.m. The Springfield, Sterling, and Manassas stores are open Monday through Friday 10 a.m. to

9 p.m., Saturday 9 a.m. to 9 p.m., and Sunday from 10 a.m. to 7 p.m.

Also known for good prices, and therefore worth checking out:

Burka's

- 3500 Wisconsin Avenue N.W., Washington, D.C.; ✆ (202) 966-7676

Circle Wine & Liquor

- 5501 Connecticut Avenue N.W., Washington, D.C.; ✆ (202) 966-0600

Continental

- Vermont Avenue & L Street N.W., Washington, D.C.; ✆ (202) 223-0616

Cork 'N Bottle

- 7421 Georgia Avenue N.W., Washington, D.C.; ✆ (202) 829-3400

Gandels

- 211 Pennsylvania Avenue S.E., Washington, D.C.; ✆ (202) 543-1000

Kovak's

- 1237 Mt. Olivet Road N.E., Washington, D.C.; ✆ (202) 399-5555

Pan-Mar

- 1902 I Street N.W., Washington, D.C.; ✆ (202) 659-2645

Penn Branch Liquors

- 3232 Pennsylvania Avenue S.E., Washington, D.C.; ✆ (202) 584-9300

Rose's

- 830 Bladensburg Road N.E., Washington, D.C.; ✆ (202) 399-7777

S & S Liquor

- 6295 Fourth Street, N.W., Washington, D.C.; ✆ (202) 882-2362

Morris Miller

- 7804 Alaska Avenue (at Georgia Avenue) N.W., Washington, D.C.; ✆ (202) 723-5000

LUGGAGE

Fine luggage can be expensive, but you don't have to "bag" the idea of finding cheap, good-quality travel gear. Most of the good deals can be found in the discount department stores (see that section earlier in the book), but you can also find some great buys from luggage specialists, a few of which Mr. C has listed here.

Bentley's Luggage & Gifts

- 1100 South Hayes Street, Arlington, VA; ✆ (703) 415-4222

- 7101 Democracy Boulevard, Bethesda, MD; ✆ (301) 365-9576

- 1811U International Drive, McLean, VA; ✆ (703) 734-2435

- 2700 Potomac Mills Circle, Woodbridge, VA; ✆ (703) 494-3851

- 10300 Little Patuxent, Columbia, MD; ✆ (410) 715-0822

- ✑ www.bentleys.com

You sure don't have to drive a Bentley to afford luggage here, where you'll find good discounts on fine bands like Samsonite, Scully, Hartmann, JanSport, Kenneth Cole, Razor, and many others. Many of Bentley's items are on sale for 50 percent off the ticketed price!

A bit of an old-fashioned emporium, Bentley's is definitely male-oriented, and geared toward the corporate customer. A man's leather briefcase with combination lock, made by Mark Phillip, was recently seen discounted from $200 to $159. The Cheapster also spotted an Andiamo 19-inch Pullman, usually priced at $495, for only $220!

A Lewis N Clark overnighter was marked down to $32 from its usual $65, while a Ricardo Beverly Hills 22-inch Expandable Wheelaboard Suiter was discounted from $300 to only $150. A Samsonite hybrid carry-on suiter was tagged at $99, down from its usual $335.

On the soft side, you can pick up a Bill Blass 29-inch wheeled duffle, usually priced at $70, for a meager $19.99, and an El Portal extra-large duffle was only $37.50 (discounted from $75).

There are some items for the ladies, such as a feminine-styled briefcase with three big inner compartments and a top zipper. List priced at $225, it sells here for $140. You'll also find luggage suitable for the whole family here, like a Hartmann leather-trim suitcase marked down from $350 to $210, and a Hartmann garment bag, selling for $198 (retail price, $330).

As these places tend to do, Bentley's also stocks fine-maker pens by Parker, Cross, and the like; as well as other travel necessities such as clock radios, hair dryers, voltage converters, toiletries, organizers, backpacks, and travel guides, all at competitive prices.

Bentley's stores are generally open from 10 a.m. to 9 p.m. from Monday through Saturday, and noon to 6 p.m. on Sundays, though hours may vary slightly by location.

Luggage Outlet

- 6210 Little River Turnpike, Alexandria, VA;
  ✎ (703) 658-4513

Luggage Outlet sells name-brand luggage, briefcases, handbags, day planners, duffels, and all the other business accouterments at below-retail prices. Samsonite is the main brand in stock—all different styles and sizes are available. A 29-inch hard-case EZ Cart with wheels Samsonite 400 series was selling here for $149.99, and the 700 series was $239.99. A 26" soft case Silhouette 7 upright with wheels was priced at $159.99.

And of course, no business trip would run smoothly without one's valet—valet garment bag, that is. The Samsonite 400 series ($80.99) and 700 series runs from your basic ($159.99) to garment bags with pockets everywhere and wheels ($239.99).

You'll also find American Tourister, Delsey, JanSport, and Benetton all for sale at below-retail prices.

Store hours are 10 a.m. to 9 p.m. Monday through Saturday, and Sunday from 11 a.m. to 6 p.m. And get this: Bring in a copy of this book and the owner will give you a 5 percent discount!

S & W Sales

- 1030 19th Street N.W., Washington, D.C.; ✎ (202) 337-6166

- ✐ www.swluggage.com

S & W has a bit of everything for the traveler who's really on the move, and this discount, family-owned business has been serving

mobile customers for 70 years. All
the famous names are here, such as
Travelpro, Samsonite, Delsey,
Atlantic, and American Tourister.
Among the items you'll find here
are hard-shell suitcases with wheels,
starting at $89 and up, soft-sided
suitcases starting at $19.88, and gar-
ment bags with wheels from $99.

Besides traveling bags, there are
60 different styles! Yes, that's a
large selection, and it includes
packing trunks and footlockers in
sizes ranging from 30 inches on up
to 43 inches with prices starting at
$39.88. Looking for a luggage cart?
They've got them in all sizes, with
handling capacity up to 275 lbs.

A large part of S & W's business
is travel accessories, including converters, adapters, straps, locks,
money belts, luggage tags, and
international electrical items. You'll
find discounts for computer bags in
ballistic or leather, brief cases on
wheels, as well as other leather
goods. You'll also find estate jewelry
sold at discount. No matter what
they sell, it's *all* discounted, and
hard-to-find items are their specialty.

S&W also repairs luggage items
in a timely manner. If you drop off
your damaged piece, you'll get it
back within 24 hours, as long as
the store is open the next day.

So when *is* the store open? Mondays through Fridays from 10 a.m.
to 5:30 p.m., and Saturdays from
10 a.m. to 1 p.m.

Tuesday Morning

- 3501 Carlin Springs Road, Falls
  Church, VA; ✆ (703) 845-3710

- 11111 Georgia Avenue,
  Wheaton, MD;
  ✆ (301) 942-1884

- 3025 Nutley Street, Fairfax, VA;
  ✆ (703) 280-2130

- 136 Maple Avenue, W Vienna,
  VA; ✆ (703) 938-6707

- 6230 Rolling Road, Springfield,
  VA; ✆ (703) 866-0379

- 25 Beall Avenue, Rockville,
  MD; ✆ (301) 424-2480

- 131 Bowie Road, Laurel, MD;
  ✆ (301) 953-7907

- 353 Muddy Branch Road,
  Gaithersburg, MD;
  ✆ (301) 921-9542

- 492 Elden Street, Herndon, VA;
  ✆ (703) 471-5571

- 750 State Route 3 South, Gambrills, MD; ✆ (410) 923-1194

- 5619 Stone Road, Centreville,
  VA; ✆ (703) 222-7730

- 14516 Potomac Mills Road,
  Woodbridge, VA;
  ✆ (703) 494-1215

- ✑ www.tuesdaymorning.com

If it's Tuesday, this must be Bel-
gium. TM's offerings include luggage for the serious (and savvy)
traveler.

Among the well-priced travel
gear Mr. C found on a recent visit,
were Samsonite duffel bags—available in an assortment of neutral
colors—reduced from $90 to $40.
A Samsonite soft-sider suitcase was
reduced from $220 to $80, while a
smaller wheeled suitcase was
marked down from $150 to $70.

Leisure Luggage brand carry-on
tote bags, listed at $90 retail, were
just $30 here; and a Pierre Cardin
carry bag sells for $90—half its
original retail price. Garment bags
are also well stocked, with brands
like Ascot and Samsonite, starting
as low as $40. All sell for at least
half of their retail prices.

Store hours are Monday,
Tuesday, Wednesday, and Friday
from 10 a.m. to 7 p.m.; Thursday
from 10 a.m. to 8 p.m.; Saturday
from 10 a.m. to 6 p.m.; and Sunday
from noon to 6 p.m.

MUSICAL INSTRUMENTS

Mr. Cheap loves the way that car dealers dress up their used car lots with a fancy sign that reads: "Previously Owned." He feels the same way about musical instruments. If you can find one in good shape, it should have many years of useful life in it. Often, a top-quality used instrument that can be repaired is a better investment than a cheaper, newer version. It will sound better and last longer. And many instruments actually *increase* in value as they age.

Bethesda Music

- 4842 Rugby Avenue, Bethesda, MD; ✆ (301) 907-0106

- ✐ www.bethesdamusic.com

Down a few side streets from Wisconsin Avenue, this shop offers low markups—sometimes as little as 5 percent to 10 percent over cost—on new instruments and accessories of all kinds. Find acoustic guitars here from around $140 and up, electrics from $180 and up.

A new Guild acoustic, for example, with a list price of $900, might go for more like $525 here. Mr. C inquired about student drum sets and they will cost you $369—a good deal for sure.

This packed little store also has some used instruments, guitars, amps, and all school band instruments, such as trumpets and flutes, with prices substantially less than a new one. However, as soon as these come in, they fly out. Bethesda Music also rents school band instruments, and they repair instruments with a 30-day warranty, including parts and labor.

Bethesda also offers instruction, taught by many of the best players in the city. A steady stream of kids and teenagers, coming and going from the back rooms, attests to the teachers' popularity. Accessories run the gamut from guitar strings to electronics, teaching method books too.

Bethesda Music is open Monday through Thursday from 11 a.m. to 8:30 p.m., Friday from 11 a.m. to 8 p.m., and Saturday from 10 a.m. to 5 p.m.

Guitar Gallery

- 3400 Connecticut Avenue N.W., Washington, D.C.; ✆ (202) 244-4200

- ✐ www.guitar-gallery.com

Located just one block from the Cleveland Park Metro, this store sells acoustic and electric guitars, specializing in Spanish flamenco and classical. The owner, Paco de Malaga, an accomplished guitarist and recording artist known throughout Spain, South America, and the U.S., opened Guitar Gallery in 1987. In his store you'll find guitars from Spanish guitar makers such as Casimiro Lozano, Pedro Maldonado, Pedro Contreras, and others. Beginners and students will have good luck in finding a decent, inexpensive first instrument here. Spanish flamenco and classical guitar classes (beginner to professional) are offered by master teachers.

GG sells a wide variety of electric and acoustic guitars, including classics like Washburn, Cort, Applauze by Takamine, and more. You'll also find all the accessories you would need for your guitar here. Looking for power? GG has amplifiers, pedals, microphones, and other electric tools.

For those of you interested in becoming a flamenco dancer, you can enroll for classes here, taught by Paco's wife, Ana, one of Spain's most outstanding flamenco dancers. And get yourself some authentic and colorful dance accessories—skirts, shoes, boots (for men), shawls, fans, castanets are all sold here, as well as flamenco CDs and cassettes. Olé!

Store hours are Monday through Friday from 11 a.m. to 7:30 p.m., and Saturday from 11 a.m. to 5:30 p.m. They're closed Sunday.

House of Musical Traditions

- 7040 Carroll Avenue, Takoma Park, MD; ✆ (301) 270-9090

- 🖃 www.musicaltraditions.com

If you're into world music, you've gotta get yourself into this fun and funky store. HMT has a little bit of everything. They sell new and used instruments, local artist's compact discs, sheet music, magazines, books, music lessons: you name it. But the styles lean a bit toward the offbeat (nice pun, huh?). Here it's all acoustic instruments (HMT has been unplugged since 1972)—offered below list prices. If you're looking for something exotic or hard to find, whether it's a ceramic Dumbek or Djembe drum or a Blue Dragon bamboo flute, this is the place. HMT carries hundreds of instruments from all over the world.

Among (slightly) more conventional instruments, there are Gibson, Alvarez, Martin, and Tacoma guitars, just to name a few, all priced at 20 to 25 percent off the listed price. In fact, the store gets a fairly steady supply of Alvarez factory seconds (only the finish is affected), all priced at substantially below retail. They do repairs too.

The other side of the store is devoted to the music itself. New

MR. CHEAP'S PICKS

Musical Instruments

House of Musical Traditions—This house seems big enough to hold all the music in the world—or, at least, its instruments.

Rolls Music—One of the biggies in the metro area for rock 'n' rollers.

Southworth Guitars—These guys have a huge inventory of used and vintage electric and acoustic guitars. There's nothing new here so you know you're saving money, and it's only quality stuff.

CDs (local artists only) are between $10 and $14.99. The emphasis, again, is on folk, acoustic, and world beat. This is also the place to find out about classes and performances in the area; between the players who hang out there and the bulletin boards and newsletters on display, you won't miss a thing.

Consignments are welcome: HMT buys, sells, and trades!

HMT is open Tuesdays through Fridays from 11 a.m. to 7 p.m., Saturdays from 11 a.m. to 7 p.m., and Sunday and Monday from 11 a.m. to 5 p.m.

Rolls Music Center

- 1065 West Broad Street, Falls Church, VA; ✆ (703) 533-9500; 800-336-0199

- 🖃 www.rollsmusic.com

Since 1975, this has been a much-relied-upon source for rock 'n' rollers. Guitars, amps, keyboards, drums, and their accessories, plus electronic mixing and recording equipment, are all here at discounts of as much at least 40 percent off retail. The store boasts over 400 guitars with names like Gibson, Ibanez, Fender, Rickenbacker, Guild, Ovation, and more, all available for test drives.

For further savings check out the secondhand band equipment and closeouts. And, of course, you can offer to trade in something of your own for store credit. You can even trade a used instrument in towards another used instrument—the ultimate money saver. Rolls will even consider paying you cash for an instrument in strong demand. Repair services for new and used instruments are done on the premises.

Rolls Music, in the tiny West End Shopping Center, is open every day but Sunday. Store hours are Monday, Tuesday, Thursday, and Friday from 11 a.m. to 9 p.m.; Wednesday and Saturday from 11 a.m. to 6 p.m.

Southworth Guitars

- 7845 Old Georgetown Road, Bethesda., MD;
  ✆ (301) 718-1667

- 🖅 www.southworthguitars.com

Don't be put off by Southworth's card, which claims it's "Where the cool man thrives." *Anyone*—women, men, professional, beginner—can find a good deal here. They have a huge inventory of used and vintage electric and acoustic guitars. There's nothing new here, so you know you're saving money, and it's only quality stuff.

And Southworth is known throughout the world as one of the best vintage guitar dealers. When Maestro Cheap last checked, among their offerings was a 1909 Martin 00-42; it was a little worn, but not too badly for an instrument nearly a century old. Southworth was offering it for a mere $14,500, which is way beyond Mr. C's wallet, but somewhere out there a new owner is waiting.

If the selection seems a bit overwhelming, the staff is very knowledgeable and helpful.

Store hours are Tuesday to Friday from 11 a.m. to 6 p.m., and Saturday from 10 a.m. to 5 p.m. Southworth is closed Sundays and Mondays.

PARTY SUPPLIES

In addition to the stores listed below, don't forget to check out the stores listed in the "Discount Department Stores" section, as well as just about any "dollar" store you come across.

Economy Party Supplies

- 1049 West Broad Street, Falls Church, VA; ✆ (703) 237-2789

Hey, these guys really like to party. Walk into the main floor of this store and you'll immediately observe that it's filled with one the largest collections of Halloween costumes in the area. Or, as they

call it, "Nightmare on Broad Street." All your favorite characters are here, along with makeup and accessories. What a hoot! Naturally, October is a big month for these, but there are outfits for every kind of special event imaginable—all for sale at discount year-round or available for rent.

Upstairs, you'll find all the basics—10,000 square feet of

everything from matching plastic cups and napkins to mylar balloons to loot bags. There are over 24 juvenile designs to choose from and Mr. Cheap's favorite is the Pirate's Cove. The staff will help you plan a theme party for kids, which is neat—everything from a soccer theme party to a cooking theme party. And it doesn't stop there, EPS has bridal shower theme supplies, making it a great source whether you are just inviting the girls or planning a coed party.

Seasonal and discontinued items are reduced as much as 50 percent, and there are extra discounts for bulk purchases, too.

Economy also offers invitation printing for all parties, and they will even help you plan your wedding. By the way, they are proud of being a female-owned company; businesses get a tax break for buying from a minority-run business. There's a tip for devoted Cheapsters.

Store hours are Monday to Friday from 9 a.m. to 9 p.m., Saturday 9 a.m. to 6 p.m., and Sunday from 10 a.m. to 5 p.m.

Factory Card Outlet

- 5604 Silverhill Road, District Heights, MD; ✆ (301) 420-0103

- 12021 Georgia Avenue, Wheaton, MD; ✆ (301) 946-8093

- 2910 Festival Way, Waldorf, MD; ✆ (301) 374-9501

- 13948 Metrotech Drive, Chantilly, VA; ✆ (703) 817-0801

- 2325 Forest Drive, Annapolis, MD; ✆ (410) 266-0737

- 8099 Sudley Road, Manassas, VA; ✆ (703) 368-1598

- ✑ www.factorycard.com

This chain takes the "superstore" approach to the greeting cards and party supplies market. Anyway, for starters at FCO, the last time Mr. Cheap checked, all holiday and greeting cards were priced at 49 cents each. Period. And they don't just have a few, yellowing leftovers from last Arbor Day or National Take Your Accountant to Lunch Day—it's a huge, current selection. Obviously, high-volume business allows them to make up the difference elsewhere. What else do they sell here? Everything you need to invite people to a party, decorate it, and serve them food and drink, all at discount prices.

Whether you want to go simple, with color-coordinated plates and napkins, or go all-out with 10-inch tapered candies in a palette of colors (79 cents each), 80-foot rolls of streamers (79 cents each), paper or plastic tablecloths, "Winnie the Pooh" napkins, and inflated helium balloons (latex balloons are 59 cents each/$5.99 a dozen, and mylar varieties are $1.99 each/3 for $5.00), chances are you'll find what you need here at discount.

Do people make fun of you for doing your Christmas shopping in January? Come in here and you'll be among friends. Leftover seasonal supplies are discounted 50 to 75 percent, and there are plenty of bargains on cards, wrapping paper, and so on.

Be sure to ask FCO where you sign up for additional discounts for schools, churches, restaurants, corporations, and other large groups. That could net you 15 percent off purchases between $50 and $100, and 20 percent for purchases over $100. Check the Web site for additional 10 percent coupons.

Store hours are Monday through Saturday from 9 a.m. to 9 p.m., and Sunday 10 a.m. to 6 p.m.

Party City

- 5522 Leesburg Pike #B, Falls Church, VA; ✆ (703) 998-0111

- 3316 Donnell Drive #600, Forestville, MD; ✆ (301) 420-6393

- 6000 Greenbelt Road #65A, Greenbelt, MD; ✆ (301) 441-2220

- 6721 Frontier Drive #B, Springfield, VA; ✆ (703) 922-3700

- 1500 Rockville Pike, Rockville, MD; ✆ (301) 770-5551

- 10700 Lee Highway, Fairfax, VA; ✆ (703) 934-4434

- 3311 Corridor Marketplace, Laurel, MD; ✆ (301) 490-1192

- 47100 Community Plaza, Sterling, VA; ✆ (571) 434-8890

- 8131 Ritchie Highway, Pasadena, MD; ✆ (410) 544-4400

- 6500 Baltimore National Pike, Catonsville, MD; ✆ (410) 455-9900

- ✍ www.partycity.com

Wherever your city may be, Party City is worth the trip when you're getting ready for a big bash. This metropolis-sized store is set up warehouse style, with floor-to-ceiling displays, but without the cold warehouse feel. And, its prices are amazing—up to 50 percent off retail pricing, and they guarantee to beat competitor's prices.

Be sure to pick up a shopping checklist when you first walk in—a very cool and useful idea. There are checklists for wedding receptions and showers, children's birthday parties, retirement parties, and seasonal events; the lists are arranged by aisle, making shopping here a breeze.

Newlyweds can put more money toward their honeymoon by shopping here for wedding decorations and accessories. Champagne plastic glasses start at $9.99 for a package of 50, wedding cake toppers start at $12.99, and cake servers start at $9.99. Party City offers personalized wedding invitation services. And for that matter, they offer printed invitations for any party event.

Basic party supplies are incredibly well stocked here. A pack of eight shower invitations are priced at $1.74. Ten-foot "Happy Birthday" banners in different designs are only $3.49. You can get fancy napkins and a matching tablecloth at good prices, or save even more with the store's own brand, available in an impressive array of brights, darks, and pastel shades.

Need some gift wrapping? Forty square feet of the stuff starts at $3.19. Taper candles were $1.99 each, and scented votive candles were 99 cents. To make sure your party packs a punch, you might to also consider getting an eight-quart plastic punch bowl with server— just $5.99 at the City. They also sell glass punch bowls at discount prices.

Bargains on kid stuff include an Elmo-shaped cake pan for $9.99, two-foot character balloons for $9.99, an eight-pack of party blowouts for $3.29, and an eight-pack of "Party Loot" bags for $3.49.

MR. CHEAP'S PICKS

Party Supplies

Economy Party Supplies—Tons of decorating stuff, plus costumes and rentals, all discounted, all year long.

Party City—Save up to 50 percent discounts off retail pricing, and they guarantee to beat competitor's prices. Party on!

Napkins and paper plates come decorated with a variety of characters, like Thomas the Tank Engine, the Little Mermaid, Beauty and the Beast, Snow White, 101 Dalmatians, and Cinderella. Paper plate prices start at $1.74 for a set of eight.

Throw a surprise party and decorate with those embarrassing birthday banners ("Look Who's 40!"—or 50!, 60!, etc.) and buy the huge "Look Who's 30!" button for ridiculously low prices.

Party City keeps on partying Monday through Friday from 9:30 a.m. to 9 p.m., Saturday from 9:30 a.m. to 8 p.m., and Sunday from 11 a.m. to 5 p.m.

We're Having a Party

- 8846 Monard Drive, Silver Spring, MD; ✆ (301) 589-5008

- ✑ www.werehavingaparty.com.

A similar operation to Party City, for you party animals north of the Potomac.

PET SUPPLIES

These are some of the best places to buy pet foods and supplies around the metro area. Mr. C also suggests that you check out some of the "dollar" stores (see the listings under "Discount Department Stores"), since many of them sell reduced-price canned food, and sometimes even leashes, collars, and doggie and kitty toys.

Investigating pet stores this time around, the C-Man learned that there are actually three categories of pet food. The first includes foods that are considered "natural" (which does not mean organic), with no fillers and preservatives. The second includes the "premium" dog foods, which have fewer fillers and additives than the third category, the "standard" brands.

Mr. C also learned that some pet food filler could even be sawdust, and that the holistic and the premium manufacturers profess that *more* of their nutritious food is absorbed, meaning you can feed your pet less, and the "cost per feeding" costs you no more than the "other foods." (Hmmm. Ohh-kay . . .) But don't listen to Dr. Cheap when it comes to this kind of advice. (After all, he may have been feeding Jackson the Shetland sheepdog little bowser kibbles and sawdust until relatively recently. Maybe that's why he was always nosing around the linseed oil under the sink.) What you buy for your furry (or feathery) loved one is ultimately your decision, so research the ingredients of various products and talk to your vet about the best choices for your pet.

Pro Feed

- 3690-G King Street, Alexandria, VA; ✆ (703) 820-3888

Pro Feed specializes in all-natural supplies for dogs, cats, and birds, featuring goods from 25 different companies such as Iams, Precise, Bil-Jac, and Solid Gold. And the store's regular prices are competitive with the major chains! In addition to dogs and cats, Pro-Feed sells pet accessories for fish, reptiles, small animals and birds.

ProFeed excels when it comes to personal service—something you won't always find in the superstores. A smaller shop also means fresher food, since they can't keep vast quantities of stock on hand. And, if your pet turns up its nose (or beak) at any of the foods you purchase here, bring the remainder back for cash refund. Now, that's service!

Store hours are Monday to Friday from 9:30 a.m. to 8 p.m., Saturday from 9:30 a.m. to 7 p.m., and Sunday from 11 a.m. to 6 p.m.

PETsMART

- 3351 Jefferson Davis Highway, Alexandria, VA; ✆ (703) 739-4844

- 6100 Arlington Boulevard, Falls Church, VA; ✆ (703) 534-0774

- 6005 Oxon Hill Road, Oxon Hill, MD; ✆ (301) 839-4900

- 6000 Greenbelt Rd #42, Greenbelt, MD; ✆ (301) 474-8334

- 5208 Nicholson Lane, Kensington, MD; ✆ (301) 770-4631

- 5154 Nicholson Lane, Kensington, MD; ✆ (301) 770-1343

- 12020 Cherry Hill Road, Silver Spring, MD; ✆ (301) 586-8262

- 6535 Frontier Drive, Springfield, VA; ✆ (703) 922-4990

- 4500 Mitchellville Road, Bowie, MD; ✆ (301) 352-7286

- 220 Kentlands Boulevard. Gaithersburg, MD; ✆ (301) 977-9677

   And other suburban locations

- ✑ www.petsmart.com

Just about everyone who owns a pet is familiar with the national pet "superstore" chain called PETs-

MART. The big savings available here have made it a very popular place to shop, indeed. PETsMART has everything you could need, and more, whether your pet is a dog or cat, bird or wild bird, reptile or fish, chinchilla or ferret, mouse or a rat (and these animals are sold at the store). You might cringe at the thought of a pet rat, but you probably haven't seen *fancy* rats, which are intelligent, fuzzy, and quite cute.

Many of the PETsMART stores have adoption centers for cats and dogs. If you're looking for a new dog or puppy, go to the store on Saturdays when breeders and pet parents are often there with their furry charges looking to make a deal. Call ahead to make sure the store has an adoption center, and to verify hours.

You'll find at least 10 different premium brands of cat and dog food here. On The Cheapster's last visit, a 20-pound bag of Eukanuba dog food was priced at $20.99. Iams was $17.29, and Pro Plan $17.49. An 8-pound bag of Iams cat food was $13.99, while Pro Plan's product was $12.49. PETsMART's own "house brand" 30-pound bag of dog food was $22.99, and that's a saver! There are lots of bird foods to choose from too, like Kaytee, ZuPreem Avian, and others. A 3-pound bag of the house food for cockatiels was $4.19, while the Kaytee version was $9.19.

Food for just about every other little creature is sold here—even for Mrs. C's pet blue tongue skink lizard. They also stock pet habitats, food, medication, vitamin supplements, cleaning, odor control supplies, dental care, and lots more.

PETsMART also offers grooming, as well as obedience training at reasonable prices, and they will trim your pet's nails for a cheap $8. (Call ahead to make an appointment.)

All stores are open Mondays through Saturdays from 9 a.m. to 9 p.m., and Sundays from 9 a.m. to 6 p.m.

Petco

- 1627 K Street NW #610, Washington, D.C.; ✆ (202) 775-0190

- 3505 Connecticut Avenue N.W., Washington, D.C.; ✆ (202) 686-0901

- 3200 Washington Boulevard, Arlington, VA; ✆ (703) 276-7387

- 5857 Leesburg Pike, Falls Church, VA; ✆ (703) 671-3361

- 5628 Silver Hill Road, Forestville, MD; ✆ (301) 420-5800

- 6612 Richmond Highway, Alexandria, VA; ✆ (703) 660-1300

- 10464 Baltimore Avenue, Beltsville, MD; ✆ (301) 937-1222

- 1929 Old Gallows Road, Vienna, VA; ✆ (703) 448-3401

- 6394 Springfield Plaza, Springfield, VA; ✆ (703) 866-0011

- 1507 Rockville Pike, Rockville, MD; ✆ (301) 984-9733

- 10708 Lee Highway, Fairfax, VA; ✆ (703) 352-3300

- 915 Washington Boulevard South, Laurel, MD; ✆ (301) 490-7452

- 275 Muddy Branch Road, Gaithersburg, MD; ✆ (301) 975-9888

- 13053 Lee Jackson Memorial Highway, Fairfax, VA; ✆ (703) 817-9444

- 2441 Centreville Road, Herndon, VA; ✆ (703) 713-1552

- ✎ www.petco.com

MR. CHEAP'S PICKS

Pet Supplies

PETsMART—The superstore for animals, their care, and feeding. The big savings available here have made it a very popular place to shop.

Pet Valu—These guys don't do a lot of advertising, and that's where they save money, passing it along to hip, cheap-savvy customers like you and The Cheapster.

PETsMART and Petco are direct competitors, and they're neck-and-neck in the races to add new stores *and* offer customers the best prices. Of course, Petco is loaded with all manner of food and accessories for dogs, cats, birds, rabbits, ferrets, gerbils, Guinea pigs, hamsters, reptiles, and fish.

In the chow department, Petco carries some of the same brand-name food as you'll find in the other pet "supermarkets" (for example, Iams, Eukanuba, Pro Plan, Bil Jac, and Science)—about 18 name-brand pet foods in all. Meanwhile, the prices here are about the same as those you'll find at PETsMART (see above). For example, a 20-pound bag of Iams dog food was priced at $17.99 here, while the same size from ProPlan was $16.99. A 24-can case of Nutro Max cat food could be had for $13.99, and a 25-pound bag of EverClean clumping kitty litter was marked down from $15.99 to $12.99.

Petco offers full-service grooming salons, as well as obedience courses, veterinary services, adoption service, and pet photography. They actually sell pets here:

fish and other small aquatic animals, reptiles, birds, and small, cuddly mammals such as mice, "fancy rats," hamsters, Guinea pigs, and the like.

Petco's Web site features a deal called "Bottomless Bowl & More," where you buy food and supplies at a discount and they are delivered right to your door.

Store hours are Monday through Saturday from 10 a.m. to 9 p.m., and Sunday from noon to 6 p.m.

Pet Essentials

- 1722 14th Street N.W.,Washington, D.C.; ✆ (202) 986-7907

- ✐ www.greenpets.com

Does your pet prefer all natural and holistic food? Do you? Well, even if neither of you have thought about the subject, the Top Dog Cheapster recommends that you take a look at this place. The foods and supplements here contain no byproducts or chemical additives, and their nutritional standards for pets are quite high—all food is human-grade quality or organic. (Not that Mr. Cheap is recommending that any humans try this stuff!)

One example of the kind of food Pet Essentials carries is Innova Dog, preserved only with natural Vitamin C and E. It's made of fresh chicken and turkey meat, plus cottage cheese and clove garlic for flavor and nutrition alfalfa sprouts to encourage your pet to graze. And it even includes natural cold-pressed sunflower oil for a shiny hair coat. You can't deny this is a good thing, and Mr. C should be buying this stuff for his furry friend, Jackson. A 16.5-pound bag sells for $21.99, and maybe—just maybe—those extra dollars will be well worth it.

Some other brands that they carry for cats as well as dogs are Solid Gold, California Natural, Precise Formula, and Canidae

(Felidae), Excel, and Sensible Choice. Mr. C found a 20-pound bag of "CatWorks Premium Cat Litter" for $9.99, and it's environmentally safe to flush down your toilet. Now that's a good thing.

If your animal appears to have a health problem, these guys will suggest nutritional enhancers and other natural remedies available in the store and that might save you future (expensive) visits to the vet. On your way out, pick up some organic Fanta-Seeds to feed the birds.

And here's one more tip: If you order at the Pet Essentials Web site, delivery within D.C. is free!

Store hours are Monday through Saturday 10 a.m. to 8 p.m., and Sunday from noon to 5 p.m.

Pet Valu

- 6120 Rose Hill Drive, Alexandria, VA; ✆ (703) 922-9566

- 11160 Veirs Mill Road, Wheaton, MD; ✆ (301) 933-2998

- 11229 New Hampshire Avenue, Silver Spring, MD; ✆ (301) 754-3690

- 7356 Little River Turnpike, Annandale, VA; ✆ (703) 941-1357

- 9337 Annapolis Rd #41, Lanham Seabrook, MD; ✆ (301) 918-8216

- 10304 Willard Way, Fairfax, VA; ✆ (703) 273-8207

- 15500 Annapolis Rd #162, Bowie, MD; ✆ (301) 464-3263

- 11130 S Lakes Drive #D, Reston, VA; ✆ (703) 476-7207

- 18272 Village Mart Drive, Olney, MD; ✆ (301) 570-1834

- 201 Kentlands Boulevard, Gaithersburg, MD; ✆ (301) 926-1216

- 20028 Goshen Road, Gaithersburg, MD; ✆ (301) 947-0495

- 14113 Saint Germain Drive, Centreville, VA; ✆ (703) 502-6979

- 5685 Santa Barbara Court, Elkridge, MD; ✆ (410) 660-8682

- 7040 Troy Hill Drive #C, Elkridge, MD; ✆ (410) 379-8002

- 940 Bay Ridge Road #A4, Annapolis, MD; ✆ (410) 626-0815

Almost all pet lovers know PetsMart and Petco, but have you heard of Pet Valu? Okay, maybe these guys can't spell very well, but they must be doing something right: There are close to 400 stores Pet Valu stores in North America, operated by franchisees, and their prices are competitive with the big superstores, sometimes even less. The stores themselves are not huge: You'll find the majority of them in the smaller strip malls. They also don't do a lot of advertising, and that's where they save money that they then pass along to hip, cheap-savvy customers like you and the Cheapster. They even honor coupons from other stores if they state the original price.

Pet Valu carries the popular dog and cat name-brand foods such as Iams, Science Diet, Eukanuba, Nutro, Purina Pro Plan and Fit and Trim Dog Chow, Nine Lives, and more. It also has its own Performatrim brand, and that will save you money. There are food and habitats for fish, birds, and small animals, dog and cat beds.

Store hours are Monday through Saturday from 9 a.m. to 9 p.m., and Sunday from 10 a.m. to 5 p.m.

SHOES AND SNEAKERS

With all the shopping he does, Mr. Cheap gives careful consideration to his footwear, and part of that equation is price, of course. Following are a number of totally superb shoe stores were you can also save some significant bucks. Not listed here are the Wal-Marts and Kmarts of the world, which also carry a number of reliable name brands at low, low prices. See the descriptions for those establishments under "Discount Department Stores."

Also, don't forget to check out places like Filene's Basement, Marshalls, Burlington Coat Factory, and Nordstrom Rack. These discounters offer both high-quality shoes at low prices and lower-quality shoes that are bargains already. See complete listings in "Clothing—New."

The Athlete's Foot

- 632 Rhode Island Avenue N.E., Washington, D.C.; ✆ (202) 635-7325

- 1100 S Hayes Street Arlington, VA; ✆ (703) 415-2245

- 2861 Alabama Avenue S.E., Washington, D.C.; ✆ (202) 583-6153

- 5115 Indian Head Highway, Oxon Hill, MD; ✆ (301) 567-0898

- 3737 Branch Avenue, Temple Hills, MD; ✆ (301) 899-2996

- 3500 E West Highway, Hyattsville, MD; ✆ (301) 559-4009

- 6167 Oxon Hill Road, Oxon Hill, MD; ✆ (301) 839-0802

- 6176 Greenbelt Road, Greenbelt, MD; ✆ (301) 313-0002

- 11160 Veirs Mill Road, Wheaton, MD; ✆ (301) 949-3786

- 7101 Democracy Boulevard, Bethesda, MD; ✆ (301) 365-9037

- 7924 Tysons Corner Center, McLean, VA; ✆ (703) 556-0116

- 6659 Loisdale Road, Springfield, VA; ✆ (703) 971-0722

- 5080 Brown Station Road, Upper Marlboro, MD; ✆ (301) 574-0160

- 5000 U.S. Highway 301, Waldorf, MD; ✆ (301) 705-8200

  And other suburban locations

- ✍ www.theathletesfoot.com

Scratch where it itches, C always says, so when you feel the urge to put your paws on a large, well-priced selection of name-brand athletic and recreational shoes—Nike, Puma, Adidas, and the like—it pays to check out The Athlete's Foot. The Cheapster won't spend a lot of space here describing this ubiquitous national chain; suffice to say that it always boasts some good clearance deals on footwear for men, women and kids, while also offering a range of pro and college sports jerseys, apparel and accessories. On the day Mr. C decided to soothe his rash desire for new running shoes, he stopped in at the closest AF and discovered a "Value Wall" filled with the things (with a

few basketball shoes thrown in). Grouped by price at $19.99, $39.99, and $59.99, most of these deals represented a 20 percent to 40 percent discount off list prices. Ahhh . . . relief!

Store hours here vary by location. The stand-alone and strip stores are usually open Monday through Thursday from 10 a.m. to 8 p.m., Friday and Saturday from 10 a.m. to 7 p.m., and Sunday from noon to 6 p.m. The mall stores routinely do business Monday through Saturday from 10 a.m. to around 9 p.m., and Sunday from noon to 6 p.m. Remember, if you're planning a visit early or late, it pays to call ahead to verify opening and closing times!

The Athlete's Foot Outlet

- 6659 Loisdale Road, Springfield, VA; ✆ (703) 971-0722

- 2700 Potomac Mills Circle #500, Woodbridge, VA; ✆ (703) 491-3668

- ✍ www.theathletesfoot.com

Even though Athlete's Foot has some good deals, you'll score an even better bargain at their clearance store, where the last time Mr. C hoofed it over there all sneakers were priced between $25 and $60. Specifically, for instance, women's old-school style Pumas GV were on special for $59.99; men's New Balance M635 running shoes were specially discounted at $44.97. Women's Avia visual sandals just $24.97. That's right, friends, just look for the color-coded dots on the boxes.

All the big names are here like Avia, Reebok, Asics, and Nike for men, women, and kids. You can even find specialty footwear, like cleats and wrestling shoes. And there are also some clothing items; Mr. C found a rack of 2002

Olympics sweatshirts for $34.99 and T-shirts for as low as $9.99. Special team organizations including leagues, church groups and corporations can take advantage of group discounts when outfitting baseball, basketball, golf, volleyball, and cycling teams on a volume basis. Additionally, if you need a beret, the going rate is $23.99.

Store hours are Monday through Friday from 10 a.m. to 9 p.m., Saturday 10 a.m. to 6 p.m., and Sunday noon to 5 p.m.

Foot Locker/Lady Foot Locker

- 1331 Pennsylvania Avenue N.W., Washington, D.C.; ✆ (202) 783-2093

- Union Station, 50 Massachusetts Avenue N.E., Washington, D.C.; ✆ (202) 289-8364

- 1776 K Street N.W., Washington, D.C.; ✆ (202) 728-1474

- 1934 14th Street N.W., Washington, D.C.; ✆ (202)319-8934

- 801 Pennsylvania Avenue S.E., Washington, D.C.; ✆ (202) 547-2551

- 1751 Columbia Road N.W., Washington, D.C.; ✆ (202) 483-4617

- 3221 M Street N.W., Washington, D.C.; ✆ (202) 333-7640

- 1525 Maryland Avenue N.E., Washington, D.C.; ✆ (202) 396-5487

- 1100 S Hayes Street, Arlington, VA; ✆ (703) 415-3668

- 3946 Minnesota Avenue N.E., Washington, D.C.; ✆ (202) 388-5653

- 4238 Wilson Boulevard, Arlington, VA; ✆ (703) 841-7256

- 5300 Wisconsin Avenue N.W., Washington, D.C.; ✆ (202) 362-7427

- 5131 Indian Head Highway, Oxon Hill, MD; ✆ (301) 839-2766

- 3520 S Jefferson Street, Falls Church, VA; ✆ (703) 379-6044

- 2020 University Boulevard E., Adelphi, MD; ✆ (301) 445-4545

- 5700 Columbia Pike, Falls Church, VA; ✆ (703) 671-8050

- 6200 Annapolis Road, Hyattsville, MD; ✆ (301) 322-2965

- 8661 Colesville Road, Silver Spring, MD; ✆ (301) 588-1994

- 5801 Duke Street, Alexandria, VA; ✆ (703) 658-1391

- 2111 Brightseat Road, Landover, MD; ✆ (301)3 22-4840

- 414 Maple Avenue, Vienna, VA; ✆ (703) 255-6525

And other suburban locations

- ✍ www.footlocker.com

A thumping hip-hop beat pulsated through Mr. C's sinewy body as he swaggered through the front door of Foot Locker, his head and shoulders moving ever so slightly to the funky groove blaring from the store's sound system. Hey, C stands for *cool*, my man, and the Crown Prince of Cheap is definitely *down* with this streetwise establishment. Decked out in purples, blues, and reds, with track lighting and that urban soundtrack permeating the air, Foot Locker is simply where it's at for checking out a hip selection of name-brand athletic and recreational shoes at discount prices. And yes, they also have all sort of footwear for the rest of you.

MR. CHEAP'S PICKS

Shoes and Sneakers

Foot Locker Outlet—As much selection as in a regular branch, at up to half off.

Nine West & Company Outlet—You love their shoes, ladies. You'll love 'em even more at discount.

Payless Shoe Source—The lowest prices on shoes you'll probably find anywhere around D.C.

Rack Room Shoes—The whole family can find cheap, good footwear here, with discounts ranging from 25 to 75 percent off.

These cats regularly offer 30 to 50 percent off a wide range of brands and styles, and there are plenty of unique deals scattered around the premises. As the C-Man cruised the aisles one evening, he noticed some Nike men's Air Max, regularly priced at $139.99, just $89.99, and Nike men's Air 40-40s, normally priced at $79.99, for just $29.99. He also spotted a clearance table offering sneakers for $19.99 and up. Women's running shoes were priced at up to 50 percent off list prices, with a good selection of Nike and Reebok running shoes for both genders available from $49.99 on up to $115—and those included styles that normally carry list prices up to the $150 mark!

Did C. Diddy mention boots? Colorado brand hiking boots were available in one of those "Buy one and get one free" deals, with one pair discounted from $84.99 to $69.99, and another slashed from $119.99 to $79.99.

And that's not all, man. Foot Locker also carries outdoor-type clothing, also at discount. For example, transition jackets normally costing $60 were priced at $29.99, and college T-shirts were tagged at just $9.99.

Lady Foot Locker is run by the same company, of course, with stores generally located next door to the main establishment. It offers similar selection and deals, as C-Man found out when the missus interrupted his funkadelic reverie with a persuasive "request" to assist her in shopping there. Well, C's gotta say that the atmosphere in the "Ladies Room" was a bit more, uh . . . sedate, with a scene more along the lines of that at The Gap: Think fluorescent lighting, tasteful Earth-toned décor, and hushed conversation. Here they had a table of boots, sandals, and sneakers that were all priced under $20, as well as Nike running shoes reduced from $89.99 to $59.99. Actra suede boots, normally $59.99, were reduced to a most-groovy $19.99. Athletic socks ("buy one and get one at half off") and other accessories were also available.

Store hours are Monday through Saturday from 10 a.m. to 9 p.m., and Sundays from noon to 6 p.m.

Foot Locker Outlet

- 2020 University Boulevard, Adelphi, MD; ☎ (301) 445-4545
- 2700 Potomac Mills Circle, Prince William, VA; ☎ (703) 490-3602
- 5700-A Columbia Pike, Falls Church, VA; ☎ (703) 671-8050
- ✐ www.footlocker.com

Foot Locker has designated a few of its stores as clearance centers for overstocks and discontinued styles. These shoes tend to be between six months and two years past current season, but few will mark you as a fashion victim. Mr. C trotted around in a pair of "Asics Gel" running shoes, originally at $89; here, they were down to $49.99. Good deal. Same treatment of women's Nike Air Max, originally $139.99 and now $99.99; women's Saucony GRID Procyon were $49.99, reduced from $69.99. And boys' Vince Carter and Michael Jordan basketball shoes were on sale for $100, marked down from $150.

FLO also clears out lots of activewear here, like men's Shield Gear Camo Tee were discounted from $21.99 to $49.99; Champion T-shirts were only $4.99. This is also the place to shop for children's clothing. At a recent NFL clearance sale, an infants Nike Cheer dress, originally $24.99, was discounted to $15.99; an infants Nike Interlock Coverall (12 to 24 months) was reduced from $22.99 to $15.99. Even though these are closeouts, hang on to that receipt, because you can get a refund on any unworn articles of clothing within 60 days. And if you're looking for extra discounts, be sure to check out their biannual sidewalk sales, it's bargain heaven!

Store hours are Monday through Friday from 10 a.m. to 5 p.m., Sunday from noon to 5 p.m.

Nine West & Company Outlet

- City Place, 8661 Colesville Road, Silver Spring, MD; ✆ (301) 587-8938

- ✑ www.ninewest.com

At their clearance store in the City Place Mall, you can get up to 30 percent and more off their regular prices—on shoes that are overstocks and closeouts but all first-quality. It's no surprise to come across clearance sales such as a boot sale

with 50 percent off select styles and sometimes even less. For instance, cool tango double-zip boots, originally $159, sell here for $69. Denim stretch boots were on sale for $139; stylish disco fever pumps were marked down to $69. Mr. C recently saw a leather cell phone case for $29, a Mercer mini flap purse for $45, and a pair of Picasso winter booties, worthy of L.L. Bean itself, marked down to $99. And nearly any multitasking, on-the-go mom can make use of a messenger baby bag tote and diaper bag for $79.

Sizes are limited, of course, but there is lots of everything in this surprisingly large store. Exchanges and refunds are available with receipt.

Store hours are Monday through Saturday from 10 a.m. to 9 p.m., and Sunday from noon to 6 p.m.

Payless Shoe Source

- 1120 G Street N.W., Washington, D.C.; ✆ (202) 783-3441

- 806 H Street N.E., Washington, D.C.; ✆ (202) 543-1385

- 401 8th Street S.E., Washington, D.C.; ✆ (202) 546-5718

- 1777 Columbia Road N.W., Washington, D.C.; ✆ (202) 387-8315

- 642 Rhode Island Avenue N.E., Washington, D.C.; ✆ (202) 269-3512

- 3220 14th Street N.W., Washington, D.C.; ✆ (202) 387-1523

- 3900 Minnesota Avenue N.E., Washington, D.C.; ✆ (202) 396-1300

- 2855 Alabama Avenue S.E., Washington, D.C.; ✆ (202) 581-2811

- 4505 Wisconsin Avenue N.W., Washington, D.C.; ✆ (202) 537-7034

- 3116 Queens Chapel Road, Hyattsville, MD; ✆ (301) 779-0111

- 6431 Georgia Avenue N.W., Washington, D.C.; ✆ (202) 723-3215

- 4238 Wilson Boulevard, Arlington, VA; ✆ (703) 243-0515

- 55129 Indian Head Highway, Oxon Hill, MD; ✆ (301) 567-7749

- 3737 Branch Avenue, Temple Hills, MD; ✆ (301) 899-1469

- 3500 E West Highway, Hyattsville, MD; ✆ (301) 559-3022

- 3501 S Jefferson Street, Falls Church, VA; ✆ (703) 379-2033

- 7943 New Hampshire Avenue, Hyattsville, MD; ✆ (301) 434-6767

- 5870 Crossroads Center Way, Falls Church, VA; ✆ (703) 931-4047

- 6230 Central Avenue, Capitol Heights, MD; ✆ (301) 336-1607

- 8661 Colesville Road, Silver Spring, MD; ✆ (301) 587-3071

  And other suburban locations

- ✍ www.payless.com

Pay less indeed! The prices at this ubiquitous, no-frills chain are super-low, and although the brands aren't world renown, the aisles are stacked high with stylish, good-quality footwear. When Mr. C last strolled through these doors, selected styles were being offered at 50 percent off the everyday prices, which already are laughably cheap, even by Mr. C's standards. However, any licensed psychologist will tell you that humor is a good thing . . . a *very* good thing.

So get a load of this: Women's sneakers were priced at $9.99 (ha!)

to $15.99; stylish leather boots were $14.99 to $24.99; and C spotted some high-heeled pumps for $9.99 (giggle) and sandals for (someone pinch the Cheapster!) $7. Kids sneakers were tagged at $9.99 and up, and there was even a wall of kids shoes priced at $3.99 and up. (ba-boom!)

And what's in store for the guys? How about sneakers priced at $10.99 to $16.99 (chortle), or a pair of rugged State Street outdoor hiking boots for $24.99? (Now that's what C calls conservation!)

You definitely don't want to shell out more for your socks than you paid for the shoes, so you might as well get the former here, too. Men's dress socks were priced at three for $10, and you could pick up two six-pair packs of athletic socks for the same price! (snicker!) Women's panty hose was on sale for $1! (lone guffaw!)

Frugally priced accessories, notably leather purses ($6.99) and sunglasses ($3) are also available, so what are you waiting for? Strike up the band and get the heck over there!

Store hours are generally 9:30 a.m. to 6 p.m. Monday through Saturday, except in the malls, where Payless is usually open 10 a.m. to 9 p.m. Monday through Saturday, and noon to 6 p.m. on Sunday.

Rack Room Shoes

- Landmark Plaza, Alexandria, VA; ✆ (703) 941-6261

- 3556 S. Jefferson Street, Arlington, VA; ✆ (703) 931-6318

- Fair City Mall, Fairfax, VA; ✆ (703) 239-8835

- ✍ www.rackroomshoes.com

The whole family can find footwear at Rack Room Shoes, with discounts ranging from 25 to 75 per-

SHOPPING: SHOES AND SNEAKERS   133

cent off. From tots to moms and pops, everyone will save big on popular lines of casual and dress shoes.

Brand-name children's shoes include Reebok, OshKosh, Asics, and Nike. A kids' pair of Steve Madden Amy shoes, originally $59.99, are now $49.99. Men, you'll find Timberland, Vans, QBX, and Lux here, and you don't have to walk to Maine to save big on Rockport walking shoes. Big savings, too, on Dexter, Reebok, and Borelli. Women, you'll find clogs by Unisa, Candies sneakers, and Etienne Aigner heels. Other women's brand names include Nine West, Nomads, Stevies, and Aerosole. Appeal Melanie shoes, originally $44.99, were reduced to $34.99 and finally $27.99. Plus, there's a cross-section of women's casual shoes ranging from Keds canvas sneakers to stuff such as Mootsies Tootsies, Esprit, and Mia.

Store hours are Monday through Saturday from 10 a.m. to 9 p.m., and Sunday from noon to 6 p.m.

Shoe Gallery

- 3251 M Street N.W., Washington, D.C.; ✆ (202) 298-6668

Despite its location on one of Georgetown's most popular stretches, the Shoe Gallery manages to keep its prices reasonable. They even offer "price protection." If you see your new shoes somewhere else for less, the store will refund the difference. How's that for fancy footwork?

Well, Mr. C has already done most of the footwork for you, as everything in this store is already 20 to 30 percent off. He also noticed both men's and women's Timberland shoes ranging from $69 to $180. There are lots of styles here for trendy teens, too: Take Steve Maddens' for instance.

Dr. Martens are also popular with Generation Xers, not to mention their younger siblings (the "Y" generation? Why not?). Basic leather boots, sans steel toe and heavy commando sole, cost about $85 to $100 for boots that come higher up the calf. Plus, there are lots of different styles to choose from, available in a range of colors. And you thought they only came in basic black?

For a less military look, Western boots by Dan Post, as well as hiking boots by Clarks of England, can also be found here at good prices.

Shoe Gallery is open Monday through Saturday from 11 a.m. to 8 p.m., and Sunday from noon to 6 p.m.

Shoe Loft

- 4807 Bethesda Avenue, Bethesda, MD; ✆ (301) 564-5383

For a no-frills kind of store, the atmosphere here is pleasantly refined. Sure, it's self-serve, from boxes piled up in the center of the floor; however, these are anything but picked-over rejects. Shoe Loft sells only first-quality, current styles of women's shoes at up to 20 percent less than the same shoes in department stores.

You can find everything you need here, from dress shoes to casual wear and sneakers. You can pick from high-fashion brands like Via Spagia, Anne Klein, Kenneth Cole, Charles Jourdan, Unisa, Vanelli, Donna Planner, Cole Haan, and Stuart Weitzman. They're all discounted, sometimes up to 40 percent off. And, though you have to find a seat and try them on yourself, the staff is friendly and helpful in finding you the right size.

Be sure to look for Shoe Loft's end-of-season clearance sales when many of these shoes are sold at up to 50 percent off.

Store hours are Monday through Saturday from 10 a.m. to 6 p.m., and Sunday from noon to 5 p.m.

Shoes by Lara

- 703 14th Street N.W., Washington D.C.; ✆ (202) 637-9787

- 913 19th Street N.W., Washington, D.C.; ✆ (202) 659-9420

- 113 18th Street N.W., Washington, D.C.; ✆ (202) 331-5002

These busy downtown boutiques specialize in better-name women footwear, stocking (pardon the pun) such brands as Nine West, Bandolino, and Moda Espana. Among the bargains recently found was a pair of Ralph Lauren flats from 40 to 50 percent off. Caressa patent leather heels were another good deal; meant to sell for $69, Lara had them for $49. A pair of Joan & David's black patent leather shoes, originally $110, were reduced to $89 and then finally $79. And ultramodern Vera Cruz suede pumps, with satin ribbon laces, were seen for $69.99, nearly $20 off the retail price.

You can also find names like Renzo Fontanelli, from the same factory that makes Amalfi, at a 30 to 40 percent savings. Now, these are Lara's everyday reductions; Mr. C hasn't even gotten to the frequent sales, proffering such deals as a rack of "Buy one, Get one free" shoes, or "buy the first pair for $29 and get the second pair 15 percent off."

Store hours are Monday through Friday from 10 a.m. to 7 p.m., and Saturday from 11 a.m. to 6 p.m.

Shoe Scene

- 1330 Connecticut Avenue N.W., Washington, D.C.; ✆ (202) 659-2194

Mr. C is always delighted to find stores that sell current, high-quality merchandise for super-low prices. In Dupont Circle, Shoe Scene is able to do this because they deal directly with manufacturers, and because they have 10 stores nationwide, and can buy in large quantities and pass the savings on. In addition, they buy closeouts from top stores in New York. Put it all together, and you've got a place worth walking to.

A pair of black leather heels by Nine West, for instance, was reduced $20 from the original price, while a pair of Eli Rucci flats were marked down by $40 from retail. Also, they have low prices on a good variety of handbags, jewelry, scarves, and other accessories. On Mr. C's visit, all leather handbags were on sale for $30 and up.

Besides great everyday prices, there are always ongoing specials to make room for new merchandise. There are also knockout sales that happen a few times a year, when you may find shoes by Jazz, Vera Cruz, Vanelli, and Annie Lago selling at $29 for one pair, or two pairs for $50.

Shoe Scene is open Monday through Friday from 10 a.m. to 6:30 p.m., and Saturday from 10 a.m. to 6 p.m.

Sport Zone

- 1501 K Street N.W., Washington, D.C.; ✆ (202) 337-9773

Sport Zone specializes in athletic clothing and footwear. Shelves are loaded with men's, women's, and children's sneakers for almost every kind of sport imaginable. Women's Reeboks ranged from $20 to $110 when Mr. C passed through; women's New Balance shoes were reduced by 10, 20, and 40 percent, depending on the style.

Indeed, the trend here seems to be a straight 50 percent off the price tag. Men's Adidas basketball sneakers and Asics Gel running shoes were marked down to $50. And for the kiddies, you can easily buy cool shoes for school, like red Converse high-tops or Reeboks, for around $15.

Extra note: There are two other Sport Zones in D.C., neither of which is a discount store.

Store hours are Monday through Saturday from 10 a.m. to 10 p.m., and Sunday from 11 a.m. to 7.

For further bargains, try this national chain:

Famous Footwear

- 18225 Contour Road, Gaithersburg, MD; ✆ (301) 330-2950

- 9658 Main Street, Fairfax, VA; ✆ (703) 323-6007

- 1513 Connecticut Avenue, Silver Spring, MD; ✆ (301) 460-4034

- 6212 Greenbelt Road, Greenbelt, MD; ✆ (301) 982-2955

- 7272 Guilford Drive, Frederick, MD; ✆ (301) 662-3050

- 13023 Fair Lakes Shopping Center, Fairfax, VA; ✆ (703) 802-6412

- 2700 Potomac Mills Circle #857, Woodbridge, VA; ✆ (703) 491-5109

And other suburban locations

- ✑ www.famousfootwear.com

Store hours are Monday through Saturday from 9 a.m. to 10 p.m., and Sunday from noon to 5 p.m.

SPORTING GOODS

Mr. Cheap is not a jock, but he has played one in his dreams—especially when he's decked out in his internationally branded sports duds that he bought at discount. (In fact, Mrs. C has taken to calling him "L'il Nike.") Getting super deals on sports equipment and clothing is not difficult around the District. Shopping choices range from megachains such as REI and The Sports Authority to used equipment outlets like Play It Again Sports to scores of specialty shops that dot the retail playing field around these parts. Here El Cheap has listed the big boys, as well as several mom-and-pop nuggets that will offer you good deals on the big brands, along with personalized service.

Big Wheel Bikes

- 3119 Lee Highway, Arlington, VA; ✆ (703) 552-1110

- 1034 33rd Street N.W., Washington, D.C.; ✆ (202) 337-0254

- 6917 Arlington Road, Bethesda, MD; ✆ (301) 652-0192

- 2 Prince Street, Alexandria, VA; ✆ (703) 739-2300

- ✑ www.bigwheelbikes.com

Though this local chain (no pun intended) has competitive prices on current model bicycles, fall is the best time to grab a terrific closeout deal on new bikes by Fuji, Iron

Horse, Yokota, and other top manufacturers. As the end of the year approaches, you can save money on a large selection of styles; these are still brand-new, perfectly good, and fully warranted.

Mr. C liked a 21-speed Fuji "Sandblaster" city bike that was marked down $40 from the original price, with a chrome-alloy frame and grip-shifting, two features that are like the "auto transmission and dual air bags" of the bicycle world. And an Iron Horse off-road "AT-200" was discounted $100 less than the list price. Plenty of city/road bike hybrids, too.

Like all bicycles sold here, these all come with one full year of free adjustments (hang on to that receipt), plus a lifetime guarantee on frames. And, if you have a bicycle to trade in, you can get store credit toward a new bike. Alternatively, if you need a bike for just an afternoon excursion, Big Wheel Bikes has a rental fleet available at $5 per hour with a $15 minimum; $25 maximum per day.

Two last ideas: the Georgetown branch periodically sells off its rental bikes at a discount—always worth a look—and all branches have some used bikes for sale as well.

Store hours are Monday through Friday from 11 a.m. to 7 p.m., Saturday from 10 a.m. to 6 p.m., and Sunday from 11 a.m. to 5 p.m.

Play It Again Sports

- 1116 West Broad Street, Falls Church, VA; (703) 241-8304

- 5750 Union Mill Road, Clinton, VA; (703) 266-8677

- 9150 Baltimore National Pike #B, Ellicott City, MD; (410) 418-9371

- www.playitagainsports.com

From humble beginnings in Minneapolis, this has grown into a national chain of some 400 stores—all buying, selling, and trading new and used sports equipment. The merchandise gets swapped around between stores, ensuring a large, balanced selection in every store.

PIAS gets good deals on new items that have been discontinued (but hey, how much can a baseball glove change?). Among these, Mr. C recently saw an Alpine Tracker exercise machine, a pair of Ultra Wheels in-line skates, and a Mizuno baseball mitt.

More than half of the stock consists of used equipment. Seen recently were boy's mountain bikes, a pair of K2 downhill skis, billiard cues, and a set of Tommy Armour 845s golf irons. The Cheapster also saw hockey sticks, basketballs, baseball bats, footballs, shoulder pads for linebackers of all ages, tennis racquets, and lots more. Best of all, you can trade in your old stuff toward anything in the store—even new items.

Play It Again Sports is open Monday through Friday from 10 a.m. to 9 p.m., Saturday from 10 a.m. to 7 p.m., and Sunday from noon to 5 p.m.

Racquet & Jog Warehouse Store

- 12115 Parklawn Drive, Rockville, MD; (301) 770-5115

Along with new, full-price gear and clothing, this branch of the local chain also mixes in closeout merchandise from its stores in Georgetown, International Square, and Bethesda. Serve yourself a discontinued model of a Wilson tennis racquet, otherwise perfectly good, at 30 percent off or more. You'll find indoor racquets, too. Or, start training for the next marathon in a

Wilson running suit—you can easily mix and match separates for up to $100–$150. And there are plenty of cotton shirts and shorts for $5 a piece—so stock up!

On the sneaker bargain tables, Mr. C noticed several pairs of women's running shoes marked from $110 to $80 and sometimes as low as $57, along with others for men and women by Nike, Avia, and Asics. Yes, these styles are a year or two old and sizes are limited, but you'll surely sprint out of here with a real deal.

Store hours are Monday through Friday from 9:30 a.m. to 9 p.m., Saturday from 9:30 a.m. to 7 p.m., and Sunday from 11 a.m. to 6 p.m.

REI: Recreational Equipment

- 9801 Rhode Island Avenue, Greenbelt, MD;
  ✆ (301) 982-9681

- 3509 Carlin Springs Road, Falls VA; ✆ (703) 379-9400

- ✐ www.rei-outlet.com

This is a rather unusual sporting goods store, focusing not on team but outdoor activities—bicycling, running, skiing, rock climbing, and camping. It's also unusual in that it's actually a membership cooperative; anyone may shop here, but if you become a member, you'll get all kinds of extra discounts and benefits.

Membership costs a one-time-only fee of $15. That gets you early notification of special sales, some of which are for members only, as well as discounts on equipment rentals and repairs. It also means that you're involved in company profit sharing, which includes an annual dividend payment—around 10 percent of whatever amount you've spent during the year.

Meanwhile, about the merchandise itself: REI carries only what it considers to be high-quality stock—brands like Marmot, Columbia, Omega Pacific, Oakley, Patagonia, Woolrich, Helly-Hansen, Specialized, and others. These are all competitively priced, even before the dividend. And there is a special "Clearance Corner" section, where you can get big discounts on closeout items. Mr. C found a pair of Nike bicycling shorts and Oxford-style leather casual shoes by Rockport. He also spotted a pair of men's Patagonia River Shorts originally $48 reduced to $34.93, and a pair of women's Patagonia Board Shorts, originally $52, for $25.95 at a recent closeout sale. A men's Northface Box Quilt Jacket was on sale for $89.93 in comparison to the initial $195 price. Clothing for toddlers is available too: A Pre-school Closeout sale featured an Obermayer Ultra Gear Zip top discounted from $39.50 to $15.93. They even offer bridal registry, for the happy and fit couple!

Store hours are Monday through Friday from 10 a.m. to 9 p.m., Saturday from 10 a.m. to 7 p.m., and Sunday from 11 a.m. to 6 p.m.

MR. CHEAP'S PICKS

Sporting Goods

Play It Again Sports—New and used gear, all at incredible prices; save even more by trading your old stuff in.

Replay Sports—This local, family-run shop can compete with the big-league resale stores. Replay Sports offers new and used sporting goods, some of which are delightfully cheap.

The Sports Authority—National megastore prices on equipment, clothing, and team memorabilia.

Replay Sports

- 3644 King Street, Alexandria, VA; ✆ (703) 998-4231

Located in the Bradlee Shopping Center, this local, family-run shop can compete with the big-league resale stores. Replay Sports offers new and used sporting goods, some of which are delightfully cheap—like used golf balls, 10 for $3.99, or individual Wilson or Ping clubs to hit them with for $10.

Some of the larger items are unused closeout deals, for example, a Bruce Jenner "Power Walk" treadmill, advertised on TV at $350, seen here for $275. Other kinds of equipment offer you a choice: Pick up a new volleyball for $20, or a used one for $10. New and used baseball mitts are all reduced by up to 40 percent after the season. Even new, current-style tennis racquets are well priced, like an Andre Agassi model by Head, selling for about $40 under a well-known superstore.

RS also has new and used rollerblades (from $30!), plus lots of used skis, boots, and bindings. You can also trade in your own used gear towards any new item in the store. Even if you have something you can't return at a department store, they'll give you credit for it here. Nice folks.

Replay is live from Monday through Friday from 10 a.m. to 8 p.m., Saturday from 10 a.m. to 7 p.m., and Sunday from noon to 5 p.m.

Sports Authority

- 6250 Greenbelt Road, Greenbelt, MD; ✆ (301) 220-4120

- 12055 Rockville Pike, Rockville, MD; ✆ (301) 231-8650

- Springfield Mall, Alexandria, VA; ✆ (703) 922-5600

- 12300 Price Club Plaza, Fairfax, VA; ✆ (703) 266-9283

- 8355 Leesburg Pike, Vienna, VA; ✆ (703) 827-2206

- ✍ www.thesportsauthority.com

This national chain is truly jock heaven—a place where you can score just about any kind of sports paraphernalia under the sun (or dome), including all manner of brand-name sports equipment and clothing from makers like Champion, Lamar, Nautilus, MacGregor, Spalding, and literally hundreds of others. The mere sight of this mega-market can bring a tear of joy to the eye of any sports fan.

The everyday prices here are nothing special, but there's almost always some kind of sale taking place, with specially priced merchandise placed in aisles all around the store.

On the day El Cheapedo jogged into his nearest location, SA was offering 20 percent to 50 percent off a wide range of its inventory. Athletic clothing for women, including tanks, tops, and running outfits, were being offered at 20 percent to 30 percent off. Other clothing was discounted up to 50 percent.

Other bargains: basketballs were available for $19.99 to $29.99; Royce Union mountain bikes were priced at 30 percent off; inline skates were available for $49.99 to $199; and sleeping bags with a comfort rating of 32 degrees could be acquired for an unbelievable $14.99! (The Cheapster feels warmer already.)

How about tearing down the slopes on a cutting-edge snowboard? You could save about 50 percent or more by picking up your implement of transportation here. Static brand snowboards were marked down from $200 to just $79; Karam models were priced at

$249, down from $350; and a Viper (normally $200) could have been yours for under $145!

If you'd rather get your exercise indoors, be aware that Sports Authority regularly knocks $100 to $500 or more off the suggested retail prices for treadmills. A Healthrider S150, normally $1,199, was tagged at $799, and a Weslo Cadence 985, listed at around $500, was discounted to $399.

Of course, Sports Authority is also the place to get the official clothing of your favorite pro or college sports team. Baseball caps feature designs for every major league team in baseball, football, basketball, and hockey; these start at around $16, higher in all-wool.

All of the footwear on the premises was offered as a "buy one and get one at 50 percent off" deal. And the prices were good: Nike Cross Trainers were marked down from $84.99 to $69.99; women's Nike's were offered at $39.99 and up; Nike running shoes were priced from $44.99; and a range of hiking boots (including the Hi-Tec and Timberland brands) were discounted from the $130 range at $70 to $90. The Cheapster pulled out his solar calculator and determined that combining special deal and discounted prices meant that he could grab two pairs of high-end athletic shoes for as low as $30 a pair. Not bad!

Store hours are Monday through Thursday from 9:30 a.m. to 9:30 p.m., Saturday from 9 a.m. to 9 p.m., and Sunday from 10 a.m. to 7 p.m.

Sunny's

- 372 South Pickett Street; Alexandria, VA; ✆ (703) 461-0088

- 13718 Baltimore Avenue, Laurel, MD; ✆ (301) 604-5771

- 8350 Bristol Court, Jessup, MD; ✆ (301) 776-7750

- 912 F Street N.W., Washington, D.C.; ✆ (202) 737-2032

- 6016 Old Silver Hill Road, District Heights, MD; ✆ (301) 967-1627

- 2090 Viers Mill Road, Rockville, MD; ✆ (301) 279-0777

- 4513 Duke Street, Alexandria, VA; ✆ (703) 461-0088

And other suburban locations

If you're really into camping, or just want to look like it, Sunny's has all the gear you'll ever need. Essentials such as sleeping bags, mess kits, and duffle bags are available in several different styles, along with tents, cookware, fishing gear, hiking boots, and much more—all at tremendous savings in comparison to similar stores. Sunny's is also a bright source for warm clothing, protective outerwear, and the like; see the listing under "Clothing—New" for info. Store hours are Monday through Friday from 10 a.m. to 8 p.m.; Saturday and Sunday from 10 a.m. to 6 p.m.

Tennis Factory

- 2500 Wilson Boulevard #100, Arlington, VA; ✆ (703) 522-2700

Here's another store that proves the local mom 'n' pops can do just as well for you as the mega stores. Tennis Factory has great prices on rackets, accessories, and clothing, as they have for 20 years. Topflight service—they'll even string a racquet for you in 24 hours. New, current racquets are discounted; a Head "Trisys" was seen for about $50 off retail. Don't miss the "Bargain Corner," where discontinued racquets are in the $100 to $150 range. Mr. C found a Spalding model here, discounted to just a little over $100. And if you're one of those purists who buy wooden racquets, this is the place where you'll find a selection, as TF has bought out remaining models from many other stores.

There are lots of children's sizes, as low as $20 to $25 each. "Kids are new players," said the salesperson, "so we must make sure to mark things down for them." The staff is made up of teaching pros who really know their stuff; they're also non-

commissioned, which means no pressure for you. The store will even let you try a racquet out for $5 a day, which will be applied to the price if you buy it. Try that from a department store!

Tennis shoe bargains abound here, with many closeout styles at extra discounts. And the store sells a fair selection of clothing, again, with clearance offering 25 to 50 percent markdowns. Talk about an ace!

Store hours are Monday through Friday from 10 a.m. to 8 p.m.; Saturday and Sunday from 10 a.m. to 6 p.m.

STATIONERY, OFFICE, AND ART SUPPLIES

Whether you're a left-brained *artiste* or a nose-to-the grindstone, right-brained business dweeb, you've still gotta find good deals on the tools of your trade. The stores listed here—mostly of the large, multiple department variety—offer large, name-brand selections and plenty of bargains.

Frame Factory Warehouse

• 5700-F General Washington Drive, Alexandria, VA; ✆ (703) 941-0737

If you can find this store, part of that stretch of warehouses in Springfield (described at length in the "Furniture" section), you'll save up to 30 percent over the regular prices at FF's suburban Virginia stores. Yet, this outlet has the same selection as the rest, all in stock, plus the full framing service.

Of course, if you're a do-it-yourselfer, you can save even more—as much as 50 percent off. Once you've chosen your materials, FF will do the cutting of frame, matte, and glass for you. All you have to do is assemble it; what an easy way to save on redecorating your home.

They will also sell you the raw materials—matte board, foam core, even cutting tools, at prices below many art supply retail stores. And if you really want something in a hurry, the store has ready-made frames in standard sizes. Friendly service, too.

Frame Factory hours are Monday through Friday from 9 a.m. to 5 p.m., and Saturday from 9 a.m. to 3 p.m.

Pearl Art and Craft Supplies

• 5695 Telegraph Road, Alexandria, VA; ✆ (703) 960-3900

• 12266 Rockville Pike #P, Rockville, MD; ✆ (301) 816-2900

• ✍ www.pearlart.com

Pearl is one of the country's leading art supply houses. Mr. C thinks of it as an art supply department store. They seem to sell everything under the sun, all at discount. Whether you want to decorate your office, a blank canvas, or a cake, you're sure to find whatever you need for the job.

The "Art Bin Sketch Pack" retails for $13.50 each but sells for $8.99 at Pearl. The store has tons of ready-made white canvases: An 8" x 18" canvas by Dixie was available at half off the list price. A Galleria set of six acrylic jars was recently on sale for $19.99, again half its retail price. At this locale, you'll also find paints, brushes, airbrush kits, the works.

Getting into crafts? Make a source of light into a piece of art when making a Memory Lamp, list price $15.99 available for $11.99. A Kolo Photo Album was $28.79, reduced from $43.98, and a Hamilton Studio Easel, originally $225, was $139. Alvin Ice Mailing Tubes, originally $14.25, were available for $9.99. Save about a dollar on sea sponges, a great alternative to paintbrushes to give walls a textured look without the expense of wallpaper.

Pearl also has an extensive collection of art guidebooks and manuals; the comprehensive *Artist's Handbook,* full of information about the latest techniques and technologies in the art world, sells here for $10 off book price. And then there's furniture—easels, drafting boards, flat files, storage systems, and more. It's all contained in an attractive catalog; the store does an extensive (but not expensive) mail-order business here and around the world.

Store hours are Monday through Saturday from 10 a.m. to 8 p.m., and Sunday from 10 a.m. to 6 p.m.

MR. CHEAP'S PICKS

Stationery, Art, and Office Supplies

Pearl Artist and Craft Supply—A true gem of a shop for all—and they mean all—your art needs.

Plaza Art—Plaza offers discounted prices on just about anything an artist or writer could ever need: all types of paper, paint, brushes, pens, glue, and more.

Office Depot; Staples—These office superstores have vast selections of business supplies, furniture, books, and tech gear, with plenty of store sales and manufacturers' rebates.

Pla-za Artists Materials

- 1990 K Street N.W., Washington, D.C.; ✆ (202) 331-7090

- 1727 I Street N.W., Washington, D.C.; ✆ (202) 331-7095

- 7925 Old Georgetown Road, Bethesda, MD; ✆ (301) 718-8500

- 1596 Rockville Pike, Rockville, MD; ✆ (301) 770-0500

- 8209 Georgia Avenue, Silver Spring, MD; ✆ (301) 587-5581

- 3045 Nutley Street, Fairfax, VA; ✆ (703) 280-4500

- 5900 Leesburg Pike, Falls Church, VA; ✆ (703) 820-4650

- ✑ www.pla-za.com

Not that this happens as much in Washington as it does in other university towns, but students actually can get a discount by flashing their school IDs at these shops. They sell just about anything an artist or writer could ever need: all types of paper, paint, brushes, pens, glue . . . lots and lots of stuff.

The prices are marked so that you can see the savings. For example, a two-ounce tube of Liquitex acrylic paint is a dollar less than what you would pay somewhere else. Topstar and Sanford highlighter pens are $1.09 each ($1.75 elsewhere). Now, these may not sound like huge savings, but students have to watch every cent—and they do add up, especially when you're buying large quantities.

In addition to the standard discounts, there are frequent special sales; low-temperature mini glue guns, with two glue-stick refill cartridges, were just $2.50 the day Mr. C visited. These normally sell for $8.25.

Damaged items are reduced even further. When Mr. C dropped by, "scratch 'n' dent" picture frames were all marked at 30 percent off. There aren't a lot of these damaged goods, but there's a decent selection.

Store hours are Monday through Friday from 9 a.m. to 7 p.m., Saturday from 9 a.m. to 6 p.m., and Sunday from 9 a.m. to 5 p.m.

Utrecht Art & Drafting Supplies

- 1250 I Street N.W., Washington, D.C.; ✆ (202) 898-0555

- ✍ www.utrechtart.com

From its base in New York, Utrecht has become one of the country's largest art supply houses, saving money manufacturing canvas and related products with low prices on other brands. The store boasts over 20,000 items at discount.

An 18" x 24" 100-sheet pad of Utrecht newsprint drawing paper sells as low as $5.98, $2 for the 9" x 12" size. Their permanent acrylic Gesso colors are $7 to $10 a pint and available in basic shades such as black, purple, blue, yellow, and white. Save money on Rembrandt oils and Chartpak lettering, Pelikan inks, Neilsen frames, Rapidograph pens, a variety of guidebooks, and much, much more. In addition to their regular low prices, Utrecht has periodic sales offering discounts of up to 60 percent on many items. The staff is friendly and very professional, too.

Store hours are Monday through Friday from 9 a.m. to 7 p.m., Saturday from 9 a.m. to 6 p.m., and Sunday from 11 a.m. to 5 p.m.

Of course, sometimes you've just got to have 57 cases of paper clips . . .

Office Depot

- 4455 Connecticut Avenue N.W., Washington D.C.; ✆ (202) 363-5758

- 11130 New Hampshire Avenue, Silver Spring, MD; ✆ (301) 681-0063

- 6700 Richmond Highway, Alexandria, VA; ✆ (703) 660-8671

- 11816 Spectrum Center, Reston, VA; ✆ (703) 481-8301

- 5812 Columbia Pike, Baileys Crossroads, Arlington, VA; ✆ (703) 379-0319

- 12137 Rockville Pike, Rockville, MD; ✆ (301) 770-5410

- 11001 Lee Highway, Fairfax, VA; ✆ (703) 591-1700

- 12275 Price Club Plaza, Fairfax, VA; ✆ (703) 830-7773

- 2901 Gallows Road, Falls Church, VA; ℘ (703) 560-5088

- 10630 Sudley Manor Drive, Manassas, VA; ℘ (703) 369-5200

- 8520 Leesburg Pike, Vienna, VA; ℘ (703) 734-6580

  And other suburban locations

- ✐ www.officedepot.com

Office Depot, along with Office Max and Staples, fits into that category of retail chains that need no introduction from the likes of Mr. Cheap. After all, they not only cover the American landscape from sea to shining sea (including scores of stores in and around the District), but also have nearly identical business models: They all offer a selection of nearly every conceivable office supply item, including paper, folders, labels, planners, and the like, plus office furniture, technology products (computers, printers, fax machines, software, cell phones, etc.), and even books. They also provide copying, printing, and binding services.

All of the office stores regularly offer manufacturers' rebates (usually the mail-in variety) that can save you $30 to $40 a pop, and hundreds of dollars during a typical shopping spree. These stores advertise heavily in the daily and Sunday papers, and that's where you'll learn about their current deals. During one such promotion, Microsoft Money financial software was available at $29.99, which was $30 off the suggested retail price; Smead colored file folders were $9.99 for a pack of 100; an Iris four-drawer storage system was discounted from $29.99 to $19.99; and you could pick up 500 sheets of the house-brand copy paper for just $2.99.

A 50-pack of Verbatim CD-R discs was just $14.99 after a $12 mail-in rebate; and Epson black ink printer cartridges were on sale for as little as $27 each.

In the market for a high-backed leather executive chair? You can pick one up at one of these stores for as little as $59.99, and several other models range up to the $200 range.

The list of good deals on business-based merchandise goes on and on, and as a guy who as worked out of the old homestead for more than 20 years, Mr. C can assure you that one of these office superstores should be a required stop on any shopping spree.

Store hours at Office Depot are generally Monday though Friday from 7 a.m. to 9 p.m., Saturday from 9 a.m. to 9 p.m., and Sunday from 11 a.m. to 6 p.m. The in-town locations usually keep shorter hours, so call ahead!

Staples

- 6800 Wisconsin Avenue, Bethesda, MD; ℘ (301) 652-3174

- 9195 Central Avenue, Capitol Heights, MD; ℘ (301) 499-8813

- 5556 Randolph Road, Rockville, MD; ℘ (301) 770-3682

- Seminary Plaza, Silver Spring, MD; ℘ (301) 588-3977

- 2545 McNair Farm Drive, Herndon, VA; ℘ (703) 713-0275

- 8461 Leesburg Pike, Vienna, VA; ℘ (703) 847-0654

  And other suburban locations

- ✐ www.staples.com

Staples, Office Max, and Office Depot are almost identical in their offering and services, which Mr. C has described in the Office Depot section above.

Store hours are Monday through Friday from 8 a.m. to 9 p.m., Saturday from 9 a.m. to 9 p.m., and Saturday from 10 a.m. to 6.

Tuesday Morning

- 3501 Carlin Springs Road, Falls Church, VA; ✆ (703) 845-3710

- 11111 Georgia Avenue, Wheaton, MD; ✆ (301) 942-1884

- 136 Maple Avenue West, Vienna, VA; ✆ (703) 938-6707

- 6230 Rolling Road, Springfield, VA; ✆ (703) 866-0379

- 25 Beall Avenue, Rockville, MD; ✆ (301) 424-2480

- 131 Bowie Road #A, Laurel, MD; ✆ (301) 953-7907

- 353 Muddy Branch Road, Gaithersburg, MD; ✆ (301) 921-9542

- 750 State Route 3 South, Gambrills, MD; ✆ (410) 923-1194

- 492 Elden Street, Herndon, VA; ✆ (703) 471-5571

- 5619 Stone Road, Centreville, VA; ✆ (703) 222-7730

- 14516 Potomac Mills Road, Woodbridge, VA; ✆ (703) 494-1215

And other suburban locations

- ✍ www.tuesdaymorning.com

TM offers a 50 percent to 80 percent "everyday" discount on upscale merchandise found in better department stores. Check out the aisles and aisles of flashy closeout bargains for which Tuesday Morning is so popular. There are also great buys on plain and fancy office supplies. You can find incredible deals on fine-maker pens and pencils, fountain pens, and roller ball pens. They also have lots to see in quality stationery sets; there are generally a good variety of colors and thicknesses. Packages of seasonal greeting cards are also priced right.

Cross writing instruments are usually about half price, while some Sheaffer sets were recently marked down from $35 to a mere $15. Both ladies' and men's styles, sold singly and in sets, tend to be well-stocked; but remember, when this store advertises a special in the paper, you can expect them to sell out fast.

Store hours are Monday, Tuesday, Wednesday, and Friday from 10 a.m. to 7 p.m.; Thursday from 10 a.m. to 8 p.m.; Saturday from 10 a.m. to 6 p.m.; and Sunday from noon to 6 p.m. Got all that?

TOYS AND GAMES

There days, good deals on toys and games are mostly limited to the large toy department stores such as Toys 'R' Us and K-B Toys (which, not coincidentally, are the main entries in this section). However, the savvy cheapster should also check out the offerings at the businesses listed in the "Discount Department Stores" section: Costco, Target, Wal-Mart, and the like, as well as just about any "dollar" store you come across. And, of course, remember that you'll likely find the best deals during post-holiday clearance sales.

Funcoland

- 9667 Lost Knife Road, Gaithersburg, MD; ✆ (301) 212-9884

- 12266 Rockville Pike, Rockville, MD; ✆ (301) 231-6691

- ✑ www.funcoland.com

Can't keep the kids in computer games? It's an expensive little habit, these Nintendos and Playstations, but there is a way to beat the system at its own game. The trick is to go with used software. Considering how quickly the novelty wears off on some of these games, the concept of paying less up front, and selling them off at the other end, may be the best way to score a win. They all look the same on the screen, and that's where it counts.

This national chain, based in Minneapolis, buys and sells games for Nintendo, Sony Playstation, and other formats, as well as the actual systems and accessories. Given their popularity, the stock of titles is enormous. Of course, availability changes all the time, and the prices, while below retail, are rather like those of old coins or baseball cards; the savings vary according to each game's popularity, supply, and demand.

The store also sells used, reconditioned equipment and accessories. Upgrade your older system instead of tossing it out and starting all over. Everything comes with a 90-day warranty, and you can always try out any game or equipment before purchasing. You'll love these stores because of the prices; your kids will love them because they're the modern version of a candy store, complete with several screens available for play.

Don't miss discounts on carrying cases, joysticks, power supplies, and other accessories, depending on stock. And you can sell them your old games, too, for payment by check or store credit. Governed by supply and demand, the amount paid out for certain games may be a small fraction of their original prices. You'll get more, by the way, if you opt for credit.

Store hours are Monday through Saturday from 10 a.m. to 9 p.m., and Sunday from 11 a.m. to 6 p.m.

K-B Toys

- 1100 S Hayes Street, Arlington, VA; ✆ (703) 418-6762

- 4238 Wilson Boulevard, Arlington, VA; ✆ (703) 527-2617

- 3765 Branch Avenue, Temple Hills, MD; ✆ (301) 899-0723

- 3500 E West Highway, Hyattsville, MD; ✆ (301) 853-3392

- 8661 Colesville Road, Silver Spring, MD; ✆ (301) 563-6862

- 6288 Arlington Boulevard, Falls Church, VA; ✆ (703) 538-5994

- 3101 Donnell Drive, Forestville, MD; ✆ (301) 568-6631

- 5801 Duke Street, Alexandria, VA; ✆ (703) 914-2109

- 7235 Arlington Boulevard, Falls Church, VA; ✆ (703) 280-9355

- 11160 Veirs Mill Road, Wheaton, MD; ✆ (301) 942-0725

- 7101 Democracy Boulevard, Bethesda, MD; ✆ (301) 469-6199

- 11301 Rockville Pike Kensington, MD; ✆ (301) 881-3120

- 1961 Chain Bridge Road, McLean, VA; ✆ (703) 848-0910

- 6701 Loisdale Road, Springfield, VA; ✆ (703) 971-5656

- 11919 Fair Oaks Mall Fairfax, VA; ✆ (703) 591-6007

- 14816 Washington Boulevard, Laurel, MD; ✆ (301) 776-8753

- 13005 Lee Jackson Memorial Highway, Fairfax, VA; ✆ (703) 263-7888

- 701 Russell Avenue, Gaithersburg, MD; ✆ (301) 840-0465

- 5000 U.S. Highway 301, Waldorf, MD; ✆ (301) 705-8040

And other suburban locations

- ✍ www.kbtoys.com

When The Cheapster and the missus set out on a grueling toy-search mission for their extended brood of nieces and nephews, they head directly to one of the big toy department stores, which in these parts means either Toys 'R' Us or K-B Toys. With a large selection and competitive prices, it's hard to go wrong at either of these outfits. K-B is generally not quite as large as the "R" store, but nevertheless has plenty from which to choose.

MR. CHEAP'S PICKS

Toys and Games

K-B Toys—This alternative to the Toys 'R' Us juggernaut offers pretty much the same selection, with mucho bargain opportunities every day of the year.

Toy Liquidators—Here toys by Fisher Price, Playskool, Disney, Nintendo, Child Guidance, Milton Bradley, Tonka, and many other popular brands are all discounted by up to 50 percent and sometimes more.

Tuesday Morning—Tons of toys for girls and boys are bargain priced at TM, whether your child wants dolls or darts.

The last time Mr. C darkened these doors, K-B was offering up to 75 percent off retail on a number of playthings, including Toy Story figures, marked down from $12.99 each to just $4.99 each; a Generation Girl Barbie or friends, regularly $9.99, on sale for $7.99 each; and an Ask Me More Eeyore (ask your kids: they'll know), slashed from $34.99 to a magnificently cheap $9.99! Also on sale were a Tonka "Mighty Backhoe" construction vehicle, discounted from $27.99 to just $14.99! For budding pop stars, you could pick up a Dance Diva home recording studio, regularly $89.99, for just $49.99.

In fact, K-B often has $9.99 sales, where you can pick up Barbie Dolls, $17 board games, and many other items super cheap. Post-season clearance sales and special promotions can save you even more.

The deals on toys go on and on, but that's not all. You can also get good prices on a range of video game systems, software, collectible action figures, sports equipment, dolls, videos and DVDs, kids furniture, models, board games, and more.

With a selection like that, and with K-B's good prices, what's not to like?

K-B's store hours are generally Monday through Saturday from 10 a.m. to 9 p.m., and Sunday from noon to 6 p.m.

Toy Liquidators

- 2700 Potomac Mills Circle, Prince William, VA; ✆ (703) 690-4077

Here's a toy store that parents will enjoy just as much as their kids. That's because toys by Fisher Price, Playskool, Disney, Nintendo, Child Guidance, Milton Bradley, Tonka, and many other popular brands are all discounted by up to 50 percent and sometimes more.

Remember Spirograph? Well, it's still around, only now it's "Mega Spirograph." Toy Liquidators has it for $15. Other game deals include the ever popular "Chutes and Ladders," "Parcheesi," and "Don't Break the Ice," each in the $10 range. The "Star Wars," "Pokemon" and NFL versions of Monopoly are available for 10 bucks as well.

There's something for all ages. To illustrate, there are lots of different Sesame Street toys, like a Kermit coin bank (certainly can't call it a "piggy bank," can we?) for $10, and "Toy Story" action figures for $5. Radio controlled cars are priced anywhere from $10 to $60, depending on quality. Polly Pocket dolls that are small enough to fit in a girl's hand yet big enough to dress with clothes, cost between $5 and $20. And, for parents' peace of mind, a Disney nursery audio monitor system was also recently seen at half price, just $25.

Then there are all types of dolls, Nintendo game cartridges, Lincoln Logs, and Tonka trucks; also, some sporting goods, like Frisbees, Voit soccer balls, and Nash skateboards. Let's go, Mommy!

Toy Liquidators is open Monday through Saturday from 10 a.m. to 9:30 p.m.; Sunday from 11 a.m. to 7 p.m.

Toys 'R' Us

- 5521 Leesburg Pike, Baileys Crossroads, VA;
  ✆ (703) 820-2428

- 8005 New Hampshire Avenue, Hyattsville, MD;
  ✆ (301) 422-4080

- 4721 Auth Pl, Suitland, MD;
  ✆ (301) 423-6614

- 10901 Georgia Avenue, Wheaton, MD;
  ✆ (301) 946-2954

- 8201 Annapolis Road, Lanham Seabrook, MD;
  ✆ (301) 459-6070

- 11810 Rockville Pike, Rockville, MD; ✆ (301) 770-3376

- 6715 Commerce Street, Springfield, VA; ✆ (703) 922-7876

- 8449 Leesburg Pike, Vienna, VA; ✆ (703) 893-2223

- 933 Washington Boulevard S., Laurel, MD; ✆ (301) 497-6325

- 11055 Mall Circle, Waldorf, MD; ✆ (301) 705-9800

And other suburban locations

- ✍ www.toysrus.com

Mr. Cheap doesn't have to tell parents about Toys 'R' Us, and you must know it's hard to beat their prices, which can range anywhere from 10 to 60 percent off list. Whether you're looking for action figures, building sets, dolls, games, puzzles, stuffed animals, educational toys, computer games, and even bikes and sports equipment— really anything you could possibly think of for kids—you will find it all here.

On a recent toy search, Mr. C noticed a G.I. Joe doll by Hasbro and a Barbie Glam Tour Bus, both $19.99. A nifty toy monorail set, normally listed at $119, was marked down to $80, and a Harry Potter "Troll on the Loose" was only $10.99.

Mr. Cheap looked around for his favorite games and found Monopoly: The dot.com Edition, for $14.98; a Lord of the Rings Board Game priced at $29.98 (list price $44); and Who Wants to be a Millionaire and Men are from Mars and Women are from Venus, both priced at $19.98. (Bring on the party!)

Most Toys 'R' Us locations are open every day from 10 a.m. to 9 p.m.

Tuesday Morning

- 3501 Carlin Springs Road, Falls Church, VA; ℅ (703) 845-3710

- 11111 Georgia Avenue, Wheaton, MD; ℅ (301) 942-1884

- 136 Maple Avenue West, Vienna, VA; ℅ (703) 938-6707

- 6230 Rolling Road, Springfield, VA; ℅ (703) 866-0379

- 25 Beall Avenue, Rockville, MD; ℅ (301) 424-2480

- 131 Bowie Road #A, Laurel, MD; ℅ (301) 953-7907

- 353 Muddy Branch Road, Gaithersburg, MD; ℅ (301) 921-9542

- 750 State Route 3 South, Gambrills, MD; ℅ (410) 923-1194

- 492 Elden Street, Herndon, VA; ℅ (703) 471-5571

- 5619 Stone Road, Centreville, VA; ℅ (703) 222-7730

- 14516 Potomac Mills Road, Woodbridge, VA; ℅ (703) 494-1215

And other suburban locations

- ℘ www.tuesdaymorning.com

TM's bargains will make you feel that much better any day with 50 percent to 80 percent discounts on everything from rugs to china to cookware to toys to luggage.

Tons of toys for girls and boys are bargain priced at TM, whether your child wants dolls or darts. Famous European collectible dolls, sold elsewhere for $15 to $90, will cost you between $6.99 and $39.99. Barbie's playsets, like Light Up Kitchen and a Fun Family Room, cost only $9.99. Mr. C saw action figures for $11.99 that included characters like Batman and Robin and some evildoers. Gund plush stuffed animals are sold here for half their retail price. You'll find interactive games here, too. Galaxy Hunt was selling for $10.99 and Road Relay was $19.99. There are infant and toddler toys, water/swim toys, books, puzzles, building blocks, and educational toys for all ages.

Store hours are Monday, Tuesday, Wednesday and Friday from 10 a.m. to 7 p.m., Thursday from 10 a.m. to 8 p.m., Saturday from 10 a.m. to 6 p.m., and Sunday from noon to 6 p.m.

UNUSUAL GIFTS

This is Mr. C's "catch-all" section, in which he's put some of stores that just don't fit anywhere else in the book. Many of the stores below are places to find truly nice gifts, while others fall more into the realm of the fun and decidedly offbeat.

Georgetown Gallery

- 3223 M Street N.W., Washington, D.C.; ℅ (202) 333-3543

Oyas Mini Bazaar

- 18th Street N.W., Washington, ℅ (202) 667-9853

Different names, same business. For exotic imports at very reasonable prices, few can compare with these fascinating shops. Hand-painted Russian dolls (you know, the hollow ones stacked inside each other) are $14.99 for a set. Chinese relaxation balls in silver ($7.99) and colored ($9.99)—roll 'em around in your hand—also make an interesting gift for that hard-to-shop-for person. For the more practical-minded, colorfully woven tote bags from Central America ($9.99) and black leather backpacks from Columbia ($69.99) are good deals.

There's lots of jewelry, of course—necklaces, rings, earrings, and bracelets, many priced around $10 and under. If you'd rather make in your own pieces, for the ultimate in a unique gift, there's also a large selection of beads and crafting paraphernalia. Plus, they offer antique paintings from various estate sales for $50 by appointment only.

The store hours for both shops are Monday through Sunday from 12:30 p.m. to 11:30 p.m.

Now & Then

- 6939 Laurel Avenue, Takoma Park, MD; ✆ (301) 270-2210

Searching high and low for an "Etcha-Sketch" key chain? You'll find 'em here. Not to mention a set of star stickers that glow in the dark, kooky rubber stamp kits, cool T-shirts, candles, incense, wind chimes, shower curtains, teapots, and picture frames. And, of course Now & Then stands ready to meet your entire stuffed animal and toy dinosaur needs; we're talking kiddie essentials.

The best part? Just about all of these things are priced under $15, making any browse here an affordable one. N & T also so has funky cards, wrapping paper, and confetti. Have a look.

Now and Then is open Monday through Friday from 11 a.m. to 7 p.m., Saturday from 10 a.m. to 6 p.m., and Sunday from 10 a.m. to 5 p.m.

MR. CHEAP'S PICKS

Unusual Gifts

Now & Then—This little shop is absolutely packed with fun and interesting gift items for all ages—most priced under $15.

Ten Thousand Villages

- 824 King Street, Alexandria, VA; ✆ (703) 684-1435

- ✐ www.tenthousandvillages.org

While Ten Thousand Villages has a zen ring from a name standpoint, this store has nothing to do with 12-step programs or getting in touch with your inner child. This nonprofit agency helps out artisans in Third World countries by selling their handicrafts. It's a local business, tied into a national chain of shops and educational programs. And because it's non-profit, and staffed by volunteers, the prices here are very reasonable indeed.

The Old Town store itself, new in 1994, is two floors of creative and delightful crafted items. Whether you want to spend $5 or $50, you're sure to find something nice for cousin Claudia (that she probably doesn't have already). Something like a polished agate stone "egg" from Pakistan that costs just $2.95, or perhaps a set of wind chimes from India for $12 to $25. At $4.95 each, linen placemats from Guatemala are a colorful housewarming gift. And $85 may sound like a lot of money for a chess set, but when the entire thing is made from black-and-white marble, it's a good deal.

TTV also has jewelry, ceramics, toys, and even musical instruments, all from faraway lands. Plus racks of unique greeting cards, many of which are crafted, too—Mr. C found a bunch with needlepoint designs actually woven on.

In all, it's a refined and cozy shop; stop in and have a free (!) cup of gourmet coffee as you wander through the warren of tiny rooms.

Store hours are Tuesdays through Saturdays from 11 p.m. to 7 p.m., and Sundays from noon to 5 p.m

A smaller store affiliated with the same organization is called Mission IYaders at 705 North Carolina Avenue S.E., Washington, D.C., telephone ✎ (202) 546-3040. They're open Tuesdays through Saturdays from 10 a.m. to 6 p.m., and Sundays from 1 to 5 p.m.

Shoe Scene

- 1330 Connecticut Avenue N.W., Washington, D.C.; ✎ (202) 659-2194

Mr. C is hardly about to suggest that anyone could ever pick out shoes as a present for someone else. (For more info on the shoes here, see the "Shoes and Sneakers" section.) But, along with stylish heels, this store has a large selection of small gift items at reasonable prices.

Wrought-iron candleholders, seen for more than $40 in some stores, can be found here for $30. Miniature models of violins, clarinets, and other instruments—resting inside tiny cases—are $30 and $40. "Victorian Essence" bath oils, in gorgeous glass bottles with flowers floating inside, are $15 and up. Imitations of (expensive) mechanical pens, with colorful enameled finishes, are a mere $12 each.

Plus gardening books, blank-book diaries, trendy-looking handbags ($25 and up), scarves, and costume jewelry. The owner of this busy little shop knows that a variety of these items bring women in for the shoes and vice versa. All this and good service, too.

Store hours are Monday through Friday from 10 a.m. to 6.30 p.m., and Saturday from 10 a.m. to 6 p.m.

Wake Up Little Suzie

- 3409 Connecticut Avenue N.W., Washington, D.C.; ✎ (202) 244-0700

A wide assortment of interesting and unusual crafts are what you'll see when you open your eyes at Suzie's. How 'bout a hand-shaped candle with five wicks—one in each finger? You can find these in a variety of lovely pastels, for under $20. Macabre, perhaps, but certainly offbeat.

For more delicate tastes, the rest of the store gleams with beautiful crafts. Figurines seen on Mr. C's visit included an adorable lion candleholder for $45 (remember, this is an artist-made, one-of-a-kind piece). Distinctive wall clocks, again hand-crafted, are priced around $30. Light-switch covers (also $30) feature themes like The Wizard of Oz—in bright emerald green, with miniature cutouts of Dorothy and all the rest laminated on, and sparkly, plastic "rubies" scattered all over. No one else is likely to bring the same thing to the party.

Jewelry includes lots of earrings, necklaces, bracelets, and brooches—in styles as varied as the artists who create them. Prices cover a similar spectrum—pins may go as high as $75, though some cost $20 or less. Earrings start at $25 and go up to the $100 range, with average prices between $40 and $60.

There are even gifts for the do-it-yourselfers out there. Would you believe a "Make Your Own Paper Shrine" kit? Mr. C saw one here for just $25.

Store hours are Monday through Friday from 11 a.m. to 7 p.m., Saturday from 11 a.m. to 7 p.m., and Sunday from noon to 5 p.m.

Entertainment

Washington is the capital of the world's most dominant cultural power. Need we say more?

Well, yes, it's not Broadway, or the Louvre, or Florence, but as a whole the District of Columbia and the surrounding region is one of the richest cultures on the planet. And best of all, not all of it requires you to be rich yourself.

Mr. Cheap has been putting on the Ritz for years at local museums, galleries, theaters, movies, concerts, and nightclubs . . . and you know what that means: good times at great prices.

Much of what is listed in this section of the book is free, or only a few bucks. In some cases, Mr. C has found activities that are a bit more expensive, but discounted from their full prices. Hey, there is no reason a limited budget should keep anyone from enjoying the arts.

ART GALLERIES

Most city dwellers know that browsing through art galleries is one of the most truly enlightening cultural activities around. Best of all, this is mostly a free entertainment: you might be hit up for the price of a cheap glass of red wine, but sometimes even the sipping is gratis.

You don't even have to dress up very much; the very rich can afford to dress any way they want. All you need to wear is the attitude of someone who *could* afford to buy something if it tickled your fancy.

Creighton-Davis Gallery

- 3222 M Street N.W. #C101, Washington, D.C.; ✆ (202) 333-3050

- ✑ http://creighton-davis.com

Recently relocated to the Shoppes of Georgetown Park Mall, this impressive Georgetown spot boasts fine art from the 15th century to the present. In fact, the gallery contends it has Washington's largest private collection, and Mr. C's not about to argue. Art by Rembrandt, Durer, Matisse, Picasso, Hockney, and Lichtenstein hangs on the wall. Catalogues are available.

From oils to watercolors, sculpture to constructions, the collection here has it all covered. Could the Cheapster buy any of this wonderful stuff? Maybe . . . or maybe not. That's between him and Dirty Money, his accountant. But it doesn't cost anything to look. Creighton-Davis is open Monday through Saturday from 10 a.m. to 9 p.m., and Sunday from noon to 6 p.m.

Govinda Gallery

- 1227 34th Street N.W., Washington, D.C.; ✆ (202) 333-1180

- ✑ www.govindagallery.com

Rock on, art fans: here is the gallery for music lovers. Photographs of The Who, Bob Dylan, and all kinds of Beatles (including fifth and sixth Beatles like Stu Sutcliffe and Pete Best) are on display here. Maybe you'd like to see ex-Stone's bassist Bill Wyman's photos of the great painter Mark Chagall, or a tribute to the late George Harrison? Have you caught Mr. C's groove yet?

This is memory lane for children of the sixties. If you remember Woodstock, or even better, if you're one of the gazillion people who were actually *there*, you have one more pilgrimage to make while you're in Washington. (Mr. C actually did attend Woodstock as a youthful cheapster in training; of course, he got in for free by shimmying through a hole in the fence. That's the truth, folks.)

And if you're too young to remember the sixties, well, here is a living photographic record of the people you missed. There are books of photographs on sale too.

Gallery hours are Tuesday through Sunday from 11 a.m. to 6 p.m.

Gudelsky Gallery

- 10500 Georgia Avenue, Silver Spring, MD; ✆ (301) 649-4454

- ✑ www.mcadmd.org

Located at the Maryland College of Art and Design, this public gallery offers as many as a dozen different shows each year, including a unique exhibition that reaches out to young artists: each December its Children's Art Exhibition features the work of kids from ages 3–15. The show is described as "non-competitive," though the works are for sale.

Other shows have focused on figurative sculpture and prints by Washington-area artists; vintage ocean liner posters; and regular exhibits of the latest efforts from MCAD students. Hours vary, but the Gudelsky is usually open Monday through Friday from 8 a.m. to 8 p.m. during special exhibitions. Call to join the mailing list for information on upcoming events.

Kathleen Ewing Gallery

- 1609 Connecticut Avenue N.W., Washington, D.C.; ✆ (202) 328-0955

- 🖃 www.kathleenewinggallery. com

Fine art photography is the specialty here, as Kathleen Ewing presents classics from the dawn of photography in the 19th century and the documentary style of the mid-20th century. Examples of the innovative work of today's best photographers can be found here, too.

The gallery was closed while undergoing extensive renovation and expansion in 2002. Call ahead to check on its schedule for reopening; even while closed, you can make your own appointment to see photos. Office hours are Wednesday through Saturday from noon to 5 p.m.

The Old Print Gallery

- 1220 31st Street N.W., Washington, D.C.; ✆ (202) 965-1818

- 🖃 www.oldprintgallery.com

If your tastes in art run more along the lines of historical vignettes, the

---

Old Print Gallery is the place for you, and would probably go hand in hand with a trip to the better-known Smithsonian across town. Here, you can find rare prints of early Washington scenery and events, plus similar selections from other American and European cities.

There's also a large selection of nautical prints, political cartoons, bird studies, and antique maps—over 30,000 prints in all. This place is one stop that the Classic Cheapster loves to make when parading through trendy Georgetown.

The gallery is open Monday through Saturday from 10 a.m. to 5:30 p.m.

Torpedo Factory Art Center

- 105 North Union Street, Alexandria, VA; ✆ (703) 838-4565

- 🖃 www.torpedofactory.org

Beat your swords into paintbrushes! This building, once used in the art of war, has been turned into a place to make art, a defense procurement heartily approved by Mr. C.

The Torpedo Factory Art Center now houses three floors of working art studios, in which some 160 professional artists create, display, and sell their works. In exchange for below-average rent, the artists happily answer visitors' questions about the creative process.

What a difference from your average, hushed gallery! All kinds of media are on view, including ceramics, fiber and glass art, jewelry, painting, photography, and sculpture.

In addition to the working studios, there are several galleries that also display and sell art. Exhibits change monthly, depending on what's available. The galleries are:

- The Art League Gallery
  ℡ (703) 683-2323

- Enamelists Gallery
  ℡ (703) 836-1561

- Factory Photoworks
  ℡ (703) 683-2205

- Potomac Craftsmen Gallery
  ℡ (703) 548-0935

- Scope Gallery
  ℡ (703) 548-6288

- Target Gallery
  ℡ (703) 549-6877

But wait, there's more! The Torpedo Factory is also home to **Alexandria Archaeology**, which serves as both a lab *and* a museum. The first municipally supported urban archaeology program in the nation, Alexandria Archaeology excavates, documents, and exhibits artifacts found all over this historic city. Located upstairs, the museum is open Tuesday through Friday from 10 a.m. to 3 p.m., Saturdays from 10 a.m. to 5 p.m., and Sundays from 1 to 5 p.m.

The Torpedo Factory is open Monday through Sunday from 10 a.m. to 5 p.m. Of course, individual artists keep their own schedules, so afternoon is the best time to visit. You can call the main number above to get information about tours. For info about lectures or other educational programs, call Friends of the Torpedo Factory Art at ℡ (703) 683-0693.

Zenith Gallery

- 413 Seventh Street N.W., Washington, D.C.; ℡ (202) 783-2963

- ✐ www.zenithgallery.com

In the heart of the Northwest's so-called Gallery Row, the Zenith is a spot to check out for its eclectic showings of contemporary works in a variety of media. Artists of every nationality exhibit here. The gallery specializes in three-dimensional mixed media work; this is art you can hang, sit on, or even wear! Zenith's collection includes sculpture, fine furniture, crafts, and tapestries. Annual shows featuring both humorous and neon art are also popular here.

The gallery is open Tuesday through Friday from 11:00 a.m. to 6 p.m., Saturday from noon to 7 p.m., and Sunday from noon to 5 p.m.

ARTS AND CULTURAL CENTERS

These centers are great places for a variety of fun and inexpensive activities—whether you're just viewing or actually participating. Many of the programs and classes are designed for adults, children, or both.

The Arlington Arts Center

- 3550 Wilson Boulevard,
  Arlington, VA;
  ✆ (703) 797-4573

Under renovation during 2002, this
wonderful space is due to reopen in
newer, expanded digs. Call for current details.

Arts Club of Washington

- 2017 1 Street N.W., Washington, D.C.; ✆ (202) 331-7282

- ✐ www.artsclubofwashington.
  org

Founded in 1916, the Arts Club of
Washington considers promoting
interest in the arts in the greater
Washington area to be its sworn
duty. Its location near the White
House, in the historic Monroe
House (after President James
Monroe, whose inaugural reception
was held here), is filled primarily
with the work of local artists
working in a wide variety of styles.
Paintings, drawings, and sculpture
cover the top three floors of
Monroe House, while special exhibitions appear in the first floor and
cellar galleries, as well as in the
adjacent MacFeeley House. Admission is free.

But wait, fellow cheapsters! The
Arts Club offers more than galleries. The activities it hosts include
a Spring Concert series at noon on
Fridays and occasional appearances
by the Washington Ballet. The galleries are open Tuesday through
Friday from 10 a.m. to 5 p.m., and
Saturday from 10 a.m. to 2 p.m.

District of Columbia Arts Center

- 2438 18th Street N.W., Washington, D.C.; ✆ (202) 462-7833

- ✐ www.dcartscenter.org

You'll get a real kick out of all the
fun, cheap events, including theater
and music, available here.
Depending on the event, tickets are
about $5 to $15, and some are free.
Theater tickets are generally $15.
Recent offerings have included
Sartre's *No Exit*. (Now *that's* a
good time!)

There are also free lectures, free
art shows in the gallery, and much
more. Give D.C.AC a call and
they'll send you a schedule of
events. The gallery is open
Wednesday through Sunday from
2 p.m. to 7 p.m.

Folger Shakespeare Library

- 201 East Capitol Street S.E.,
  Washington, D.C.;
  ✆ (202) 544-7077

- ✐ www.folger.edu

The Folger Shakespeare Library has
perhaps the world's finest collection of Shakespearean books and
research materials. Scholars come
from around the world to study and
work here. Does this mean you
have to be a scholar, dressed in full
neck ruffle, to enjoy the place? No,
sayeth Mr. Cheap. "I say no more
than truth, so help me God!"
(Gloucester, in *King Henry VI, Part
II.* act 3, scene 1).

For example, there are the stage
performances, poetry and fiction
readings, and concerts. Oliver
Goldsmith's *She Stoops to Conquer*
was presented here recently, in an
acclaimed production directed by
Britain's Richard Clifford, and that
was followed by a new production
of *Othello*. Music by the Folger
Consort, which specializes in works
from the 15th and 16th centuries, is
offered regularly. And there are
family programs as well, with lots
of lower-priced events for children
and their parents.

Aye, but here's the rub: Some
events are pricey, as much as $40

to $50 for the best seats. That's why Mr. Cheap keeps himself in good shape so that he can buy a $10 standing-room spot. And there are also discounts of up to 25 percent for senior citizens and students, and member and group discounts can be had as well. (These discounts do not apply to the Pen/Faulkner literary series, the Folger's prestigious program of readings by some of the country's most important writers.)

This is one of the most remarkable cultural centers in the world. Anyone in the Washington area should make time to see it. A calendar of events is available on request. The Folger is open to visitors Monday through Saturday from 10 a.m. to 4 p.m.

Glen Echo Park

- 7300 MacArthur Boulevard,
  Glen Echo, MD;
  ✆ (301) 492-6282

- ✐ www.nps.gov/glec

In 1891 the National Chautauqua Assembly was created as a center where people could participate in the sciences, arts, languages, and literature. The assembly didn't last too long, alas, and the location became an amusement park in 1899. In the early 1970s, it morphed again into Glen Echo Park, which restores the original charter: a place for folks to exchange ideas, and participate in educational and artistic activities.

Classes in the arts and dance, the classic Chautauqua idea, are offered in the spring (catalog available by calling 301-492-6229.) The Spanish Ballroom hosts square dancing, swing dancing, concerts of swing and zydeco music, and other events as well. There are puppet shows, theater for children (see listings under *Children's Activities*) and the young and the young-at-heart can

ride the vintage 1921 Glen Echo Carousel, a reminder of those amusement park days. The carousel is in operation May through September, Wednesday and Thursday from 10 a.m. to 2 p.m., and Saturday and Sunday from noon to 6 p.m.

You want more? The park is also home to the Clara Barton National Historic Site. For those who missed that day in history class, Clara Barton founded the American Red Cross in 1881 and served as its leader for 20 years. This house was her last residence as well as headquarters for the Red Cross from 1897 to 1904. It is open Monday through Sunday, with hourly tours starting at 10 a.m. and ending at 4 p.m.

Ellipse Arts Center

- 4350 North Fairfax Drive,
  Arlington, VA;
  ✆ (703) 228-7710

- ✐ www.arlingtonarts.org

Opened in 1990, the Ellipse Arts Center is a visual and performing arts facility offering as many as six exhibitions a year. Its programs cover both historical and contemporary themes, with the goal of providing area artists a showcase for their work. Along with regular exhibits, EAC presents movies, lectures, and performances that deal with related topics.

A recent exhibition was called *Contemporary Wood Turning*, featuring work by the artist David Ellsworth. As usual, the public was invited to an artist's talk, a reception, and a preview showing.

Admission to the Ellipse is free. It's open to the public Wednesday through Friday from 10 a.m. to 6 p.m., and Saturday from 11 a.m. to 5 p.m.

Gunston Arts Center

- 2700 South Lang Street, Arlington, VA; ✆ (703) 228-1850

- 🖰 www.arlingtonarts.org

This center has been referred to as an "arts incubator" because it has given birth to two different theater groups in recent years. Both the Signature Theatre and the Washington Shakespeare Company originated here before moving on to other spaces.

The Gunston, however, keeps humming along, with programs in two available theater spaces, a dance studio, and costume and set construction shops. Renovation is currently taking place, but the theaters and costume shop will remain open throughout. Tickets for a recent production (*Scape Vietnam* by Jane Franklin Dance, in collaboration with visual artist Brece Honneycut) were reasonably priced at $16, $12, and $8.

Ticket prices vary, but it's generally less expensive to see a show here than in most theaters. Call the above number for more info.

The Kennedy Center

- The John F. Kennedy Center for the Performing Arts, 2700 F Street, N.W., Washington, D.C.; ✆ (800) 444-1324 or ✆ (202) 467-4600

- 🖰 www.kennedy-center.org

What goes on at the Kennedy Center? Probably easier to ask what doesn't. Here you will find regular good deals for cheapsters with a little patience. For example, the Center offers an annual series of youth and family programs, including storytelling, magic, theater, and musical programs—with tickets often running at a most reasonable $12.

Of course the Center has the expected assortment of world-class performance art, with prices to match. However, you can even find good deals for those if you're willing to sit in the cheap seats. The American Ballet Theatre regularly performs pieces by Balanchine, Morris, and Tudor, and ABT's highly stylized *Corsaire* (featuring pirates, harem girls, a kidnapping or two, and a chance for virtuoso dancing by the male members of the company) was very well received, with tickets priced at $27 to $75.

The Lyon Opera Ballet performs Maguy Marin's *Cendrillon.* Set to music by Prokofiev, this Cinderella is like no other—provocative and slightly sinister but good fun nonetheless. Tickets for that ranged from $23 to $36.

The Kennedy Center also lays claim to the largest discount ticket program in the country, made possible primarily through private contributions. Specially priced tickets are available for most performances, to the tune of 50 percent off for students, senior citizens, some military personnel, and anyone with a fixed income. Also available are a limited number of half-price tickets to previews of first performances, as well as for some same-day events (if they're not sold out). Of course, dedicated cheapniks will *need* the discounts, because ticket prices can range up to $75 for an evening of theater, and $60 for weekend matinees.

Library of Congress

- 101 Independence Avenue S.E., Washington, D.C.; ✆ (202) 707-8000

- 🖰 www.loc.gov/today

The Library of Congress is the largest library in the world. Over 121 million items in the library's collection stretch out along 532 miles of bookshelves! The big news for you, dear readers, is that the library also sponsors some 350 public events each year. These include concerts, poetry readings, exhibitions, and lectures, and all are free of charge.

Many of these events are held at noontime, especially convenient for those who work in the Capitol Hill area. Great way to spend your lunch hour! Lecturers of note have included author Herman Wouk, former U.S. poet laureate Rita Dove, and documentary filmmaker Elaine Prater Hodges. The library's American Folklife Center presents concerts that celebrate the diverse cultures of the United States. And, don't miss the free movies shown in the Mary Pickford Theater. Free tours of the library are also given regularly; call the Visitor Services Office at ✆ (202) 707-5458 for information.

Tours of the Jefferson building are Monday through Friday at 10:30 a.m., 11:30 a.m., 1:30 p.m., 2:30 p.m., and 3:30 p.m.; and Saturday and Sunday at 10:30 a.m., 11:30 a.m., 1:30 p.m., and 2:30 p.m.

Martin Luther King, Jr. Memorial Library

- 901 G Street N.W., Washington, D.C.; ✆ (202) 727-0321

- Anacostia Branch, 1800 Good Hope Road S.E.; ✆ (202) 698-1190

- Benning Branch, 3935 Benning Road N.E.; ✆ (202) 727-4787

- Capitol View Branch, 5001 Central Avenue S.E.; ✆ (202) 645-0755

- Chevy Chase Branch, 5625 Connecticut Avenue N.W.; ✆ (202) 282-0021

- Cleveland Park Branch, 3310 Connecticut Avenue N.W.; ✆ (202) 282-3080

- Deanwood Kiosk, 4215 Nannie Helen Burroughs Avenue N.E.; ✆ (202) 724-8526

- Francis A. Gregory Branch, 3660 Alabama Avenue S.E.; ✆ (202) 645-4297

- Georgetown Regional Branch, 3260 R Street N.W.; ✆ (202) 282-0220

- Juanita E. Thornton-Shepherd Park Branch, 7420 Georgia Avenue N.W.; ✆ (202) 541-6100

- Lamond-Riggs Branch, 5401 South Dakota Avenue N.E.; ✆ (202) 541-6255

- Langston Community Library, 2600 Benning Road N.E.; ✆ (202) 724-8665

- Mt. Pleasant Branch, 16th & Lamont Streets N.W.; ✆ (202) 671-0200

- Northeast Branch, 330 Seventh Street N.E.; ✆ (202) 698-3320

- Palisades Branch, 4901 V Street N.W.; ✆ (202) 282-3139

- Parklands-Turner Community Library, 1700 Alabama Avenue S.E.; ✆ (202) 698-1103

- Petworth Branch, 4200 Kansas Avenue N.W.; ✆ (202) 541-6300

- R.L. Christian Community Library, 1300 H Street N.E.; ✆ (202) 724-8599

- Southeast Branch, 403 Seventh Street S.E.; ✆ (202) 698-3377

- Southwest Branch, 900 Wesley Place S.W.; ✆ (202) 724-4752

- Sursum-Corda Community Library, 135 New York Avenue N.W.; ✆ (202) 724-4772

- Takoma Park Branch, 416 Cedar Street N.W.; ☏ (202) 576-7252

- Tenley-Friendship Branch, 4450 Wisconsin Avenue N.W., ☏ (202) 282-3090

- Washington Highlands Branch, 115 Atlantic Street S.W.; ☏ (202) 645-5880

- Watha T. Daniel Branch, 1701 Eighth Street N.W.; ☏ (202) 671-0212

- West End Branch, 1101 24th Street N.W.; ☏ (202) 724-8707

- Woodridge Regional Branch, 1801 Rhode Island Avenue N.E.; ☏ (202) 541-6226

- ✍ www.dclibrary.org

Dedicated Cheapsters already know that the library is the first stop for cultural bargains in any city. Read the day's newspapers, borrow a CD or a video, all for free—and books haven't even been mentioned yet! But there's more. District libraries sponsor free workshops, lectures, book discussion clubs, and author readings throughout the year.

The Library hosts art exhibits, concerts (the Morehouse College Glee Club sang at the main branch recently), and programs for preschool children, including book readings and puppet shows. Older children and teens can get tutoring on how to use the Internet and high school students can get help researching colleges. Need help filling out your tax return? The library has someone to assist you. There are programs for senior citizens too. What's more, there are of branches around all around D.C. with similar programs. For a calendar of events by branch, call the location near you.

> ## MR. CHEAP'S PICKS
>
> ### Arts and Cultural Centers
>
> **Ellipse Arts Center**—Art galleries, movies, theater, all under one roof.
>
> **Glen Echo Park**—Once an amusement park, now a center for budget-priced culture, arts, and literature.
>
> **Washington Performing Arts Society**—Their programs offer family-priced concerts and dance.

Prince George's County Memorial Library System

- Administrative offices: 6532 Adelphi Road, Hyattsville, MD; ☏ (301) 699-3500

- Beltsville Branch, 4319 Sellman Road; ☏ (301) 937-0294

- Glenarden Branch, 8724 Glenarden Parkway; ☏ (301) 772-5477

- Greenbelt Branch, II Crescent Road; ☏ (301) 345-5800

- Hyattsville Branch, 6530 Adelphi Road; ☏ (301) 779-9330

- Magruder Branch, 4310 Gallatin Street; ☏ (301) 277-3432

- New Carrollton Branch, 7414 Riverdale Road; ☏ (301) 459-6900

- Oxon Hill Branch, 6200 Oxon Hill Road; ☏ (301) 839-2400

- Spauldings Branch, 5811 Old Silver Hill Road (District Heights); ☏ (301) 568-9533

- Surratts-Clinton Branch, 9400 Piscataway Road (Clinton); ☏ (301) 868-9200

- ✍ www.prge.lib.md.us

Like the District of Columbia Public Library (see the listing for Martin Luther King Memorial Library above), the Prince George's County branches in Maryland offer a plethora of cultural activities, all free and open to the general public. Most branches offer "Drop-In Story Time," morning readings for young children on a weekly basis. Some offer evening and weekend events for all ages. Book discussion groups, art exhibits, and author appearances take place throughout the system, along with seasonal events—like a "Scary Stories Night" around Halloween.

You can get a bimonthly newsletter of the events at all branches by phoning the number above. Libraries closest to D.C. are listed above.

Rosslyn Spectrum Theatre

- 1611 North Kent Street, Arlington, VA; ✆ (703) 228-6960

- 🖉 www.arlingtonarts.org

Since re-opening in 1997 as a shared conference center/theater site, this former cinema has hosted mostly live theater by independent Arlington companies, visiting artists, and community-specific groups. Here you can find Horizon's Theater, which features theater from a woman's perspective, Le Neon Theater, a French-American theater company, Trumpet Vine, which takes an innovative approach to presenting the classics, and ASIA, dedicated to telling Asian stories in American theater.

Recently, a Keegan Co. production of Brian Friel's *Give Me Your Answer, Do* was presented here, with a top ticket price of $22; not cheap, but not too bad for live theater either. It cost $35 to see Broadway's Donna McKechnie sing and dance here, but that's half of what it would cost to see her in New York.

Ticket prices to see other presentations are often closer to the cheapster ideal (free if possible, almost free if not) and the variety of events on tap is extraordinary.

Show times vary, so call the theater or check the Web site for a calendar of events.

Washington Performing Arts Society

- 2000L Street N.W., Suite 810, Washington, D.C.; ✆ (202) 833-9800

- 🖉 www.wpas.org

The Washington Performing Arts Society bills its lineup as "Something for Everyone," and it delivers on its promise. There are 11 different subscription series with more than 80 performances each season, ranging from jazz to gospel, world music to classical music.

Whatever you want to hear, it's here: The Chieftains, the Boys Choir of Harlem, Murray Perahia, and Wynton Marsalis have all performed for the WPAS. Many of the shows are very reasonably priced.

Events are held at locations across the D.C. area, including the Kennedy Center. WPAS memberships are available, offering discounts and benefits, and there are group discounts and senior citizen and student plans as well. Box-office hours are Monday through Friday from 9:30 a.m. to 5 p.m. Tickets may be ordered online at the Web address above.

Washington Project for the Arts

- 400 Seventh Street N.W., Washington, D.C.; ✆ (202) 347-4813

Founded in 1975, the Washington Project for the Arts long operated on a shoestring in its efforts to showcase new and experimental works. Today, it presents an active community of local talent and has grown to attract both well-known and emerging artists on the basis of its daring reputation. One good example: the 1989 exhibit of the show *Robert Mapplethorpe: The Perfect Moment,* which these folks grabbed after another D.C. gallery dropped it. Controversial as it was, the exhibit brought 45,000 people through the WPA's doors.

More than an art gallery, though, the Project offers a series of workshops and events based on all kinds of artistic themes and contemporary issues. Recent performances included African-American poetry and music ensemble, an exhibition of video from Germany, and authors reading (and signing) their latest books. Events generally cost $5 for members, and $7 for all others.

CHILDREN'S ACTIVITIES

See also the "Museums" and "Outdoors" chapters for listings of activities suitable for children and families.

A Likely Story Children's Bookstore

- 1555 King Street, Alexandria, VA; ✆ (703) 836-2498

- ✍ www.alikelystorybooks.com

This bright, cozy bookshop, a locally owned, independent bookstore, is an anomaly in this chain store age: a small bookstore that is surviving.

Located between downtown Alexandria and the Metro station, this store provides a variety of activities to entertain even the most rambunctious kids. There are storytelling hours for all ages, and many popular authors and illustrators come to talk about their work. If your little ones won't sit still that long, watch for one of Likely's more, well, *active* activities. These could include a rubber stamp demonstration or a workshop on making ornaments out of quilts.

Your kids will love this place and you will too. Movies have been made about romantic little bookstores like this one. Well, here's the real thing. Store hours are Monday through Saturday from 10 a.m. to 6 p.m., and Sunday from 1 p.m. to 5 p.m.

Adventure Theatre

- Glen Echo Park, 7300 MacArthur Boulevard, Glen Echo, MD; ✆ (301) 320-5331

Washington's longest-running children's playhouse, Adventure Theatre offers magical stories in a style that all kids can enjoy. The seating is specially designed for little ones, and shows last about an hour, perfect for the short attention spans of little kids. A recent production of Raggedy Ann and Raggedy Andy was great fun, for parents and for kids.

Tickets are $6 for all. Show times are Saturday and Sunday at 1:30 p.m. and 3:30 p.m. The office is open Monday through Friday from 9 a.m. to 5 p.m., so you can make reservations.

Bethesda Academy of Performing Arts Imagination Stage

- White Flint Mall, 11301 Rockville Pike, Bethesda, MD; ✆ (301) 881-5106

- 7300 Whittier Boulevard, Bethesda, MD; ✆ (301) 320-2550

If you can't bring the kids to the theater, bring the theater to the mall! The Bethesda Academy of Performing Arts Imagination Stage features professional actors in an intimate setting that encourages audience participation. And kids love shows like *Aladdin,* which played here recently. Some shows, like *The Sorcerer's Apprentice* and *Kids' Clubhouse,* feature BAPA's Deaf Access Company, which performs in both voice and sign language.

Tickets are just $6.50 each, $5.50 for groups of 10 or more. Show times are Saturdays and Sundays at 12:30 p.m. and 3:00 p.m. Shows usually sell out, so it's important to make reservations. The box office is open during the week from 10 a.m. to 6 p.m.

Capital Children's Museum

- 800 Third Street N.E., Washington, D.C.; ✆ (202) 675-4120

- ✑ www.ccm.org

It's Saturday. It's raining. You've yelled, "Don't touch!" for the 79th time. It's time to grab the kids and head for the Capital Children's Museum, where the little ones can touch, smell, draw, run, jump,

scream, explore, and otherwise have fun. Through innovative hands-on exhibits, CCM entertains kids and educates them at the same time. And they may not even know it!

One of the most popular exhibits in recent years has been "Chuck Jones: An Animated Life." Kids learn about animation through the work of the legendary creator of Bugs Bunny and Daffy Duck. Visitors can create an animated film, draw their favorite characters, and create sound effects. Other exhibits include *Japan: Through the Eyes of a Child,* and a Mexican program that includes making hot chocolate.

Admission is $7 for adults, $5 for seniors (55+), free for children two and under and for members. On Sunday tickets are half-price before noon, with no other discounts.

The museum's regular hours, Labor Day until Memorial Day, are Tuesday through Sunday from 10 a.m. to 5 p.m.

The Children's Theatre

- Thomas Jefferson Community Theatre, 125 South Old Glebe Road, Arlington, VA; ✆ (703) 548-1154

The Children's Theatre offers kids an opportunity to perform. A recent show, *Joseph and the Amazing Technicolor Dreamcoat,* gave kids nine and up the opportunity to audition, no acting experience necessary, for a part in a show featuring professional actors. Of course, children can just come see the play, if they prefer. Someone has to be in the audience, right?

Tickets are $7 for children and $10 for adults. Show times are Friday at 7:30 p.m., Saturday at 3:00 p.m. and 7:30 p.m., and Sunday at 3:00 p.m.

MR. CHEAP'S PICKS

Children's Activities

Adventure Theatre and the Puppet Company Playhouse— Magical stories and marionettes make these two Glen Echo Park spots special.

National Zoo—Scores of incredible animals, and it's free!

Now This! Kids!—Improv comedy/ theater for children.

Discovery Theater

- Arts and Industries Building, 900 Jefferson Drive S.W., Washington, D.C.; ✆ (202) 357-1500

- ✍ www.discoverytheater.org

The Smithsonian's Discovery Theater, is dedicated to offering the best in live performing arts for young people. Each season more than a dozen productions feature puppets, storytellers, dancers, actors, musicians, and mimes in performances that present classic stories for children, folk tales from all over the world, American history and cultures, and innovative theater techniques. Some are written specially for Discovery Theater. Often interactive, Discovery Theater performances unite ideologies, enact themes that reflect the diversity of its audiences, open avenues of self-reflection, and are enjoyable means for parents and teachers to demonstrate life's lessons.

Shows take place Monday through Friday at 10 a.m. and 11:30 a.m. Ticket prices, where applicable, might typically run between $4 and $5 for a weekday performance and up to $10 for a special Saturday show. For reservations, call Monday through Friday from 9 a.m. to 5 p.m.

Explore & Moore Children's Museum

- 12904 Occoquan Road, Woodbridge, VA; ✆ (703) 492-2222

The kids are gonna love this hands-on entertainment center, which boasts more than 20 interactive exhibits, including a dinosaur fossil find, puppet theatre, dress-up closet, sandbox, bubble room, medical center, shadow freeze room, an eight-foot climbing wall, toddler room, take-apart table, magnet play, space room, beauty parlor, and a dance studio.

They're open Monday through Friday from 9 a.m. to 3 p.m., Saturday from 10 a.m. to 6 p.m., and Sunday from noon to 5 p.m. Admission is a cheap $5 per person, and kids under two years of age are free. Explore & Moore also offers group rates available for parties of 10 or more (advance registration required), and a 20 percent discount for seniors. Grandpa on the climbing wall—now that's a sight!

FCS Family Concert Series

- 6201 Belcrest Road, Hyattsville, MD; ✆ (301) 927-6133

Held at the First United Methodist Church, this annual concert series offers a variety of shows, every two months from fall to spring. They are oriented toward families and have such diverse performers as storytellers, musicians, blues singer/songwriters, an area dance and theater company's renditions of *Aesop's Fables*, and other stories for the young ones.

"They're meant to be for children, though I've invited adult friends who really enjoyed themselves," an organizer once told Mr. C. Tickets for each hour-long show are a mere $4, or $10.50 for all three over the course of the season. You can call the Community School, which organizes the series, at ✆ (301) 699-6086. The church seats about 350, and it usually fills up.

Leesburg Animal Park

- 19270 James Monroe Highway, Leesburg, VA; ✆ (703) 433-0002

- ✍ www.leesburganimalpark. com

Here kids get to walk among chickens, goats, llamas, sheep, cow, deer, antelope, squirrel monkeys, and other cuddly creatures. Some eat right out of your hand, and the newborns drink out of bottles that you feed them. Admission is $5 all the time for kids over two years of age. On weekends, adults are charged $7. They're closed on Mondays.

Mount Vernon Community Children's Theatre

- 1900 Elkin Street, Alexandria, VA; ✆ (703) 360-0686

- ✑ www.geocities.com/mvcct

Through acting classes, workshops, and performing opportunities, Mount Vernon Community Children's Theatre introduces kids to the joys of the lively arts. Their season of three productions leans toward Broadway-style musicals with large casts.

MVCCT holds open auditions for each play, encouraging children from ages 7–16 to participate. Professional directors rehearse the shows, which are ultimately presented with top-notch music and sets. A recent production of *Tom Sawyer* was very well received.

Ticket prices are $8 for adults and $7 for children and senior citizens. Group discounts are available. The box office is open daily, with voice mail for reservations if no one is in. Shows run on Friday and Saturday at 7:30 p.m., and Sunday at 3 p.m.

National Aquarium

- 14th & Constitution Avenue N.W., Washington; ✆ (202) 482-2826

This is the nation's oldest aquarium, established in 1873. A small but interesting collection includes more than 50 tanks containing over 200 species of salt- and freshwater fish, including piranha, shark, eel, and Japanese carp.

See the full listing under *Museums.*

National Aquarium, Baltimore

- Pier 3, 501 East Pratt Street, Baltimore; ✆ (410) 576-3800

- ✑ www.aqua.org

Okay, so *this* National Aquarium is a little farther afield from D.C., and the prices aren't super cheap. Still, you've gotta make the hour's drive, because here kids can explore more than 10,000 aquatic animals, including sting rays, jelly fish, dolphins, and sharks. According to the aquarium, you can avoid the worst crowds by visiting before 11 a.m. and after 3 p.m., and in the fall and winter. If you have little ones, bring an infant carrier or borrow one of the aquarium's free backpacks since strollers are not allowed in the aquarium. Ticket prices are $16 for adults, $9.50 for kids three to eleven years of age, and kids two and under get in free. They also offer group discounts!

For most of the year the aquarium is open from 9 a.m. to 5 p.m., but hours vary according to the season. Check out the Web site for details!

National Theatre

- 1321 Pennsylvania Avenue N.W. Washington, D.C.; ✆ (202) 628-6161

- ✑ www.nationaltheatre.org

On Saturday mornings from September to April, families can visit the Helen Hayes Gallery for theatre, music, dance, clowning, juggling, storytelling, magic, and educational shows. Performances are free and are held at 9:30 and 11 a.m. Seating is limited for these popular shows, so arrive early to get your tickets, which are distributed 30 minutes before each show. Call ✆ (202) 783-3372 for recorded program information.

National Zoo

- 3001 Connecticut Avenue, Washington, D.C.; ✆ (202) 673-4800

- ✐ www.fonz.org/visit.htm

Tigers, lions, gorillas, orangutans, elephants, bears, seals, and giraffes are just a few of the scores exotic animals that live at the world-class National Zoo, and admission is absolutely free! You and the kids will also see the giant pandas, Mei Xiang and Tian Tian, as well as the Sumatran tiger cub, Berani, and Kandula, the male Asian elephant born on November 25, 2001. The best time to visit is the morning when the animals are most active, people are fewer, and parking spaces are still available. Wear comfortable shoes, as you'll probably do a lot of walking (though there is a tram).

See the full listing in the "Outdoors" section.

Free! From May 1 to September 15, the grounds are open from 6 a.m. to 8 p.m. and the buildings are open from 10 a.m. to 6 p.m. From September 16 to April 30, the grounds are open 6 a.m. to 6 p.m.; the buildings from 10 a.m. to 4:30 p.m.

Now This! Kids!

- Blair Mansion Inn, 7711 Eastern Avenue, Silver Spring, MD; ✆ (202) 364-8292

- ✐ www.nowthisimprov.com

If you think improv comedy is strictly for grownups, think again. Now This! is a professional comedy troupe that performs "totally improvised, interactive children's musical theatre." Its shows will have your kids laughing, singing along, and, perhaps, performing. Kids love becoming part of the show and parents love the ticket prices—just $11 (including dessert) or $17.75 (including lunch). Now This! offers birthday packages and group rates as well.

The ensemble also performs for grown-ups but there is no fixed schedule for that. Arrangements are made by calling the theater; imagine, a show just for you and your friends! This group has received rave reviews. Show time is Saturday at 1:30 p.m.

Planet Play

- 6030 Burke Commons Road, Burke, VA; ✆ (703) 425-0007

- Springfield Mall, Springfield, VA; ✆ (703) 313-6770

- 6206 Multiplex Drive, Centerville; ✆ (703) 502-7888

This free activity center features a two-story slide, a moon bounce, and a pit of balls. Hey, what more do you need? Well, (for the older kids) how about Laser Tag, miniature golf, and bumper cars?

The Puppet Company Playhouse

- Glen Echo Park, 7300 MacArthur Boulevard (at the junction of Goldsboro Road), Glen Echo, MD; ✆ (301) 320-6668

- ✐ www.thepuppetco.org

Behind the lovely antique carousel in this small park is a building called the Spanish Ballroom, and inside of that is this small treasure of a theater. Your kids will love the shows at the Puppet Company Playhouse. You will love the super-cheap ticket prices; you can see every show without dipping into the kids' college fund. The professional troupe goes way beyond traditional hand puppets, at various times using rod puppets, marionettes, shadow puppetry, and other styles to tell favorite children's tales. Proving the popularity of this place, its annual holiday show, *The Nutcracker,* sells out for almost every performance.

Tickets are just $5 for adults and children. Discounts are available for groups of 20 or more (with an advance reservation), so it's a great idea for a school field trip. And check out that carousel; it's fully operational and lots of fun. Open year-round, show times are Wednesday through Friday at 10 a.m. and 11:30 a.m., and Saturday and Sunday at 11:30 a.m. and 1 p.m.

The Rainbow Company

- Burke Village Center 11, 9570 Burke Road, Burke, VA; ✆ (703) 239-0037

- ✐ http://home.earthlink.net/ ~reciact

You've probably heard "interactive" used to describe a zillion video games. You may also despair of ever finding activities your kids can enjoy without sitting in front of the tube. The Rainbow Company has an alternative with its "interactive children's theater." Kids in the audience volunteer to become part of the show, which doesn't begin until a selected child counts to three and the whole crowd chants, "Once upon a time . . ."

Although the performance is largely improvised, professional actors guide the young participants

through the story. They are well trained to deal with any situation, handy skills in a room full of excited kids. After "the end," everyone is invited to come up on stage and try on costumes, examine the sets, and chat with the actors. It's great fun for everyone—even the parents—and a good way to introduce the little tykes to live entertainment.

Tickets are just $3.50 and free for children under two. Performances are given on Saturday, Sunday, and Monday afternoons. Shows for school groups can be arranged, too.

U.S. Airways Playstrip

- Dulles Town Center Mall, Sterling, VA ✆ (703) 404-7120

- ✐ www.shopdullestowncenter. com

Smack in the heart of the Dulles Town Center Mall is a mini airport terminal complete with control tower, baggage cart, and a slide-and-jump-in cockpit for junior pilots. Admission is free.

West End Dinner Theatre

- 4615 Duke Street, Alexandria, VA; ✆ (703) 370-2500

- ✐ www.wedt.com

Like many of the other theaters listed in this chapter, West End Dinner Theatre is a "grown-ups" playhouse that also presents children's theater on weekend afternoons. Tickets are just $9 (sorry, no meal is included), and productions include classics *like Aladdin, The Wizard of Oz* and *Babes in Toyland*. Dinner is served two hours before the show goes up, Tuesday through Sunday at 6 p.m. (show time 8 p.m.) Matinees are on Wednesday and Sunday, with lunch at noon (show time 2 p.m.).

Young Artists Theatre

- Route 29 & 216, Cherry Tree Center, Laurel, MD;
  ☏ (301) 604-2844

- ✍ http://youngartiststheater.com

Here you'll enjoy musicals and shows as performed by professional child actors. Many of the actors here have gone on to perform on television, in professional theatre, and with touring companies.

Open Saturdays and Sundays, YAT offers special discounts and arrangements for scout troops and birthdays. Recommended audiences are children ages two and older.

COLLEGE PERFORMING ARTS

Senator Cheap has found that the best-kept secret for all things performance-artsy are the area's colleges and universities. The local campuses regularly offer music, dance, theater, and film programs that don't require much wealth to attend (unlike the colleges themselves). Some events are for students only (don't forget your ID!), but most are open to the general public for free or a very small charge. If you want to experience a wide range of culture in your life on a regular basis, and for most cases under $10, this is a great way to do it.

American University

- College of Performing Arts, 4400 Massachusetts Avenue, N.W., Washington, D.C.;

- ☏ (202) 885-ARTS

- ✍ www.american.edu

Each year AU offers a season of plays, musicals, operas, orchestra, choral, and dance concerts, most designed to enhance classroom learning with actual experience. Most performances occur in one of two locations, the Experimental Theatre or the Kay Spiritual Life Center, AU's chapel.

About 10 performances are scheduled for each spring and fall season, with offerings such as *The Glass Menagerie, The Fantasticks,* and *A Chorus Line* and other Broadway revivals, as well as original works produced by the students themselves.

The AU Players, Chamber Singers, Chorus, and Dance Thesis performances provide a variety of opportunities to experience the full breadth of performance art. Most D.C.-area classical music fans would not want to miss a highlight of each season, the AU Symphony Spring and Fall Concerts. One such program included homage to Tchaikovsky, with selections from his Symphony Number 5.

Ticket prices vary, from about $3 with student ID to $12 for non-student day of show performances.

Catholic University

- 620 Michigan Avenue, N.E.,Washington, D.C.;
  ☏ (202) 319-5000

- ✍ www.cua.edu

Hartke Theatre is the setting for CU's high-caliber theatrical productions. Generally performing once a month, the department draws upon works from both contemporary artists and classical writers. Ibsen's

A Doll House, as well as (daringly) a musical version of George Orwell's *Animal Farm*, are just two of the programs produced during the research for this edition of the book.

Although CU's music department focuses exclusively on classical music, the Benjamin T. Rome School of Music's productions held at Ward Hall have much to offer: They present more than 200 performances annually, ranging from solo recitals to opera. Students have also presented concerts in Rome and at the Vatican for Pope John Paul II, at the John F. Kennedy Center for the Performing Arts, at Washington's Basilica of the National Shrine of the Immaculate Conception, and in major U.S. cities. Many of these events are free of charge; larger productions, such as the operas, range up to $20 a ticket.

Call the concert info line at ℡ (202) 319-5367.

Gallaudet University

- 800 Florida Avenue N.E., Washington, D.C.; ℡ (202) 651-5000

- ✐ www.gallaudet.edu

This nationally acclaimed school for the deaf offers a unique style of theater performance. The Gallaudet Dance Company relies on vision as their primary mode of conversation and communicate through dancing in a range of styles, including dance that uses American Sign Language as its foundation.

The Theater Arts Department assembles three productions a year; one in the fall, one in the winter, and a children's play in the spring. Recent performances at the Black Box Theatre include *Goya in the House of the Deaf Man.* Student actors perform using sign language,

while professional hearing actors provide vocal interpretations.

Tickets cost $7 ($5 for the children's play). Discounts are available for students and kids.

George Mason University

- 4400 University Drive, Fairfax, VA; Box Office, ℡ (703) 218-6500

- ✐ www.gmu.edu

If you crave the best in music, theatre, dance, and global/ethnic entertainment, GMU has something for you. The Center for the Arts organization brings major national and international artists to its Concert Hall building; sometimes at the higher prices these acts command. But there are some exceptions. Lesser-priced entertainment here and at other university halls is provided by local theater groups (notably, artists-in-residence The Theater of the First Amendment), along with various local music groups ranging from orchestras to military bands. Some of these performances are even free to all, which more than satisfies Mr. C's appetite for good value.

GMU presents its performing arts offerings in a variety of "series." Most popular are the Magnificent Music Series, where today's best and brightest stars perform the greatest musical works from yesterday and today, and the Dynamic Dance Series, where the foremost talents in dance explore the art of movement. Experience the many genres of dance, from the most innovative to the traditional, from the familiar to the obscure, from regional to international. And the Virginia Opera Series, where Virginia's most renowned opera company offers works from the masters.

Pick up your tickets in the Grand Lobby of the Concert Hall, or call ✆ (703) 218-6500.

Georgetown University

- 37th & O Streets N.W., Washington, D.C.; ✆ (202) 687-0100

- ✐ www.georgetown.edu

As if there wasn't enough to do outside the walls of GU, a whole world waits for you once you enter the campus, with most programs going for merely a song.

Bring music to your ears at Gaston Hall with the help of the semi-pro Georgetown University Orchestra. The GUO has recently presented a program of jazz-tinged chamber music for $5.

The Mask and Bauble Dramatic Society produces two major plays each semester. As an example, the Donn B. Murphy One-Acts Festival is organized each year by the MBDS to promote student-written plays. And at $4 for everyone, who can afford *not* to go, listen and enjoy? Call ✆ (202) 687-6783 for information.

Your friends could never accuse you of being a stuffed shirt after attending the Ballet Folklorico Mexicano de Georgetown, featuring not only traditional dances from diverse regions of Mexico but also a live Mariachi band. (Why not end the night with a margarita at one of the local restaurants?)

Black Movements Dance Theatre and the Georgetown University Dance Company both present modern dance performances. Admission prices range from absolutely free to about $7 for the GU Dance Company's biannual extravaganza of jazz, ballet, and tap. Call ✆ (202) 687-1625 for info.

Georgetown Players Improvfest is where the Georgetown Players Improv Group hosts a comedy extravaganza, featuring college and professional troupes from around the country.

Tickets for most programs at Georgetown range from $5 to $8. Just try to improv(e) on that!

George Washington University

- 600 22nd Street. N.W., Washington D.C.; ✆ (202) 994-6178

- ✐ www.gwu.edu

GWU is the place to be for all kinds of concerts, Mr. C style. The "Lisner at Noon" series offers free weekday lunchtime concerts open to the public in the world-class Lisner Auditorium. It showcases local pianists and dance troupes; for upcoming shows, call the Lisner's 24-hour concert line at ✆ (202) 994-1500.

GW's music department presents both student and faculty artists: the University Singers, Symphonic Orchestra, Chamber Players, the *a cappella* Troubadours, and more. Most concerts are held at the Dorothy Betts Marvin Theatre, where tickets can be purchased in advance. General admission is usually $5, although subscription rates are available for the artist series (which can bring tix down to under $2 per concert!) Call the department at ✆ (202) 994-6245 for info.

The Department of Theatre and Dance produces four major plays, including a musical, and two dance recitals. GW's modern dance troupe, the Dance Company, is often joined by guest artists. Most of these shows cost $8 to $10; subscriber discounts reduce the per-ticket price. For more info, call this department at ✆ (202) 994-6178.

Howard University

- 2400 Sixth Street. N.W., Washington, D.C. ✆ (202) 806-0971

• ✑ www.hu.edu

Howard University hosts about seven programs each year. The Department of Theatre Arts is housed in the Division of Fine Arts complex (Lulu Vere Childers Hall), located on Howard University's main campus in D.C.

Recent performances include *Once on This Island,* written by Stephen Flaherty and Lynn Ahrens, and choreographed and directed by Mike Malone. General admission is $12.50 for the public, $7.50 for students. Some programs, including *A Night of One Acts,* presented by the Howard Players, are offered for $3.

Most events occur at either the Ira Aldridge Theatre or the Experimental Performance Space. Call the school at ✆ (202) 806-7700 for concert dates, times, and to confirm ticket prices.

Marymount University

• 2807 North Glebe Road, Arlington, VA; ✆ (703) 284-1611

• ✑ www.marymount.edu

APB, not to be confused with an "all-points bulletin," stands for Marymount's Activities Programming Board. The "FYI" Web site is the best source for numerous concerts and performances by nationally known artists, including folk, jazz, and classical musicians; renowned theater groups; and popular comedians. Not widely publicized, most events are actually free and open to the public. They take place in the Student Center on the Marymount campus. Call the Student Activities Info Line at ✆ (703) 284-1517.

Montgomery College

• Performing Arts Center, 51 Mannakee Street, Rockville, MD; ✆ (301) 279-5301

• 7600 Takoma Avenue, Takoma Park, MD; ✆ (301) 650-1368

MC boasts a huge offering of performing arts options at multiple venues across two campuses.

The Guest Artist Series features the best in professional dance, music, and theatre. All performances are reserved seating. For example, widely acclaimed as "America's Greatest Bluegrass Band," the members of The Seldom Scene have played regularly at the Robert E. Parilla Performing Arts Center for a mere $18 ($16 for students).

The College Performing Arts Series brings you stimulating theatre, dance, and music performances featuring the students of Montgomery College. It's a wonderful and affordable introduction to the excitement of live theatre and the performing arts. Hippies (and former hippies) can enjoy such offerings as the recently produced *Hair* at the counterculture-friendly price of $8 ($6 students and seniors).

The Saturday Morning Children's Series has something for the young *and* the young at heart! Designed for shorter attention spans, these performances are 50 to 60 minutes in length and offer general admission seating. Master puppeteer Jim West's *Dinosaurs* recently invaded the Montgomery campus, priced at $6 ($5 for kids and seniors).

You can also enjoy free music concerts featuring jazz, wind ensemble, symphony, and chorus concerts.

And as if this weren't enough, a Summer Dinner Theatre package is just the ticket for those of you who can't wait for the fall semester to start enjoying popular Broadway caliber productions like *On The Town* and *South Pacific.*

Call ✆ (301) 251-7676 for ticket information.

Mount Vernon College

- 2100 Foxhall Road, N.W., Washington, D.C.; ✆ (202) 625-4655

- ✍ www.mvc.gwu.edu

Part of George Washington University, The GWU Program Board is the largest student organization on the GW campus and provides GW and MVC students (and the public) with a broad and diverse selection of programs and events. These events include lectures, concerts, films, outdoor festivals, and many other types of entertainment.

The Spring Film series offered at the Newman Center features revealing documentaries such as *The Auction Block*. No Doubt, one of the most popular alternative bands in the country, recently rocked the Smith Center.

And the Annual Festival of the Arts, held at Kogan Plaza, offers music, dance, and various crafters and food vendors for those of you into more festive, and in some cases interactive, fodder. All for free!

Be sure to call the above number to verify what events are open to the public.

Trinity College

- 125 Michigan Avenue, N.E., Washington, D.C.; ✆ (202) 939-5277

- ✍ www.trinitydc.edu

Trinity features several free or inexpensively priced concerts throughout the school year. "Concerts in the Well" is a noontime student recital series held in Trinity's main building. Classical fare ranges from soloists to a group called the Chamber Players, whose makeup consists of different instrumental combinations every year. Other recitals, some in the evening, feature members of the faculty. All

of these events are usually open to the public.

Recitals and concerts are also held at other campus performing spaces, such as O'Connor Auditorium or the Notre Dame Chapel. Here, you may catch *a cappella* faves, The Belles (a student-run group), or the Pan American Symphony Orchestra (artists-in-residence). Performing four to five concerts a year, the orchestra showcases composers and artists from Latin America. Their concerts cost about $10, but are discounted for students.

In addition, Trinity's Drama Society produces two small-scale works a year, with tickets that won't cost more than $5. The number above is for the school's public relations department; they'll give you info on the next production.

University of the District of Columbia

- Van Ness Campus, 4200 Connecticut Avenue, N.W., Washington, D.C.; ✆ (202) 274-5000

- ✍ www.udc.edu

UDC's Department of Mass Media, Visual, and Performing Arts presents just that range of entertainment. The music department showcases about nine recitals each semester, most of which can be enjoyed for free. You may have to extend your lunch break (most of the performances are around noontime) so you can enjoy the jazz and gospel of the University Chorale, the Voices, and instrumental jazz ensembles. And the UDC music department faculty regularly performs at the University Auditorium.

Less frequent, but every bit as enjoyable, are the stage works presented by the theatre department. They usually perform two plays each semester in the Little Theatre, a setting as intimate as it sounds. UDC also produces a series of one-act plays, as well as larger works written by theater majors. Culturally diverse themes set the scene at downright deviant ticket prices—ranging from free to $5 for larger works.

And at no charge, interested patrons can attend photography exhibits or sit in on related seminars on such topics as digital imaging. Call for an events calendar.

University of Maryland at College Park

- University Boulevard, College Park, MD; ✆ (301) 405-5548

- ✎ www.umcp.umd.edu

You would really be hard pressed to find an institute of higher learning in the D.C. area offering more in the way of the performing arts. Most dance, concert, and theatre events here are held at the

Clarice Smith Performing Arts Center.

UM pulls in such renowned national acts as virtuoso violinist Midori, accompanied by pianist Robert McDonald, her long-time partner and winner of the William Kapell International Piano Competition at Maryland. Tickets for special events such as this range from $20 to $40 and are well worth it.

The Leipzig Quartet, Germany's foremost young string quartet, are all former first chairs of the famed Leipzig Gewandhaus Orchestra, and latest winners of the Grand Prix du Disque. This awesome foursome recently performed a program of German quartet masters, all to the tune of $25.

But Mr. C has found much more to do in College Park, at a fraction of that cost.

The Philharmonia Ensemble, a student-run chamber orchestra, presented a concert featuring School of Music faculty artist Rita Sloan on piano. Works included Mendelssohn's Symphony No. 3 ("Scottish"), Tchaikovsky's *Serenade for Strings,* and Martinu's *Toccata e due Canzoni.* All were free and open to the public. And for all of you film buffs, PE has also produced programs exclusively featuring film compositions.

The music department is "in tune" with presentations of its own. The biannual Handel Festival, at Memorial Chapel, features the UMD chorus and the Smithsonian Chamber Orchestra, with top tickets priced around $20. However, tickets are under $10 if you don't mind sitting in the "C" sections of the chapel (that's "C" for "cheap seats," which suit Mr. C just fine). Other concerts, held at the Stamp Student Union, include the "UMD Bands Showcase" and the annual "Pops" concerts. Tickets range from free up to around $7 or so. Call the music department at ☎ (301) 405-5568.

Back at the chapel is the "Monday Night Music Series," offering free concerts of high caliber—some recitals and open rehearsals feature artists who play for the big spenders! The series features everything from jazz to chamber music to the occasional sing-along session for those who'd like to join in. To inquire about Monday events, call ☎ (301) 314-9866.

And there's still more; the dance department is also, um, hopping. Besides staging three major student concerts, U of M also hosts major artists-in-residence. To find out more, this department number is ☎ (301) 405-3180. Check the UMD Web site often for last minute additions.

COMEDY

Why did the Cheap One cross the road? Why, to attend an economic rib-tickler, of course.

For standup comedy, the best cost-cutter in the biz remains the open mike night, when you can get in for a very low cover charge and see the jocular "stars of tomorrow." Of course, funny is in the funny bone of the beholder, and you may have to be patient to see something that really tickles your fancy. Fortunately, the shows are usually hosted by headliners, so you're sure to get plenty of good laughs no matter what. Most clubs have open mike shows earlier in the week. Best to call your favorite venue to see what they offer.

Chelsea's

- 1055 Jefferson Street, N.W., Washington, D.C.; ☎ (202) 298-8222

Comedy of the Capitol Steps is on tap during the first few hours of weekend evenings at this dance club. This ensemble of former Washington interns and Congressional aides spoofs politics through musical satire. These guys have become very popular, and they've appeared at the White House several times, as well as on national television. Performances are on Friday and Saturday.

Dinner and the show cost $50, while the show only costs $37.50. For information about the group, and some samples of their work, consult their Web page at ✐ www.capsteps.com.

Fun Factory

- 3112 Mount Vernon Avenue, Alexandria, VA; ☎ (703) 684-5212

In recent years, several restaurants have opened in this rapidly gentrifying neighborhood a few blocks northwest of Old Town. The acts here aren't world famous, and some are funnier than others (which are not so funny, actually), but the club is surrounded by interesting and varied restaurants, so even if you choose to eat elsewhere, you can park and make a fun, cheap evening of it. Performances are Thursday to Saturday, with an $11 cover charge.

Headliners Holiday Inn

• 2460 Eisenhower Avenue
  Alexandria, VA;
  ✆ (703) 379-4242

Yes, it is a Holiday Inn, but it's
also managed to turn itself into a
halfway decent comedy club. Since
there are so few of that ilk in the
area, it has actually managed to
generate a steady, casual clientele
while providing some yuks along
the way.

Performances are Friday and
Saturday, with a $10 cover charge.

The Improv

• 1140 Connecticut Avenue,
  N.W.,Washington, D.C.;
  ✆ (202) 296-7008

Perhaps D.C.'s premiere comedy
club, and part of a national chain,
this reasonably priced venue brings
top acts to Washington at a convenient midtown location. Acts here
are often comedians you've seen on
TV, and you'll recognize most of
the names. Tickets are generally
priced at $12 to $15, but you can
score discounts if you flash your
college I.D. You can have dinner if
you attend the early shows, or wait
for the 10:30 performance on weekends and dine at one of the great
restaurants nearby. The Improv is
open Tuesday through Saturday,
with tickets priced $12 to $15.

Lazy Susan Dinner Theater

• U.S. Highway 1 at Furnace
  Road, Woodbridge, VA;
  ✆ (703) 550-7384

How about a dinner and musical
comedy combo for about 30 bucks?
That's just within the range of Mr.
C's value criteria, and you can get
that kind of deal here at this long-
time northern Virginia spot. Call
for reservations, and show up early
so that you have plenty of time for

food and conversation before the
curtain comes up!

Lazy Susan is open nightly,
except on Monday. Tickets are
$30.95, except on Saturdays, when
they cost $32.95.

Teddy's House of Comedy

• 617 I Street N.W.,Washington,
  D.C.; ✆ (202) 289-1695

• ✑ teddyshouseofcomedy.com

Teddy Carpenter, the former HBO
and BET personality, runs this fun,
intimate comedy club with a special
interest in African-American
comedy, located in the heart of
D.C.'s Chinatown district. (You'll
find it between the Great Wall
Seafood Restaurant and MVP's
Sports Bar.) The décor consists of
cement walls and candlelit tables,
with the first of about 50 rows of
seats placed right up against the
tiny stage. Up there you'd better
mind your manners, or try to be as
nondescript as possible, or you'll
most likely be fodder for the come-
dian performing inches from your
quaking boots. If you really want
to save money, stick to open mike
nights, which are free. When
nationally known comics perform,
you'll pay a typical cover charge.

West End Theater

• 4615 Duke Street, Alexandria,
  VA; ✆ (703) 370-2500

• ✑ www.wedt.com

Catch dinner and a musical at this
nice little dinner theater located close
by Old Town. Productions such as
*Joseph and the Amazing Technicolor
Dreamcoat* have been very well
received by area critics, and the food
is good as well. As an added bonus,
you can stroll the streets of Old
Town after the show. The theater
offers evening performances, as
well as Sunday and Wednesday

lunch matinees. WET is open nightly, except on Monday. Tickets range from $29 to $35. See the *Children's Activities* section for information about shows for children.

Wiseacres Comedy Club and Lounge

• 8401 Westpark Drive, McLean, VA; (703) 734-2800

This McLean mainstay in the Tyson's Westpark Hotel features a New York City skyline—complete with King Kong climbing up the Empire State Building—behind its small stage, perhaps to give you the impression that you're in the big city rather than the leafy suburbs. Showtimes here are usually 9 p.m. on Friday, and 8 p.m. and 10:30 p.m. on Saturday. Occasionally they'll offer a two-for-one admission deal, so make sure to ask about that when you call. Admission normally runs around $10 to $15.

DANCE

Arlington Dance Theatre

• Gunston Arts Center, 2700 S. Lang Street, Arlington, VA; (703) 548-1017

Founded in 1956, this community arts organization houses a professional dance group that performs seasonal concerts and such holiday shows as *The Nutcracker.* A typical season, from September through June, includes five shows with tickets just $25 for adults; $16 for children and seniors.

The Arlington Dance Theatre includes a school with an extensive slate of classes, and accomplished students may audition for youth ballet, jazz, and tap dance companies. These companies present two major productions each season, as well as several outreach performances, with season tickets running just $12. Call for more information.

Dance Place

• 3225 Eighth Street, N.E.,Washington, D.C.; (202) 269-1600

• www.danceplace.org

The *Washington Post* has called this place D.C.'s "hub of dance activity." Indeed. Dance Place offers shows every weekend, and at very reasonable prices. Housed in a converted industrial building, DP has been doing this for some 20 years now, with obvious dedication.

Its four resident dance companies—Carla & Company, Deborah Riley Dance Projects, Coyaba Dance Company, and the Youth Step Team—form the core of its annual programming efforts, with numerous other shows throughout the year, often touching on ethnic

---

MR. CHEAP'S PICKS

Cheap Tip o' the Day: Half-Price Tickets

TICKETplace, the booth for half-price tickets to nearly every venue in D.C., is located in the Old Post Office Pavilion on Pennsylvania Avenue at 11th Street, NW. The booth also sells some full-price advance tickets for events handled by Ticketmaster.

For booth hours and what's for sale, call (202) 842-5387. A Web page at www.cultural-alliance.org/tickets has daily updates on what's available not just in Washington but at half-price booths all over North America and London.

themes. Seating is general admission, with ticket prices around $15 or less.

The Youth Dance Festival includes performances of hip-hop, tap, African, step, ballet, and modern dance by kids' groups from all over Washington. Havana Select performed a concert of Cuban song and dance, ending with a conga line that audience members were invited to join. Tickets for that were $16 adults, $12 seniors and students, $6 children.

Dance Place also offers classes in modern and ethnic dance, often employing live music. Call the Dance Place or check out its Web site for information on upcoming shows.

The Kennedy Center

- The John F. Kennedy Center for the Performing Arts, 2700 F Street, N.W., Washington, D.C.; 800-444-1324 or 202-467-4600

- ✑ www.kennedy-center.org

Most programs offered at this venerable D.C. performing arts institution, home to the National Symphony Orchestra, occur at the Opera House or Eisenhower Theatre. While not normally cheap, the Kennedy Center offers some occasional good deals for cheapsters with a little patience. For example, the Center offers an annual series of youth and family programs, including storytelling, magic, theater, and musical programs—with tickets often running at a most reasonable $12.

Of course the Center has the expected assortment of world-class performance art, with prices to match. However, you can even find good deals for those if you're willing to sit in the cheap seats. The American Ballet Theatre regularly performs pieces by Balanchine, Morris, and Tudor, and ABT's highly stylized *Corsaire* (featuring pirates, harem girls, a kidnapping or two, and a chance for virtuoso dancing by the male members of the company) was very well received, with tickets priced at $27 to $75.

The Lyon Opera Ballet performs Maguy Marin's *Cendrillon.* Set to music by Prokofiev, this Cinderella is like no other—provocative and slightly sinister but good fun nonetheless. Tickets for that ranged from $23 to $36.

Be sure to stop by the Kennedy Center Education Resource Center (on the Terrace level). The ERC offers revolving exhibits dedicated to all things artistic. A recent dance-related exhibit *Capturing Nureyev: James Wyeth Paints the Dancer,* presented the Russian-born dancer portrayed in sentimental style by the American painter. Visitors could also browse through Nureyev memorabilia, including costumes and photographs. Most exhibits are free.

Manassas Dance Company

- 9004 Mathis Avenue, Manassas, VA; ✆ (703) 257-1811

- ✑ www.manassasdance.com

It's the mission of the Manassas Dance Company to improve the quality of life in Manassas/Prince William County through the art of ballet. They accomplish this by providing accessible and affordable cultural arts performances to the public as well as by offering free performances to schoolchildren.

MDC has offered such programs as *The Nutcracker* and *Sleeping Beauty,* usually at area schools. It's really a great way to introduce your kids to higher culture, without the high price!

The National Theatre

- 1321 Pennsylvania Avenue, Washington, D.C.; ✆ (202) 628-6161

- ✑ www.nationaltheatre.org

The management at the not-for-profit NT take great pains to remind you that this is "your" National Theatre. And the programs offers here reflect the performing arts from all walks of life.

Recently, the touring company of the Broadway hit *Contact,* Susan Stroman's highly entertaining musical about passion, danced in. There is very little dialogue in this show and no lyrics, just dance. Superb dance—humorous, engaging, and ultimately chilling. May not sound like much, but this is a great show. Who needs lyrics and dialogue? Tickets ranged from $25 to $75.

NT also offers a limited number of half-price tickets to seniors, students, and the military.

FESTIVALS

The festival season in and around D.C. is all year long. These usually outdoor events are a great way to spend a day eating, shopping, and generally being entertained for as little as you'd like to spend. Please be aware that these are annual festivals, and it may be a good idea to give call to confirm dates and locations.

THE DISTRICT

Adams Morgan Day

- Columbia Road and Florida Avenue N.W., Washington, D.C.; ✆ (202) 789-7000

Held in funky, hip Adams Morgan in northwest D.C., this annual event celebrates the neighborhood's multicultural character. Here's where you can hear great music—reggae, jazz, R&B, and salsa—and lose yourself in some of the city's best international cuisine.

Carnival Extravaganza

- Emery Park, Georgia and Missouri Avenues N.W., Washington, D.C.; ✆ (202) 726-2204

Washington's large Caribbean population turns out in full force for this annual carnival that is reminiscent of Caribbean and Brazilian celebrations, though on a smaller scale. Participants wear elaborate costumes with sequins and peacock-like feather headpieces.

Festival of American Folklife

- National Mall, Independence and Constitution Avenues, Washington, D.C.; ✆ (202) 357-2700

Each summer on the Mall, usually for two weeks around the Fourth of July, the Festival of American Folklife serves as a "living exhibit" in entertaining and educating—for free, as such an event should be. Rather than some kind of dry history lesson, the festival presents the everyday culture and traditions of people living in a particular region of the country. In 2002, for example, it focused on the connections between the cultures of Asia, Europe, and America based on historical trade routes.

The festival includes crafts, cooking, music, demonstrations, people in period dress, and more—all starting around 11 a.m. and continuing until 9 p.m. daily.

Latin-American Festival

- Adams Morgan, Columbia Road N.W. and the National Mall, Washington, D.C.; ✆ (301) 588-8719

Latin-American music, dance, art, food, and theater are the focus of a two-day heritage festival that takes place in the eclectic Adams Morgan neighborhood and on the grounds of the Washington Monument.

National Cherry Blossom Festival

- Various parks and downtown locations, Washington, D.C.; ℡ (202) 619-7222

Held around the Jefferson Memorial and the Tidal Basin, this is probably D.C.'s most famous festival, and if you haven't heard of it you've probably been living under a rock somewhere. It honors the blooming of the city's 3,000 Japanese cherry trees—a sight to behold. The festival reaches its climax with the Cherry Blossom Festival Parade (usually the first Saturday in April), but numerous related parties and ceremonies begin around the last week of March. The trees bloom anywhere from late March to early April, depending on Mother Nature. Mr. C advises you to avoid the parking hassles by taking the Metro.

The Shakespeare Theater Free-for-All

- Carter Barron Amphitheatre, 16th Street and Colorado Avenue N.W., Washington, D.C.; ℡ (202) 334-4790

Carter Barron and D.C.'s Shakespeare Theater collaborate to stage free, professional performances of Shakespearean masterpieces for two weeks every June. These open-air productions draw huge crowds, in spite of the fact that you have to drive into D.C. to pick up those free tickets the same day of the performance.

Smithsonian Kite Festival

- 15th Street and Constitution Avenue, N.W., Washington, D.C.; ℡ (202) 357-2700

Founded by aviation pioneer Paul E. Garber, and sponsored by the Smithsonian Institution, this high-flying fun is free for both competitors and spectators. Creativity is the festival's thrust, with scores of mind-boggling designs filling the sky around the Washington Monument, where kite makers and flyers of all ages compete for prizes and trophies. This festival is usually held around the last Saturday in March, and often the cherry blossoms are blooming around the same time, making for an absolutely beautiful way to enjoy the nation's capital while getting into the springtime spirit.

Taste of D.C. Festival

- Freedom Plaza at Pennsylvania Avenue, 9th and 14th Streets N.W., Washington, D.C.; ℡ (202) 724-5347

Washington's top restaurants lay it on the line in this public tasting, which also includes free concerts, arts and crafts exhibits, and games for the kids. Proceeds go to various charities.

Admission is free, but food samples start at $4.

Washington International Film Festival (Filmfest D.C.)

- Various theaters and reception halls, Washington, D.C.; ℡ (202) 724-5613

It's been said that Washington D.C. is kind of like a "Hollywood East," where the civic focus is always rife with rumors about who among the glitterati is doing what, and with whom. In this case east and west (the real thing) meet, and all of Washington is the focus of the cinematic world during this two-week festival of international and American film. Washington is one of the top U.S. movie markets and one of the most filmed cities in the world.

MARYLAND

Annapolis Waterfront Festival

- Annapolis Yacht Basin, Compromise and Main Streets, Annapolis, MD; ✆ (410) 268-8828

The capital city, about an hour's drive from D.C., honors its maritime heritage during this three-day festival, which features handicrafts from around the nation. Exhibitors displaying handmade materials fill an entire block at the foot of Main Street and a tented area adjacent to the City Dock, which is flanked by Compromise Street. You'll find wearable art, paintings, carvings, and all manner of decorative items.

Kunte Kinte Heritage Commemoration and Festival

- St. John's College, 60 College Avenue, Annapolis, MD; ✆ (410) 349-0338.

- ✑ www.kuntakinte.org

Made into a household name with the airing of TV's 1977 landmark miniseries *Roots*, Kunte Kinte was brought into the harsh New World at the Port of Annapolis. The festival honors his legacy and the rich traditions of generations of succeeding African-Americans. There are educational programs for children and adults, as well as African-American crafts exhibits and demonstrations. Food vendors represent many ethnic backgrounds, and entertainment ranges from gospel singers to calypso.

Admission is $5 for adults and $3 for seniors and children.

Maryland Renaissance Festival

- Crownsville Road at Maryland Highway, Crownsville, MD; ✆ (410) 266-7304

- ✑ www.rennfest.com/mrf

This well-attended festival for those into a little medieval role-playing usually occurs around the last weekend of August, running into October. Jousting events, jugglers, and medieval foods and crafts are just some of the many fun activities awaiting visitors at this 20-acre "village" located in the heart of suburban Crownsville.

Admission is $13.95 for adults, $4.95 for children ages 7 to 15, and free for kids 6 and under.

Sugarloaf's Crafts Festival

- Montgomery County Fairgrounds, Gaithersburg, MD; ✆ (301) 990-1400

- ✑ www.sugarloafcrafts.com

This mother of all crafts festivals, held in April and October each year, claims to be the largest in the East, featuring around 500 artisans from all across the country, with strict standards for quality—only a small fraction of applicants are accepted each year. Activities include crafts, demonstrations, musical events, children's theater, and more. The Cheapster recommends that you wear a good pair of walking shoes to better traverse the huge festival grounds. Admission is $7.

VIRGINIA

International Children's Festival

- Wolf Trap Farm Park for the Performing Arts, 1624 Trap Road, Vienna, VA; ✆ (703) 255-1900.

- ✑ www.wolf-trap.org

At America's only national park for the performing arts, kids take center stage for a three-day outdoor festival celebrating the global arts. Sponsored by the Arts Council of Fairfax County, the popular event features a variety of performances and educational workshops presented by groups from the local area, throughout the United States and around the world. Most of the performance groups are largely made up of children.

Admission is $10 for adults and $8 for children age 3 and older.

Oktoberfest

- Reston Town Center, Market Street, Reston, VA;
  ✆ (703) 787-6601

More than 20,000 people usually attend this four-day beer, polka, and sauerbraten festival in lively Reston

Town Center. This is a big, open area where you can let the kids run, and there's plenty to amuse them, from balloons to dancers and musicians. Admission is free.

Red Cross Waterfront Festival

- Oronoco Bay Park, Oronoco Street at the waterfront, Old Town Alexandria, VA;
  ✆ (703) 549-8300

One of Alexandria's top summer events, the Red Cross Waterfront Festival brings in a weekend full of music (including some top-name rock, country, folk, and reggae acts), ethnic foods, canoe rides, juried arts and crafts, fireworks, tall ships, and even a 10K run to work off all the calories.

Admission is $5 to $8 for adults, and practically free for kids.

MOVIES

It seems that in the past few years, a few movie houses have gotten the drift that some of us want more than Milk Duds when we venture out to see a film. Extended menus, stadium seating, and even cocktail options have made their way into aisles. Unfortunately, there's not much to be done about the ever-rising prices of first-run Hollywood movies. Some theaters do cut the price a bit on their first shows of the day, if you can go early. But don't despair! There are lots of alternative options for the budget moviegoer, as well as better ways to spend your $8 than at your local chain-owned venue.

American Film Institute

- National Film Theater—The Kennedy Center, New Hampshire Avenue & F Street N.W., Washington, D.C.;
  ✆ (202) 785-4600

- ✐ www.afionline.com

A major force in the preservation of movies and the development of

new talent, the American Film Institute presents several series of American, foreign, and independent films. These range from classics to the latest from the avant-garde. A recent program included films from the European Union. General admission is $7 and $6 for AFI members, seniors, and students under 18. Membership allows you to purchase tickets two weeks in advance and reserve seats four days in advance. Membership also includes program guides, discounted tickets, and invitations to sneak previews and premieres.

Arlington Cinema 'N Drafthouse

- 2903 Columbia Pike, Arlington, VA; ✆ (703) 486-2345

Arlington Cinema 'N Drafthouse is set apart from most other theaters in the area by the fact that you can quaff a brew while watching your favorite Hollywood movies. The comfortable chairs and lounge setting more than make up for the theater's slightly rundown condition. Smoking is permitted but only in the center section of seats. The screen size is comparable to a moderately large theater and the venue is usually crowded.

Perhaps it is the beverages served, or maybe just the relaxed seating structure, but experiencing a movie here is vastly different than at other theaters. It feels more like a shared group experience. Parking is a major drawback, with few spaces nearby, so an early arrival is imperative for weekend shows. Tickets go on sale at 6:45 p.m. Those younger than 21 must be accompanied by a parent or guardian.

Biograph

- 2819 M Street, N.W., Washington, D.C.; ✆ (202) 333-2696

Biograph is the Grande Dame of D.C. art houses. Specializing in culturally diverse festivals and film series, it shows a wide array of classic, foreign, independent, and animated features.

General admission to all shows is $6, with tix just $3 (!) for those under 12 and over 60. And anyone may buy a book of passes—good at matinees, late shows, and Monday through Thursday night showings—giving you 10 admissions for $25. That's just $2.50 per show! An infrared hearing system is available for the hearing-impaired. Call or stop in for an informative newsletter of upcoming events and schedules.

Visions

- 1927 Florida Avenue, Washington, D.C.; ✆ (202) 667-0090

- ⌨ www.visionsdc.com

Visions is a view of a movie lover's paradise. It features first-run quality films, both independent and foreign run daily, with repertory festivals celebrating bodies of work by actors, directors, genres, and so forth.

The theater offers two screening rooms: one with 250 seats and the other with 115. (A skybox above the larger house is available for individual viewing and group rentals.)

In addition to a liquor license and lounge, Visions serves Mediterranean/Indian cuisine with an emphasis on nutrient-rich foods that can be consumed quickly for those on a tight schedule. The restaurant has comfy seats conducive to conversation and discussing films.

Tickets are $8.50, with a $2 discount available for seniors, students, and military. $5.50 matinees are also available, as well as discounted "Smartpasses" for the frequent viewer.

Just experience viewing a film at Vision versus a megamall googolplex . . . and you'll be back for a Smartpass. Mr.C has seen the future of moviegoing, and he hopes it's Visions.

SECOND-RUN DISCOUNT CINEMAS

Second-run movies are the same Hollywood releases that you see in the shopping malls and downtown cinemas, after they've finished their "first runs" in those major venues. Well before they make their way to pay-per-view and DVD, they often show up at some of the theaters listed below. Not only do you get one last chance to see recent hits you may have missed—still on the big screen—but the tickets usually cost less than half of those at the big-deal houses. Call to confirm show times and prices.

Andrews Manor Twin Cinemas

- Andrews Manor Shopping Center, 4801 Allentown Road, Camp Springs, MD; ✆ (301) 736-6373

Loews Cineplex Foundry

- 1055 Thomas Jefferson Street, Washington, D.C.; ✆ (202) 333-8613

Loews Cineplex Waldorf

- Shopper's World, Route 301,Waldorf, MD; ✆ (301) 645-5530

Herndon Twin Cinema

- Dulles Park Shopping Center, 1086 Elden Street, Herndon, VA; ✆ (703) 471-1776

Hoff Theater

- University of Maryland, College Park, MD; ✆ (301) 314-4633

Hoyts Laurel Cinema

- Laurel Shopping Center, Laurel, MD; ✆ (301) 604-5090

Loehmann's Plaza Twin Cinema

- Loehmann's Plaza, 7291 Arlington Boulevard, Falls Church, VA; ✆ (703) 560-2118

Loews Manassas Movie

- 8890 Mathis Avenue, Manassas, VA; ✆ (703) 368-9292

Marymount University

- 2807 North Glebe Road, Arlington, VA; ✆ (703) 284-1517

NEI Holiday Cinemas

- 100 Baughmans Lane, Frederick, MD; ✆ (301) 694-0100

P & G Flower Cinemas

- 8725 Flower Avenue, Silver Spring, MD; ✆ (301) 588-1666

P & G Laurel Town Center Theater

- Town Center Shopping Center, 13314 Laurel Bowie Road, Laurel, MD; ✆ (301) 776-2500

P & G Montgomery Mall Cinemas

- Montgomery Village Avenue, Gaithersburg, MD; ✆ (301) 948-9200

P & G Old Greenbelt Theater

- 129 Centerway Street, Greenbelt, MD; ✆ (301) 474-9744

P & G Riverdale Theatre

- Riverdale Plaza, Riverdale and Kenilworth Avenue, Riverdale, MD; ✆ (301) 864-2421

Showcase Beacon Mail Theatres

- Beacon Mall, 6738 Richmond Highway, Arlington, VA; ✆ (703) 768-7612

Town Center Cinema

- 21800 Town Center Plaza, Sterling, VA; ✆ (703) 444-1117

University Mall Theatres

- 10659 Braddock Road, Fairfax, VA; ✆ (703) 273-7111

MUSEUMS

Mr. C firmly believes museums are our greatest treasures—and not just because many of them are free. Below you'll find highlights of these behemoths, as well as entries for a few museums you may not have heard of.

If you really enjoy a particular museum that does have an admission fee, consider becoming a member. This usually gets you, and perhaps your family, free admission anytime for the price of a couple of visits. It's a money-saver, and it helps out your beloved institution as well.

Art Museum of the Americas

- 201 18th Street N.W., Washington, D.C.; ✆ (202) 458-6016

- ✐ www.museum.oas.org.index.html

Free admission is just one reason to check out this museum, located a stone's throw from the White House and just behind the House of the Americas (see the listing under "Walks and Tours"). In keeping with the international theme set down by that home to the Organization of American States, the museum is dedicated to Latin American and Caribbean art. See contemporary works on all kinds of themes by artists and sculptors from Mexico, Venezuela, the Galapagos Islands, and more. And if you're in need of a rest and a moment of serenity, be sure to check out the secret garden behind the museum. It's a spot where you can indulge in an oasis of floral beauty during the warmer months of the year.

Museum hours are Tuesday through Saturday from 10 a.m. to 5 p.m.

Bethune Council House

- 1318 Vermont Avenue N.W., Washington, D.C.; ✆ (202) 332-1233

- ✐ www.nps.gov/mamc/bethune/welcome/frame.htm

A prominent political leader of the early 1900s, Mary McLeod Bethune's dream was to preserve and document the history of black women in America. Her Victorian townhouse is now home to the country's largest collection of original documents dedicated to the achievements of African-American women. It is also the headquarters for the National Council of Negro Women, which she founded.

Educators, religious leaders, political activists, entertainers, and artists: Black women have long been among all of these, and you can learn about them here. BMA also shows the work of contemporary African-American women through art exhibits, films, concerts, lectures, and symposia. Guided tours are available for groups of 10 or more (call 202-673-2402 in advance). There is a nominal charge for tours; most other programs are free and open to the public.

Museum hours are Monday through Saturday from 10 a.m. to 4 p.m.

Capital Children's Museum

- 800 Third Street N.E., Washington, D.C.; ✆ (202) 534-8600

- ✒ www.ccm.com

See the listing under *Children's Activities*.

College Park Airport Museum

- 1985 Corporal Frank Scott Drive, College Park, MD; ✆ (301) 864-6029

- ✒ www.avialantic.com/collpark.html

The world's oldest operating airport was established here in 1909, when two guys by the names of Orville and Wilbur brought their "aeroplane" to this field. It led to the creation of the first Army Aviation School, one of many firsts to occur at this site; and, though it's in the history books, the airport continues to operate today.

Much newer is the museum, filled with displays and artifacts on these and other important contributions to aviation. Admission is free.

And don't miss the annual "Air Fair," held each fall, with stunt shows and historic aircraft on display. Call the above number to request a copy of their newsletter, "The Wright Flyer," or visit their Web site for more event info. For instance, if you need a unique spot to celebrate your child's day of birth—the museum hosts aviation birthday parties for 3- to 12-year-old kids.

Museum hours are Monday through Sunday from 10 a.m. to 5 p.m.

The Corcoran Gallery of Art

- 500 17th Street N.W., Washington, D.C.; ✆ (202) 639-1700

- ✒ www.corcoran.org

Known the world over, the Corcoran is one of the three oldest art museums in the country (the other two are the Museum of Fine Arts in Boston and the Metropolitan Museum of Art in New York). Its collection is nothing short of breathtaking, offering a comprehensive look at American art from colonial times through the twentieth century: prints, drawings, sculpture, photography, and more. There are also some European masterworks on view (for equal time).

The Corcoran also hosts lectures, workshops, poetry readings, and music concerts. Many of these programs are way out of Mr. C's price range, but a little hunting through their events calendar will uncover some gems. Recent events have included a poetry reading, special artist lectures, private exhibition viewings, and a family holiday decorations workshop. All of these programs were in the not-unreasonable $10 to $15 range. And, don't miss the jazz series, priced at about $20 per show. (See the listing under *Music*.)

Admission to the museum is $5 for adults, $3 for senior citizens and students, and $1 for students ages 13 to 18; Family groups of one or two parents and children under 18 can get in for $8. Members and children under 12 are free. There is sometimes an extra charge for featured exhibitions. Believe Mr. C when he tells you it's worth every penny.

At press time, Frank Gehry had been commissioned to design the newest (and final) addition to the gallery—something to definitely look forward to. Mr. C sorta kinda likes Gehry's work, although he admits that at times he wonders if the construction crew made a colossal mistake in assembly.

The Corcoran is open Monday through Sunday from 10 a.m. to 5 p.m., but closed every Tuesday; on Thursdays, it extends its hours to 9 p.m.

Daughters of the American Revolution Museum

- 1776 D Street N.W., Washington, D.C.; ✎ (202) 628-1776

- ✎ www.dar.org

This free museum showcasing decorative arts and crafts in America occupies the DAR Constitution Hall, adjacent to the White House. The collection holds some 50,000 (!) objects; 33 period rooms display furniture, ceramics, toys and dolls, and other artifacts. You can see replicas of rooms from an 1850 California mansion, as well as one from Massachusetts circa 1775.

The DAR library is filled with antique periodicals, books on family histories, and special collections. Constitution Hall has hosted everything from the National Sports Awards to Tom Joyner's classic soul tour to a comedy performance

---

MR. CHEAP'S PICKS

Museums

The National Aquarium—One fish, two fish, red fish, blue fish! See all the fish—and more—at the nation's oldest aquarium.

National Geographic Explorers Hall—You've read the magazine, now see the exhibits. Orbit the earth, touch a tornado, and explore ecology—all free.

Phillips Collection—One of the finest private art collections in Washington, in a mansion as appealing as the art on the walls.

United States Holocaust Memorial Museum—It's not often that the hottest ticket in town is free. Get in line early, and prepare for a powerful, sobering experience.

---

given by Robin Williams (excellent choice for a good laugh!).

Call the above number for more information; the museum is open Monday through Friday from 8:30 a.m. to 4 p.m., and Sunday from 1 to 5 p.m.

Decatur House Museum

- 748 Jackson Pl. N.W., Washington, D.C.; ✎ (202) 842-0920

- ✎ www.decaturhouse.org

One of several National Trust for Historic Preservation properties, the Decatur House is an interesting part of the historical landscape of the District. It has been the home of a naval hero, three secretaries of state, several members of Congress, and a vice president. World leaders have dined and danced here. The ground floor preserves the Federal-era style of the original occupants, the Decaturs, while the second floor features the Victorian decor of its later residents, the Beales. Special events are often held at this historic site and the Carriage House is also available for group rentals.

The museum is open Tuesday through Friday from 10 a.m. to 3 p.m., and Saturday and Sunday from noon to 4 p.m. All tours of the Decatur House are offered free of charge.

Dumbarton Oaks

* 1703 32nd Street N.W., Washington, D.C.; ✆ (202) 342-3212

* 🖰 www.doaks.org

This 19th-century Georgetown mansion features a variety of artistic and architectural endeavors from both sides of the Atlantic. You can see paintings, sculpture, and antique furniture from Spain, Italy, and France, as well as an 18th-century parquet floor and a ceiling painted in 16th-century French style.

A wealth of art and objects from the East Roman, or Byzantine, Empire also demands a look. So does the Music Room, which once played host to composer Igor Stravinsky, a friend to the mansion's owners. Finally, take the time to tour the Dumbarton Oaks Gardens—in fact, take a lot of time. The exquisitely landscaped formal gardens take up 10 acres; the property itself covers 53 acres, dotted with exotic trees and flowers. Ahhh, surrounded by beauty and serenity!

Admission to the gardens is $5 for adults; $3 for children and senior citizens. Garden hours are Monday through Sunday from 2 to 6 p.m. (March 15 through October) and from 2 to 5 p.m. (November 14 through March). Admission to the museum is free of charge; donations are kindly accepted. Museum hours are Tuesday through Sunday from 2 to 5 p.m. all year round.

Ford's Theatre National Historic Site

* 511 Tenth Street N.W., Washington, D.C.; ✆ (202) 347-4833

* 🖰 www.fordstheatre.org

Ford's Theatre, famous as the site of Abraham Lincoln's assassination, has been fully restored with original and reproduced furnishings of the period. The building also houses the Lincoln Museum, which displays John Wilkes Booth's pistol, along with exhibits that give a flavor of Civil War–era Washington.

Both theater and museum are generally open Monday through Sunday from 9 a.m. to 5 p.m., although the theater is sometimes in use for matinee performances as the Ford's Theatre Society presents a full slate of plays to this day. Ticket prices, alas, are not cheap but usually worth the money. At press time, tickets for a swing and jazz musical entitled *Hot Mikado* promises "an explosion of laughter, song and dance"—at $25 per ticket. To obtain a full schedule of shows, the box office number is (800) 955-5560.

Tour admission is free, however, for both the theatre and Petersen House across the street. It was there that Lincoln spent his final hours, in the company of friends and doctors. This building has also been completely restored. When extra docents are available, there are 15-minute talks given at a quarter past the hours of 9 a.m. to 11 a.m. and 2 p.m. to 4 p.m.

Fort Ward Museum & Historic Site

* 4301 West Braddock Road, Alexandria, VA; ✆ (703) 838-4848

* 🖰 www.fortward.org

Fort Ward was taken under the wing of the City of Alexandria in 1961 and has since been both restored and preserved as befits an important Civil War site. Today, this fifth-largest of 162 forts built by Union forces features a completely restored northwest bastion and over 95 percent of its original walls. Both the fort and accompanying museum occupy a 45-acre park setting just east of I-395.

On Sundays it's possible to browse through artifacts, a research library, and a range of educational programs. One recent exhibition entitled *To Aid and Comfort: The U.S. Sanitary Commission,* gave an overview of how civilians provided food, clothing and medical supplies to Union troops. Mr. C also suggests periodically checking Fort Ward's monthly calendar for special happenings ranging from lecture series such as "Women in Civil War America" to announcements of upcoming exhibit openings, such as *Civil War Mess Equipment.*

A path runs along the earthwork walls and can take as long as 45 minutes to walk. Admission to the fort, and the museum, is free. Hours for the historic site itself are Monday through Sunday from 9 a.m. to sunset. Museum hours are Tuesday through Saturday from 9 a.m. to 5 p.m., and Sunday from noon to 5 p.m.

Frederick Douglass National Historic Site

- 1411 W Street S.E., Washington, D.C.; ☎ (202) 426-5961

Known in its day as Cedar Hill, this spot was the home of famed abolitionist Frederick Douglass from 1877 until his death in 1895. His second wife, Helen Pitts, preserved their home in his memory; thanks to her efforts, visitors today can see many of the home's original furnishings.

Belongings displayed here include Abraham Lincoln's cane, given to Douglass by Mrs. Lincoln following the president's assassination; a leather rocking chair from the people of Haiti; and a hand-carved German clock, a gift from Ottilia Assing.

Tours begin at the visitor center, which features exhibits and a documentary film about Douglass's life. Tours of the home are given on an hourly basis. Admission is $2 for both children and adults. Museum hours are Monday through Sunday from 9 a.m. to 5 p.m. (April 1 to September 30) and from 9 a.m. to 4 p.m. (October 1 to March 31).

The Historical Society of Washington, D.C.

- 1307 New Hampshire Avenue N.W., Washington, D.C.; ☎ (202) 785-2068

- ✐ www.hswdc.org

Headquartered in the Heurich Mansion, former home to beer baron Christian Heurich, the Historical Society offers a library and exhibit gallery, as well as guided tours of its Victorian splendor and of the city itself.

Recent get-togethers have included walking tours of historic apartment buildings in the Northwest area of 16th and 17th Streets; a bus tour of the "niftiest" churches among the staggering 269 places of worship along 16th Street; and a lecture and book signing by a Civil War historian with a specialty on Washington. Many events are free to members and nonmembers alike, although some tours can run on the expensive side.

Tours of the house museum are free. House hours are Monday through Saturday from 10 a.m. to 4 p.m.; the Research Library hours are the same.

Meridian House/ White-Meyer House

- 1624 and 1630 Crescent Place N.W., Washington, D.C.; ✎ (202) 939-5568

- ✎ www.meridian.org

Designed by John Russell Pope, these two historic mansions sponsor tours, lectures, exhibits, concerts, and more. Both homes now belong to the Meridian International Center, which promotes international understanding through cultural exchanges.

Recent exhibits include *True Colors: Mediations of the American Spirit* and *Cultural Business Protocol-Asia*. Works by Leonid Pasternak, Pablo Picasso, and Henry Moore have been seen here. In addition, the houses and their furnishings are wonderful examples of early twentieth-century architecture and decor.

House hours for both are Wednesday through Sunday from 2 to 5 p.m.

Mexican Cultural Institute

- 2829 16th Street N.W., Washington, D.C.; ✎ (202) 728-1628

- ✎ www.embassy.org

The Mexican Cultural Institute has two art galleries filled with exhibits that show off the artistic heritage of our neighbor to the south. The permanent collection includes paintings, sculptures, and photographs. A recent special exhibit, *Bolteros . . . Yesterday, Today and Always: A Tribute to Bolero Musical Genre*, included pieces by prominent Mex-

ican artists reinterpreting music of their childhood.

The galleries are free and open to the public. Hours are Tuesday through Friday from 9:30 a.m. to 5:30 p.m., and Saturday from 11 a.m. to 5:30.

NASA/Goddard Space Flight Center

- Soil Conservation Road, Greenbelt, MD; ✎ (301) 286-3979

- ✎ www.gsfc.nasa.gov

Named for the "Father of Modern Rocketry," the Goddard Space Flight Center was built by NASA *wayyyy* back in 1959! Along with displays of rockets and spacecraft, the lab's visitor center has lots of fun hands-on stuff, like a gyro-chair that lets you experience the sensation of steering with no gravity, and a maneuvering unit that lets you try to retrieve a satellite in space.

At press time, it's still possible to have a look at the general exhibits. While this is the case, the Space Flight Center no longer offers special events such as model rocket launches, stargazing groups, lectures by scientists, or videos of new NASA projects. Nor can you tour some of the actual laboratories, including stops at the Test and Evaluation Facility, NASA Communications Network, Flight Dynamics Facility, and satellite control centers for such spacecraft as the Hubble Space Telescope. These tours and activities have been suspended until further notice, but Mr. C is optimistic that the events will soon resume in the near future. So be sure to periodically check on the status from time to time—visit their Web site, or call ✎ (301) 286-8981 for further information. Visitor center hours are Monday through Saturday from 9 a.m. to 4 p.m.

The National Aquarium

- U.S. Department of Commerce Building, 14th Street & Constitution Avenue N.W., Room B-077, Washington, D.C.; ✆ (202) 482-2825

- ✑ www.nationalaquarium.com

Established in 1873, the National Aquarium was the first one in the country. Now, Mr. C doesn't want you to mistake this place for Sea World; this is a small and basic collection. Nevertheless, the aquarium has some 1,200 creatures: sea turtles, alligators, tropical clownfish, leopard sharks (don't they sound nasty), and all the rest. At the "Touch Tank" you can hold hermit crabs, horseshoe crabs, and sea urchins. Don't miss the shark feedings on Monday, Wednesday, and Saturday at 2 p.m., or the (gulp) piranha feedings on Tuesday, Thursday, and Sunday—also at 2 p.m.

And if you're around in July, try to visit on "Shark Day." This popular annual event educates the public about sharks, their habits, and the need to protect them from extinction. Something else to consider: If you're searching for a worthy cause, it's now possible to support the aquarium with their "Adopt-A-Fish" program. For a nominal sum of $30 (tax deductible, of course!), you can sponsor or "adopt" your own fish. Proceeds are directly allocated towards the maintenance of the facility. Or if you prefer other aquatic life forms, firebelly toads, sea stars, mudskippers, wood turtles, and poison arrow frogs are also on offer. Call the aquarium to find out about this program and other special events.

Admission prices are a real catch: $3 for adults and 75 cents for kids ages 2–10. But any price would be a bargain, really. National Aquarium hours are Monday through Sunday from 9 a.m. to 5 p.m.

National Archives

- Seventh Street & Constitution Avenue N.W., Washington, D.C.; ✆ (202) 501-5205

- ✑ www.nara.gov

Sometime in 2003, the Rotunda of the National Archives is due to reopen with a redesigned and improved display of the basic documents of our nation: The Declaration of Independence, the Constitution, and the Bill of Rights—collectively known as the Charters of Freedom—are on display here, in all their aged glory. They're sealed under glass in helium-filled cases; at night they are lowered some 20 feet into a 55-ton vault below. Hey, when you build a nation, you don't want to lose the instructions.

But there's a lot more. This rotunda also houses a cross-section of books, public records, federal documents, maps, photographs, movies, and sound recordings created by the government over the past 200 years or so—all available for reference and research. There's even a copy of the Magna Carta, the early British document that is the basis for our own Bill of Rights. (It's on loan from Ross Perot; no wonder he always wanted to work in Washington.)

There's no admission charge. For general information, call ✆ (202) 501-5000. National Archive hours are Monday through Sunday from 10 a.m. to 5:30 p.m.

The National Building Museum

- 401 F Street N.W., Washington, D.C.; ✆ (202) 272-2448

- ✑ www.nbm.org

One of the lesser-known museums in Washington, this is one Mr. C's favorite places to explore and just hang out.

The National Building Museum claims to be the only museum dedicated to American building achievements. Exhibits focus on architectural elements and styles, urban development, feats of engineering, and historic preservation. Permanent displays include *Building A Landmark: The National Building Museum's Historic Home*—a treatise on the history of the museum's home itself, which is a building of architectural significance in its own right. Another "must see" permanent installation is entitled *Tools as Art VI: Instruments of Change*. You get the idea!

In addition, NBM leads a "Demonstration Cart," also known as *Arches & Tresses: The Tension Builds*. Other programs include symposia, lectures, films, and free concerts.

Admission to the museum is free, though there is a nominal charge for some events. NBM hours are Monday through Saturday from 10 a.m. to 5 p.m., and Sunday from 11 a.m. to 5 p.m.

National Capital Trolley Museum

- 1313 Bonifant Road & New Hampshire Avenue, Wheaton, MD; ✆ (301) 384-6088

- ✎ www.dctrolley.org

Streetcars once shuttled people around the District; today, the Metro has taken over as the transport of choice. This museum preserves the symbols of that bygone era with American electric streetcars from the 1890s onward, as well as 19th-century trams from Austria and Germany.

Start your tour at the visitor's center, filled with photos and artifacts, plus an operating model trolley and a slide show. Then, take a two-mile ride through the countryside on one of the museum's 15 cars. Admission to the visitor's center and exhibits is free; the trolley fare is $2.50 for adults, $2 for children under 17.

Special events at the museum include film programs, musical events, antique car shows, and the annual "Holly Trolleyfest," with toy trains and Santa himself. Museum hours are Saturday, Sunday, and summer holidays from noon to 5 p.m.; in December it's open Saturday and Sunday from 5 p.m. to 9 p.m for the "Holly Trolley." During July and August additional hours on Wednesday are from 11 a.m. to 3 p.m.

National Gallery of Art

- Fourth Street & Constitution Avenue N.W., Washington, D.C.; ✆ (202) 737-4215

- ✎ www.nga.gov

Betcha didn't know you're an art collector. Well, the National Gallery of Art, and its nifty collection, belongs to the people of the United States of America. No, that doesn't mean you can pick up a Renoir for the laundry room. It does mean that you can come and enjoy the collection free of charge at all times! The National Gallery's permanent collection includes European and American paintings, sculpture, and decorative arts.

Temporary exhibits include works from countries and cultures throughout the world, enhancing the visitor's appreciation for art. Special programs include gallery talks, lectures, films, and family activities. The gallery also sponsors a series of free classical music concerts; see the listing under *Music*.

National Gallery hours are Monday through Saturday from 10 a.m. to 5 p.m., and Sunday from 11 a.m. to 6 p.m.

National Geographic Explorers Hall

- 1145 17th Street N.W., Washington, D.C.; ✆ (202) 857-7588

- ✐ www.nationalgeographic.com/explorer

Like a science project come to life, "Geographica" is filled with fun ways to explore the geography and ecology of the earth. Appropriately, it is located in Explorers Hall on the first floor of the National Geographic Society's headquarters. Geographica is an interactive exhibit where you can touch a tornado, explore the solar system, gaze at the stars, and check the weather.

Space buffs shouldn't miss Earth Station One, a 72-seat amphitheater that takes you into orbit 23,000 miles above the earth—well, at least it feels that way. Earth Station One is also home to National Geographic's 11-foot, freestanding globe.

Admission is free; NG's Explorers Hall hours are Monday through Saturday from 9 a.m. to 5 p.m., and Sunday from 10 a.m. to 5 p.m.

National Jewish Museum

- 1640 Rhode Island Avenue N.W., Washington, D.C.; ✆ (202) 857-6583

- ✐ www.bnaibrith.org/museum

Not far from Dupont Circle, the galleries of this museum display the artistic, historical, and ethnic lives of Jews in America and around the world. This diverse culture is seen through religious objects, archaeological artifacts, paintings, photographs, and sculptures.

Since its opening in 1957 on the ground floor of the B'nai B'rith's international headquarters, the museum has grown steadily. Relatively new sections include the *Jewish American Sports Hall of Fame* and *Unpacking on the Prairie: Jewish Women in the Upper Midwest.*

Admission is free. Guides offer tours in Hebrew, French, and Russian; call for schedule information. Museum hours are Sunday through Friday from 10 a.m. to 5 p.m.

National Museum of Health and Medicine

- Walter Reed Army Medical Center, Building 54, 6825 16th Street N.W., Washington, D.C. ✆ (202) 782-2200

- ✐ www.natmedmuse.afip.org

If you're a fan of any hospital show, from *M*A*S*H* to *ER,* then this is the museum for you. And if you hate going to the doctor, you'll at least be glad to see how far we've come. NMHM explores the past, present, and future of the healing arts, through anatomical displays and interactive exhibits. It's sort of like an owner's manual to your body. You can even perform simulated surgery—gulp!—on ADAM, a computerized cadaver used to teach medical students surgical techniques.

Temporary exhibits focus on current and recent health issues, some of which are highly controversial. One examined medical experimentation during the Holocaust. On a much lighter note, the museum also sponsors occasional art shows, such as *The World From Within: The National Art Exhibition by the Mentally Ill.*

Visitors should be forewarned: Some of the displays are a bit graphic for the, um, faint of heart. But, remember, the goal is a realistic presentation of the body and disease. Admission is free. Museum hours are Monday through Sunday from 10 a.m. to 5:30 p.m.

The National Museum of Women in the Arts

- 1250 New York Avenue N.W., Washington, D.C.; ℡ (202) 783-5000

- ✎ www.nmwa.org

Though it opened in its newly renovated building in 1987, the NMWA had its origin in the 1960s, when individuals began collecting works for the first museum of its kind—devoted to recognizing the achievements of women artists of all nationalities and time periods. In addition to 10 exhibitions a year, the museum also collaborates with such organizations as the Source Theatre Company (see the listing under *Theater*) and the Smithsonian (see below) to present plays, educational programs, and musical events dealing with, yes, women in the arts.

Exhibitions have included *Cartoons from the Women's Suffrage Movement,* and a stirring presentation of the early photography of Julia Margaret Cameron. A unique show entitled *Brave Little Girls,* was especially designed for children ages 8–12.

The NMWA's permanent collection is certainly the most significant of its type in the world; its library archives, open to all, hold over 13,000 files on artists, as well as books, audio, and videotapes. Admission for adults is $5, seniors (60 and over) $3. Students with ID, NMWA members, and youth under 18 are admitted for free.

NMWA hours are Monday through Saturday from 10 a.m. to 5 p.m.; on Sunday from noon to 5 p.m.

The Navy Art Gallery

- Washington Navy Yard, 901 M Street S.E., Building 67, Washington, D.C.; ℡ (202) 433-3815

- ✎ www.history.navy.mil/ branches/org6-4.htm

The Navy Art Gallery exhibits works from their collection of over 10,000 pieces of art. That assortment includes fine and historical pieces, some going back to Revolutionary War time, as well as works from the Combat Art Program. The Combat Art Program began during World War II and its artists have recorded naval history ever since. The works in this part of the collection chronicle the Navy on the front lines of battle and on the front lines of science, like paintings depicting space exploration.

Anyone who loves big ships, aircraft, and submarines will enjoy visiting this gallery.

Gallery hours are Monday through Friday from 9 a.m. to 4 p.m.; closed on Saturday and Sunday.

The Navy Museum

- Washington Navy Yard, Building 76, Kidder Breese S.E., Washington, D.C.; ℡ (202) 433-4882

- ✎ www.history.navy.mil/ branches/nhcorg8.htm

This museum tells the history of the United States Navy, from its inception to the present day. The exhibits take you through wars and conflicts; polar, undersea, and space explorations; and scientific discoveries, all part of the Navy's storied past. Other exhibits explore the role of black men and women in the Navy, and the Navy's role in World War II.

Fans of *The Hunt for Red October* shouldn't miss the submarine display, which includes the Intelligent Whale, built during the

Civil War, as well as subs from Japan, Germany, and Italy.

Admission to the Navy Museum is free. Tours, both guided and self-guided, are available, including a weekday highlights tour. Call for details or to schedule a group tour. Museum hours are Monday through Friday from 9 a.m. to 4 p.m.; closed on Saturday and Sunday.

The Octagon Museum

- 1799 New York Avenue N.W., Washington, D.C.; ✆ (202) 638-3221

- ✍ www.nmwa.org

Built in the early 1800s, the Octagon became a temporary residence for President James and Dolly Madison after the British burned the White House in 1812. Madison signed the Treaty of Ghent in the upstairs parlor of this house, ending the War of 1812.

Today, the Octagon serves as the museum of the American Architectural Foundation. Along with tours of the house and other special exhibits, the museum features gallery talks, lectures, and walking tours. The fee for some of these activities includes the price of admission, regularly $5 for adults and $3 for students and senior citizens. Others charge an additional fee that can range from nominal to pricey. As a rule, talks and lectures are cheap and walking tours, led by renowned architects and architectural historians, are more expensive. AAF members generally enjoy reduced prices.

Exhibits here showcase cross-sections of architecture—ranging from the "here and now" to the past. To illustrate, a current show entitled *Skyscrapers: The New Millennium* consists of architectural drawings, plans, photographs, models, and a treatise of how up to 30 modern day high-rise buildings have been constructed. A former show, *Thomas Jefferson's Academical Village: The Creation of an Architectural Masterpiece, 1817-1826,* explored Jefferson's plans in creating the academic village of the University of Virginia in Charlottesville, Virginia. Related programs included walking tours of academic villages in D.C. and a lecture exploring the political implications of building the University.

House and gallery hours are Tuesday through Sunday from 10 a.m. to 4 p.m.

Phillips Collection

- 1600 21st Street N.W., Washington, D.C.; ✆ (202) 387-2151

- ✍ www.phillipscollection.org

Strong in 19th- and 20th-century European paintings, as well as works of American modernists, the Phillips Collection boasts one of D.C.'s finest private art collections—but that's just one of the reasons to check this place out. Also worthwhile are its concerts, lectures, and other special events that increase this charming old mansion's appeal.

The permanent collection includes masterpieces from Renoir, Van Gogh, Cezanne, and Delacroix, running all the way up through a handful of works by Georgia O'Keeffe—recently showcased in a special exhibition on modernists. On Sundays, your museum experience is augmented by chamber music concerts, including works of composers such as Brahms. These begin at 5 p.m.; free with cost of museum admission of $7.50 for adults, $4 for seniors over 62 and full-time students, and no charge for those 18 and under.

There's more: On every Thursday from 5 p.m. to 8:30 p.m., the very popular "Artful Evenings" present gallery talks, brief videos, and opportunities for "socializing" with speakers and other attendees. A cash bar is available, and gentle jazz and classical music set the atmosphere. Admission is $5; there's no formal admission on weekdays; donations are suggested.

Phillips Collection hours are Tuesday, Wednesday, Friday, and Saturday from 10 a.m. to 5 p.m.; Thursday from noon to 8:30 p.m.; and Sunday from noon to 7 p.m.

The Textile Museum

- 2320 South Street N.W., Washington, D.C.; ✆ (202) 667-0441

- ✐ www.textilemuseum.org

The Textile Museum displays pieces from antiquity to the present, from regions all over the globe: India, Indonesia, China, Japan, Africa, Latin America, and other countries, as well as the American Southwest. Historically significant pieces include archaeological textiles from pre-Columbian Peru.

Museum exhibits only hint at the depth of these holdings. Unfortunately, because of the fragile nature of the pieces, there are no permanent exhibits. Recent exhibits include *Technology as Catalyst: Textile Artists on the Cutting Edge, Deceptively Simple: The Complexities of Plain Weave,* and *Hidden Threads of Peru: Q'ero Textiles.*

Admission is free, with a suggested contribution of $5. Textile Museum hours are Monday through Saturday from 10 a.m. to 5 p.m. and Sunday from 1 p.m. to 5 p.m.

United States Holocaust Memorial Museum

- 100 Raoul Wallenberg Place S.W., Washington, D.C.; ✆ (202) 488-0400

- ✐ www.ushmm.org

This museum is physically and emotionally exhausting . . . but also amazingly powerful. Expect to spend at least three hours here, and even with that you will not come close to seeing and reading everything. Exhibits chronicle the rise of the Nazi party in Europe, its brutal beliefs and practices, and its aftermath.

One of the most moving exhibits, *Daniel's Story,* puts you into the life of a fictitious boy, from his family's first troubles to internment in a concentration camp. It serves as both a human-scale introduction to the subject and something to do while waiting to go into the main part of the museum. Because it's in the lobby, with free admission, this also makes for a sort of quick and easy alternative visit.

The entire museum is free of charge, but due to the large crowds it generates, you do need scheduled tickets during peak periods in the summer and holidays. No passes are necessary to enter the museum building and to look at the special exhibitions. While this is the case, "timed passes" are required for entrance into an integral part of the museum; a permanent exhibition entitled *The Holocaust.* Each day the museum distributes these "timed passes" on a first come, first serve basis at the 14th Street entrance. They're limited, however, and not easy to come by. Your best bet is to get them online at: ✐ www.tickets.com or call (800) 400-9373. Mr. C advises making arrangements a few weeks in advance if you've got a specific date and time in mind—as weekends are busiest; the small service fee you pay is worth it.

USHMM hours are Monday through Sunday from 10 a.m. to 5:30 p.m.

One last note from Mr. C: Be sure to wear comfortable shoes. You will spend the entire time on your feet; and, crowded or not, there is a lot of standing. Eating beforehand is also a good idea, since there is so much to see. Fortunately, there is a cafeteria just outside the exit when you're done.

Washington Dolls' House & Toy Museum

- 5236 44th Street N.W., Washington, D.C.; ✆ (202) 244-0024

Just purchasing your tickets to this museum, with its antique post office window, is enough to bring a smile to the faces of the young and young at heart. Inside, you'll be dazzled by the large collection of antique dollhouses, toys, and games. Toys here are mainly American and from the Victorian era, though other countries and styles are represented. Miniatures are the biggest (ha, ha) part of this museum, including the aforementioned dolls' houses, shops, stables, schoolrooms, a hotel, a mansion, and more. Annual highlights include the Christmas display, complete with a revolving musical tree. Other seasonal exhibits celebrate the baseball season, Easter, and Halloween. You'll also see several hundred dolls, in their original clothes, displayed in houses, shops, and rooms.

Admission to the museum is $5 for adults, $3 for seniors, and $2 for children under 14. Museum hours are Tuesday through Saturday from 10 a.m. to 5 p.m., and Sunday from noon to 5 p.m.

Woodrow Wilson House

- 2340 South Street N.W., Washington, D.C.; ✆ (202) 387-4062

- ✐ www.woodrowwilsonhouse. org

The 28th president of the United States, Woodrow Wilson is probably best known for helming the nation through World War I. The Wilson House, where he lived after office, offers a glimpse of Wilson's private life and a variety of important materials from his White House years.

Presidential mementos include gifts of state from around the world, as well as various personal effects of the world statesman who created the League of Nations. Designed in 1915, the house is authentically furnished with items capturing American life in the 1920s.

Museum hours are Tuesday through Sunday from 10 a.m. to 4 p.m.

THE SMITHSONIAN INSTITUTION

- ✐ www.si.edu

Mr. C loves garage sales; maybe that's why he loves the Smithsonian even more. The 17 Washington facilities of the Smithsonian—the world's largest museum complex— are the nation's attic.

Even sweeter: admission to every one of the museums, most located right on the National Mall, is free.

Established in 1846 through the generous contributions of England's James Smithson, it has continued to grow; sometime in 2004, the National Museum of the American Indian will open on the Mall.

In addition to the display of its collection, the Smithsonian offers a full schedule of "living exhibits," including artists and musicians on the Mall each summer; publications, such as a monthly magazine devoted to art, history, and science; and a variety of documentary series aired on public radio stations across the country.

The Institution's oldest building is known as the Castle (1000 Jefferson Drive S.W.), and it's comprised of the Information Center, various administrative offices, and two theaters offering video overviews of the complex—a good idea to help you decide what to see first, since it is just not possible to hit everything in a day.

Hours are Monday through Sunday from 9 a.m. to 5:30 p.m.; all other branches are open from 10 a.m. to 5:30 p.m., unless otherwise indicated. For more information, call ✆ (202) 357-2700.

Anacostia Museum

- 1901 Fort Pl. S.E., Washington, D.C.; ✆ (202) 287-2060

- ✏ www.si.edu/anacostia

Opened in 1967, the Anacostia Museum is one of two D.C. Smithsonians not located on the National Mall, instead found in the historic community of Anacostia. Devoted to the history and culture of African-Americans, it features changing exhibits that document the experiences of people living in the "Upper South," including Maryland, Virginia, the Carolinas, Georgia, and Washington, D.C. And for a worthwhile attraction also on the museum grounds, check out the George Washington Carver Nature Trail. Regular trail walks are available. Call ✆ (202) 287-3369 for information and reservations.

Arts and Industries Building

- 900 Jefferson Drive S.W., Washington, D.C.; ✆ (202) 357-1300

Constructed second in the National Mall complex, the Arts and Industries Building was conceived after the Philadelphia Centennial celebration in 1876, in order to house the exhibits given to the government at that time. Consequently, a large number of Victorian items are on display, including a steam locomotive and carriages from the original Centennial festivities. The museum is not restricted to history, however. An Experimental Gallery in the South Hall features changing arts and humanities exhibits.

Freer Gallery

- Jefferson Dr. at 12th Street S.W., Washington, D.C.; ✆ (202) 357-3200

- ✏ www.asia.si.edu

Home to both an ever-expanding collection of Asian art as well as one of the world's best collection of 19th and early 20th century American art, the Freer Gallery opened in 1923. Founded by industrialist Charles Lang Freer, the museum lives as a testament to his belief that the works of many American artists of the time were "visually harmonious" with those of Asian artists. To further explore Asian culture and history, amble across the indoor access to the Sackler Gallery (see below). Regular events at the two museums include international films, book signings, and concerts—all free.

Hirshhorn Museum and Sculpture Garden

- Independence Avenue & Seventh Street S.W., Washington, D.C.; ✆ (202) 357-3200

- ✏ www.hirshhorn.si.edu

While much of the Smithsonian is steeped in history, the Hirshhorn opened in 1974 with a goal of encouraging interest in contemporary art. Philanthropist Joseph Hirshhorn gave his entire collection to the United States in 1966, and today the cylindrical-shaped museum features a vast amount of modern sculpture, including works by Henri

Matisse and Auguste Rodin, as well as paintings. More art from American and European masters can be found in the two-level Sculpture Garden covering nearly four acres—which is open 7:30 a.m. until dusk.

National Air and Space Museum

- Independence Avenue & Seventh Street S.W., Washington, D.C.; ✆ (202) 357-1300

- ✑ www.nasm.si.edu

There's really something for everyone here in the Smithsonian's largest and most popular museum. Want to see the Wright Brothers' plane, or Lindbergh's *Spirit of Saint Louis?* They're here. The Apollo lunar exploration module? Yup.

Changing exhibits in recent years have included *Explore the Universe,* which highlighted the ways in which digital technology has expanded our worldview from that of a star filled sky to galaxies beyond. And at the Lockheed Imax Theater, it's possible to partake in virtual travel experiences with show offerings such as "To Fly," "Cosmic Voyage," "The Magic of Flight" and Adventures in Wild America." Mr. C was pleased with the nominal fees for the Imax shows: adult tickets were $7.50 each; youth ages 2 to 12 and seniors ages 55+ are $5 per person.

Treasures regularly on display include the Wright brothers' 1903 *Flyer I,* Charles Lindbergh's *Spirit of Saint Louis,* Amelia Earhart's Lockheed 5B Vega, the high-flying *X-15* spy plane, and John Glenn's *Mercury* spacecraft. Suspended from the ceiling of the lobby is *Voyager,* the lightweight aircraft that flew around the world in December of 1986 without stopping or refueling. Other galleries include the history of military and civilian aviation.

As you enter from the Mall you'll walk directly to the *Apollo 11* command module Columbia, used on the first manned lunar landing mission. In July of 1969 the spacecraft carried Neil Armstrong, Edwin "Buzz" Aldrin, and Michael Collins to the moon. This is the same type of spacecraft used in the ill-fated *Apollo 13* mission. The lunar rock sample near the Mall entrance was cut from a rock picked up from the surface of the moon by the crew of *Apollo 17* in December of 1972. You can save billions from your travel budget and still tell your friends and neighbors you touched a piece of the moon.

If all goes well, in December 2003 the new Steven F. Udvar-Hazy Center will open at Washington Dulles International Airport in Northern Virginia. The huge, 760,000-square-foot facility will permit the display of more than 200 aircraft, including an SR-71 Blackbird, the B-17 Flying Fortress Swoose, a Phantom F-4 fighter, and the B-29 Superfortress *Enola Gay.* The 10-story aviation hangar will be about 2½ football fields in length, featuring three viewing levels for visitors.

The *Enola Gay* B-29 that dropped the first atomic bomb on Hiroshima, Japan, had been on display at the original museum from 1996 to 1998. The 99-foot-long plane, with a wingspan of 141 feet and a top speed of 375 miles per hour, was the largest plane ever restored by the Smithsonian.

Subsequent phases of construction will include a space hangar, to showcase the space shuttle *Enterprise* and some 130 other significant space vehicles, as well as a state-of-the-art restoration hangar and an archives center.

The planned opening is meant to coincide with the centennial of the Wright brothers' flight at Kitty

Hawk, North Carolina. Planners hope the center will draw as many as 3 million visitors per year.

Paul E. Garber Preservation, Restoration, and Storage Facility

- Old Silver Road at Street, Barnabas Road, Suitland, MD; ✆ (202) 357-1400

- ✎ www.nasm.si.edu/nasm/ garber/Garber.html

In his travels, Mr. C has come across heaps of "no-frills" shops and restaurants. This, however, is his first encounter with a no-frills museum! Why would people come to a warehouse, with no heat or air conditioning, and traipse around for two or three hours? Well—besides the fact that it's free—this is the place to step behind the scenes of the nation's most popular museum: the Smithsonian's National Air and Space Museum.

The Paul E. Garber Facility restores and preserves artifacts for the mother museum in Washington. Also on display at the Garber Facility are fascinating pieces that just can't be fit into the Air and Space museum itself. Babies like a scale model of the Vostok spacecraft that carried the first man into space; a Soviet MiG-15 jet; and a World War I "Jenny" training airplane. Plus real satellites, rocket engines, and fighter planes—approximately 140 in all. You can also take a behind-the-scenes look at the restoration workshop.

Admission and tours are absolutely free. Tours are restricted, however, to ages 16 and up. Reservations are required; the Garber Facility recommends calling at least three weeks in advance.

Warehouse hours are Monday through Friday from 10 a.m. to 5 p.m., and Saturday and Sunday from 10 a.m. to 1 p.m.

National Museum of African Art

- 950 Independence Avenue S.W., Washington, D.C.; ✆ (202) 357-4600

- ✎ www.nmafa.si.edu

Devoted to research, collection, and exhibition of African art, this museum became part of the Smithsonian in 1979 and features over 7,000 works in wood, metal, ceramics, cloth, and ivory. Permanent exhibitions include one celebrating the creative pottery of women of central Africa. Regular lectures, workshops, and tours introduce both school children and adults to African art and its history.

Entrance is through a small African adobe-like structure located behind the Smithsonian Castle. Among the items on display are traditional African masks used in rituals of daily life and in supplication for harvests and fertility. An important permanent exhibition at the museum is *The Ancient West African City of Benin, A.D. 1300–1897,* a replication of items from the royal court of the capital of the Kingdom of Benin before British colonial rule. On display are images of kings and attendants in sculptures, figures, and plaques.

Smithsonian American Art Museum

- Eighth & G Street N.W., Washington, D.C.; ✆ (202) 357-2247

- ✎ www.americanart.si.edu

Sometime in 2004, the oldest national art collection (formerly the National Museum of American Art) will reopen in renewed digs in the Old Patent Office Building, the fourth-oldest public building in Washington. (The only older official buildings in the capital are the White House, the U.S. Capitol, and the Treasury Building.)

A new entrance and lobby at Eighth and F Streets will introduce visitors to the art and portrait gallery collections.

The museum is home to the world's largest collection of American art, the national museum's three floors present over 200 years of achievement by artists such as Gilbert Stuart, Georgia O'Keeffe, and Edward Hopper. Everything from colonial art and 19th-century landscapes to 20th-century realist and abstract contemporary work is found here, in the historic Old Patent Office Building which the Smithsonian's purchase saved from being leveled in favor of a parking lot.

National Museum of American History

- 14th Street & Constitution Avenue N.W., Washington, D.C.; ✆ (202) 357-2700

- ✐ www.americanhistory.si.edu

America's scientific, technological, and cultural heritage is explored here through a wide variety of artifacts and exhibits—everything from a Model T Ford to Captain Kirk's chair. People who love to haunt antique malls will have no trouble spending hours here.

A recent addition deals with tasty pop culture: Julia Child's own kitchen from 1961. Other treasures include Thomas Edison's phonograph, Judy Garland's ruby slippers from *The Wizard of Oz,* a massive steam locomotive and the relatively tiny John Bull steam engine, and a World War II "Enigma" cryptographic decoder.

Conservators have been working for years to restore the original Star-Spangled Banner, the large American flag raised over Fort McHenry near Baltimore in the last hours of the nighttime attack by British Naval forces on September 13, 1814. Their work in progress is usually open to visitors.

National Museum of Natural History

- 10th Street & Constitution Avenue N.W., Washington, D.C.; ✆ (202) 357-2700

- ✐ www.mnh.si.edu

This museum really slowed Mr. C down. Animal lovers will find both joy in the wide range of exhibits, images, and information here, and sorrow, in the rather somber exhibit of animals that are either extinct or well on their way to that fate. Probably the most spectacular attractions are the prehistoric skeletons, particularly of those "terrible lizards" known as dinosaurs, of course, but also the wonderfully gothic woolly mammoth and ground sloths. Inside the museum, the real dinosaur on display is *Diplodocus longus,* a 145 million-year-old skeleton from the late Jurassic period. The skeleton was collected in 1923 in Utah at what is now Dinosaur National Monument.

Also shown are a stone head from Easter Island in the South Pacific, artifacts from American-Indian cultures, and a collection of birds from the common to the rare, including a few extinct species such as passenger pigeons and great auks.

For some, the crown jewel of the museum is the Janet Annenberg Hooker Hall of Geology, Gems, and Minerals. The collection begins with the famed Hope Diamond—the world's largest deep blue diamond. But it goes beyond there, exhibiting more than 7,500 gemstones from half-carat sparklers to 23,000-carat eyepoppers.

National Portrait Gallery

- Eighth & G Streets N.W., Washington, D.C.; ☎ (202) 357-2247

- ✐ www.npg.si.edu

Sometime in 2004, the home of some of the best-known faces of American history is due to reopen within the Old Patent Office Building.

Treasures include Gilbert Stuart's portraits of George Washington, Edgar Degas's portrait of Mary Cassatt, sculptures and paintings in the Hall of Presidents, a collection of early photographs by Mathew Brady, and the *Time* magazine cover collection.

National Postal Museum

- 2 Massachusetts Avenue N.E., Washington, D.C.; ☎ (202) 357-2700

- ✐ www.si.edu/postal

Stamp collectors will think they've died and been returned to sender when they see the world's most comprehensive assortment of philatelic paraphernalia (in other words, stamps). Exhibits are devoted to the history of mail service, from colonial times to present, whether by planes, trains, or Pony Express. Recent presentations have included a history of mass-produced valentines and tributes to the many historical figures immortalized on stamps. You'll even find the postal uniform worn by actor John Ratzenberger in his role as Cliff Claven in the television sitcom "Cheers."

Suspended from the ceiling of the 90-foot-high atrium are three airmail planes, including a 1911 Wiseman-Cooke, a 1924 De Havilland mail plane, and a 1930s Stinson Reliant. On the floor of the museum are artifacts that include a Concord-style mail stagecoach of the type that first appeared in the 1820s and

remained in use in the United States well into the early 1900s.

The National Philatelic Collection was established at the Smithsonian in 1886 with the donation of a sheet of 10-cent Confederate postage stamps. Gifts from individuals and foreign governments, transfers from government agencies, and occasional purchases have increased the collection to more than 16 million items. In addition to the stamp collection, the museum has postal stationery, historic postal material that predates stamps, vehicles used to transport the mail, mailboxes, meters, greeting cards, covers, and letters.

Open daily from 10 a.m. to 5:30 p.m., the museum is located several blocks to the northeast of the National Mall on the lower level of the former City Post Office Building, which operated from 1914 through 1986; the structure was considered a marvel of its time and a prime example of Beaux-Arts architecture. It was designed by Daniel Burnham, also responsible for Union Station a few steps away. Together, the two massive buildings frame the U.S. Capitol to the south.

National Zoological Park

- 3000 Connecticut Avenue N.W., Washington, D.C.; ☎ (202) 673-4717

- ✐ www.natzoo.si.edu

  See the listing under *Outdoors*.

Smithsonian American Art Museum's Renwick Gallery

- 17th Street & Pennsylvania Avenue N.W., Washington, D.C.; ☎ (202) 633-8070

- ✐ http://americanart.si.edu/collections/renwick/main.html

The Renwick Gallery focuses on crafts and decorative arts from

Americans past and present. Two large rooms are entirely furnished in the styles of the 1860s and 1870s; other exhibits have dealt with contemporary crafts, such as the collection of George and Dorothy Saxe. Accomplished ceramic and glass artists give free lectures from time to time as well.

Freer Gallery of Art and Arthur M. Sackler Gallery

- 1050 Independence Avenue S.W., Washington, D.C.; ✆ (202) 357-3200

- ✐ www.asia.si.edu

The Freer became the Smithsonian's first art museum when it opened in 1923. Its initial collection of Asian and American art was a gift from Detroit industrialist Charles Lang Freer.

Its companion collection was founded through a gift from Arthur M. Sackler, a medical researcher, publisher, and art collector. Regular exhibits have featured metalwork and ceramics from ancient Persia, and the sculpture of South and Southeast Asia.

The Freer's collection of Asian art is considered among the best in the world, including some 28,000 pieces of Japanese, Chinese, Korean, South and Southeast Asian, and Near Eastern art, dating from the fourth millennium B.C. to the early 20th century. The American collection features paintings and other works by James McNeill Whistler, including *Harmony in Blue and Gold: The Peacock Room,* a dining room decorated by Whistler for a London patron—the room was dismantled and shipped to the museum in 1919.

The Sackler Gallery's treasures include early Chinese bronzes and jades, Chinese paintings and lacquerware, ancient Near Eastern ceramics and metalware, and sculpture from South and Southeast Asia. Since its opening, the gallery's collections have expanded through purchases and donations and now include the Vever Collection, an assemblage of Islamic illustrated books dating to the 11th century; 19th-century Japanese prints; paintings from India, China, Japan, and Korea; arts of rural India; and contemporary Chinese ceramics.

MUSIC

From Bach to bluegrass, Washington has a robust and exciting music scene. That's not surprising when you consider that the driving engine of the local economy—government and politics—draws bright and capable people from around the nation and across the globe.

You'll find plenty of venues, both large and small, at which you can catch your tunes of choice without wearing out your wallet.

CLASSICAL MUSIC

Alexandria Symphony Orchestra

- Various locations; Information, ✆ (703) 548-0045

- ✐ www.alexsym.org/home.html

If classical music is your love, here's an arrangement you'll enjoy. The Alexandria Symphony Orchestra presents a full slate of events around the area: half a dozen concerts a year, educational performances for children, free summer recitals, and other special productions. Prices are reasonable, too; you can see four of the major concerts for as little as $45.

A recent season included a "Haute Jazz" with pianist Stella Sinakova, a "supper with the symphony" fundraiser, and "Concert Conversations" one hour prior to concert performances. Other performances previously given include a "Scottish Heritage Tribute," a "George Washington Birthday Celebration," and a show focusing on *Romeo and Juliet* as interpreted by Mozart, Brahms, Vivaldi, and Gershwin. Children's concerts enable kids to meet the musicians and learn about the instruments. Call the office for more information.

Levine School of Music

- 1690 36th Street N.W., Washington, D.C.; ✆ (202) 337-2227
- 🖰 www.levineschool.org

This nonprofit community school sponsors a variety of concerts from its youngest of students (age four and up!) to the recitals of the internationally renowned musicians on its faculty. In between, there are outstanding high school and com-

---

MR. CHEAP'S PICKS

Classical Music

National Gallery of Art Concert Series—For over 50 years, the National Gallery has presented a free series of Sunday evening concerts.

Washington National Cathedral Concerts—As beautiful as the music it offers, the Cathedral hosts frequent concerts featuring choirs and guest artists.

---

munity member ensembles, such as the Metropolitan Wind Symphony and the Levine Opera Workshop, which are featured monthly. Ticket prices are inexpensive—in fact, several concerts are free. For instance, the ever popular "Encore Series: World of Jazz," with performances held at the Kennedy Center, is not one to miss!

Many of Levine's shows take place at locations other than the school's performance space. The Church of the Epiphany Series, a program of lunchtime concerts, features Levine's artists-in-residence and faculty showcasing instruments like this church's large pipe organ. A small donation is suggested. A newer series, "Grand Foyer at the Kennedy Center," presents Levine's honor students and faculty in free recitals.

Levine's "Spring Sing" featuring the Senior Singers Chorale, the Virginia Women's Vocal Ensemble Choirs, and the Southeast Male Quartet encompass genres of music ranging from classical, gospel, choral, and Broadway tunes.

You say you can carry a tune yourself? Stretch those vocal chords at Levine's "choral sing-in" (featuring African-American traditional music) or try a community voice class in classical music. In 2002, Levine offered a vocal master class entitled PROJECTION where students learned to project both voice and character. Classes are held on a drop-in basis: Sing-in sessions cost $15 each, community voice sessions $5. Need a home piano tune-up? Levine's head piano technician can be contracted for the task. This way, you can practice singing at home! Otherwise, be sure to call the main office for a monthly calendar of events and for series and class information.

The Metropolitan Chorus

- Gunston Arts Center, 2700 South Lang Street, Arlington, VA; ✆ (703) 933-2500

- 🖰 www.arlingtonarts.org

It began as a volunteer group in 1966, with the desire to bring great choral works to area residents. Today it boasts over 100 members, with a season featuring four regular concerts, the occasional special performance, and a couple of free shows—although none of the prices hits a particularly high note.

Four afternoon shows are spread from November to June, ranging from a focus on Vivaldi to a sampling of great opera choruses. Each single-performance ticket costs $15; seniors, students, and military $10; and children 6 or under free. Alternatively, it's $25 for the full schedule. A few samples of special seasonal events include: *Music Under the Stars* (when it doesn't rain, of course!) and *Choral Top Twenty Count-Down* (featuring TMC's top favorites since it's inception in 1966—and that means lots of free tunes that won't disappoint!)

National Academy of Sciences Concerts

- 2100 C Street N.W., Washington, D.C.; ✆ (202) 334-2436

- 🖰 www.nationalacademies.org

Who says you need cash to be cultured? Not so, as the "Arts in the Academy" program at the National Academy of Sciences presents a series of free concerts. Mainstays of the series include the National Musical Arts, a 10-member chamber ensemble in residence at the academy, as well as outstanding local soloists. The U.S. Marine Chamber Orchestra, which frequently performs at the White House, has also appeared in the series.

The concert setting is the academy's 670-seat auditorium, boasting near-perfect acoustics. Generally, this program runs from October through May; because concert times vary, you should call for a schedule of events. All concerts begin at 3 p.m.; doors to the building and exhibition galleries open at 2 p.m. No reservations required.

National Gallery of Art Concert Series

- Fourth Street and Constitution Avenue N.W., Washington, D.C.; ✆ (202) 842-6941

- 🖰 www.nga.gov

For over 50 seasons, Washingtonians have gathered on Sunday evenings to enjoy free concerts at this fine museum. Many concerts feature the National Gallery Orchestra or the National Gallery Vocal Arts Ensemble, along with internationally known guest artists. To illustrate a sampling of shows: the Jerusalem Trio recently performed works by Ben-haim, Mendelssohn, and Shostakovich; the Amsterdam Loeki Stardust Quartet presented music by baroque composers, and finally the Zurich String Trio played works by Beethoven, Schnittke, and Dohnanyi. A global repertoire such as this rounds out the whole experience nicely (and cheaply), don't you think? Concerts are held on Sunday evenings at 7 p.m. in the West Garden Court. Admission is first-come, first-serve, beginning at 6 p.m., so try to arrive an hour beforehand.

Netherlands Carillon

- Arlington National Cemetery, North Entrance, Arlington, VA; ✆ (703) 285-2598

- 🖰 www.gcna.org

See the listing under *Walks and Tours: Arlington National Cemetery.*

Summer Opera Theatre Company at Ward Hall

- Ward Hall, Catholic University, 620 Michigan Avenue N.E., Washington, D.C.; ✆ (202) 526-1669

- ✐ www.summeropera.org

At CU's Hartke Theatre, during the months of June and July the SOTC presents two professional productions with established opera singers. The company has received high marks from area and national opera critics. Recent performances have ranged from Massenet's *Manon* performed in French and Strauss' *Ariadne auf Naxos* performed in English. Other previous shows include Verdi's *La Traviata* to Poulenc's *Dialogues of the Carmelites*. Ticket prices max out at an eye-popping $35 to $55, but some seats cost as little as $10 for area college students. Admission is free for senior citizens, high school students, and handicapped children.

Washington National Cathedral Concerts

- Massachusetts and Wisconsin Avenue N.W., Washington, D.C.; ✆ (202) 537-6200

- ✐ www.cathedral.org

Besides being a major tourist attraction to thousands of visitors of all faiths, this architectural landmark hosts concerts frequently. "The Great Organ" is featured most Sundays at 5 p.m. The organ itself was originally built in 1938–1939. After years of additions, it now boasts something like 10,660 pipes. These guest recitals are free, as are the organ demonstrations conducted by the cathedral's own organists on Wednesdays at 12:30 p.m. (excluding the month of August).

The Cathedral's Choir of Men and Boys is the highlight of liturgical services throughout the week, especially Sundays. People of all denominations and faiths attend services just to hear this professional group perform. Call ✆ (202) 364-6616 for recorded information on services.

Another resident symphonic chorus, the Cathedral Choral Society, performs major classical works at select times in the nave of the cathedral. Tickets to see this 200-voice ensemble can be pricey, but less so if you don't mind sitting farther away. Most general admission prices run around $15. The Choral Society also hosts other visiting choirs from around the world; and one recent concert featured pianist Dave Brubeck, who has "taken five" from his jazz career to compose religious choral works. For information about the Choral Society, call ✆ (202) 537-8980.

The Cathedral's annual Summer Festival is held during the months of June and July. This free event usually takes place in the nave of the cathedral or outside on the cathedral grounds, and features up and coming professional artists of all types. Call the music office at ✆ (202) 537-6216 for information on all of these programs.

MILITARY BANDS

United States Air Force Band

- Various locations; Information, ✆ (202) 767-5658

- ✐ www.bolling.af.mil/band

Dating back to the 1940s, the Air Force Band has dazzled millions worldwide. From their home at Bolling Air Force Base, the band now performs all around the area, and sponsors other performing groups and guest artists. Most concerts are free, making this a Force to be reckoned with, in Mr. C's opinion.

During the school year, AFB chamber ensembles perform free concerts every second and fourth Wednesday afternoon of the month at the Anderson House Museum (2118 Massachusetts Avenue N.W.). Free concerts during the summer months feature pop and jazz ensembles such as High Flight and The Airmen of Note and traditional groups such as The Singing Sergeants. Summer concerts are generally presented Tuesday nights in front of the U.S Capitol and Friday nights at the Sylvan Theater, in front of the Washington Monument. And when winter blows in, Christmas concerts are not too far behind. These usually take place during the first week of December, at DAR Constitution Hall (18th and D Streets N.W.).

More impressive yet is the band's free "Guest Artist" series. It's presented on Sunday afternoons during the months of February and March, again at the DAR Constitution Hall.

United States Army Band

- Brucker Hall, Fort Myer, Arlington, VA; ✆ (703) 696-3399

- 🖅 www.army.mil/armyband

The Army's Brucker Concert Hall at Fort Myer is another great place to be for free music. Throughout the year, recital and concert series generally take place at 8 p.m. on Tuesdays and Thursdays, respectively. The recitals by soloists and small groups include wind and string musicians. The concert series features many different Army ensembles such as the chorale, brass band, blues jazz ensemble, and full orchestra. Some annual events to watch for include the Tuba Euphonium Conference, the National Trumpet Competition, and the "Spirit of America" celebration.

Call for exact location and times for the later events.

United States Marine Band Marine Barracks

- Eighth and I Street S.E., Washington, D.C.; ✆ (202) 433-4011

- 🖅 www.marineband.usmc.mil

The Marine Band is the country's oldest professional musical organization, and a critically acclaimed one at that; best of all, many of its events are free. Comprising several traditional and specialty groups, the Marine band sponsors various seasonal concert series. Winter Chamber Music Series concerts are held on Sunday afternoons at 2 p.m. in January and February; they take place in the Sousa Band Hall at the Marine Barracks, near the Washington Navy Yard. Call ✆ (202) 433-5809 for more information.

The Orchestra Concert Series is held annually at the National Academy of Sciences (2100 C Street N.W.). Spring band concerts are generally held at the George Mason Center for the Arts in nearby Fairfax; call ✆ (703) 993-8888 for more information. Summer concerts happen Wednesdays at 8 p.m. at the U.S. Capitol Building and Sundays at the Sylvan Theater (on Washington Monument grounds). Also during the summer, parades featuring the Drum and Bugle Corps and the Marine Corps Silent Drill team are held on Friday nights at the Marine Barracks. And finally, Autumn Chamber Music Recitals can be heard every Sunday at 2 p.m. in the Sousa Band Hall.

United States Navy Band

- Washington Navy Yard, 901 M Street S.E., Washington, D.C.; ✆ (202) 433-6090

- 🖅 www.navyband.navy.mil

Not to be outdone by its military brethren, this is yet another premier musical organization offering free concerts around the D.C. area. Its musical ensembles include the 56-piece traditional Navy Band, the Commodores Big Band Jazz Ensemble; bluegrass sounds from Country Current, and of course, the Sea Chanters chorus. Locations for these concerts vary, and some require free ticket stubs for admittance.

Regularly scheduled events include two summer concert series. The Navy Band performs on Mondays at 8 p.m. at the U.S. Capital building; other "specialty units" perform on Thursdays at 8 p.m. at the Sylvan Theatre (on the Washington Monument grounds). Call ✆ (202) 433-2525 for recorded concert information.

FOLK MUSIC

The Barns of Wolf Trap

- 1635 Trap Road, Vienna, VA
- ✑ www.wolftrap.org

Located just down the road from the renowned Filene Center for the Performing Arts, this 352-seat indoor theater (actually built from two historic barns) provides a great opportunity for reasonable priced music. For as little as $15 you can see nationally known folk, blues, and Americana acts such as Lucy Kaplansky, Christine Lavin, Tom Chapin, Karla Bonoff, Tom Paxton, and many others. Check out the schedule and ticket prices on the Wolf Trap Web site. The bar at The Barns of Wolf Trap opens 60 minutes prior to each performance, and you can be seated 30 minutes before the show. Parking is free!

The Birchmere

- 3701 Mt. Vernon Avenue, Alexandria, VA; ✆ (703) 549-7500
- ✑ www.birchmere.com

This D.C.-area music landmark isn't quite cheap, but Mr. C can recognize good value at any price. After all, where else can you see internationally renowned folk artists in an intimate atmosphere? We're talking about performers such as Mary Chapin Carpenter, Lyle Lovett, Shawn Colvin, Jerry Jeff Walker, Dave Matthews, Vince Gill, John Prine, Emmylou Harris, Linda Ronstadt, k.d. Lang, and even Joan Baez—they've all played here.

Tickets start at around $20 and range up to $37.50.

The Del Ray Coffeehouse

- 100 East Windsor Avenue, Alexandria, VA; ✆ (703) 549-4848
- ✑ www.radiodelray.com

Held at the United Methodist Church in the Del Ray neighborhood, local musicians perform on the second Saturday of each month, from September to May. For example, Rancho Del Rays "Country & Americana" tunes will surely get your head bopping! Not enough for ya? Nationally known artists drop in from time to time also. The Del Ray enticed Mary Chapin Carpenter several years ago, just as she was rising to widespread fame.

Two to three artists usually fill out the bill, and sounds can range from South American-style classical and jazz guitarists to "Western Swing Cajun" and acoustic rock. Music runs from 7:30 p.m. to 10:00 p.m., admission is about $7 for the whole shebang, including coffee. Now, there's a bargain.

Institute of Musical Traditions

- 7040 Carroll Avenue, Takoma Park, MD; ✆ (301) 270-9090

- ✍ www.imtfolk.org

Held during the months of December and January, the "Monday Night Concert Series" is an annual event that offers up quality folk and acoustic music in an intimate setting. Rising stars seen here have included award-winning guitarists Peter Mealy, Catie Curtis, and Vicky Pratt Keating. Tickets are $12, or $14 if it's a double bill; refreshments are served. These concerts take place at the Unitarian Universalist Church, 10309 New Hampshire Avenue, in Silver Spring, MD; Paint Branch Unitarian Universalist Church, 3215 Powder Mill Road in Adelphi, MD; NOAA Auditorium, 1305 East West Highway in Silver Spring, MD; River Road Unitarian Universalist Church, 6301 River Road in Bethesda, MD.

Other kinds of events sponsored by the society include annual holiday concerts, with tickets as low as $12; the extremely well-reviewed Ensemble Galilei has performed at these. Call ✆ (301) 754-3611 for more information on upcoming concerts.

Iota Restaurant & Bar

- 2832 Wilson Boulevard, Arlington, VA; ✆ (703) 522-8340

- ✍ www.iotaclubandcafe.com

This dilapidated old storefront has been reborn as a hip lunch and dinner place—not to mention a cool nightspot for the suburban crowd that longs for a bit of downtown atmosphere. The menu offers a little bit of everything trendy— soups and salads, sandwiches, and full meals—all priced around

10 bucks and under (see the listing under *Restaurants—Virginia*). The full bar is well stocked with microbrews and selected wines.

The Iota complements these with music and poetry most nights of the week. At the time of Mr. C's visit, regular events included a songwriters' showcase on Monday evenings; free open-mike music on Wednesdays; and live bands on Tuesday, Thursday, and Saturday, all starting at 9 p.m. Plus poetry readings at 8 p.m. on Sunday, with a featured writer followed by an open mike. Cover charges usually range from $8 to $10 if the event isn't already free. Hours from 11:30 a.m. to 2 a.m., with food served until closing, further making Iota a natural hangout.

Ireland's 4 Provinces

- 3412 Connecticut Avenue N.W., Washington, D.C.; ✆ (202) 244-0860

- ✍ www.irelandsfourprovinces. com

As its name suggests, traditional Irish and folk music are the rule at this club, every Tuesday through Sunday night year-round. There's a $5 cover on Fridays and Saturdays, but the rest of the week there's no charge at all. Local Irish bands fiddle (or whatever) from 8 p.m. or so; food is served Monday though Sunday from 5 p.m. to 11:30. And on a final note, Mr. C wishes a "top-o-the day" to his fellow Cheapsters!

Ireland's Own

- 132 North Royal Street, Alexandria, VA; (703) 549-4535

- www.pattroysirishpub.com

Local bands? Irish folk music? Seven nights a week, with no cover except once a year on St. Patty's Day—and Mr. C thinks that's fair enough to make Ireland's Own your own. Entertainment starts around 8:30 p.m. and rolls along until closing. And check out the authentic Irish food—corned beef, cabbage, shepherd's pie, and the like, served from 11 a.m. until 11 p.m.

Ireland's Own also hosts the occasional Celtic festival (count on March 17, for one), with a marathon of bands playing all day long. A major attraction, according to one employee, is the "Unicorn Song" (y'know, with those green alligators and long-necked geese), which the bar owner gets up and sings every Friday and Saturday night. "He's kind of a nut," she explains. (Mr. C has withheld her name to save her job . . .)

Kelly's Irish Times

- 14 F Street N.W., Washington, D.C.; (202) 543-5433

- www.kellysirishtimes.com

Every Tuesday through Sunday evening, Kelley's features live music that ranges from traditional Irish sounds to folk and acoustic

music. Jolly patrons often sing along to tunes such as "When Irish Eyes Are Smiling." There's never a cover charge to come in and enjoy the entertainment. Check it out. You'll grin from ear to ear as the Irish do!

Kramerbooks & Afterwords Cafe

- 1517 Connecticut Avenue N.W., Washington, D.C.; (202) 387-1462

- www.kramers.com

The "books" part of Kramerbooks are priced at retail, and the same goes for its "Afterwords Cafe." However, the sweet-sounding deal Mr. C does like is the free, live local music that can be enjoyed here Wednesday through Saturday nights. Sets run through four hours, starting at 8 p.m. on Wednesday, 9 p.m., Thursday, and 10 p.m. on Friday and Saturday. Plus, if you get hungry, breakfast, lunch, and dinner is served daily.

Acoustic, folk, blues, or a touch of jazz are among the styles you can expect on various eves. Dawdle over cappuccino and pastries in the cafe; getting a seat, a good view, and the free music make it worth the splurge. Standing room is available in the books area. And, for those 'round the clock caffeine junkies, Kramerbooks is open all night on Friday and Saturday.

Potomac Overlook Concert Series

- Potomac Overlook Regional Park, 2845 Marcey Road, Arlington, VA; (703) 528-5406

- www.nvrpa.org

Concerts, coffeehouses, and condors—all can be found at Potomac

Overlook, located at the end of Marcey Road in northern Arlington. Summer concerts are held every other Friday from late May through September and feature area bands performing folk, bluegrass, and light rock. Held outdoors on a grassy field at dusk (around 7 p.m.), these generally attract a good crowd. There is a suggested donation of $5.

In the fall and winter months, the "Coffeehouse at Potomac Overlook" series moves indoors, to the park's Nature Center, again with a donation requested. Folk music is the specialty. These take place on the third Saturday of every month in the center's auditorium, where you'll also see exhibits and ongoing programs on human and natural history. Percussion Festivals are periodically held on Saturday during the summer months from 5 p.m. to 8. Call the above number for more information.

Seaport Inn

- 6 King Street, Alexandria, VA; ✆ (703) 549-2341

If you're looking for inexpensive casual entertainment along Old Town's waterfront, this is it. The Seaport Inn's pub room presents live music every night of the week except Tuesdays; the sounds vary from solo folk and pop to "open mike" nights (Mondays), with no cover charge or drink minimum ever.

The room itself, in a historic building that dates from the 18th century, couldn't be more atmospheric. It's a warm and cozy tavern, a bit bustling at times, good for just hanging out. A bar menu of sandwiches and nibbles is moderately priced, too. Music runs 'til 8:30 p.m. to 11:30 p.m. or so early in the week, more toward 1 a.m. on Friday and Saturday.

Tiffany Tavern, Murphy's

- 1116 King Street, Alexandria, VA; ✆ (703) 836-8844

Is musical variety the spice of your life? This cozy Alexandria pub offers good, inexpensive food and a whole range of relaxed, live entertainment six nights a week. Best of all, these performances are free.

Mondays, Wednesdays, and Thursdays are open-mike nights, generally featuring folk and acoustic artists. Tuesdays break this up with traditional Irish bands, while Fridays and Saturdays offer bluegrass bands pickin' and grinnin' their way across the small stage. They're closed on Sunday. There is no cover charge and no drink minimum, so feel free to sit and sip.

Across the street and down a ways, Murphy's (713 King Street, Alexandria, VA; 703-548-1717) is another warm and friendly tavern, with live Irish music every night and no cover charge, except on St. Patty's Day. Hours are Monday through Sunday from 8:30 p.m. to 11:30.

JAZZ AND BLUES MUSIC

Cafe Bukom

- 2442 18th Street N.W., Washington, D.C.; ✆ (202) 265-4600

- ✑ www.bukom.com

If you're looking for a change of pace in your musical outings, the cool rhythms of Cafe Bukom offer many welcome options. Namely, you can "savor the flavor of West Africa" at this unique establishment. Live entertainment six nights a week includes jazz on Tuesdays, and various world beats Wednesdays through Sundays. Reggae and African sounds are the most common. Better yet, there's never a cover charge.

In addition to drinks, a wide variety of authentic African food is available; put it all together and you're in an excellent place for leaving the city behind. You'll find yourself experiencing "a slice of pure heaven!"

Fridays and Saturdays jump until 3 a.m.; on other nights the place closes up between 1 and 2 a.m. It's closed on Mondays.

Carter Barron Amphitheatre

*   4850 Colorado Avenue N.W., Washington, D.C.; ✆ (202) 393-2700

*   🖮 www.interchange.org

Tickets to concerts at this 4,000-seat outdoor arena, located at the southern end of Rock Creek Park, are not the cheapest—they usually run around $20. However, you do get a lot of bands for the buck. Annual events include a "Jazz Explosion" and a "Reggae Summerfest" with half a dozen groups each day, as well as zydeco and Native American festivals.

Performances have included The Dells and Pascal Boker's Blues Under the Stars. Delbert McClinton and Don McLean have also been among various all-star lineups, covering a similar variety of pop

---

MR. CHEAP'S PICKS

Jazz and Blues Music

Cafe Bukom—Jazz and a variety of world beats descend on this cool spot—which also features authentic African food—six nights a week, free of charge.

Fat Tuesday's N'awlins Saloon— The music and the food will fool you into thinking you're in the Deep South.

---

genres. Call the above number during the off-season for the coming summer's schedule.

The Carter Barron often plays host to events sponsored by other organizations, such as the *"Washington Post* Weekend Weekends." Four evening concerts each summer feature Caribbean, Latino, jazz, and R & B sounds; all are free of charge. The *Post* has also held weekday lunchtime concerts in area parks on occasion; you can call them at ✆ (202) 334-7969.

Corcoran Gallery of Art Jazz Series

*   500 17th Street N.W., Washington, D.C.; ✆ (202) 639-1827

*   🖮 www.corcoran.org

The Corcoran offers two terrific jazz series, which won't leave you toe-tapping with a hole in your shoe. There is a free jazz series held in the Frances and Armand Hammer Auditorium on Wednesdays, from 12:30 p.m. to 1:30 p.m.; jamming is courtesy of Washington's best local groups.

For jazz with a gospel flavor, plus great eats to boot, try brunch at the "Cafe at the Corcoran." Every Sunday from 11 a.m. to 2 p.m., you can chow down on waffles, chicken, catfish, and Creole sausage while you enjoy live music. All this unbridled joy can be had for a reasonable $20 per person, and $10 for kids. Seating is on a first-come, first-served basis.

There are several other musical series offered through the Corcoran. Though not always inexpensive, there are the occasional lesser-priced concerts. The Hesperus Ensemble, the Washington Chamber Symphony, and the Contemporary Music Forum have all performed here, with tickets priced in the $20 range. Stop in for a calendar of events, or visit the Web site listed above.

Fat Tuesday's N'awlins Saloon

- 10673 Braddock Road, Fairfax, VA; ✆ (703) 385-5717

- 🖥 www.fattuesday.com

Five nights a week, Fat Tuesday's brings the down-home sounds of New Orleans up north. They offer a mix of rock, blues, and jazz—not to mention the food that made "The Big Easy" famous. Various specials on both food and entertainment will keep you from feeling like a po'boy (that's a hometown sandwich on French bread, in case you don't know).

Wednesdays, Fridays, and Saturdays generally feature blues or Dixieland jazz, while Thursdays switch to college-style progressive rock. Sunday is "Fat's Blues Night," featuring the house band, and there is no cover charge. Other nights have a $5 to $7 cover (depending on the band), unless you show up before 8:30 p.m., in which case it's free. Music starts around 9.

Food bargains come Mondays, when po'boy sandwiches are half-price, and Tuesdays, when "Raw Bar Night" offers specials on oysters, clams, and shrimp from 4 p.m. to closing. Also on Mondays, try a new microbrew of the month, and if you're a student, say, at nearby George Mason University, check the deals on Wednesdays.

Fort Dupont Summer Theater

- Minnesota Avenue & F Street S.E., Washington, D.C.; ✆ (202) 426-7723

Fort Dupont offers free jazz concerts on Friday and Saturday nights in the summer. Past performers have included luminaries like Wynton Marsalis and many others. At press time, it was uncertain whether this series would continue; it falls under the umbrella of the National Park Service, which has been going through funding changes. Call for ✆ (202) 426-5961 for more scheduling information.

ROCK AND POP MUSIC

The Barking Dog

- 4723 Elm Street, Bethesda, MD; ✆ (301) 654-7979

In the heart of downtown Bethesda, this joint (formerly called Nantucket Landing) offers live music or a DJ every Tuesday through Saturday night, with no cover charges. This establishment has dark wood décor with forest green trim—and promises a lively, friendly atmosphere. During the week, one can come by happy hour bargains such as $2.50 draft beers and $3 rail drinks. On the Saturdays and Sundays, DJs serve up an array of music ranging from top 40s to old time favorites from the '80s and '90s.

Patronizing the "BD" could easily cause one to have a Pavlovian reaction—you'll just continue going back again and again in hopes of a reward.

The Black Cat

- 1811 14th Street N.W., Washington, D.C.; ✆ (202) 667-7960

- 🖥 www.blackcatdc.com

It's truly a stroke of luck to find a bar where you can hear up-and-coming alternative rock bands for just a few dollars. National acts like Pavement, Bad Religion, and Fugazi have played here, and lots of popular local groups also appear regularly. Generally speaking, live music can be heard five to six nights per week. Cover charge is $8 to $10, most often at the lower end of the scale. And, there's no charge to hang out and listen from the bar.

Chief Ike's Mambo Room

• 1725 Columbia Road N.W., Washington, D.C.; ✆ (202) 332-2211

This Adams Morgan club is as eccentric as its offbeat name suggests, packing crowds in with live rock, jazz, and blues early in the week, and disco dancing toward the end. Mondays and Tuesdays focus on blues, while Thursdays and weekends have local DJs presenting a variety of house music. There's generally free admission Monday through Thursday. Upstairs, "Chaos & Pandemonium" changes the pace by bringing in alternative rock DJs on Fridays and Saturdays. There's a $5 cover on weekends.

Cowboy Cafe

• 2421 Columbia Pike, Arlington, VA; ✆ (703) 486-3467

• 4792 Lee Highway, Arlington, VA; ✆ (703) 243-8010

• ✐ www.cowboycafe.net

These pair of roadhouse-style joints serves lunch and dinner seven days a week (see the listing under *Restaurants—Virginia*), but it's the live music every Thursday, Friday, and Saturday—with no cover—that gets Mr. C's feet a-stompin' and toes a-tappin'! The average month sports 8–10 different local bands at each location, not counting the regular country-rock house band that plays every Thursday night at 9 p.m. Giddyup!

Gecko's

• 13188 Marina Way, Wood-bridge, VA; ✆ (703) 494-5000

Just a short crawl west of Alexandria, Gecko's offers two huge dance floors and live bands three nights a week, with covers running $5 to $7, depending on the group. Tuesdays feature acoustic rock; Fridays, artists churn out Top 40, college rock, and R & B; and Sundays present live acts on one floor, with a DJ spinning discs on the other. Two dueling DJs battle on Saturdays to please a variety of tastes, while Wednesdays feature one of those love-it-or-hate-it attractions, karaoke.

Gecko's also offers a full menu of Southwestern and Tex-Mex food, with dinner deals weeknights from 3 to 11 p.m. Closed on Mondays.

Lulu's New Orleans Cafe

• 1217 22nd Street N.W., Washington, D.C.; ✆ (202) 861-5858

• ✐ www.lulusclub.com

Don't let the name fool y'all—Lulu's rocks. A DJ spins progressive rock 'n' roll tunes for the dance crowd, on weeknights, there's no cover charge, and on Fridays and Saturdays, it's a mere $5. Live bands pop in from time to time; the cover ranges from $8 to $10, depending on the group. Oh, and if you think a joint with "New Orleans" in the name must play some Dixieland, don't despair: Live jazz is offered during Sunday brunch.

9:30 Club

• 815 V Street N.W., Washington, D.C.; ✆ (202) 638-2008

• ✐ www.930.com

Hip, hot, and happening, 9:30 has live bands on weekends and many weeknights, and plenty of action every night of the week. The sound here is mostly alternative rock, with some ska, rap, and whatever else thrown in. The place attracts artists like Midnight Coalition, Bush, Moore and More, Beatlejam, South Elbow and the Eels.

Tickets to live shows run anywhere from $10 to $25. Yikes! Don't worry, fellow Cheapsters—there are several gigs in the $15 range. Lower-priced shows generally happen midweek, naturally. Still, a recent calendar listed some Friday and Saturday night gigs for just $10, so you never know. Take a chance; today's unknowns could be tomorrow's Madonna.

There are some freebies for you night crawlers. Come down to the 9:30 after hours (each weekend from 12:30 a.m. to 3 a.m.) when it turns into "Insomnia." There's no cover charge, just plenty of music and videos. Beats counting sheep.

If you want to keep in touch with what's going on at the 9:30, find out online at the Web site listed above. They also host a conference on digitalNATION, a free online service. You can even download songs from various bands for a quick listen. More info on all this is also available in their newsletter "Volume." Call or stop in to get a copy.

Oxford Tavern

- 3000 Connecticut Avenue N.W., Washington, D.C.; ✆ (202) 232-4225

- ✎ www.oxfordtavern.com

Light years from the hallowed halls of old England (and not just geographically), the Oxford Tavern has lots of great live entertainment and there's never a cover charge. Live shows take place on

Tuesdays, Thursdays, and Saturdays; the selection is a mix of blues, jazz, and plenty of good ol' rock 'n' roll. On Friday nights, a DJ keeps it hopping with a similar mix of sounds. Hence, the locals fondly call this watering hole "Zoo Bar." Entertainment starts around 9 p.m. and jumps 'til 1:30 a.m.

Rumors

- 19th & M Street N.W., Washington, D.C.; ✆ (202) 466-7378

- ✎ www.rumorsrestaurant.com

This midtown spot features a DJ setting the stage every night but Monday, and does its part to please a Cheapster's heart by eschewing a cover at all times—unless you show up after 10 p.m. on Friday and Saturday, when it's only $4. The music is generally Top 40 dance, and the place definitely hops. No lie.

OUTDOORS

Dumbarton Oaks Gardens

- 1703 32nd Street N.W., Washington, D.C.; ✆ (202) 342-3212

- ✐ www.doaks.org

  See the listing under *Museums.*

Fort Dupont Park

- Minnesota and Massachusetts Aves. at Randle Circle, Washington, D.C.; ✆ (202) 426-7745

One of Washington's largest parks, Fort Dupont offers 376 acres of wooded land, which serve as a friendly haven for picnics, nature walks, and various outdoor sports. Although the Civil War fort itself is no more, the former site is marked by earthworks and an explanatory plaque. Dupont was one of 68 forts encircling Washington in the 1860s; runaway slaves found safety within its walls.

Today, the grounds feature a sizable garden, a skating rink, and a sports complex, among other amenities. A hiking-biking trail surrounds the park, while an activity center includes park rangers leading workshops and walks; nature

---

MR. CHEAP'S PICKS

Outdoors

Kenilworth Aquatic Garden— Think of it as a very wet arboretum. Free admission to commune with lilies, lotuses, and more.

National Zoo—One of the country's best, and free.

Rock Creek Park—There's an activity here to suit anyone: boating, horseback riding, tennis, golf, nature trails, and even art?

---

studies; and Civil War exhibits. Most presentations are free; there is a small charge for the ice rink and sports complex activities. Summers feature weekend jazz concerts at an outdoor stage, free to all. The center's hours vary by season; it's open Tuesdays through Saturdays in the summer, weekdays only the rest of the year.

As for those other 67 forts, some of their ruins may be seen while walking the marked trails that make up the Fort Circle Parks. Fort Ward is the most impressive reconstruction; see the listing under "Museums." Maps are available showing the approximate location of the various forts.

The Historical Society of Washington, D.C.

- 1307 New Hampshire Avenue N.W., Washington, D.C.; ✆ (202) 785-2068

- ✐ www.hswd.org

  See the listing under *Museums.*

Kenilworth Aquatic Gardens

- 1900 Anacostia Drive S.E., Washington, D.C.; ✆ (202) 426-6905

- ✐ www.nps.gov/kepa

Not far from the United States National Arboretum (see below), Kenilworth Aquatic Gardens is a 12-acre garden devoted to water-living plants. Over 40 ponds are filled with water lilies, lotus flowers, and other aquatic flora. Cattails and yellow flag irises edge the ponds. Completing this watery world, the garden naturally attracts an interesting ecosystem of turtles, snakes, frogs, and ducks.

Bordering all this is the Kenilworth Marsh, the last remaining tidal marsh in the District. Walk the garden's River Trail for spectacular views of the marsh, the Anacostia River, and nearby wooded swamps.

The trail is equally suited to bird watching, walking, bicycling, and discreet romantic rendezvous.

Kenilworth Aquatic Gardens are open to the public, free of charge. Visitors are welcome to picnic in designated areas. The gardens are open daily until late afternoon, but evening walks can be arranged. The best time to visit is June and July for hardy water lilies, and July into August for tropical plants and lotuses.

National Zoological Park

- 3000 Connecticut Avenue N.W., Washington, D.C.; ✆ (202) 673-4717

- ✐ www.natzoo.si.edu

Hop on the subway to get out to the zoo, a good 20-minute ride from the majority of the Smithsonians on the National Mall, but well worth the trip. One of the few places to see white Bengal tigers (well, besides Siegfried and Roy's Vegas act), it also features a giant panda, Komodo dragons, and other furry friends—all in all, nearly 3,000 animals of 500 different species. And it's all free.

The stars of the zoo evoke a daily panda-monium: Tian Tian and Mei Xiang arrived in 2001. The pandas, born in captivity in the Wolong Reserve in China's Sichuan province, are on a 10-year loan to the National Zoo, which pays the Chinese government $10 million in rent; the money, from corporations and other private donors, is earmarked for projects to preserve the wild panda population in China.

The female, Mei Xiang (which means "beautiful fragrance") is about four years old, and the male, Tian Tian ("more and more") is

about five years old. They are expected to reach breeding age about the year 2003, which should set off even more frenzy.

The giant pandas are on exhibit daily from 9 a.m. to 4:30 p.m.

Famed landscape architect Frederick Law Olmsted laid out the original design for the National Zoo along a valley cut by Rock Creek in the 1890s. Today Olmsted Walk is the central pathway of the zoo, and all the animal trails branch off from it.

The National Zoological Park also makes great efforts to preserve endangered species. An impressive tropical rain forest exhibit is as educational as it is entertaining, to minds both young and old alike. Plus, the daily elephant-training demos at 11 a.m. aren't to be missed! The grounds are open daily, 8 a.m. to 8 p.m., from April 15 through October 15; until 6 p.m. the rest of the year. The animal buildings themselves are open from 9 a.m. to 4:30 p.m.

The zoo lies between two Metro stops. Here's Mr. C's plan to make the most of your dwindling life force: when you head for the zoo, get off at the Cleveland Park station and walk downhill to the zoo entrance. At the end of the day, walk downhill to the Woodley Park–National Zoo station.

Rock Creek Park

- 5100 Glover Road N.W., Washington, D.C.; Headquarters, ✆ (202) 426-6832

Run by the National Park Service, this long, winding oasis begins at the Maryland border, near Chevy Chase, and runs south all the way to the Potomac River in Georgetown—though the bulk of it ends at the National Zoo (see above), which is part of its grounds.

A good place to start is the Rock Creek Nature Center (✆ (202) 426-6829). Here you'll find wildlife exhibits, a library, films, and programs run by the Park Rangers, including nature walks, crafts, and live animal programs. Its planetarium is popular with astronomy buffs of all ages. All activities at the Nature Center are free and open to the public, six days a week; it's closed on Mondays.

Rock Creek Park offers a number of ways for you to take part in sports and other outdoor activities. There's the Rock Creek Golf Course (✆ (202) 882-7332) and the Rock Creek Park Horse Center (telephone 362-0117), each of which charges a nominal fee. At Thompson's Boat Center (telephone 333-4861), you can rent canoes and rowboats to go off exploring the creek, the Potomac, and even Theodore Roosevelt Island. They rent out bicycles, too. The boathouse is open daily through the year, weather permitting.

There are also tennis courts, which you can reserve by calling guest services at ✆ (202) 722-5949. Other playing fields can be reserved through the Department of Recreation at ✆ (202) 673-6788. Reservations are required for some picnic areas; call ✆ (202) 673-7646 for these details.

And there's more! The park is also home to the Pierce Mill (✆ (202) 426-6908) and the Art Barn (✆ (202) 244-2482). Inside Pierce Mill, flour and cornmeal are ground up just as they were in the 1820s. You can tour the millhouse, and even buy these grains to take home. Next to the mill, a carriage house has been converted into the Art Barn, where local artists display and sell their work. Exhibits rotate monthly; drawing classes and other art activities are also offered. Both the Pierce Mill and Art Barn are closed Mondays and Tuesdays.

The United States National Arboretum

• 3501 New York Avenue N.E. Washington, D.C.; ✆ (202) 245-2726

• ✆ www.usna.usda.gov

Administered by the Secretary of Agriculture, the United States National Arboretum has two main functions: educating the public and conducting research on trees and shrubs. Along with the educational programs, fellow Cheapsters will like the fact that they can explore the arboretum free of charge. Stroll through 444 acres of grounds planted with hollies, boxwoods, maples, crabapple, and cherry trees; as well as azaleas, magnolias, irises, day lilies, rhododendrons, and other fantastic flora.

Highlights include the National Bonsai and Penjing Museum and the National Herb Garden—which itself includes the Knot Garden, an example of the style popular in 16th-century England. Specialty gardens display herbs and plants used as dyes, medicines, seasonings, fragrances, beverages, and in industry. In these gardens you'll find aloe, oregano, indigo, wild strawberries, basil, chives, licorice, sesame, English lavender, ginger, hops, and coffee. Maybe this place belongs in Mr. C's restaurant section!

While the Arboretum is usually open year round, it was temporarily closed at Mr. C's press time but was projected to reopen soon. Regular hours are Monday through Friday from 8 a.m. to 5 p.m., and Saturday and Sunday from 10 a.m. to 5 p.m. Call ahead for information about the reopening schedule and guided tours. Hours for the National Bonsai Collection are daily from 10 a.m. to 3:30 p.m.

READINGS AND LITERARY EVENTS

Being both a man of letters *and* cheap, Mr. C certainly knows where to partake of low-cost intellectual endeavors. While not exactly the Algonquin Club, most of these places will provide a stimulating literary experience.

Borders Books and Music

- 1800 K Street N.W., Washington, D.C.; ☎ (202) 466-4999

- White Flint Mall, 11301 Rockville Pike, Rockville, MD; ☎ (301) 816-1067

- 8311 Leesburg Pike, Vienna, VA; ☎ (703) 556-7766

- 600 14th Street N.W., Washington D.C.; ☎ (202) 737-1385

- 1201 South Hayes Street #C, Arlington, VA; ☎ (703) 418-0166

- 5333 Wisconsin Avenue N.W. #5, Washington, D.C.; ☎ (202) 686-8270

- 5871 Crossroads Center Way, Falls Church, VA; ☎ (703) 998-0404

- 11054 Lee Highway, Fairfax, VA; ☎ (703) 359-8420

- 4420 Mitchellville Road, Bowie, MD; ☎ (301) 352-5560

- 3304 Crain Highway #A, Waldorf, MD; ☎ (301) 705-6672

- ✑ www.borders.com

This fast-growing superstore chain presents a packed schedule of readings, live music, and more. Events cover a wide range of topics, like *All Things Considered* host Robert Siegel reading from his book *The NPR Interviews.* Borders sponsors several ongoing activities, including the "Business Lunch," a weekday lunch-hour discussion series.

Music fans will want to check Borders out, too. The "Jazz Conversations . . . and Performance" series brings in some of today's hottest jazz stars to perform and talk about their music. Then, there's the "Lunchtime Musical Proms" series, on various weekdays at noon, featuring local guitarists, pianists, vocalists, and more. And the place jumps with live swing music on Fridays at 6:30 p.m.

This is just the tip of the iceberg; there's so much going on. Stop in to pick up a copy of their monthly newsletter, which details upcoming events. Store hours are Monday through Thursday from 9 a.m. to 10 p.m., and Friday and Saturday from 10 a.m. to 7 p.m.

Chapters

- 1512 K Street N.W., Washington, D.C.; ☎ (202) 347-5495

- ✑ www.chaptersliterary.com

Chapters proclaims itself a "literary bookstore," and as far as the plebeian Mr. C can tell, this holds true. The shelves are filled with poetry, fiction, literary criticism, and biographies of famous writers. Moreover, the events calendar is laced with the names of literary lights like Tobias Wolff and Fran Lebowitz. Generally, these readings take place three to four times a week, drawing crowds of about 75 to 100 people—and sometimes as many as 250!

If you're surprised that this seemingly small store can hold that many people, don't be fooled. The back of the store, where readings are held, is large and enjoys the

218 MR. CHEAP'S WASHINGTON D.C.

natural lighting from skylights. One sales clerk termed it "an oasis of civility," and any bias is easily forgiven here. Store hours are Monday through Friday from 10 a.m. to 6:30 p.m., and Saturday from 11 a.m. to 5 p.m.

Iota

- 2832 Wilson Boulevard, Arlington, VA; ✆ (703) 522-8340

- ✐ www.iotaclubandcafe.com

The name indicates a single particle, but when it comes to local poetry readings, Iota offers a far greater quantity than that. The second Sunday of every month showcases scheduled poets, followed by open readings; bring your notebooks and get up on that stage. Some dates feature specific themes, such as "Asian American Poetry," but any topic is fair game. Best of all, these readings are free. And the inexpensive food is just as creative; see the listing under *Restaurants—Virginia*. Hours are Monday through Sunday from 9 a.m. to 2 a.m.

Kramerbooks & Afterwords Cafe

- 1521 Connecticut Avenue N.W., Washington, D.C.; ✆ (202) 387-1462

- ✐ www.kramers.com

  See the listing under *Music*.

Lambda Rising

- 1625 Connecticut Avenue N.W., Washington, D.C.; ✆ (202) 462-6969

Lambda Rising is one of the most well known gay and lesbian bookstores in the country. As befits their reputation, they've had readings by the likes of Sandra Bernhardt,

Armistead Maupin, and Rita Mae Brown. An average of two to three events per month are all free and open to the public. Lambda also sponsors occasional musical events; groups heard here recently include the Flirtations, the quartet seen in the movie *Philadelphia*. And every December, the Gay Men's Chorus stops in to sing Christmas carols.

Lambda Rising is also a great place to go for information on the gay and lesbian community in and around the District. They have maps, newspapers, a community bulletin board, and more. Hours are 10 a.m. to midnight, seven days a week.

Lammas Bookstore

- 1426 21st Street N.W., Washington, D.C.; ✆ (202) 775-8218

Billing itself as the "women's bookstore for the '90s," Lammas features a wide selection of multicultural, feminist books and more. Readings and special events run the gamut of topics for, by, and about women; there's generally something every week, depending on the season. Recent events featured mystery writer Penny Mickelbury and biographer Dale Harper. Self-defense instructor Rosalind Wiseman gave a demonstration from her book *Defending Ourselves*. Store hours are Monday through Saturday from 10 a.m. to 9 p.m., and Sunday from 11 a.m. to 7 p.m.

Live . . . from National Geographic

- Grosvenor Auditorium, 1600 M Street N.W., Washington, D.C. ✆ (202) 857-7700

If magazines could come to life, then this series would be the breath and blood of the periodical that has chronicled the world for more than a century. "Live . . . from National Geographic" presents films that are even more dazzling than the printed page; lectures by archaeologists, historians, photographers, and others who've "been there"; and also children's activities. Ticket prices run a little under $15 and National Geographic Society members can obtain special discounts. Some lectures are grouped by subjects into series allowing you to buy tickets at a further discount. In addition, children under 12 get tickets for half-price.

Now, Mr. C thinks these tix are worth every penny, but his heart really goes pitter-patter for the "Tuesdays at Noon" presentations, which are free! This series includes showings of National Geographic television specials, educational films, and more. As the name implies, these events take place every Tuesday at noon, same location.

Bring the kids to NG's "Saturday Family Programs." These shows are a broader range of music, storytelling, and more, to amuse, delight, and educate. For more information and a color brochure detailing these events, call the ticket office at the number above.

Luna Books and Democracy Center

- 1633 P Street N.W., Washington, D.C.; ✆ (202) 332-2543

- ✑ www.skewers-cafeluna.com

The name may sound imposing to the not so politically inclined, but don't be intimidated. Luna Books and Democracy Center considers itself "dedicated to enhancing the spirit of community." In other words: It's a place to hang out and talk.

It's also a place to listen. LBDC presents readings, lectures, music,

---

MR. CHEAP'S PICKS

Readings and Literary Events

Iota—The second Sunday of every month showcases scheduled poets, followed by open readings

Live . . . from National Geographic—Presents lectures and films by archaeologists, historians, photographers, and others who've "been there."

Politics and Prose—Everything from prominent national speakers to local authors, and all events are free of charge.

Writer's Center—A wonderful resource for writers, WC hosts readings and discussions for those who appreciate good writing.

---

and discussion groups. There's something going on just about every day, and the space is available to groups who need a meeting space. In-store presentations include author readings, informational lectures, live music, and performance artists. Except for the occasional benefit, all programs are free. Regular group meetings include an "Ecofeminist Coffeehouse," book discussion groups, and writing groups. Store hours are Monday through Sunday 10 a.m. to 11 p.m.

Montgomery College

- 7600 Takoma Avenue, Takoma Park, MD; Humanities Office, ✆ (301) 650-1364

See the listing under *College Arts*.

Olsson's

- 1200 F Street N.W., Washington, D.C.; ✆ (202) 347-3686

- 1239 Wisconsin Avenue N.W.,Washington, D.C.; ✆ (202) 337-8084

- 418 Seventh Street N.W., Washington, D.C.; ✆ (202) 638-7610

- 1307 19th Street N.W., Washington, D.C.; ✆ (202) 785-1133

  And other suburban locations

- ✐ www.olssons.com

Olsson's many locations in the D.C. area offer a large selection of quality remainders for sale, but literary Cheapsters should also check out their free readings and (somewhat less frequent) live music performances.

There's something happening every week at various branches. Most events are held at the downtown store on F Street, near the Metro Center station, so call that number for more information.

Politics and Prose

- 5015 Connecticut Avenue N.W., Washington, D.C.; ✆ (202) 364-1919

- ✐ www.politics-prose.com

For over 10 years, P & P has hosted readings, lectures, and book discussion groups on a wide variety of topics. Three evenings a week, grab a cuppa joe from the coffeehouse side and head over to the bookstore side for everything from prominent national speakers to local authors. All events are free of charge.

Authors previously featured include Vermont poet Ellen Voigt, Washington mystery writer Jody Jaffe, and feminist leader Gloria Steinem—all in the same week!

Authors usually read from their works and are available afterward for discussions and signings. Certain events require free tickets, which can be picked up in advance at the store. Book groups read and discuss fiction on one Tuesday and Thursday of each month, spirituality on the third Sunday, and women's studies on the first Monday. Monthly calendars are available online; see the Web site address listed above.

Reprint Book Shop

- 455 L'Enfant Plaza S.W., Washington, D.C.; ✆ (202) 554-5070

With 40 years of service under its belt, Reprint Book Shop certainly knows its books. This is a general-interest bookstore, with every subject you can imagine represented; they do specialize in computer books, travel, and Afro-American studies—not the most common of combinations, but it seems to work.

Since this is a downtown joint, author appearances tend to be held in the afternoons to attract the lunchtime crowd. Recent appearances include celebrity authors like David Cassidy (a.k.a. Keith Partridge from the Partridge Family); other well-known authors have included journalist Carl Rowan and dancer Judith Jamison. Reprint hosts many local writers, too. Store hours are Monday through Friday from 9 a.m. to 6 p.m.

Soho Tea & Coffee

- 2150 P Street N.W., Washington, D.C.; ✆ (202) 463-7646

- ✐ www.sohotnc.com

You can be forgiven for wondering why the Soho ever bothers to close at all, since its hours are a striking 6 a.m. to 4 a.m., seven days a week. If that's not enough to get your pulse racing, take note of its lineup of poetry readings, open-mike nights, and live entertainment—not to mention (but here Mr. C goes) regular shows of artwork and photography by area artists. And hey, there's no admission charge for any of it.

Every other Wednesday, the open-mike nights feature poetry, comedy, and song; Fridays and Saturdays generally present local folk artists, with an acoustic guitar setting the tone. Other nights occasionally feature music as well; call for schedules.

Vertigo Books

- 7346 Baltimore Avenue, College Park, MD; ✆ (301) 779-9300

You may already know that Vertigo Books has a huge selection of books at low prices (if you don't, see the listing under *Shopping—Books*). You should also know that they have a diverse selection of programs, readings, and other events, all free to the public. Vertigo does ask that if you attend a reading and plan to purchase the author's book, you do buy it from them, rather than from a competitor. Fair enough.

The store's specialties include international politics, world literature, and Afro-American studies. These are reflected in its books as well as in the events on its calendar. Recent literary luminaries seen here include Julia Alvarez, Art Spiegelman, and Eleanor Kerlow; there's something going on at least four times a week. And if you want to talk some more about the latest titles, join the monthly book group, which meets on Sunday afternoons.

In addition to all this, Vertigo Books has also formed a partnership with the Prince George's County Memorial Library system to offer readings in Maryland. This is a wonderful opportunity for people who can't get into D.C. on a regular basis. Call ✆ (301) 699-3500 for details and directions, or visit their Web site: ✑ www.page.lib. md.us. Store hours are Monday through Saturday from 10 a.m. to 7 p.m., and Sundays from noon to 5 p.m.

Writer's Center

- 4508 Walsh Street, Bethesda, MD; ✆ (301) 654-8664

- ✑ www.writer.org

If you're a wordsmith in the area, you may already know about this place. They offer more than 50 different writing and editing workshops. But even if you don't aspire to be the next Grisham . . . or Mr. Cheap . . . the Writer's Center is a great place to come to for readings and discussions.

On Friday nights at 7:30, listen or join in on the "New Words Coffee house." Its offerings can include anything: poetry, improv comedy, staged play readings, or even an open mike (so dust off that masterpiece). The rest of the calendar is filled with similar events; the Writer's Center focuses on lesser known writers and smaller presses. Except for the occasional special event, all readings and discussions are free and open to the public.

As mentioned above, the Writer's Center also offers literary workshops, as well as classes on writing and editing on the job. These courses are fairly reasonably priced, and you'll get discounts if you become a member before you register.

SPORTS AND PLAY: SPECTATOR SPORTS

No, Mr. C can't get you into the Redskins game for free. A cheaper, and more accessible, alternative is college sports; there are highly competitive schools throughout Washington, and most have very affordable prices for football, basketball, hockey, and more. There are often many different sports locations on each campus; the ticket offices, at the phone numbers listed below, can give you all the details. And, don't overlook minor league sports, particularly baseball. The tickets are cheap and the games can be just as much fun as—and less commercialized—than the pro versions.

A few teams to check out:

American University

- 4400 Massachusetts Avenue N.W., Washington, D.C.; ✆ (202) 885-3030

- ✐ www.american.edu

With the exception of men's basketball, it costs absolutely zip to watch American's NCAA Division I varsity teams in action. Tickets to see Eagle basketball at Bender Arena are $8 at the time of this writing, with discounts for kids. The men's soccer team, another favorite, plays at the newly renovated Reeve's Field, which now sports (excuse the pun) an expanded seating complex. Call the information line above for the scoop on other events.

Catholic University

- 620 Michigan Avenue N.E., Washington, D.C.; ✆ (202) 319-5610

Admission to see most varsity teams at this NCAA Division III school is free. Cardinal football games, at DuFour Field, are only $8; men's and women's basketball games, at DuFour Center, are a mere $5. Better yet, students are admitted for free with a valid ID.

Columbia Union College

- 7600 Flower Avenue, Takoma Park, MD; ✆ (301) 891-4196

- ✐ www.cuc.com

It won't cost much to watch the 10 varsity teams in action at this NCAA Division II school. Many of their games are free, except for the more popular teams: Men's and women's basketball, and women's volleyball tickets are priced at a whopping $5.

Gallaudet University

- 800 Florida Avenue N.E., Washington, D.C.; ✆ (202) 651-5603

- ✐ www.gallaudet.edu

An NCAA Division III school, Gallaudet offers 15 spectator sports, most of which are free. Big events, such as football at Hotchkiss Field, cost $10. Men's and women's basketball games, at the Field House, are generally around $5.

George Mason University

- 4400 University Dr., Fairfax, VA; ✆ (703) 993-3270

- ✐ www.gmu.edu

For almost nothing (and sometimes exactly nothing), George

Mason gives you several NCAA Division I varsity teams to enjoy. GMU Patriots basketball games are usually $15 at Patriot Center Arena, specifically designed for viewing basketball. Season tickets are also available. Men's and women's soccer, and women's lacrosse games all cost $8, but the other 11 varsity team games, including baseball, are freebies.

Georgetown University

- 37th & O Street N.W., Washington, D.C.; ✆ (202) 687-2492

- ✍ www.georgetown.edu

Though some two dozen sports are played here—most with free admission—Georgetown is best known for one sport: basketball. Among the former Hoya standouts are such NBA stars as Patrick Ewing and Alonzo Mourning. Tickets for this Big East action top out at $20, but start at a reasonable $10. The Hoyas play at the USAir Arena (formerly the Capital Centre) in Landover, Maryland. Call ✆ (202) 687-HOYA (4692) for tickets and parking discount information. Track and lacrosse teams are also a big draw at Georgetown; call the main number (at top) to find out more.

George Washington University

- 600 22nd Street N.W., Washington, D.C.; ✆ (202) 994-2702

- ✍ www.gwu.com

You can see some serious Division I excitement for practically nothing at GW. Tickets to men's basketball games top the list at around $15, but women's basketball costs only $10 (the "glass ceiling" in reverse?), and women's volleyball is $8. Most other matchups are free, including baseball games, gymnastic meets, and rowing crew regattas. Call the above number for schedules and locations.

Howard University

- 2400 Sixth Street N.W., Washington, D.C.; ✆ (202) 806-7198

- ✍ www.howard.edu

Bison sports, part of the Mid-Eastern Athletic Conference, are a free spectacle with the exception of football and basketball. You can see the football team, ranked in Division IAA, for a general admission price of $15. Same price for men's and women's basketball games, at Buff Gymnasium.

Marymount University

- 2807 North Glebe Road, Arlington, VA; ✆ (703) 284-1515

- ✍ www.marymount.edu

Marymount is a small Division III school—but hey, you can see all 11 varsity teams for free! The big draws are its men's and women's basketball, and men's lacrosse teams.

MR. CHEAP'S PICKS

Spectator Sports

Georgetown University—Free admission to every sport save one; and Hoyas basketball, though often nationally ranked, still costs less than the NBA.

Minor League Baseball—Less expensive, and more pure, than the Bigs.

Trinity College

- 125 Michigan Avenue
  N.E., Washington, D.C.;
  ✆ (202) 884-9711

- ✍ www.trinitydc.com

A member of the Women's College
Conference, in the NCAA's Division III, the Saints offer ticket
prices that are indeed heavenly:
Their games cost you not one
penny. Of the six varsity sports, the
crew team is the only Division I
competitor—and rowing meets are
a free ride.

University of the District of Columbia

- 4200 Connecticut Avenue
  N.W., Washington, D.C.;
  ✆ (202) 274-5024

- ✍ www.udc/index-b.htm

UDC is a NCAA Division II school
with eight varsity teams. The men's
and women's basketball games are
the main "hoopla" here, if you will.

Tickets to see both teams are
only $10 and can be purchased at
their gymnasium, the Physical
Activities Center, on the night of
the games. All other Firebird and
"Lady" Firebird sports are free.

University of Maryland at College Park

- University Boulevard, College
  Park, MD; (800) 462-TERP
  (8377)

- ✍ www.umd.edu

There are many varsity teams to
cheer about at this NCAA Division
IA school—24, to be exact. It's no
wonder that this nationally recognized college can command ticket
prices around $30 (less than the
NFL, but not by much). But don't
despair; discounts are available for

students (free with an ID, in
advance only) and their guests
(usually a $5 discount off the best
seats). And, in recent years, UM
has offered $5 discount vouchers
through local businesses—well
worth inquiring about. Men's basketball games usually cost $25, but
tix are only $15 for non-conference
contests. Less-expensive live action
includes $10 admission to women's
basketball, men's lacrosse, and
baseball games.

Major and Minor League Baseball

The Senators (the ball-playing
ones) are long gone; most Washingtonians follow the nearby **Baltimore Orioles** in their modern,
much-lauded ballpark, Camden
Yards, at 333 West Camden Street,
Baltimore, MD. Tickets, which
can be hard to get, range from
$10 to $30. ✆ (410) 685-9800.
✍ www.orioles.com

Less expensive, and more fun
for those who are tired of overpaid
prima donnas, is baseball at the
minor league level. The season
starts a bit later, and ends a month
earlier, than the major league
schedules. There are several teams
whose home parks are less than an
hour's drive from the District.

The **Bowie Baysox** of the
Eastern League are a Class AA
team, two levels below the big
leagues. Affiliated with the Baltimore Orioles, they play at Prince
George's Stadium, which seats
about 10,000; it's located at the
interchange of Routes 301 and 50,
Bowie, MD. Tickets generally go
for $10. ✆ (301) 805-2233.
✍ www.baysox.com

The **Frederick Keys**, also affiliated with the Orioles, play in the
Class A Carolina League. At this
level, the players are mostly rookies
as green as the grass on the field,

but hey, even Cal Ripken Jr. had to start somewhere. Their home is Harry Grove Stadium, at 6201 New Design Road, Frederick, MD. It's about an hour from D.C., and tickets cost around $10. ✆ (301) 662-0013. 🖳 www.frederickkeys. com

The **Prince William Cannons**, the Class A affiliate of the Chicago White Sox are among the Keys' Carolina League rivals. They play about half an hour from D.C., at G. Richard Pfitzner Stadium, 7 County Complex Court, Woodbridge, VA. General admission tickets are $8 to $10. ✆ (703) 590-2311. 🖳 www.potomaccannons.com

PARTICIPATORY SPORTS

Meanwhile, there is more to "sports" than watching from the stands (or your couch, for that matter). Why not consider some inexpensive ways to get in on the action?

Babe's Billiards

• 4600 Wisconsin Avenue N.W., Washington, D.C.; ✆ (202) 966-0082

• 🖳 www.babesbilliards.com

There is some serious pool played at this clean, rather fancy establishment, and until 4 a.m., no less. Rates are $12 an hour per person, which is not unreasonable. (Cue rentals are $3, or make like Paul "Fast Eddie" Newman and bring your own.)

Babe's also serves a full lunch and dinner menu, not to mention breakfast from midnight to 3 a.m. (see the listing under *Restaurants*). Weekday happy hours feature half-price appetizers and cheap pitchers. Darts and snooker are popular as well.

Hours are Monday through Sunday from 11 a.m. to 4 a.m.

CityGolf

• Old Post Office Pavilion, 1100 Pennsylvania Avenue, Washington, D.C.; ✆ (202) 479-2596

With its upbeat atmosphere, City-Golf is an inexpensive way for everybody to have fun right in town. Practice your putt in a professionally styled indoor miniature golf course, complete with sand traps and replicas of D.C.'s landmarks. Other activities include billiard tables and video games. For those over 21, check out the 19th Hole sports bar, which features happy hour specials and TVs for watching those other kinds of sporting events. Admission rates are reasonable; group rates and party packages are also available.

Hours are Mondays from 11 a.m. to 10 p.m., Tuesday through Thursday from 11 a.m. to 11 p.m., Friday and Saturday from 11 a.m. to 12 a.m., and Sunday from noon to 8 p.m.

Georgetown Billiards

• 3251 Prospect Street N.W., Washington, D.C.; ✆ (202) 965-POOL (7665)

This swanky billiard hall features 19 pool tables, two lanes for dart games, and "the best jukebox in town." Not to mention (but Mr. C will anyway) a large menu of good bar food. Definitely a cool hangout for the gang. The pool table rental rate is $20 an hour, for up to four players (split the tab for a super-cheap night out); $5 extra for each additional player. Rack 'em up. Hours are Sunday through Thursday from noon to 2 a.m., and Friday and Saturday from noon to 3 a.m.

Montgomery Aquatic Center

- 5900 Executive Boulevard, Bethesda, MD;
  ✆ (301) 468-4211

If the idea of keeping fit interests you, but hefty health club fees do not, Montgomery Aquatic's offerings and admission rates will fit you as snugly as a swim cap. Inside, there's a 50-meter pool with eight lanes; two hydrotherapy pools; and a shallow-water leisure pool, perfect for tots. After your swim, hang out in the large spectator area, or, during warmer months, the outdoor sun deck. Outdoor basketball and neighboring racquetball courts are free on a first-come, first-served basis; there's also a children's play area. Inside, you'll find an exercise gym, saunas, and locker rooms.

How much for this oasis? Depends on where you live. Montgomery County residents pay $5 per admission, and $4 for those under 17 and over 60. For non-county residents, it's $6.50 and $5.50, respectively. Discounted passes are available with membership; call the Montgomery County Department of Recreation at ✆ (301) 217-6840. The center is open daily, but you should call for specific open-swim and lap-swim hours.

THEATER

To save money on professional theater in town, consider a little known option: volunteer ushering. Many theaters use regular folks to help rip tickets, hand out programs, or guide people to their seats. In exchange for your services, you can watch the show for free. Responsibilities are light; you'll have to dress nicely, arrive a bit early to learn the layout of seats, and then go to it. As soon as the performance begins, find a seat for yourself and enjoy the show—you're all done. Ushering can even make a fun cheap date, and it's a guaranteed conversation starter afterwards! Best of all, you'll save yourself some cash and help the theater out at the same time. Call ahead to find out if that show you've been eyeing uses volunteers and when they have slots available.

If ushering is not for you, but saving money is still important, try this option:

Ticketplace

- 1100 Pennsylvania Avenue N.W., Washington, D.C.;
  ✆ (202) 842-5387

- ✐ www.cultural-alliance.org/tickets

Similar to the discount ticket booths found in many major cities, Ticketplace offers half-price, day-of-performance tickets to shows at various theaters around the metropolitan D.C. area. The box office is located inside the Lisner Auditorium on the George Washington University campus.

A menu board tells you what's available for that evening (a less-complete list is on a recording at the number above; you have to buy your tickets in person anyway). It's not uncommon to find half-price deals for the Arena Stage, the Olney Theatre, Ford's Theatre, and the various Kennedy Center stages, to name but a few. Occasionally, theaters will offer "Pay What You Can" performances through Ticketplace.

A service charge (10 percent of the original price) is added to each ticket, and be forewarned, Ticketplace accepts cash only. Advance full-price tickets for many shows are also available here. Hours are Tuesday through Friday from noon to 6:00 p.m., and Saturday from 11 a.m. to 5 p.m. It's closed on Sunday and Monday.

Meanwhile, here are some of the good, inexpensive theater companies around the Washington area:

Arena Stage

- 1101 Sixth Street & Maine Avenue S.W., Washington, D.C.; ✆ (202) 488-3300

- ✍ www.arenastage.com

Now in its fifth decade of operation, the Arena Stage is well known as one of the country's leading regional theater operations. Its three-stage complex hosts nearly a quarter of a million patrons each season. Productions range from European classics by Voltaire, Lorca, and Noel Coward to contemporary American plays.

Unfortunately, tickets run in the neighborhood of $40 to $45 a pop, which would usually have Mr. C hunting down a video version. That's why he is thrilled to note that a limited number of half-price

"rush" tickets are available 90 minutes before curtain time. These are sold directly from the box office only.

Another low-cost option is the Arena's "PlayQuest" series, which runs in December and January and offers two shows in the cabaret-style Old Vat theater for free. It's a great chance to see new productions still in the development process. Seats for these plays go fast; call to see what's coming up.

Ford's Theatre National Historic Site

- 511 Tenth Street N.W., Washington, D.C.; ✆ (202) 426-6924

- ✍ www.fordtheatre.org

  See the listing under *Museums*.

Gala Hispanic Theatre

- 1625 Park Road N.W., Washington, D.C.; ✆ (202) 234-7174

- ✍ www.galatheatre.org

Nearing its twentieth anniversary, Gala Hispanic Theatre presents professional-quality Latino theater, dance, music, and poetry. Most performances are done in Spanish, but Gala also offers a simultaneous English translation. After many of the shows, the performers and directors come back out to discuss the work with the audience (again, in a bilingual format). Previous performances have included "Mano a Mano," an exploration of the culture of tango through dramatic poetry, prose, and live music.

General admission tickets are $27. Students, senior citizen, and group discounts are available, too. GHT's theater is up in the Mt. Pleasant area, not far from the National Zoo.

National Theatre

- 1321 Pennsylvania Avenue
  N.W.,Washington, D.C.,
  ✆ (202) 628-6161

- ✍ www.nationaltheatre.org

D.C.'s famous National Theatre
opened in 1835; it's the Capital's
oldest cultural institution. The
National Theatre presents touring
Broadway hits on a regular basis;
accordingly, tickets can be nearly
as expensive as New York itself.
But don't despair, fellow Cheapsters! For starters, these big-time
shows frequently offer half-price
tickets on certain nights to senior
citizens, students, military personnel, and economically and
physically disadvantaged persons.
Call the box office for more
details.

Meanwhile, once a week from
September to April, both young and
old can enjoy special events here
that are absolutely free. Each Saturday morning, the National offers
music and theater especially for
children. A recent show demon-
strated string instruments in performing *Peter and the Wolf* and
The William Tell Overture; puppets,
folk tales, and magic are also
among the free offerings. And on

Monday nights the public is welcome to enjoy various one-act
plays, music, readings, and dance
performances. One recent orchestral
treat, entitled "Music of the Night,"
featured the songs of Andrew
Lloyd Webber.

Seating for both series is on a
first-come, first-served basis; Mr. C
recommends showing up early. Further information is available at
✆ (202) 783-3370, with a recorded
hotline at 783-3372.

Olney Theatre Center for the Arts

- 2001 Olney-Sandy Spring
  Road (Route 108), Olney, MD;
  ✆ (301) 924-3400

- ✍ www.olneytheatre.org

This rustic, charming location
halfway between D.C. and Baltimore is worth the trip for a number
of reasons, not the least of which is
the quality of its presentations.
Seven offerings from March to
September run the gamut from
American and British classics to
comedies, musicals, and more, all
performed by a resident troupe. It
takes place in a setting considerably
fancier than your standard converted barn; tickets, therefore, are
in the $30 to $35 range, with some
discounts available.

Somewhat more inexpensive
options exist, though; the monthly
Acorn Family Projects, for instance,
is held on Saturdays throughout the
year. As the name suggests, concerts featuring music and dance for
the whole family are presented,
with tickets running around $15.
Also, the National Players—the
oldest running classical touring
company in the country—perform
annually, including a deal in which
students get in free. Call for more
info.

MR. CHEAP'S PICKS

Theater

Source Theatre Company—Your
source for innovative entertainment in D.C., tickets are reasonably priced; the month-long
festival in July is renowned.

Ticketplace—Half-price, day-of-
show tix to some of the hottest
(and most expensive) venues in
town

Publick Playhouse

- 5445 Landover Road, Cheverly, MD; ✆ (301) 277-1710

- ✍ www.ptparks.com

Once an abandoned movie cinema, this renovated stage now presents music, theater, dance, and children's events for all ages. And with general admission seats priced at $4, there's sure to be a happy ending for parents.

Renowned professional troupes such as American Family Theater and Theatreworks/USA present musical productions like *Pinocchio* and *The Wizard of Oz*, usually in weekday and Saturday matinee performances. Friday and Saturday nights switch to concerts by internationally famous groups like DanceBrazil and the Urban Bush Women, with tickets ranging from $30 to $35.

There are also student, senior, and group discounts. In addition, local groups of all kinds also rent the theater for their own shows; musical revues, gospel choirs, and student ballet can often be seen here for about $8. Located right off the Baltimore-Washington Parkway, the Publick operates year-round.

Hours are Monday through Friday from 10 a.m. to 5 p.m.

The Shakespeare Theatre

- 450 Seventh Street N.W., Washington, D.C.; ✆ (202) 393-2700

- ✍ www.shakespearetheatre.org

A glance through their impressive brochure may make you worry about high prices, but the Shakespeare Theatre—which became independent from the Folger Shakespeare Library in 1985—has managed to keep tickets at reasonable levels while continuing to pack in Bard buffs season round. Crowds have praised these talented casts, not buried them.

As for those ticket prices, the best deal is to go during preview week, when tickets can be had for as little as $15. Not the best seats in the house, but it's not like you'll have any trouble hearing the chimes at midnight. Seats for regular shows are a still-reasonable $15 to $45; and, if you've got the legs for it, standing room admission runs $10.

The annual "Arts on Foot" festival includes activities presented by a vast array of other troupes, as well as open rehearsals of current plays. Call the box office for information on package deals and group rates.

Source Theatre Company

- 1835 14th Street N.W., Washington, D.C.; ✆ (202) 462-1073

- ✍ www.sourcetheatre.org

Calling itself "the face of provocative theatre in Washington," this has indeed been a prime source for exciting drama over the past two decades. STC is committed to innovative original plays, as well as modern interpretations of classical works. Moreover, it offers deals on tickets, which belie the notion that quality theatre has to cost a fortune.

Source takes on dramas and comedies that hit some tough topics. A recent season included *Snowfall*, dealing with romance and racism at a small New England college; Paul Rudnick's comedy about AIDS (yes), *Jeffrey*; plus adaptations of *The Merchant of Venice* and *Dr. Jekyll and Mr. Hyde*.

STC's month-long "Washington Theatre Festival" in July presents a remarkable 70 new plays and musicals of all kinds, at 10 different area locations. Individual tickets run $25 for adults, $20 for seniors, and $17.50 for students. Each show's third performance is followed by discussions with the playwrights, directors, and actors; the month winds up with an awards ceremony.

Finally, as a community service, the troupe offers free tickets through social service agencies; they also present special plays created in an after school program for homeless children. Good show!

Theater of the First Amendment

- George Mason University, 4400 University Drive, Fairfax, VA; ✆ (703) 993-2195

- ✐ www.gmu.edu/cfa

This professional company performs exclusively at TheaterSpace, a small venue on George Mason's campus. They usually produce three stage works from September through April, each of which can be seen for a not-so-bad $25 ticket price, considering the caliber of the performances. Better yet, Mr. C appreciates discounts of $15 for students of any college (with ID), and $3 off per ticket for large groups.

TFA is a first-rate ensemble, choosing dramas that grapple with social issues, like their satirical *Boomtown.* Call GMU's box office at ✆ (703) 9938-888 for tickets. And, for even less-expensive theater, see the George Mason University listing in the "College Performing Arts" chapter.

Washington Stage Guild

- 924 G Street N.W., Washington, D.C.; ✆ (202) 529-2084

- ✐ www.potomacstages.com

Having recently celebrated its tenth year in show biz, the Washington Stage Guild presents four plays each season, running from October through May. "Neglected classics" are the focus here, according to

someone from the theatre; he proudly cited an example from several years ago, when WSG produced Oscar Wilde's *An Ideal Husband* instead of the better-known *The Importance of Being Earnest.* More recently, *Husband* has seen a new popularity with many troupes.

George Bernard Shaw, T.S. Eliot, and other older playwrights have been given new life by the Guild. Tickets run $22 to $25 for all seats on most nights; but if you're going with nine friends, you'll get a truly impressive group rate—half price!

West End Dinner Theatre

- Foxchase Shopping Center, 4615 Duke Street, Alexandria, VA; ✆ (703) 370-2500

- ✐ www.wedt.com

The West End Dinner Theatre has no problem attracting quality shows to its stage—which it bills as the "area's largest!—nor any problem attracting crowds to its appealing productions. Broadway musicals and comedies are the rule here; *Singin' in the Rain, Annie Get Your Gun,* and *The Secret Garden* have all been presented. Shows are generally booked for a three-month run.

Tickets cost $29 per person for dinner and the performance ($32 on Saturdays). Not bad for your whole night out. Occasional coupon deals found in the *Washington Post* give SIO-per-couple discounts; there are also special rates for groups of 20 or more.

Woolly Mammoth Theatre

- 1401 Church Street N.W., Washington, D.C.; ✆ (202) 393-3939

- ✐ www.woollymammoth.net

Having recently celebrated its 15th anniversary, this Mammoth seems in no danger of extinction. The troupe seeks to produce "highly charged" new plays, and hoofs along the cutting edge with shows that run the gamut from merely sensational to all-out controversial.

Popular efforts such as their recent *Lynnwood Pharmacy* hint that if director David Lynch wrote plays, this would be his stage. *Rush Limbaugh in Night School,* a one-man show by San Francisco comic Charlie Varon, was another recent hit.

Top seats run $25 to $30, something of a theater bargain for the area; however, an even better deal is available at the WMT's "Pay What You Can" preview performances. Each show does this before opening night; true to the name, you can indeed pay whatever you wish to buy tickets (don't be too cheap, now). Reduced price tickets are also available for many shows on the "off nights" of Sundays, Mondays, and Tuesdays, to the tune of $17 to $20.

WALKS AND TOURS

This section is designed as much for the "tourists in their own home-town" as for out-of-town visitors. There's a lot to see out there!

Arlington House

- Arlington National Cemetery, Arlington, VA; ✆ (703) 235-1530

- ✐ www.arlingtoncemetery. org/historical_information/ arlington_house.htm

Once the home of Confederate leader Robert E. Lee and his wife Mary Custis Lee, Arlington House now serves as a memorial to the general, as well as a landmark filled with Civil War artifacts.

The National Park Service is still in the process of fully restoring the house to its original glory. In the meantime, there is plenty to see on a self-guided tour of this huge mansion. You'll get a brochure with a summary of Lee's life; staff members, in period clothing, are on hand to answer any questions.

During the non-peak season, guided tours are available for groups; call for reservations. During the season, groups may reserve a brief introductory talk on the front portico. The grounds of Arlington

House include a restored flower garden and historic slave quarters. Admission is free. It's all within the grounds of the Arlington National Cemetery, and open daily; hours vary by season.

Arlington National Cemetery

- Jefferson Davis Highway, Arlington, VA; ✆ (703) 692-2131

- ✐ www.arlingtoncemetery.com

One of the most-visited places in an area replete with must-sees, Arlington National Cemetery is the final resting place of many of our nation's heroes. Here you'll see the graves of John and Robert Kennedy, Jacqueline Kennedy Onassis, Justice Thurgood Marshall—and, of course, hundreds of thousands of military men and women who lost their lives in the service of their country.

Also here is the Tomb of the Unknowns, where the remains of unidentified soldiers who died in World Wars I and II, Korea, and Vietnam rest today. The changing of the guard takes place every half hour in the summer and every hour in the winter, 24 hours a day. ANC is home to the Nurses Memorial, commemorating the nurses of the Army, Navy, and Air Force; and the Challenger Memorial, honoring the seven astronauts killed in that space shuttle tragedy.

Just outside of the cemetery, on the north side, you'll find the Netherlands Carillon. The 49-bell tower was a gift from the Dutch people to show their gratitude for American aid during World War II. On Saturdays from April through September, professional carilloneurs ring out concerts for the public. During performances, visitors can go up into the tower and watch the action. It's all free of charge.

Bureau of Engraving and Printing

- 14th & C Streets S.W., Washington, D.C.; ✆ (202) 874-3188

- ✍ www.bep.treas.gov

If you believe the government spends money faster than it can make it, wait 'til you take this tour. The Bureau of Engraving and Printing prints all of the paper moola for the country. Matter of fact, they print all the government's securities, including stamps, bonds, and Treasury obligations. Take the 20-minute, self-guided tour, and you'll see pages of money rolling fresh off the presses. Exhibits detail the whole sordid history of money-making.

And how much green will you have to part with to see it all? Zilch. These tours are free and open to the public! Hours are Mondays through Fridays from 9 a.m. to 2 p.m. Reservations are not necessary, but during the peak tourist season you will need tickets, available from the kiosk on 15th Street.

Or, call your senator or representative to arrange a guided "Congressional" tour.

Capitol River Cruises

- Washington Harbor, Wisconsin Avenue & K Street N.W., Washington, D.C.; ✆ (301) 460-7447

- ✍ www.capitolrivercruises.com/crc/blink.html

Departing from Georgetown and heading down the Potomac, this narrated, one-hour cruise gives you great, camera-ready views of the Kennedy Center, Lincoln Memorial, and Capitol Building. The $8-per-hour and $25-per-day charge should be especially worth it for tired out tourists—just for the chance to keep sightseeing while resting your feet. The ship has an open-air deck, and there's even a cocktail bar on board—a capital idea indeed. Tours are given on the hour from noon to 8 p.m., every day but Tuesday; closed during the winter months.

Dumbarton House

- 2715 Q Street N.W., Washington, DQ ✆ (202) 337-2288

- ✍ www.dumbartonhouse.org

Dumbarton House was probably one of the first houses on the heights above Rock Creek in Georgetown. Today, it's a house museum that's open for tours, lectures, and concerts. It's also the headquarters for the National Society of the Colonial Dames of America.

The collection includes Federal-period furniture in the Sheraton and Hepplewhite styles, decorative arts from the late 1700s and early 1800s, and Chinese porcelain. Exhibits highlight famous occupants, including Joseph Nourse, first Registrar of the U.S. Treasury.

Guided tours are offered Tuesday through Saturday from 10 a.m. to 1:00 p.m. Admission is a suggested donation of $5. Better yet, students are admitted free; and group rates are available.

And there's more! Dumbarton House also sponsors a lecture series and live concerts, all free and open to the public. Lectures feature notable historians and experts on the 18th and 19th centuries, while the concerts highlight the music of those same eras. Programs are scheduled about once every two Mondays, call for a schedule.

Enid A. Haupt Garden

- 1000 Independence Avenue S.W., Washington, D.C.; ✆ (202) 357-2700

- ✍ www.si.edu/horticulture/gardens/Haupt/hpt_home.htm

If you show up at the National Mall before the various Smithsonian museums open, a stroll through the garden built across the tops of two of them—the Sackler Gallery and the Museum of African Art—is an ideal time-killer. But the Enid A. Haupt Garden, named for its financial patron, is more than just that. The lush, park-like setting is awash with flowers, trees, and plants of all kinds. It opens at 7 a.m. every day of the year, with closing hours determined by the setting sun.

Federal Bureau of Investigation Headquarters

- Tenth Street and Pennsylvania Avenue N.W., Washington, D.C.; ✆ (202) 324-3000

- ✍ www.fbi.gov/fbinbrief/tour/tour.htm

A tour of the Federal Bureau of Investigation will fascinate anyone who played cops and robbers as a

---

MR. CHEAP'S PICKS

Walks and Tours

Arlington National Cemetery— One of the capital's most visited locations features the final resting place of figures both famous (John F. Kennedy) and anonymous (the Tomb of the Unknowns).

Capitol River Cruises—This river expedition affords scenic views of the District, and your boarding pass is under $10.

Enid A. Haupt Garden—Take a breather from the Smithsonian with a stroll through this park, built on top of the Sackler and the Museum of African Art.

Old Post Office Building—Fantastic (and free!) downtown view from the clock tower.

United States Supreme Court— The buck—not to mention the appeals process—stops here. Take the tour and, if your timing is right, sit in on the weighty decisions that change lives.

---

kid. Naturally, the tour portrays the always-controversial FBI in the best possible light, emphasizing things like citizens' cooperation and firearm safety.

The tour lasts about an hour and is given on a first-come, first-served basis. Reservations are strongly recommended for groups of 15 or more. If you're only in town briefly and want to assure your place for a tour, you can make an advance reservation through your senator or representative.

But wait: because of security concerns, tours were suspended after September 2001 except for school groups. The Feds hoped to resume tours for the public in mid-2002. Mr. C suggests you have a look online, or you can always call the tour office at ✆ (202) 324-3447 for more information. When in operation, tour hours are Monday through Friday from 9 a.m. to 4:15 p.m.

Jefferson Memorial

- Potomac Park, Tidal Basin, Washington, D.C.; ✆ (202) 426-6841

- ✍ www.nps.gov/jefm

Thomas Jefferson's contributions to American history are diverse, but he's probably best known as the principal author of the Declaration of Independence. The Jefferson Memorial, dedicated in 1943 on the bicentennial of his birth, is the majestic tribute to his many accomplishments. The circular colonnaded structure features a 19-foot bronze statue of the third president and engraved passages from four of his writings on the walls.

Accessible from Ohio Drive in Potomac Park, the memorial is staffed from 8 a.m. to midnight daily. Unless of course, there's a government shutdown, but what are the chances of that? Admission is free.

Lincoln Memorial

- 23rd Street between Constitution Avenue and Independence Avenues, Washington, D.C.; ✆ (202) 426-6841.

- ✍ www.nleomf.com

Congress commissioned this memorial in 1867, but with typical government alacrity (even then!), work did not begin until 1914. The now famous 19-foot statue was completed in 1922, and it was dedicated

with the president's only surviving son in attendance.

The seated marble figure is surrounded by 36 columns, representing the number of states in the union at the time of Lincoln's assassination. Today visitors can see the names of the 50 states on all the walls, as well as a passage from the "Gettysburg Address" carved into the stone. As well it should be, the memorial is free and open to the public, around the clock; park rangers staff the building to answer questions from 8 a.m. to 12 midnight daily.

Meridian House and the White-Meyer House

- 1624 & 1630 Crescent Place N.W., Washington, D.C.; ✆ (202) 939-5568

- ✍ www.meridian.org

See the listing under *Entertainment—Museums*.

National Law Enforcement Officers Memorial

- 605 East Street W., Washington, D.C.; ✆ (202) 737-3400

- ✍ www.nleomf.com

Near Judiciary Square, dedicated in 1991, this monument's blue-gray marble walls are inscribed with the names of over 13,000 policemen and women who have been killed in the line of duty. Thousands of plants and trees, with an 80-foot reflecting pool, make this a remarkable oasis in the city. The message carved into the wall explains, "It is not how these officers died that made them heroes, it is how they lived."

Tellingly, plenty of space has been left for further updates. The memorial took on an even greater resonance after the events of September 11, 2001.

Among the names, particular notice is given on these walls to officers by notorious villains from Billy the Kid to John Dillinger, and to various "firsts" in law enforcement fatalities.

The memorial is always free. The Visitors Center is open from 9 a.m. to 5 p.m. on Saturdays, and noon to 5 p.m. on Sundays. The center is located at the above address; the memorial is two blocks away, between 4th and 5th streets.

Old Post Office Building

• 1100 Pennsylvania Avenue N.W., Washington, D.C.; ✆ (202) 606-8691

• 🖳 www.oldpostofficedc.com

Constructed around the turn of the 20th century, the Old Post Office Building became "old" rather quickly, as the district post office moved to Union Station in 1914 and the postmaster general left soon after that. In the early 1970s, the National Endowment for the Arts led a preservation effort and saved the building from demolition; in 1984, after much renovation, it opened for public tours.

The building features a clock tower and electric power plant, both "firsts" when the building was completed in 1899. The clock tower, in particular, is a popular part of this sightseeing adventure. At 315 feet it offers a glorious view of the District. It is also home to the immense Congress Bells, replicas of those found in Westminster Abbey. They were a gift from Great Britain in 1976, honoring America's bicentennial.

Downstairs, a pavilion features a variety of shops and restaurants. It also houses the headquarters of the NEA. Tours are free and given daily beginning at 10 a.m. with the last one at 5:45 p.m.

Old Stone House

• 3051 M Street N.W., Washington, D.C.; ✆ (202) 426-6851

Tucked into the heart of Georgetown, halfway between the Key Bridge and Rock Creek, you'll find what is believed to be the oldest surviving building in the District. It was built in 1765, which is old enough for Mr. C. A free guided tour will take you through its six rooms, furnished with Colonial-era pieces. The house is closed on Mondays and Tuesdays.

Organization of American States

• 1889 F Street N.W., Washington, D.C.; ✆ (202) 458-3000

• 🖳 www.oas.org

The Organization of American States was originally formed in 1826, although it was 1890 before the goal of some level of regional solidarity for North, Central, and South America was realized. Built by contributions from member countries and from Andrew Carnegie, a strong supporter of inter-American unity, the building is open to the public for free tours.

One highlight is the "Hall of Heroes," lined with busts of such leaders as George Washington and Simon Bolivar; another is the "Hall of the Americas," featuring flags from the various American nations. Out on the grounds, marvel at such sights as the beautiful Aztec garden. Admission is free; guided tours are available on request. Hours are Monday through Friday from 9:30 a.m. to 5 p.m.

St. John's Church

• 1525 H Street, N.W., Washington, D.C.; ✆ (202) 347-8766

It's known as "The Church of the Presidents," because every U.S.

chief executive since James Madison has attended services here. Established in 1816, St. John's was originally built in the shape of a Greek cross, a shape that can still be perceived despite numerous enlargements and alterations over the years. Spectacular stained glass windows, most made in France around 1885, are its most impressive adornments.

The church remains an active parish of the Christian faith, with some 6,000 communicants today. The public is welcome to enjoy the guided tours, given Sundays at about 12:30 p.m.—directly following the 11 a.m. service. These are free, as are organ recitals held every Wednesday at 12:10 p.m., from October through July, and lasting 45 minutes.

Union Station

- 40 Massachusetts Avenue N.E., Washington, D.C.; ✆ (202) 371-9441

- ✍ www.unionstationdc.com

Union Station is not quite as active a train station as it was at its peak, but then again it has never looked quite so appealing either. The sheer grandeur, history, and smorgasbord of restaurants and stops ensures your visit will have nearly the same hustle and bustle of yesteryear. Open 24 hours a day, this beautiful old building on the northern outskirts of Capitol Hill is definitely a spot worth pulling into.

An extensive restoration project was completed in 1988, and since that time Union Station—originally opened in 1907—has hosted a number of major cultural and civic events, including dinners and charitable benefits in its cavernous Main Hall.

The 96-foot-high room features great arched doorways, granite columns, and 36 statues of Roman legionnaires. Amble into the East Hall for even more beauty, with intricate, Pompeiian-style murals and a skylight ceiling.

If you're in the mood for shopping, you won't be disappointed: The station's 100 or so retail stores make this one of D.C's popular spots, although don't expect to find many "Mr. Cheap's Picks" here.

Finally, drop down a level to the snazzy food court, offering international cuisine and American fast food—more than 40 different choices. If you'd like to set a spell, check out the two-level Center Café, in the Main Hall, which offers a pleasant perspective on the surroundings; more economical dining options include Pizzeria Uno and the Station Grill, among others. The food courts and shops hours are Monday through Saturday from 10 a.m. to 9 p.m. and from noon to 6 p.m. on Sunday. Guided tours of Union Station are available at $2 per person, but they require a group of 15 to 20 people and must be scheduled in advance. Call ✆ (202) 289-1908 for this information.

The United States Capitol

- National Mall, between Constitution and Independence Avenues, Washington, D.C.; ✆ (202) 225-6827

- ✍ www.aoc.gov

An estimated 7 to 10 million people a year visit the U.S. Capitol. The Greek and Roman-styled building, built in 1793, spreads out to four acres—enough to easily hold two of those research papers Congress likes to fund—maybe three.

Tours were suspended for a while after the events of September 11, 2001, but have resumed—under strict security. Call ahead to confirm schedules and current rules.

As we go to press, tours were conducted from 9:00 a.m. to 4:30 p.m. Monday through Saturday, including all federal holidays except Thanksgiving Day and Christmas Day. Visitors must obtain free tickets for tours on a first-come, first-served basis at the East Front Screening Facility, which is located near the fountains on the East Front plaza of the Capitol. All security screening is done at this facility, and visitors are then escorted by the Capitol Police and the Capitol Guide Service to the Rotunda to begin their tour. All tours are free.

Touring the many levels takes you through the basement crypt, with its historic exhibits; the old Supreme Court chamber; and the Brumidi Corridors, where intricate murals line each wall.

Senate and House of Representatives working sessions are open to the public, but free gallery passes must be obtained in advance; call your senator or representative. Self-guided tours are also available.

United States
Navy Memorial

- 701 Pennsylvania Avenue N.W., Washington, D.C.; ✆ (202) 737-2300, or ✆ (800) 821-8892

- ✐ www.lonesailor.org

"Damn the torpedoes—full speed ahead!" Those words of Admiral David Farragut during the Civil War remain a well-known rallying cry, even today. The exhibits, bronzed engravings, and sculptures at the Navy Memorial match that sense of drama.

Near the National Archives, this outdoor memorial features an immense granite map of the world, a solemn statue of "The Lone Sailor," and two great sculpture walls with bronze reliefs depicting

Farragut's Mobile Bay battle, Captain John Paul Jones ("I have not yet begun to fight!"), and more. A concert stage hosts military band performances two or three times a week, between Memorial Day and Labor Day.

Meanwhile, the adjacent Visitors Center offers even more: interactive video displays, an impressive U.S. Presidents Room, and a glass "Wave Wall" highlighting two centuries of Naval achievements. A movie theater with a two-story screen shows the film "At Sea" every 45 minutes for a nominal charge.

The memorial is open Monday through Saturday from 10 a.m. to 6 p.m. and from Sunday from noon to 5. Admission is free.

The United States
Supreme Court

- One First Street N.E., Washington, D.C.; ✆ (202) 479-3300

- ✐ www.supremecourtus.gov

The Supreme Court, designed by Cass Gilbert and completed in 1935, is one of the most majestic public structures in all of Washington. The front façade is like a Roman temple, with 16 great Corinthian-style columns. At the top of the white marble stairs are a pair of seated sculptures, the *Authority of Law* to the left, and the *Contemplation of Justice* on the right. All around the building are friezes and sculptures that glorify the rule of law as well as some of the leading lights of the court.

The 13-ton bronze ceremonial doors are ornamented with scenes from history, literature, and law, including the Magna Carta, the Shield of Achilles representing Greek law, the Praetor's Edict for Roman law, and the Justinian code for religious law. And that's just the outside. The main hall within is lined with busts of former chief justices and more columns.

The court did not have a place of its own before 1935, meeting in various locations—including some Washington taverns and two different rooms within the U.S. Capitol—during its first 146 years of existence.

Two large exhibit areas detail the history of the court itself, a 23-minute film runs continuously, and talks are given in the courtroom every hour on the half-hour, unless the court is in session. There are also plenty of opportunities to see some real live action. From October to May, oral arguments are presented Mondays through Wednesdays; in June, the court takes the bench to rule on all cases heard during the term. The Supreme Court is open to the public Monday through Friday from 9 a.m. to 4:30 p.m. Admission to the whole circus is free.

Informal tours are given by court employees when the justices are not in session.

On the lower level is a gift shop with books and souvenirs, including some very official-looking clipboards and binders inscribed with the words "Supreme Court," enough to impress any of the dozens of lawyers retained by Mr. C.

The Supreme Court offers a reasonably priced snack bar and cafeteria on the lower level. It's a good place to stop between visits to the Court and the Capitol. Don't expect to sit down next to one of their honors, though; the justices have their own private dining rooms.

Vietnam Veterans Memorial

- 21st Street & Constitution Avenue N.W., Washington D.C.; (202) 426-6841

- www.nps.gov/vive

Few memorials can match the solemn power of the Vietnam Veterans Memorial, with nearly 250 feet of polished black granite walls engraved with the names of more than 58,000 men and women who lost their lives in the fateful war. It was dedicated in 1982; two years later, an American flag and a powerful bronze sculpture of three soldiers were added to the plaza entrance, a short walk from the Lincoln Memorial.

The names are chiseled in stark capital letters, "In the order they were taken from us." An alphabetical guide helps visitors search for particular names. Almost as stirring as the memorial itself are the tokens of remembrance left every day by relatives and friends. These are gathered and stored by the National Park Service.

More recently, the Vietnam Women's Memorial, a sculpture featuring two women tending to a wounded soldier, was added; it lies directly adjacent to its predecessor in the Constitution Gardens. In July of 1995, the Korean War Veteran's Memorial opened to the public, although it remains incomplete at the time of this writing. The exhibit features a wall adorned with faces of veterans, as well as sculptures of soldiers marching toward a reflecting pool.

The Voice of America Studios

- 330 Independence Avenue S.W., Washington, D.C.; (202) 619-3919

- www.voa.gov

On February 24, 1942, the words "Here speaks a voice from America" began the first broadcast of the Voice of America—79 days after the U.S. entered World War II. Today, VOA broadcasts in 46 languages around world, in the belief that "the long interests of the United States served by communicating with peoples of the world by radio."

Voice of America primarily broadcasts news, but it also features programs on economics, science, medicine, technology, agriculture, and music. VOA Europe also highlights music, lifestyles, and sports, designed for a younger audience interested in American culture.

VOA offers free public tours on Monday through Friday from 8:30 a.m. to 9:30 a.m., 10:30 a.m. to 11:30 p.m., and 1 p.m. to 2:40 p.m. The tour lasts about 45 minutes and includes a film, a stroll through the studio during a live broadcast, and a glimpse into the newsroom. Reservations are recommended.

Washington Monument

- 15th Street near Constitution Avenue N.W., Washington, D.C.; ✆ (202) 426-6841

- 🖱 www.nps.gov/wash

At over 555 feet tall, you can see this great white obelisk from just about anywhere in the city. Its cornerstone was set July 4, 1848, but the 3,300-pound marble tower wasn't finished until 1884. It was then capped with a pyramid of cast aluminum, a rare metal at the time.

Obviously, you can gaze up at the Monument as long as light permits, but if you want to take the elevator up, it's open daily from 8 a.m. to midnight from April through August; and from 9 a.m. to 5 p.m., September through March. Admission is free. Ride to the 500-foot level and take a commanding look out over the city; then walk down in scheduled tours, led by interpreters who point out nearly 200 different memorial stones from a variety of sources.

The monument underwent a massive repair and renovation project that was completed in 2002; it's the same as ever, except now the elevator works real fine and there are better visitor facilities throughout.

Washington National Cathedral

- Wisconsin and Massachusetts Avenues N.W., Washington, D.C.; ✆ (202) 537-6207

- 🖱 www.cathedral.org/cathedral

The Washington National Cathedral, fully completed in 1990 after 80 years of construction, is the sixth-largest cathedral in the world. Mr. C recommends taking a tour so you won't miss out on the incredible details of the place. For example: The primary pipe organ (they have more than one!) consists of more than 10,500 pipes . . . the entire cathedral is intentionally asymmetrical, as is the style with gothic architecture . . . statues of the disciples leave an empty space for Judas . . . there are some 1,500 pieces of specially designed needlepoint, showing the faces of presidents, the Wright brothers, Louisa May Alcott, and Edgar Allan Poe (with a little black raven and skull stitched in).

The Cathedral is a functioning church, and so tours are obviously not given during services. Daily mass is from 11:45 a.m. to 12:45 p.m. Otherwise, Mondays through Saturdays, tours are offered between 10 a.m. and 3:15 p.m.; and on Sundays, 12:30 p.m. to 2:45 p.m. Tours take about 45 minutes, with a requested donation of $5 for adults, and $3 for children.

Along with the tours, special events include exhibits in the Rare Book Library; "Medireview workshops" on Saturdays, in which you can do stuff like make your own gargoyle; "Kirken' o'the Tartan," a Scottish bagpipe ritual, in April; and the St. Nicholas Festival at Christmas. Plus organ demonstrations, concerts, and chorale recitals. For more information on special events, call ✆ (202) 364-6616.

Washington Post Tours

- 1150 15th Street N.W., Washington, D.C.; ✆ (202) 334-7969

- 🖰 www.washpost.com

SEE the famous newsroom where Woodward and Bernstein worked to bring down the Nixon administration! THRILL to the experience of walking among the presses where Watergate became the stuff of legend—and proved that the pen truly is mightier the sword. Moreover, just enjoy a FREE tour of one of the country's largest and most respected newspapers.

Each Monday, tours are given every hour on the hour between 10 a.m. and 3 p.m., except at noon. (Lunch is sacred in the newspaper biz.) The walk takes about 45 minutes, during which you see the presses (alas, these are silent until nighttime), the newsroom, and the production room. It's best to call ahead for reservations; children under 11 are not permitted.

The White House

- 1600 Pennsylvania Avenue N.W., Washington, D.C.; ✆ (202) 456-7041

- 🖰 www.whitehouse.gov

Alas, the terrorist events of 2001 resulted in a sharp curtailment of access to the most famous house in Washington. But we can hope that someday there'll be a return to a Washington form of normalcy.

You can still walk around the fence that surrounds the building and learn about its history at the nearby Visitors Center at 1450 Pennsylvania Avenue.

But as this edition goes to press, the only scheduled tours of the White House are offered by advance reservation to school groups.

The Visitors Center is open from 7 a.m. to 5 p.m., seven days a week. It features a 30-minute film to familiarize you with White House history. For information on special White House events, such as occasional tours of the gardens, call ✆ (202) 456-2200.

Restaurants

When ya gotta eat, ya gotta eat. For the dining chapters of the book Mr. C decided not to dig in alphabetically, but rather by geographical area. After all, when you're hungry, you want to eat now, no matter how appetizing some place halfway across town may sound.

The city has been divided into broad sections, so that you can just pick up the book and find the cheap choices and best values in your area.

And if you're planning a day or night out on the town, you can coordinate this section with the Entertainment listings.

All of the restaurants in this book are places where you can eat dinner for around $15 per person (or, in many cases, far less), not including tax and tip. Lunch prices, of course, can be even lower. Even so, all of these eateries serve filling meals of "real" food, not phony fast-food junk.

That $15 limit also does not include alcohol, which is going to be expensive just about anywhere. Have you ever pondered the fact that you can buy a six-pack of decent beer for $5 to $10, but restaurants typically charge about $5 per glass? Restaurants make a disproportionate amount of profit on alcohol—sometimes their entire profit. That doesn't mean you have to order a beer, a glass of wine, or a cocktail; politely concentrate on the cheap eats if you want the best deal.

HAPPY HOURS

Happy hour is a beloved institution in the District, perhaps more so than in any other city Mr. Cheap has explored. Many an unpaid intern has found sustenance on a diet of Buffalo wings and nachos. Of course, few bars offer enough food to make a full meal, so consider a "pub crawl" to fill your tummy. If you keep your bar bill at a reasonable level, this is about as close to a free lunch—or a free dinner—as most of us will ever experience.

It's impossible to publish a definitive list of these offerings because changes can occur from day to day; it's a good idea to call ahead before making plans. And be aware that prices can—and will—change.

A few notes on pub jargon: "Premium" beers are those other than your "domestic," mass-produced brands like Budweiser or Coors or low-priced but still decent brews like those from Pabst or Miller. "Rail" or "well" drinks refer to simple mixed drinks using whatever brands the house prefers. "Top shelf" cocktails are those mixed with requested high-end brands such as Absolut vodka or Johnny Walker Scotch.

17th Street Bar & Grill

* 1615 Rhode Island Avenue N.W., Washington, D.C.; ✆ (202) 872-1126

Located close to Dupont Circle in the Governor's House hotel, this fine little joint holds happy hour from 4 to 7 p.m. Monday through Friday, featuring domestic bottled and draft beer for $2, and microbrew drafts, house wine, and rail drinks all for $3. As if that weren't good enough, you can also scarf up some of their $3.99 appetizers, including chicken wings, homemade potato chips, grilled brochette, calamari, and other delectables.

Bar Nun Club 2000

* 1326 U Street N.W., Washington, D.C.; ✆ (202) 667-6680

This hip music club, a hangout for the twentysomething crowd, could be considered to be a kind of a happy hour heaven, where the sacred period actually lasts all night. This means 2-for-1 deals on domestic beers and rail drinks, as well as $1 off the top shelf drinks. They also offer live jazz and poetry on Monday and Friday evenings. The place features two levels of music and dancing with bars on both floors, and TVs throughout the club. The DJ prefers house, hip hop and r&b, rave, reggae, and world tunes.

The Black Rooster Pub

* 1919 L Street N.W., Washington, D.C.; ✆ (202) 659-4431

Wake up to this happy hour! The Black Rooster features cheap drinks, with a wide variety of premium beers priced from $2.50 to $3.75. Happy hour is Monday through Friday from 4 to 8 p.m.

The Bottom Line

- 1720 I Street N.W., Washington, D.C.; ✆ (202) 298-8488

Here, happy hour is a true Cheap-meister's paradise. There's a different low-price food special every weekday, which can include mussels, clams, shrimp, Mexican fare, Buffalo wings, and half-price burgers. Libations are also available at fantastic prices: microbrews and imported beer goes for no more than $3 every day, and certain afternoons feature specials on margaritas and Skyy vodka. Stop by weekdays between 4 p.m. and 8 p.m. and see what's cookin'.

Buffalo Billiards

- 1333 New Hampshire Avenue N.W., Washington, D.C. ✆ (202) 331-7665

Located near Dupont Circle, this joint offers happy hour from 4 to 8 p.m. on weekdays, where you'll find Bud and Bud Lite drafts for $2.50, and microbrews, rail drinks, and wine for $3. On Mondays you can also score some half-priced burritos and quesadillas.

Bullfeathers

- 410 First Street S.E., Washington, D.C.; ✆ (202) 543-5005

This popular "neighborherd pub" (their pun, not Mr. C's) offers $2.25 Sam Adams drafts, $2.50 Absolut Citron drinks, and $3.75 burgers, always drawing large, lively crowds. Call ahead of time for daily food specials.

Cafe Amadeus

- 1300 I Street N.W., Washington, D.C.; ✆ (202) 962-8686

Stop in for Cafe Amadeus' happy hour between 4 and 6 p.m. on weekdays. Free hors d'oeuvres are available along with some pretty impressive drink specials: Heineken and Samuel Adams drafts for $1.99, and mixed drinks for just $2.25. So what's not to get happy about? The bar is open Mondays through Fridays from 3 p.m. until 9 p.m.

Capitol City Brewing Co.

- 2 Massachusetts Avenue N.W., Washington D.C.; ✆ (202) 842-2337

- 1100 New York Avenue N.W., Washington, D.C.; ✆ (202) 628-2222

- ✎ www.capitolcitybrew.com

Located in the Capitol Hill district, here you can check out all manner of eager beaver interns while partaking of good spirits and some cheap eats. Happy hour runs Monday through Friday from 4 to 7 p.m., featuring $2.75 pints and half-priced appetizers such as pot stickers, quesadillas, and hummus, as well as 25-cent tacos.

MR. CHEAP'S PICKS

Happy Hours

The Bottom Line—You can get a lot of good food cheap here, if you know when to go.

Georgetown Seafood Grill—In addition to specially priced drinks, these folks also offer a 50-cent raw bar at certain hours. The only thing Mr. C likes more than slurping up Chesapeake oysters and clams on the half shell is when he can do so at bargain prices!

Southside 815—This Old Town Alexandria joint offers cheap drinks and tasty appetizers at discount.

Clyde's

- 3236 M Street N.W., Washington D.C.; ☎ (202) 333-9180

- 70 Wisconsin Circle, Chevy Chase, MD; ☎ (301) 951-9600

- 1700 N. Beauregard Street, Alexandria, VA; ☎ (703) 820-8300

- 8332 Leesburg Pike, Vienna, VA; ☎ (703) 734-1900

- 11905 Market Street, Reston, VA ☎ (703) 787-6601

- 10221 Wincopin Circle, Columbia, MD; ☎ (410) 730-2828

And other suburban locations

- ✑ www.clydes.com

After a hard day at work, soak up some of that quaint Georgetown ambiance (even if you're not actually at the original Georgetown location) while partaking of tasty gourmet eats at discounted prices. Come to Clyde's weeknights from 4 to 7 p.m. for a happy hour that features half-price specials on such delectable offerings as crab cakes, Caesar salad, and burgers!

Cowboy Café

- 2421 Columbia Pike, Arlington, VA; ☎ (703) 486-3467

- 4792 Lee Highway, Arlington, VA; ☎ (703) 243-8010

Mommas, let your babies grow up to be cowboy . . . café . . . visitors. (See, there's this old song . . .) The Cowboy Cafe is a popular and rowdy entertainment spot, a home to Texas feeding at its riproarin' best. Here from 4 to 7 p.m. on weeknights you can quaff Bud or Miller for $1.50 a mug/$2 a pint, plus $2.50 rails, $2.25 for house wine, and $2 for domestic bottles. Enjoy half-price burger night on Monday.

Fanatics Sports & Billiards

- 1520 K Street N.W., Washington, D.C.; ☎ (202) 737-7678

- ✑ www.diningmetro.com/fanatics/

A great place to hang out and watch the game, Fanatics has discounted appetizers during its weeknight happy hour, as well as good prices on beverages: Beer starts at $2, with imported varieties priced at $2.50, while mixed drinks are $2.25. Those are prices Mr. C can wrap his hand around. Stop by between 3 p.m. and 8 p.m.

Garrett's

- 3125 M. Street N.W., Washington, D.C.; ☎ (202) 336-6122

This Georgetown joint offers Bud and Bud Lite drafts for $1.50, domestic bottles for $1.70, house wine for $1.50, and rail drinks for $1.75 from 5 to 7 p.m. weeknights.

Georgetown Seafood Grill

- 1200 19th Street N.W., Washington, D.C.; ☎ (202) 530-4430

The Miller Lite, Rolling Rock, and Miller Lite drafts here are $3 weekdays from 4 to 7 p.m., which is an unspectacular deal. However, these folks also offer a 50-cent raw bar during those hours: Chesapeake oysters and clams on the half shell go oh-so-well with a brew or two.

Hamburger Hamlet

- 10400 Old Georgetown Road, Bethesda, MD; ☎ (301) 897-5350

- 1601 Crystal Square Arcade, Crystal City, VA; ☎ (703) 413-0422

- 9811 Washingtonian Boulevard, Gaithersberg, MD; ☎ (301) 417-0773

- ✑ www.hamburgerhamlet.com

Hamburger Hamlet has not one, but two great happy hour deals between 3 and 7 p.m. First, during these hours all beer and "rail" drinks are $2.50 to $2.75. You can also enjoy half price on appetizers, which are just as good as the standard offerings, but smaller portions. Mr. C likes to put together a couple of these plates into his very own mix-and-match tapas meal. The little nachos come highly recommended, loaded with beans, cheddar, guacamole sour cream, and chili. Baby cheeseburgers, hot dogs, chicken wings, and stuffed jalapenos are a few other scrumptious choices.

Kramerbooks & Afterwords Cafe

- 1517 Connecticut Avenue N.W., Washington, D.C.;
  ✆ (202) 387-1462

- ✍ www.kramers.com

Cool and literary as it is, Afterwords Cafe is still a bit pricey; however, you can still stop by, soak up the scene, and actually find some good deals on drink and light bites. Between 4 p.m. and 7 p.m., and again from 11 p.m. to 1 a.m. during the week, you may partake of happy hours that include beer, wine, and mixed drinks for $3.85, as well as a selection of five delicious appetizers offered at $5 each. Choose from gourmet versions of old favorites—smoked salmon tortillas, Thai basil grilled shrimp, and chilled Asian spring rolls with julienne breast of chicken, just to name a few.

Lulu's

- 2200 M Street N.W., Washington, D.C.; ✆ (202) 861-5858 (LULU)

A little slice of New Orleans has made its way to Foggy Bottom. The ornate, wrought iron spiral staircase, stained glass windows, and authentic-looking old-fashioned signposts certainly make you think you're on Bourbon Street rather than M Street.

Thursday and Friday nights are especially popular in the bar area, where the singles' scene is definitely happening. Tuesday happy hours take place all night long; tequila drinks are $3.50, tequila shots $3, and the going rate for Corona beer is $3. Their Wednesday happy hour has $3 Tom Collins and $4.50 Cosmos.

Mr. Smith's of Georgetown

- 3104 M Street N.W., Washington, D.C.; ✆ (202) 333-3104

- 8369 Leesburg Pike, Tysons Corner, VA; ✆ (703) 893-1204

- ✍ www.mrsmiths.com

A popular Georgetown hangout, Mr. Smith's features a happy hour on weeknights from 4 to 7 p.m. with half-price appetizers, $1.50 "rail" drinks, $1.50 for house wine, and $1 off draft beer. Same deal in the 'burbs.

Republic Gardens

- 1355 U Street N.W., Washington, D.C.; ✆ (202) 232-2710

Features an open bar, a decent-sized complimentary buffet until 7 p.m., and some of D.C.'s hottest DJs.

Recessions

- 1700 K Street N.W., Washington, D.C.; ✆ (202) 296-6686

One of Washington's renowned speakeasies (nestled in the basement of an unmarked building), Recessions offers a happy hour every night of the week from 5 to 8 p.m. with $1.50 domestic drafts, $1.99 rail drinks, and burgers at 50 percent off.

Red Hot & Blue

- 1120 19th Street N.W., Washington, D.C.; ☎ (202) 466-6731

That's right, it's an old-fashioned Memphis pit bar-b-que right here in D.C. This is a fun kind of place; its walls lined are with autographed photos, some of them are even the real thing. Happy hour deals include $1 off drafts and appetizers at 50 percent off from 4 to 7 p.m.

Southside 815

- 815 South Washington Street, Alexandria, VA; ☎ (703) 836-6222

- ✐ www.southside815.com

This lively place, located in Old Town Alexandria, is a great restaurant with an excellent happy hour. From 4 to 7 p.m. weeknights you'll find domestic drafts for just $1.75, Coors bottles and rail drinks for $2, and Sam Adams, Guinness, and Bass drafts for $3.75. You'll also get half off on burgers, 25-cent chicken wings, mini-nachos for a buck, and much more. There are at least a dozen TVs scattered around the bar.

Timberlake's

- 1726 Connecticut Avenue N.W., Washington, D.C.; ☎ (202) 483-2266

Timberlake's happy hour starts at 3 p.m. and goes 'til 7 p.m.; along with a dollar off all drinks, you can get 25 percent off appetizers. These finger foods include "Onion Strings" ($2.95), chili con queso ($3.95), baked brie ($4.95), and chicken wings ($5.25, lots of flavors). Timberlake's is open until 2 a.m. Sundays through Thursdays and until 3 a.m. on Fridays and Saturdays.

Toledo Lounge

- 2435 18th Street N.W., Washington, D.C.; ☎ (202) 986-5416

This neighborhood bar in colorful Adams Morgan features happy hour every weekday: 6 to 9 p.m. on Monday through Wednesday, and 6 to 8 p.m. on Thursday and Friday. All happy hours feature $2 domestic drafts, and $3 for rail drinks. You can eat cheap here as well: on Mondays, Toledo offers half-price appetizers all night; on Tuesdays, you can get half price on the Toledo Eagle sandwich, and on Wednesdays you can enjoy grilled cheese and Lounge dogs for half price.

GOVERNMENT CAFETERIAS

There's nothing like seeing your tax dollars at work. And talk about service: There's even someone pushing buttons in the elevator for you at the Capitol building—and there are only three floors! If all this gets you steamed, why not go to these buildings and take advantage of some of the deals available to hardworking, tax-paying citizens. Eateries at these popular workplace/tourist spots offer better-than-average cafeteria food, and lower-than-you'd-expect prices. Also, keep in mind that although some of these addresses may be in different quadrants (Northwest, Southeast, etc.), they're all still in the same general area. Note, too, that security concerns may make access to some of the buildings a bit more difficult than in years past.

Capitol Coffee Shop

- Capitol Building, Room HB11, Washington, D.C.;
  ✆ (202) 225-3919

Tip-free

The service may be cafeteria style, but once you're in the small, elegant dining room, you can easily forget that part. Soft lighting, brass chandeliers, pillared walls, "domed" ceiling, and rich carpeting all add elegance you don't find in most quick-serve joints. Hot main courses change daily, but you can always count on finding grilled steak sandwiches for less than $15, a slice of sausage pizza, or tossed salad for under $3.

Capitol Coffee Shop hours are Monday through Sunday from 7 a.m. to 7 p.m. when Congress is in session.

Dirksen Senate Office Building Cafeterias

- First Street & Constitution Avenue N.E., Washington, D.C.;
  ✆ (202) 224-4249

Tip-free

This building offers two distinctly different dining rooms, both connected by a long hallway, on the basement level. The main cafeteria, the North Servery, is a vast and bustling enterprise—modern, wood-paneled, and broken up into sections of various sizes. Here, you can fill a tray with quick goodies like pasta primavera, fried flounder, barley mushroom casserole, stuffed peppers, and other such "blue plates," each around $5. There's also a well-stocked "gourmet" salad bar, plus soups and sandwiches. It's opened to the public from 7:30 a.m. to 3 p.m. each weekday. On particularly busy days—those rare occasions when all the senators are working—public access may be restricted during the lunch rush.

Down the hall is the Senators' Dining Room, which is quite a step up in class. This room is more sedate, with a maitre d' who will seat you at a booth or a linen-topped table. Service is buffet-style, though, offering things like smoked salmon over penne with cream sauce, or herb-roasted pork loin, plus tossed salads, cooked vegetables, and desserts. The tab for all this is a mere $10.95 for adults and $7.25 for children. There's also a "Create Your Own Sundae" bar, separately priced at $2.95.

In all, that's not bad for a power lunch! And yet, Mr. C didn't see anyone in here who looked, well, *senatorial* . . . perhaps it had something to do with the lack of martinis. The Senators' Dining Room serves food Monday through Friday only, from 11:30 a.m. to 2:30 p.m. VIP Note: A letter from your state's senator is required to dine here; contact his or her office before you head out for lunch.

House of Representatives Restaurant

- Capitol Building, Room H118, Washington, D.C.;
  ✆ (202) 225-6300

Tip-free

Good luck finding this one. It's at the south end of the building; from there, ask one of the guards for directions. Once you get here you'll realize you've found a true gem.

Only the Bennett dining room is open to the public, but oh, what a room . . . fresh flowers, linen tablecloths, padded wood chairs with arm rests, and rich blue wall paper. Considering this opulence, the menu is surprisingly reasonable. Soup of the day is $1.50; bean soup is the real classic here. For a lighter meal, enjoy one of the salads, like spinach, strawberry, and Mandarin orange salad, with poppy seed honey vinaigrette ($6.95). Or, try one of the specials—lemon-broiled scallops with pesto fettuccini ($8.75) was especially tasty. Reubens ($6.25) should not be missed, either.

There's no official dress code, but most men wear jackets and ties. Hours are from 8 a.m. to 2:30 p.m.; when Congress is in session the restaurant is closed to the public from 11 a.m. to 1:30 p.m.

Library of Congress Cafeterias

- James Madison Building, First Street & Independence Avenue S.E., Washington, D.C.; ✆ (202) 707-8300

Tip-free

Hungry bookworms have a couple of dining options on the sixth floor of this modern building. The basic cafeteria is a large, comfortable room offering a pretty good lunch variety—grilled turkey sandwiches, individual pizzas, chicken fajitas, and the like, all priced around $3 to $4. More substantial choices include a rotisserie half-chicken for $5; or perhaps a daily special such as chicken, two vegetables, bread, and a soda, all for $6.25. This room is open to the public Monday through Friday for breakfast from 9 to 10:30 a.m.; hot food is served from 12:30 to 2 p.m., soda and snacks are available from 2 to 3:30 p.m.

Down the hall, also on the sixth floor, is the much nicer Montpelier Room. This is one of the finest of the government cafeterias: Its tables are set with pink linen tablecloths and napkins, while its plate-glass windows offer impressive views of the Capitol dome and the southern half of the District. The food is set up in a central buffet, which may yield roast turkey, barbecued spareribs, soups, salads, vegetables, and the like. Lunch costs $8.50 here, allowing you one visit to the buffet table; desserts and beverages cost extra. Still, for atmosphere like this, with decent food, 10 bucks ain't bad. The Montpelier Room serves breakfast by special request, RSVP to the number listed above; and there's no freeze-out time at the lunch hour, unlike some of these operations.

Hours are Monday through Friday from 11:30 a.m. to 2 p.m.

Longworth House Office Building Cafeteria

- South Capitol Street & C Street S.E., Washington, D.C.; ✆ (202) 225-4410

Tip-free

Here in the cafeteria that serves the House of Representatives office building, there's a curious blend of power and prep school. Important-looking men in blue pinstripe suits discuss the latest movements of the stock market while sitting beside a "Jack and Jill" ice cream freezer. Such confections probably follow a hearty luncheon of a cup or bowl of soup for $.90 and $1.10 respectively—maybe with a chef's salad for $3. If these power lunchers are really trying to be frugal, they might have opted for a hot entrée available for $4.50 to $4.95, or a deli sandwich and chips for $2.45 to $4.30.

It's all in a large, cavernous lunchroom whose lime-green-and-lemon yellow color scheme has apparently not changed in years. Potted palm trees and large plants do help the atmosphere a bit. As with all government cafeterias, there is a security check at the door of the building, which you enter from South Capitol Street.

Public dining hours are Monday through Friday from 7:30 a.m. to 2:30 p.m. The cafeteria is also open on Saturdays when Congress is in session; be sure to avoid any hassles by calling ahead for hours.

Supreme Court Cafeteria

- First Street N.E., between East Capitol Street and Maryland Avenue, Washington, D.C.; ✆ (202) 479-3246

  Tip-free

Slightly bigger than other government dining rooms, the Supreme Court Cafeteria isn't quite as elegant as some of the others described in this section. It's still nicer than the average cafeteria and Mr. C didn't hear any complaints from the Chief Justice. (You're not likely to find yourself sitting next to one of the supremes, though; they have their own private dining room elsewhere in the building.)

Stopping by for breakfast is a treat. Mr. C recommends the blueberry pancakes if you prefer something to satisfy a sweet tooth craving, or try the bacon and cheese omelets if you're in the mood for something savory—either choice is only $3. Lunch includes burgers, deli favorites, and pizza. Other interesting choices in the $3 range include seafood lasagna, bourbon barbecued chicken (hmmm, let's hope the alcohol cooks out!), or lentil chili served over brown rice, which cost about the same as the more pedestrian options.

Open for breakfast Monday through Friday from 7:30 a.m. to 10:30 a.m. and from 11:30 a.m. to 2 p.m. for lunch. Please note: the cafeteria is briefly closed to the public from noon to 12:15 p.m. and

from 1 to 1:10 p.m. to allow court workers to get their lunch.

Here are a few more government cafeterias in D.C. with similarities to those described above: decent, quick food, low-low prices.

THE CANON BUILDING

Canon Cafeteria

- Canon Building, 1st Street & S.E., Independence & C Street, Washington, D.C.; ✆ (202) 225-1406

Open to the public on Monday through Friday from 7.30 a.m. to 2.30 p.m.; it's advisable to call beforehand to confirm the schedule, as it can unexpectedly vary from day to day.

THE CAPITOL BUILDING

The Capital Market Members Dining Room

Capitol Building, Senate side, First Floor, Washington, D.C.; ✆ (202) 224-4870

Tip-free

Open to the public on Mondays and Fridays only from 8 a.m. to 2 p.m. when Congress is in session; the room may be closed for official business.

THE RAYBURN BUILDING

Rayburn Cafeteria

- Independence Avenue at South Capitol Street, Washington, D.C.; ✆ (202) 225-7109

  Tip-free

Rayburn Cafeteria hours are Monday through Friday from 7:30 a.m. to 2:30 p.m. Closed to the public from 11:45 a.m. to 1:15 p.m., so office workers can squeeze in and get lunch.

CAPITOL HILL

Armand's Chicago Pizzeria

- 226 Massachusetts Avenue N.E.
  Washington, D.C.;
  ✆ (202) 547-6600

This other Chicago pizzeria has offered a great deal for lunch for two decades. Mr. C starves himself in anticipation of Armand's luncheon buffet where just $5.99 gets you all the pizza and salad you can stuff yourself with. Several varieties of hearty deep-dish pies are brought out piping hot, along with a full salad bar; kids (age 6–11) get the buffet for half price, while fivers-and-under can nibble for free.

Grab this deal any weekday from 11 a.m. to 2:30 p.m.; on weekends, the buffet is extended to 3:30. Can ya beat that? Sure: they usually have beverage deals, like dollar drafts. Get crazy!

Bread & Chocolate

- 666 Pennsylvania Avenue S.E.,
  Washington, D.C.;
  ✆ (202) 547-2875

See the listing under *Restaurants—Upper Northwest*.

Bullfeathers

- 410 First Street S.E., Washington, D.C.; ✆ (202) 543-5005

Bullfeathers has a little fun with its name, and prides itself on being a popular neighborherd pub (their pun, not Mr. C's). The menu covers all the basics, though the offerings are superior to most bar menus.

Bull Wings (more kick than Buffalo wings?) come in two sizes and have three degrees of heat: mild, spicy, and "Suicide." Burgers come with fries, and are all $7 to $8. Sandwiches, like marinated chicken or crab cake, are a dollar or two more. The desserts are something special, too. Mr. C loved "Neil's Pieces Sundae," with peanut butter cups and peanut butter ice cream, topped with chocolate sauce, fresh whipped cream, and nuts, for $5.95.

Stop by for Sunday brunch from 10 a.m. to 3 p.m. to sample other delicious and unusual concoctions. Try Cajun quiche for $7.25, in which Louisiana crawfish, sweet onion, and Swiss and provolone cheeses are baked in French Quarter custard and served with fresh fruit. Bullfeathers periodically offers happy hour deals at Mr. C's kind of prices. For instance, the $2.25 Sam Adams, $2.50 Absolut Citron drinks, and $3.75 burgers always draw large, lively crowds. Call ahead of time for daily food specials. Hours are Monday through Sunday from 11:15 a.m. to 12:30 a.m.

Burrito Brothers

- 205 Pennsylvania Avenue S.E.,
  Washington, D.C.;
  ✆ (202) 543-6835

- 50 Massachusetts Avenue N.E.,
  Washington, D.C.;
  ✆ (202) 289-3652

Olé! This is quick Mexican food at its best. But, you probably don't need Mr. C to tell you this—just ask anyone who's standing in the long line outside. And these fantastic brothers don't even take advantage of their popularity by upping the prices. The last time Mr. C stuck his nose in, there was nothing over $7—nada! Choose from super burritos with beans and rice ($5.25), or beef ($6.20). You can also get pork burritos ($5), or "healthier" chicken tacos ($3.75). The portions are huge, and the food is fantastic. Order, get a number, and wait. There are only a few stools for dining in, if you decide to go against the carryout trend. But when you manage to snag a seat, expect to be watched by hungry, envious people in line.

Burrito Brothers' hours are Monday through Thursday from 11 a.m. to 9 p.m., Saturday from 11 a.m. to 6 p.m. Closed on Sunday.

Kelly's Irish Times

- 14 F Street N.W., Washington, D.C.; ✆ (202) 543-5433

Kelly's is a fun Irish football pub (soccer to Americans). The menu is basic, but the food is good and cheap. There are lots of appetizers, including pub favorites like spicy Buffalo wings ($6.95), potato skins with sour cream and chives ($6.35), and chili nachos ($6.75). Half-pound bacon cheeseburgers, served with fries, are delicious. Ham and Swiss cheese sandwiches, served with potato salad, are also a good choice. Both are $6.75. Look for daily specials, too. Shrimp salad on a croissant ($9.95) and a chili cheeseburger with fries ($6.95) were featured when Mr. C stopped by. Mrs. C loves to savor a pint of Guinness for only $4.

Hours are Monday through Thursday from 10 a.m. to 2 a.m.; Friday and Saturday from 10 a.m. to 3 a.m.

Le Bon Café

- 210 Second Street S.E., Washington, D.C.; ✆ (202) 547-7200

This small yet popular restaurant is a little bit of the Left Bank on the fringe of Capitol Hill. Look for the striped awning and handful of patio tables out front, although with just a few tables in total, most of its business is carryout. Scan the menu for pithy sayings, such as "Coffee induces wit." *Touché!*

The prices will impress you, both on pastries (scones with cur-

> ### MR. CHEAP'S PICKS
>
> *Capitol Hill*
>
> **Government Cafeterias**—The Capitol Building, the Rayburn Building, the Supreme Court . . . they all serve surprisingly good food for little money. And you never know who you may bump into!
>
> **Le Bon Café**—Behind the Capitol, you'll find this nifty little bistro for soups, sandwiches, and pastries.

rants or dried cherries, each $1.65) and more substantial breakfasts (poached eggs on farm toast for $3.25). On weekends, try an egg-cellent egg casserole with Italian sausage and peppers ($2.25).

Lunchtime brings a unique lineup of sandwiches. Mr. C enjoyed grilled summer vegetables (yellow squash, zucchini, eggplant, sun-dried tomato, and basil) on focaccia bread, a reasonable $6.25. Soup of the day and a half-sandwich come together for $5.95; a daily quiche is just $1.65.

Le Bon Café hours are Monday through Saturday from 7:30 a.m. to 6:30 p.m.; Sunday from 8:30 a.m. to 3:30 p.m.

The Market Lunch

- 225 Seventh Street S.E., Washington, D.C.; ✆ (202) 547-8444

If you like fish, you like it cooked up fresh. And you can't get it much fresher than at the venerable Eastern Market, which has sold the freshest meat, fish, and produce in town since 1873. Tucked into a corner of the main market building, Market Lunch looks like an after-thought: a walk-up counter and a rickety collection of wooden tables and chairs for shoppers who want a quick bite until they can get some "real" lunch somewhere else.

But that's just not the case. In fact, this hidden gem has been reviewed in publications from the *New York Times* to the *Condé Nast Traveler*. It offers huge luncheon platters, mostly priced under $10. The fried shrimp plate ($9.50) is big and tasty; the jumbo back fin crab cake platter ($9.25) is as good as you'd find at any four-star seaside restaurant. Even at these reasonable prices, such plates include homemade bread and two side orders. Or, if you really do want a snack, grab a fried filet sandwich for $5.25. The North Carolina style barbeque (pulled pork with red pepper vinegar base versus tomato Alabama style) is also a menu item not to miss out on.

Market Lunch also serves up hearty breakfasts, no doubt to stoke the furnaces of the folks who put in a hard day's work here. Two eggs, toast, and home fries will only set you back $1.95; even less for eggs and yummy scrapple. Or go fancy with a plate of pecan waffles ($4.25) and add a cup of espresso for just $1.

The place always seems to be full, or at least crowded—with people who know the real thing and want that genuine market atmosphere. As a result, this is not a place to linger over your catch; signs ask that you move along when you're done.

Maybe another reason for the crowds is the limited access to these goodies: Market Lunch hours are Tuesday through Friday from 7:30 a.m. to noon; Saturday and Sunday from 11 a.m. to 3:30 p.m. They're open Tuesdays through Saturdays from 7:30 a.m. to 2:30 p.m.

My Brother's Place

- 237 Second Street N.W., Washington, D.C.; ✆ (202) 347-1350

My Brothers Place offers special discounts on light bites the first three days of every week: For instance, on Monday's you can buy either half-priced burgers or three tacos for only $3.99; on Tuesdays you can get 30 chicken wings for $19.99 and refills for $7.99; and finally, on Wednesdays a basket of 20 spicy shrimp are available for $12.95.

The weekend usually gets started early on Thursday with $1.50 bottles of Bud and Bud Lite, followed by $4.95 pitchers of domestic beer. On Friday you'll enjoy $12 "all-you-care-to-drink" bargains with rail drinks and 17 beers on draft. So by the time Friday rolls around, you're ready to visit for a bit of "down time" before the start of the next week's resumes. Catholic University students, civil servants, and Hill workers flock here and the reasons are obvious; they know a Mr. C favorite when they see it.

Hours are Monday through Sunday from 11 a.m. to 1 a.m.

Sherrill's Restaurant and Bakery

- 233 Pennsylvania Avenue S.E., Washington, D.C.; ✆ (202) 544-2480

Here's one of those longtime legends that somehow turns cheapness into charm. Sherrill's is little more than your basic luncheonette, a holdover from decades past—outfitted with old wooden paneling, old wooden booths, and old wooden waitresses (only kidding).

It's the kinda place where you can roll in, park at the well-worn counter, and order up a few slices of fresh roast turkey and gravy, with two vegetables on the side, for a mere $8.50. Or perhaps a pork sandwich for $3.25, or a bowl of homemade chili con carne for $3.85, with fresh baked bread. That's the other thing this joint is known for: Up at the front, Sherrill's bakery serves pastry treats for folks on the go.

With its location just behind Capitol Hill, most of Sherrill's patrons are congressional workers. But the place is also open on weekends (when it serves up steak and eggs for $6.95). It's really a cool hangout, if you're the Mr. C type.

Sherrill's hours are Monday through Friday from 6 a.m. to 7 p.m.; Saturday and Sunday from 7 a.m. to 7 p.m.

Thai Roma

- 313 Pennsylvania Avenue S.E., Washington, D.C.;
  ✆ (202) 544-2338

First, to clear up the name thing: Thai cuisine is served at this Capitol Hill spot, which was formerly an Italian restaurant. Since their Thai pizzas were getting the best responses a few years back, the Italian part of the menu was scrapped. And they've taken to Thai, well, like a duck takes to water. Hey . . . that's just good business!

Appetizers run $5 to $7, and include egg rolls, skewers of chicken and pork satay, and spicy Thai choices like *yurn pla murek*, calamari with lemon grass. (That's sort of Italian.) Mr. C's eye was caught by the house curry dishes, including green curry chicken ($9.95) and a seafood combo with red panang curry paste, basil, and lemon grass leaves ($12.95). There's also a wealth of vegetarian options, like tofu with cashews ($8.95) and *sam sa hai*, Chinese eggplant and mixed vegetables, all sautéed in a curry coconut sauce ($9.95). There are even a few pasta

options, further holdovers from the past, in the $10 range.

Thai Roma hours are Monday through Friday from 11:30 a.m. to 10:30 p.m.; Saturday and Sunday from noon to 11 p.m.

Tune Inn

- 331½ Pennsylvania Avenue S.E., Washington, D.C.;
  ✆ (202) 543-2725

According to local legend, this popular Capital Hill establishment is the very place where bipartisan power couple James Carville and Mary Matalin had their first date. Deer heads dot the walls of this dark, cavernous venue and may have served as a topic of discussion for their first debate—NRA and gun control. Who knows, but it's purported that they didn't stick around for long. . . !

Regardless, the atmosphere is always fun and the food is cheap. It doesn't take long for this tiny venue to get packed with a young, boisterous crowd, as the Tune Inn is an ideal spot for both breakfast and lunch specials. The cheeseburger and fries are guaranteed to please and have gained undisputed popularity amongst those working on the Hill. In any case, whether you're a political junkie or not, the $1 off drink deals means that everyone can eventually get on the "same channel."

Union Station Food Court

- 50 Massachusetts Avenue N.E., Washington, D.C.;
  ✆ (202) 289-1908

- ✑ www.unionstationdc.com

While Union Station is primarily known as the pulse of the district's Metro, Amtrak, and local commuter train services (serving routes to Virginia and Maryland), the shops and food court are not to be missed, as there's a virtual rail yard of cheap eats to be had there.

When entering Union Station from the street level of the main entrance, walk straight back until you spot a staircase descending down to the lower level, towards the entrance of the Union Station Metro station. Here, you'll find an array of cafes and casual dining venues. The list of dining establishments is long, and Mr. C has decided to note them here for quick reference. Be sure to drop by, since this is a "feeding frenzy" from a bargain perspective.

Cafes:

Au Bon Pan
✆ (202) 898-0299

Caffee Renee
✆ (202) 216-0002

Corner Bakery Café
✆ (202) 371-8811

Johnny Rockets
✆ (202) 289-6969

Sbarro—The Italian Eatery
✆ (202) 289-0767

Casual Dining:

Acropolis
✆ (202) 785-7333

Auntie Anne's
✆ (202) 289-9838

Ben & Jerry's
✆ (202) 842-2887

Boardwalk Fries
✆ (202) 371-2860

Bucks County Coffee Co.
✆ (202) 682-1326

Burrito Brothers
✆ (202) 289-3652

Cajun Grill
✆ (202) 842-0028

Cookie Café
✆ (202) 682-3060

Flamers Charburgers
✆ (202) 371-8253

Frank and Stein Dogs and Drafts
✆ (202) 289-3661

Georgetown Seafood Grill
✆ (202) 842-2344

Gourmet Corner
✆ (202) 898-2010

Great Steak & Potato
✆ (202) 371-9830

Haagen Dazs
✆ (202) 789-0953

Indian Delight/Bombay Express
✆ (202) 842-1040

Kabuki Sushi Bar
✆ (202) 789-1159

King Bar-B-Q
✆ (202) 898-9300

Larry's Cookies
✆ (202) 289-7586

Le Petit Bistro
✆ (202) 371-1233

Mamma Ilardo's Pizzeria
✆ (202) 371-9072

New York Deli
✆ (202) 216-0909

Nothing But Donuts
✆ (202) 408-9464

Panda's Rice Bowl
✆ (202) 789-0382

Paradise Smoothies
✆ (202) 289-7560

Pasta T' Go-Go
✆ (202) 289-4720

Primo Cappuccino
✆ (202) 898-0292

Salad Works
✆ (202) 898-0550

Soup Nutsy
✆ (202) 216-0160

Sweet Factory
✆ (202) 371-8660

The Great Steak and Fry
✆ (202) 371-9830

Vaccaro's
✆ (202) 371-2855

Wingmaster's Grill
✆ (202) 371-9614

DOWNTOWN AREA

Including Foggy Bottom, Farragut, and the Mall

AV Ristorante Italiano

- 607 New York Avenue N.W., Washington, D.C.; ✆ (202) 737-0550

This large, simple restaurant and lounge is the real thing for Italian food. Start off with a cocktail from their full bar, and perhaps a stuffed artichoke for $5. Follow these with a big plate of pasta; around an average price of $6.75, with enough food to make you cry "Mama!"

Or, try the fine, thin veal parmigiana, served with a big plate of spaghetti, all for $9.25. Mussels over linguine goes for just $8.75. And sausage pizzaiola, using sausage made on the premises, is a house specialty at $8.25.

Speaking of pizzas, AV has lots to choose from in that department as well. A small white pizza, plenty for one or as an appetizer for two to share, is $8. Other kinds of pies range from $9 or so up to $10 (for the extra large!), and they are terrific.

Still have a little room? Look no further than AV's homemade tiramisu. Mmmm!

AV offers specials on a daily basis. Have a look at the menu board in the entrance hall, or call prior to arriving at the restaurant.

The neighborhood is not considered one of the District's finest, but if you're at all skittish, take note that the precinct police station is on the next block. The restaurant is open weekdays for lunch and dinner, until midnight; Saturdays offer dinner only, from 5:30 to midnight. They're closed on Sundays.

The Black Rooster Pub

- 1919 L Street N.W., Washington, D.C.; ✆ (202) 659-4431

Hear ye! Hear ye! The Black Rooster Pub brings a touch of England to the District. Five dartboards stand at the ready, and the bar features European imports, including Bass, Guinness, and Harp. Actually, that's about as British as it gets. With the exception of fish and chips ($5.95), the menu is pretty all-American. The dinner menu includes a tempting list of appetizers like beer batter onion rings ($2.50) or potato skins ($3.75).

Skip the main course and order nachos smothered in homemade chili, cheddar, jalapenos, black olives, salsa, and sour cream ($6.95). Pub fare includes a variety of sandwiches, like the "Classic Pub Club"—smoked turkey, honey-baked ham, Swiss and American cheese, and bacon. All sandwiches are $6.95 or under. The flame-grilled half-pound burgers can't be beat: A plain sirloin burger starts at $5.95, while variations on this classic are $6.95—bacon cheeseburgers, mushroom and mozzarella, and Tex-Mex are just a few of your choices.

Happy hour at The Black Rooster is offered Mondays through Fridays from 4 to 8 p.m. During that window of time you'll enjoy cheap drinks, with a wide variety of premium beers priced from $2.50 to $3.75.

Black Rooster is open Monday through Thursday from 11:30 a.m. to 2 a.m., Friday from 11:30 a.m. until 3 a.m., and Saturday from 6 p.m. to 3 a.m.

The Bottom Line

• 1720 I Street N.W., Washington, D.C.; ✆ (202) 298-8488

The Bottom Line offers classic pub fare and a place to unwind after a long day. The menu prices will definitely help you maintain a healthy bottom line, with nothing over $10: Burgers ($7 to $8), Mexican favorites ($7.50 beef and bean burrito), and large salads ($7.95 average) are among the good choices.

The best budget-buster is happy hour (weekdays between 4 and 8 p.m.), where this joint becomes a true Cheapmeister's paradise. There's a different low-price food special every weekday, which can include mussels, clams, shrimp, Mexican, Buffalo wings, and half-price burgers. Of course, the libations are also available at fantastic prices: Microbrews and imported beer goes for no more than $3 every day, and certain afternoons feature specials on margaritas and Skyy vodka. Wow.

Hours are Monday through Sunday from 11:30 p.m. to 3 a.m.

The Brickskeller

• 1523 22nd Street N.W., Washington, D.C.; ✆ (202) 293-1885

• ✐ www.thebrickskeller.com

If the city had a beer museum, it would be the Brickskeller, family owned and operated since 1957. The decor consists of bottles and cans from all over the world, beer ads, and posters. Sample one of the over 850 domestic and imported beers available. Prices start at a couple dollars and go up from there (*waaay* up, actually, so be sure to check the price before you order).

If you'd like some food to help wash down that brew, no problem. The food is very inexpensive, very tasty, and very filling. Mr. C ordered a thick crust, nine-inch cheese pizza ($5.95!) and found he could not finish it, what with all the gooey, melted cheese, and pretzel-like crust. The "Baconcheddarburger" ($5.50) is as much of a mouthful as its name. Those with a more discriminating palate will enjoy swordfish, with vegetable of the day and steak fries ($10.50), or sirloin steak with salad and fries ($14.95). Or try the buffalo stew ($7.95), seafood platter ($11.95), and filet of salmon and the Bricks Bucket of mussels ($6.25).

Beer shows in the past have featured "Great Beers from Women Brewers," or partake in Belgian and Sierra Nevada beer tastings for $24.95.

Be sure to get here early if you want a seat—the place sure fills up fast. Hours are Monday through Thursday from 11:30 a.m. to 2 p.m., Friday and Saturday from 11:30 a.m. to 3 a.m., and Sunday from noon to 6 p.m.

Cafe Amadeus

• 1300 I Street N.W., Washington, D.C.; ✆ (202) 962-8686

Cafe Amadeus undertakes the challenging task of preparing a "symphony of flavors in harmony with your health," as their motto says. Can this be done while still serving German cuisine? The cooks here succeed by grilling food, cutting down on the salt, and using lean cuts of meat.

With high quality come prices a bit higher than Mr. C likes, but most dishes are still under $10. For a classy, downtown restaurant, that's pretty good. Mr. C enjoyed German meatballs ($8.95), served in a sour cream sauce with capers. Yummy! Hungarian beef goulash ($9.95) was also quite tempting. If beef isn't your favorite, there are lots of turkey and chicken dishes. Turkey tips in mustard sauce ($9.95) and chicken almandine ($12.95) are especially good choices.

Stop in for Cafe Amadeus' happy hour between 4 and 6 p.m. on weekdays. Free hors d'oeuvres are available along with some pretty impressive drink specials: Heineken and Samuel Adams drafts for $1.99, and mixed drinks for just $2.25. So what's not to get happy about? All food products arrive daily and you're guaranteed the freshest meal possible; the owner of Cafe Amadeus is known to take tremendous pride in this fact.

Open Monday through Friday from 7 a.m. to 9:30 p.m., Saturday from 9 a.m. to 9:30 p.m., and Sunday from 11 a.m. to 9:30 p.m.

The folks here also own the nearby Cafe Mozart, at 1331 H Street N.W., telephone ✆ (202) 347-5732. Prices are a bit higher, but still reasonable. The menu is filled with German specialties, including sausage, schnitzel, sauerkraut, liverwurst, and German potato salad. Hours there are Monday through Friday from 7:30 to 10 p.m., Saturday from 9 to 10 p.m., and Sunday from 11 a.m. to 10 p.m.

Capitol City Brewing Company

- 2 Massachusetts Avenue N.W., Washington, D.C.; ✆ (202) 842-2337

- 1100 New York Avenue N.W.,Washington, D.C.; ✆ (202) 628-2222

- ✐ www.capitalcitybrew.com

Getting into Capitol City Brewing Company can be tricky: It's located in the back of the I 1100 building, and the outside entrance on the corner of 11th and H Streets is the quickest, most direct route inside.

The pub itself is very large, with high ceilings and a rather industrial

theme, appropriate since this is an actual brewery. Eight varieties, different each month, are on tap; other microbrews are available in bottles. In keeping with the pub theme, order popular finger foods including stuffed potato skins ($5.95), atomic wings ($7.50), or a basket of fries ($3). Order one of these and a cup of pale ale chili ($3.50), and you're set for dinner.

The entrees are a bit over $10, but not unreasonable. Fresh salmon with veggies and potatoes is a bargain for $11.95. There are less pricey alternatives—light yet filling dinner salads are a good choice. Spicy chicken salad ($9.95), with grilled chicken, Thai peanut dressing, and shiitake mushrooms, is an exotic twist on a familiar favorite. Burgers are $5.95; turkey clubs are a dollar more. Mr. C liked the grilled hofbrau bratwurst sandwich ($13.95), smothered with sauerkraut and Swiss cheese. Happy hour offerings include half-price appetizers and $2.75 pints from 4 to 7 p.m. Monday through Thursday.

Capitol City's restaurant hours are Monday through Saturday from 11 a.m. to 1:30 p.m., and Sunday from 11 a.m. to 12 midnight.

Chipotle

- 1937 M Street, N.W., Washington, D.C.; ✆ (202) 466-4104

- ✍ www.chipotle.com

See the listing under *Restaurants—Dupont Circle.*

DJ's

- 2145 G Street N.W., Washington, D.C.; ✆ (202) 429-0230

DJ's small cafeteria atmosphere hardly hints that you can order delectable dishes from all over the world. In fact, many international cuisines are represented; hot and cold soups, made with Oriental noodles or rice, seem to be the specialty. Mr. C enjoyed a large bowl of makuksu, a noodle soup with spiced chicken (or beef), which would have been $5.20—but as a special of the day, the price was $4.99.

Mexican and Middle Eastern foods are also on the menu, like *burrilos* (made with chicken breast for $5.20) and falafel ($4.50). Breakfast is available until 11 a.m. during the week and until noon on the weekends. You can get a stack of pancakes for $2.50, but why not try the *cho-ban* Oriental breakfast, with rice, vegetables, dakuwan, egg, and miso soup for $3.50? Most dishes can be made to accommodate vegetarians, with extra veggies thrown in.

Stop by for a delicious meal at a bargain. DJ's restaurant hours are Monday through Saturday from 8 a.m. to 7 p.m.

Fanatics Sports & Billiards

- 1520 K Street N.W., Washington, D.C.; ✆ (202) 737-7678

- ✍ www.diningmetro.com/fanatics

Like any good sports bar, Fanatics is visually entertaining. TVs perch in all corners and tons of sports posters cover the walls. But you don't come back to look, you come here to eat. Fanatics does not disappoint. The food is delicious, the portions are huge, and the prices are quite reasonable.

Mr. C thought the burgers were just fabulous. These monstrous, hand-formed half-pounders are $6.95, topped with your choice of Swiss cheese and bacon, grilled mushroom, onion, or barbecue bacon cheddar, to name a few. Other sandwiches include the New York Italian hoagie ($7.50), stuffed with all the usual suspects: ham, salami, capocolla, provolone, onion, hot pepper, and Italian dressing. Sandwiches are served with fries and coleslaw. In the way of entrees, tasty choices include chicken teriyaki served with rice and vegetables, or fried shrimp platter served with fries and coleslaw (each $10.95).

Save room for dessert; you're not going to want to pass these goodies up. Midnight chocolate layer cake, Mississippi mud ice cream pie, strawberry delight torte, chocolate mousse pie—take your pick, each one is $4.50 per slice.

Fanatics has discounted appetizers during its weeknight happy hour, as well as good prices on beverages: Beer starts at $2, with imported varieties priced at $2.50, while mixed drinks are $2.25. Not bad! Stop by between 3 p.m. and 8 p.m. for those deals. On a Wednesday or Thursday night, head upstairs to the Comedy Cafe to enjoy "open mike night" and local comedians.

Fanatics' restaurant hours are Monday through Sunday from 11:30 a.m. to 2 a.m.

Le Sorbet

- 1776 G Street N.W., Washington, D.C.; ✆ (202) 789-1313

Ooh la la! What a great little French cafe! There are several wooden tables for dining in, though carryout is big business here. Very few of the many sandwiches are over $4.50. Specialty fillings include pate champagne, crab meat "sea legs," and Camembert cheese. These sandwiches aren't huge, but they're absolutely delicious and make a light meal that's *très bon*. And, with the prices so low, you can easily add soup of the day ($2.30), house salad ($1.65), or an almond croissant ($1.35) for a more substantial meal. For something a little fancier, homemade quiche and salad ($4.50), or croque monsieur, grilled ham and Swiss cheese on toast "French style" ($4.50), are tasty choices. Your sweet tooth is also in for a treat—assorted cookies and croissants are made fresh daily.

Le Sorbet hours are Monday through Friday from 7:30 a.m. to 5:30 p.m. Closed on Saturday and Sunday.

Lindy's Bon Appetit

- 2040 I Street N.W., Washington, D.C.; ✆ (202) 452-0055

Since 1974, Lindy's has been a GWU landmark, known for inexpensive and delicious carryout. Start the day with three pancakes and ham, bacon, or sausage ($2.50). Maybe the ham and cheese omelet, served with home fries and toast ($2.75), is more your style. Either way, Lindy's breakfast is a treat for your wallet and tummy.

And how's this for variety: There are more than 20 different kinds of burgers, available in single and double sizes. The basic model is $3.96, but why not try some of

the more interesting combinations? Exotic "Blue Beard" is topped with bleu cheese and brandy spread; "Capitol Punishment" sets your mouth ablaze with green peppers, hot red peppers, and ground black pepper; and good ol' Robert ("Bob" to his friends?) features A-1 Steak Sauce, sautéed mushrooms, and onions. All these choices are $3.95, the average single burger price—a couple more dollars for a double. There are also plenty of sandwiches, from turkey club ($4.95) to gyro ($4.95), plus soups, nachos, and desserts.

Lindy's hours are Monday through Friday from 8 a.m. to 8 p.m., and Saturday from 11 a.m. to 4 p.m. They're closed on Sunday.

Lulu's

- 2200 M Street N.W., Washington, D.C.; ✆ (202) 861-5858 (LULU)

A little slice of New Orleans has made its way to Foggy Bottom. The ornate, wrought iron spiral staircase, stained glass windows, and authentic-looking old-fashioned signposts certainly make you think you're on Bourbon Street rather than M Street.

The food here is just as beautiful and festive-looking as the rest of the joint. Mr. C enjoyed one of the daily specials, a large and artistically arranged plateful of crawfish *étouffée*—tasty crustaceans in thick, spicy gravy, served around rice and colorful peppers ($12.95). Traditional chicken and sausage gumbo, served with rice pilaf ($10.95), or a catfish po'boy sandwich, served with curly fries ($9.95), are also excellent choices. If you can spare a few more dollars, the desserts should not be missed; Lulu's bread pudding ($3.25), saturated with whiskey or Amaretto sauce, tastes heavenly.

Sunday brunch features omelets loaded with everything, andouille sausage to tomatoes. These are topped with Cajun hollandaise sauce and served with spicy potatoes, fresh fruit, and French bread for $10.25. This brunch will fill you up for the rest of the day. It will fill your ears, too, with live jazz music from 11:30 a.m. to 2 p.m.

Thursday and Friday nights are especially popular in the bar area— the singles' scene here is definitely happening. Tuesday happy hours take place all night long; tequila drinks are $3.50, tequila shots $3, and the going rate for Corona's are $3. Their Wednesday happy hour has $3 Tom Collins and $4.50 Cosmos. Brunch specials are in the $15 range.

LuLu's hours are Monday through Thursday from 4 p.m. to 2 a.m.; Friday and Saturday from 4 p.m. to 3 a.m.

MR. CHEAP'S PICKS

Foggy Bottom

Lindy's Bon Appetit—For more than 20 years, Lindy's has served up delicious, inexpensive takeout to the GWU crowd.

Lulu's—Bourbon Street meets Foggy Bottom. New Orleans specialties are the focus of this moderately priced venue.

Manhattan Deli

- 2001 L Street N.W., Washington, D.C.; ✆ (202) 659-3030

Tip-free

Well, it's not New York, but the Manhattan Deli serves up large portions of filling and tasty deli delights. Deli sandwiches, the main menu event, start at $4.50 and go up to $5.25 for triple-decker clubs. Try the "Empire State Building" with turkey, ham, and Swiss, or the "Broadway" with roast beef, turkey, and cheddar (each $5.25).

You can get breakfast here, too. The "Good Morning Breakfasts" combos of eggs, home fries, bacon, sausage, ham, and toast, are about $3.75. Unfortunately, the "Are You Talkin' to Me? Breakfast" is only available in the real New York.

Omelets are about a dollar more and come with home fries and toast. The Manhattan Deli is located in a city that, unlike New York, does sleep.

Hours are Monday through Friday from 6:30 a.m. to 5 p.m. during the week, and Saturday from 8 a.m. to 3 p.m.

Recessions

- 1700 K Street N.W., Washington, D.C.; ✆ (202) 296-6686

One of Washington's renowned speakeasies (hence nestled in the basement of an unmarked building), Recessions beats the recession by serving large portions of filling food at very low prices. First, a word about the location: The restaurant is located inside the 1700 Building down a long flight of stairs; follow the pictures of vintage autos.

Appetizers are available for $4.50; steak is available for under $10. Half-pound sirloin burgers come with a variety of toppings including cheese, bacon, onions, and mushrooms, and cost between $4.95 and $5.95. Same price for a beef gyro platter complete with homemade pita bread, feta cheese, and yogurt cucumber sauce. Don't miss the homemade crab cakes with baked potato or steak fries and coleslaw for $6.95. "Giant Sandwiches" certainly live up to their name; try the grilled marinated chicken breast for $5.75.

You can also choose one of four daily specials, all under $7. These have included lasagna, shrimp creole with rice, and barbecued ribs. There's a happy hour every night of the week with $1.50 domestic drafts, $1.99 rail drinks, and burgers at 50 percent off.

Hours are Monday through Sunday from 7 a.m. to 9 p.m.

Red Hot & Blue

• 1120 19th Street N.W., Washington, D.C.; ☎ (202) 466-6731

That's right, it's an old-fashioned Memphis pit bar-b-que right here in D.C. This is a fun kind of place; its walls lined are with autographed photos real—and fake. They declare their food "the best you'll ever have in a building that hasn't already been condemned." Rhythm and blues play good and loud on the speakers, including one outside the front door. On tap? Sam Adams, Lone Star, and other fine brews.

As for that food, Mr. C drooled over RH & B's hickory-flavored ribs; a rack is just $11.99 (or $18.99 for two people). The sumptuous order comes with barbecued beans, coleslaw, and fresh-baked bread. Other platters include moist pork shoulder, beef brisket (both $8.59), and a half chicken ($8.99), all with the same sides.

Just want a sandwich? No prob. How about pulled pork in two sizes ($5.50/$6.25), beef brisket for the same prices, or chicken for $1

more. All of these choices, as well as several burgers (all under $10), come with potato salad or baked beans. Don't forget to save room for dessert, as $3.99 gets you a slab of fudge brownie pie, pecan pie, or apple cobbler. Happy hour deals include $1 off drafts and appetizers at 50 percent off from 4 to 7 p.m.

Red Hot and Blue's hours are Sunday through Thursday from 11 a.m. to 10 p.m., and Friday and Saturday from 11 a.m. to 11 p.m.

Red Sage Border Cafe

• 605 14th Street N.W., Washington, D.C.; ☎ (202) 638-4444

• ✐ www.redsage.com

The Red Sage is a sprawling, two-story restaurant set up like a natural cave in the side of a mountain, with sand-colored curved arches and walls. Unfortunately, such beauty does not come cheap. There is a budget option, however. Upstairs, the Red Sage's Border Cafe is bright and airy with a high ceiling and tall windows. The menu is similar to the Red Sage. The food is as skillfully prepared and artfully presented, and the prices are considerably lower. So in this case, Mr. C advises you head north!

Border Cafe menu items include soups and salads, pizza, sandwiches, quesadillas, and desserts. It's easy to find something for $10 or under. Soup or salad could each be a full meal: Red Sage steak and black bean smoked chili ($6.95), and house-cured duck Caesar ($10) with dried apples, red chili pecans, and Parmesan, are both delicious. The Red Sage chorizo pizza ($9.20) will certainly wake up your taste buds; it's topped with smoked cheeses, black bean paste, red chili oil, roasted peppers, and cilantro: Order a tall glass of ice water with that one. Try the *tuscano torta* ($8.75), with grilled chicken breast, smoked prosciutto, sun-dried tomato spread, and cheese, served on roasted garlic herb focaccia. Mr. C enjoyed "Mark's Barbecued Brisket Quesadilla" ($8.50); house-smoked beef brisket, covered with special tangy-sweet barbecue sauce, folded inside flour tortillas, drizzled with a swirl of cream, and served with *salsa fresca*. Plus, their wild mushroom chipotle tamale with jicama salad never disappoints.

Red Sage Border Café's lunch menu offers a baked plaintain tamale starter with goat cheese, grilled tomatillo-mint relish, and black bean sauce for $6.50, lobster spring rolls for $9, fresh rock shrimp chowder for $8, fish and chips with dried lemon dust for $15, and a grilled Virginia buffalo burger with peppery fries, Vidalia onion rings and smoked BBQ sauce for $14.

Desserts are just as creative and delicious. The more memorable and mouthwatering treats are chocolate mousse cake with wild raspberry sauce ($5.50); warm pear cobbler with dried cherries and hazelnut crust ($5.50); and ice cream sandwiches with chewy raisin spice cookies, molasses ice cream, and rum raisin sauce ($5). Skip right from an appetizer and order one of these babies or just come here for dessert!

The Border Cafe is open for lunch and dinner during the week; dinner only on the weekends.

Reeves Restaurant Bakery

- 1306 G Street N.W., Washington, D.C.; ✆ (202) 628-6350

Established in 1886, Reeves is one of the oldest bakeries in Washington. In that time, it has garnered a reputation for good food and low prices and has become a popular spot for breakfast, lunch, or an early dinner.

Just about everything is under $10, just like it was in the old days!

The "all you can eat" breakfast buffet is a deal: $6.95 per person during the week, $7.95 Saturdays and holidays. It's loaded with a wide variety of standard breakfast favorites, like bacon and eggs. Items off the menu are also well priced. French toast is just $5.25; even better, add hot peaches, apples, blueberries, or fresh strawberries ($6).

The rest of the menu includes sandwiches, salads, burgers, and pasta dishes. Some of Mr. C's favorites include lasagna with homemade Italian meat sauce ($8); creamy Manhattan clam chowder ($4 per cup); and the pizza steak sub, with mozzarella and homemade meat sauce ($6).

Now for Reeves' true claim to fame—baked goods! A mind-boggling variety of homemade pies and cakes includes lemon meringue, pecan, peach, and apple pie; carrot, devil's food, and German chocolate cake; plus tarts, éclairs, and bread pudding. Most of the goodies are $3 and $4 for a serving. These confections are baked right there on the premises.

Reeves is open Monday through Saturday from 7 a.m. to 6 p.m. Closed on Sunday.

Sichuan Pavilion

- 1820 K Street N.W., Washington, D.C.; ✆ (202) 466-2038

Cheap Chinese food is easily found, but cheap, authentic Chinese is another matter. With a chef directly from China, Sichuan Pavilion has no problem with authenticity or price.

Start off your meal with Chinese cabbage marinated in sweet-and-sour sauce, or crispy shrimp packs, each for $5.95. For a real treat, try the chef's specials, such as crispy duck ($12.95). All the familiar favorites are included on the regular menu, like General Tso's and sesame chicken, both $10.95. Sweet-and-sour shrimp ($15.95) and kung pao scallops ($14.95) are tasty choices if you're in the mood for seafood; and the popular some-assembly-required moo shi pork is just $14.95. Lunches are a few dollars less.

For the better deal, stop by for Sunday brunch between noon and 4 p.m. That's when you can get an appetizer, soup, one entree (a huge choice, including beef with snow peas and kung pao chicken), dessert, and wine or a mimosa, all for just $10.95.

Hours are Monday through Sunday from 11:30 a.m. to 10 p.m.

Star of Siam

- 1736 19th Street N.W., Washington, D.C.; ✆ (202) 785-2839

- 2446 18th Street N.W., Washington, D.C.; ✆ (202) 986-4133

- 1735 North Lynn Street, Arlington, VA; ✆ (703) 524-1208

See the listing under *Restaurants—Dupont Circle*.

Thai Kingdom

- 2021 K Street N.W., Washington, D.C.; ✆ (202) 835-1700

Unlike some ethnic eateries, Thai Kingdom's offerings are delicious and delicately flavored, not just spicy or hot. Every item is $10 and under, even the seafood dishes. Try the interesting "Anna and the King," featuring fresh sea scallops, wrapped in minced chicken, fried up with fresh basil for $8.50. Or boneless duck in plum broth, for $3.50. Traditional Pad Thai with shrimp ($7) is done to perfection. The portions here are not huge; however, they will fill you up, leaving just enough room for dessert. Mr. C recommends the Thai custard.

Fret not if you're fearful of the really spicy stuff—dishes can be seasoned to your taste, and stars on the menu or ominous names, like "Crying Tiger" or "Killer Prawn," warn you of dishes that may be too hot to handle.

Visit the Kingdom for lunch and dinner. Hours are Sunday through Thursday from 11:30 a.m. to 10:30 p.m., Friday and Saturday from noon to 11 p.m., and Sunday from noon to 10 p.m.

Treats Bakery and Cafe

- 1745 H Street N.W., Washington, D.C.; ✆ (202) 659-0558

- 300 D Street SW #101, Washington, D.C.; ✆ (202) 479-1005

- 409 Third Street S.W., Washington, D.C.; ✆ (202) 488-2887

- 50 Massachusetts Avenue N.E., Washington, D.C.; ✆ (202) 898-2570

Despite its name, Treats is not an ice cream shop or bakery. It's a cafeteria serving up a variety of entrees that are tasty, filling, and very inexpensive. The ever-changing menu may include "Treatzza," vegetarian pizza topped with tomatoes, green peppers, and mushrooms ($2.50); or vegetable lasagna ($4.25). Meat lovers are not left out: Mr. C enjoyed a salami, mortadella, and provolone sandwich, topped with Italian dressing ($3.99). For breakfast, Treats creates some tasty sandwiches to go. A two-egg sandwich is $1.95; with ham and cheese it's just $2.25. There's also a selection of giant muffins (they're a handful!), including peach, oat bran, banana nut, and cherry cream cheese for $1.25 each (there are some sweets here, after all).

Go ahead and treat youself! Hours are Monday through Friday from 6 a.m. to 5 p.m.

MUSEUM CAFETERIAS

Like the government buildings described earlier in this section, many area museums feature upscale, inexpensive cafeterias. Unlike the ones in government buildings, however, these don't close to the public in the middle of the day. Good to know if you suddenly find you're starving at high noon.

CORCORAN GALLERY

Cafe des Artistes

- 500 17th Street N.W., Washington, D.C.; ℡ (202) 639-1700

- ✍ www.corcoran.org

Full menu service available on Monday, Wednesday, Friday, and Saturday from 11 a.m. to 2 p.m.; Thursday from 11 a.m. to 8 p.m.; and Sunday from 10:30 a.m. to 2 p.m. for buffet brunch ($21.95). This price includes museum admission.

THE KENNEDY CENTER

KC Cafe

- New Hampshire Avenue & F Street N.W.,Washington, D.C.: ℡ (202) 416-8555

- ✍ www.kennedycenter.center.org

Take advantage of the Chef's Table specials with pasta, fish, and meat made to special order. Other unique offerings include the smoothie bar, coffee bar, salad bar, and gourmet sandwiches—all at a reasonable charge.

NATIONAL AIR AND SPACE MUSEUM

Flight Line

- Independence Avenue and Seventh Street S.W., Washington, D.C.; ℡ (202) 371-8778

- ✍ www.nasm.si.edu

The most popular museum in Washington . . . and anywhere else we know of in the cosmos . . . rebuilt its cafeteria in 2002 to bring together a trio of American faves: McDonald's, Donato's Pizzeria, and Boston Market. Wow. This makes SI's Air and Space museum a "one-stop-drop-'n'-chomp." Definite plus from seating perspective—there's capacity for up to 1,000 people to sit comfortably. This bit of trivia should send you over the moon!

Hours are Monday through Sunday from 10 a.m. to 5 p.m.

NATIONAL GALLERY OF ART

Concourse Buffet

- Fourth Street and Constitution Avenue N.W., Washington, D.C.; ℡ (202) 842-6043

- ✍ www.nga.gov/ginfo/cafes.htm

  Tip-free

Here, you'll a cost-effective bite to eat. Hours are Monday through Saturday from 10 a.m. to 3 p.m., and Sunday from 11 a.m. to 4 p.m. Hours are extended in the summer months.

National Gallery of Art Cafeterias

- Fourth Street and Constitution Avenue N.W., Washington, D.C.; ✆ (202) 842-6043

- ✒ www.nga.gov/ginfo/cafes.htm

Tip-free

Includes the Cascade Espresso Bar, the Terrace Cafe, and the Sculpture Garden Pavilion Cafe. You're bound to find a cup of java, burger, fries, dogs, soup, sandwiches, or salads at any of these locales. Hours vary; all three are open for lunch. Call ahead of time for exact schedule.

NATIONAL PORTRAIT GALLERY

Patent Pending

- Eighth & G Streets N.W., Washington, D.C.: ✆ (202) 275-1738

- ✒ www.npg.si.edu

Tip-free

Mr. C apologizes for painting a picture of a place you can't visit. At press time, the National Portrait Gallery is closed for renovation until further notice. Projected reopening is set for fall of 2004, or sometime in 2005.

DUPONT CIRCLE

Including Adams Morgan and Shaw/U Street Area

Adams Morgan Spaghetti Garden

- 2317 18th Street N.W., Washington, D.C.; ✆ (202) 265-6665

Cheap and filling—this sure is Mr. C's kind of place! Here, you can treat yourself to large portions of pasta for around $7, including the house specials—baked pastas such as lasagna, ravioli, and manicotti. These can even be ordered in combination with spaghetti, for the maximum carbo-loading experience.

Mr. C opted for the manicotti, which boasted a smooth cheese filling and a thick layer of mozzarella on top. Angel hair pasta with fresh tomatoes included plenty of tomato chunks and visible pieces of minced garlic. Speaking of which, the Garden's garlic bread is powerful stuff dripping with plenty of butter and herbs. The house wines are nothing to write home about—much less a book about—

but they certainly are a bargain at $2.75 a glass.

The decor, while not checkered-tablecloth romantic, does feature candles on each table. Service is nice and quick. And, when the weather is warm, you can mangia from the Spaghetti Garden's rooftop patio.

Hours are Monday through Saturday from 11 a.m. to 2 p.m.

Ben's Chili Bowl

- 1213 U Street N.W., Washington, D.C.; ✆ (202) 667-0909

Ben's, or "Home of the Famous Chili Dog," has made the soul food scene up on U Street for over 30 years, serving up hearty homemade breakfasts and lunches for next to nothing. Grab a booth or sit at the counter, while B.B. King plays on the jukebox (well-stoked with such further royalty as Albert King and King Curtis) and friendly folks hang out and chat.

An 8-ounce bowl of their trade-mark chili con carne goes for a mere $2.95; 12 ounces for $3.75, which includes potato salad and coleslaw; the same price can get you a grilled burger slathered with the red stuff. Or, for $2.75, try an order of chili-topped French fries—beat that, McD's.

For breakfast, you can get two eggs any way you want them, with scrapple, home fries, grits, fruit, and a biscuit, all for $3.95. Wow. Great coffee, too—none of your gourmet stuff, just a fine cuppa java. Ben's Chili Bowl hours are Monday through Sunday from 6 a.m. to 6 p.m.

As the rest of this neighborhood has taken off, a fast-food version of Ben's, called Ben's Bakery and Ice Cream, has opened up a couple of blocks away in the Reeves Center building, at 2000 14th Street N.W.; telephone ✆ (202) 667-2313. It has most of the same food, but none of the same charm. Stick with the original if you're looking for down-home atmosphere.

Burrito Brothers

- 1524 Connecticut Avenue N.W., Washington, D.C.; ✆ (202) 332-2308

- 3273 M Street N.W., Washington, D.C.; ✆ (202) 785-3309

- 205 Pennsylvania Avenue S.E., Washington, D.C.; ✆ (202) 543-6835

  Tip-free

See the listing under *Restaurants—Capitol Hill*.

Chipotle

- 1629 Connecticut Avenue N.W., Washington, D.C.; ✆ (202) 387-8261

- ✍ www.chipotle.com

This stylish and fun establishment served stylish and fun Tex-Mex—and at good prices. Try some of their delectable chunky guacamole ($1.25) along with freshly made tortilla chips, and wash it down with an ice-cold beer or margarita. Your can then get to the main courses, including burritos, tacos, and fajitas (ranging from $4.25 to $5.25), along with Chipotle's steaming cilantro and lime-flavored rice. Not too shabby.

Chipotle is open 11 a.m. to 10 p.m. every day.

D.C. Cafe

- 2035 P Street N.W., Washington, D.C.; ✆ (202) 887-5819

  Tip-free

Open 24 hours; every day of the week, D.C. Cafe specializes in Mediterranean and deli-style food. Most people do carryout or call for delivery, but there is some seating inside this little joint. The food is tasty and the prices are excellent.

A la carte items are perfect for a snack or light meal. Stuffed grape leaves and chef salad are each $4.99, while crushed lentil soup is $3.50. Most sandwiches are also $3.50; $5.99 for larger sizes. Steak and cheese, pastrami on rye, and falafel with hummus and tahini, are just a few choices. Complete meals are a bit more, like chicken shawarma ($6.50), marinated chicken breast wrapped in a tortilla with garlic sauce, served with rice or fries, and salad. D.C. Cafe is always open; at 4 a.m., sometimes that's its best feature.

The Diner

- 2453 18th Street N.W., Washington, D.C.; ✆ (202) 232-8800

If there's a dining establishment with a laid back "home away from home" type ambiance, then this place would be it. The dress code, more or less, is "anything goes" as it would be in your own house. Yep this means you can roll out of bed and show up in your pajamas, slippers, and mud-mask. In keeping with the homebody theme, you can easily order any of the following for under $10: Grilled cheese sandwich, macaroni and cheese, French toast, fresh turkey sandwich, burger, fries, onion rings—you name it! Due to immense popularity, the lines tend to get long. So you might want to stop in during off peak times.

The Diner is open seven days a week, 24 hours.

1800 Cafe

- 1800 N Street N.W., Washington, D.C.; ✆ (202) 223-2388

With about 10 stools and no booths, the 1800 Cafe is a tiny greasy spoon (a baby spoon, perhaps?). And, in classic diner tradition, the portions are enormous, and the prices super-cheap. Breakfast platters include toast and hash browns—a Western omelet ($4.75) or ham and eggs ($4.50) are just a few of the choices. Egg sandwiches start at $2.25. Muffins, donuts, bagels, and French toast are other options.

Most of the menu is dedicated to "overstuffed sandwiches." All your basic cold cuts and sandwich salads are represented, as are burgers ($3.50) and crab cakes ($3.75). Nothing is much over $5, and all certainly live up to their name. For a full meal, the priciest items on the menu are a whopping $5.25 for the roast beef or turkey platters, each served with two vegetables. Mr. C enjoyed chicken cordon bleu, also with two veggies, for $4.95. The 1800 Cafe hours are Monday through Friday from 7 a.m. to 3 p.m.; closed on Saturday and Sunday.

El Bodegon

- 1637 R Street N.W., Washington, D.C.; ✆ (202) 667-1710

Located kinda off the beaten track (about six blocks up and over from the Dupont Circle Metro stop) is El Bodegon, a little slice of Spain that's been around since 1962. Textured stucco walls, arched doorways, and a fireplace create a cozy atmosphere.

Specialties of the house include classic Spanish dishes like paella valenciana—chicken, sausage, and vegetables—cooked with rice in a saffron sauce ($12.95); and arroz con pollo, a casserole of chicken with rice ($8.95). For a delicious sampling of El Bodegon's Spanish cuisine try their selection of tapas. These include fried mussels ($6.95), ham croquette ($5.95), and homemade beef pastries ($6.25). For lighter appetites, white bean salad ($4.95) and gazpacho ($4.95) will leave you enough room (and money) for one of the specialty after-dinner coffees. In addition to all that good food, the staff is friendly and very accommodating.

El Bodegon hours are Sunday through Thursday from 11:30 a.m. to 11 p.m., and Friday and Saturday from 11:30 a.m. until midnight.

El Tamarindo

- 1785 Florida Avenue N.W., Washington, D.C.; ✆ (202) 328-3660

- 7331 Georgia Avenue N.W., Washington, D.C.; ✆ (202) 291-0525

- 4910 Wisconsin Avenue N.W., Washington, D.C.; ✆ (202) 244-8888

The best in Mexican and Salvadoran food in the D.C. area? So says a friend of Mr. C. A hearty selection and incredible hours help put this place over the top.

And there are bargains to be found, including chicken ($9.95) and beef ($10.25) fajitas—or bring a date to share the fajita combo for two ($18.95), with the above plus pork and shrimp. Several different tasty dinner options include Yucatan chicken, with vegetables, onions, and tomatoes in a ranchera sauce, served with rice and beans for $8.95.

Plus burritos ($8.50) and various chimichangas, including one stuffed with crab and shrimp for $9.95; and a medley of enchiladas, highlighted by the "Super de Pollo," with chicken rolled and topped with enchilada sauce, melted cheese, sliced avocado, and sour cream ($8.50). To die for. Mr. C highly recommends the sangria pitchers, only $14.95. Olé to that!

Hours are Monday to Sunday from 11 a.m. to 2 a.m.

Florida Avenue Grill

• 1100 Florida Avenue N.W., Washington, D.C.; ✆ (202) 265-1586

Since 1944, this little diner has been keeping area folks happy with glorious, Southern-style food, served in a friendly and simple manner. Everyone should schedule time for the opportunity to grab this grill's grub.

Those breakfasts, served with a choice of grits, apples, or home fries and hot biscuits, include two eggs served with bacon or sausage ($4), corned beef hash ($5), or two pork chops ($6). Three hotcakes with bacon are just $4. An enormous chef's special features country ham and eggs, grits, home fries, and a hot biscuit and coffee all for $7. The scrapple is $1.95; the fried apples cost $1.50.

For lunch, go with a sausage and egg sandwich for $3, or barbecued spare ribs for $5.50. As a dinner, the ribs go for $10, meatloaf $8.50, and pan-fried chicken a mere $7. All of these entrees come with two sides, including candied sweet potatoes, macaroni and cheese, pickled beets, and more. The more adventurous may want to try pig's feet—let Mr. C know how they were!

The Florida Avenue Grill hours are Tuesday through Saturday from 6 a.m. to 9 p.m.

Food for Thought at the Black Cat Club

• 1811 14th Street N.W., Washington, D.C.; ✆ (202) 797-1095

Now you can get brain food and musical nourishment all rolled into one. Well, this seems pretty logical. Mr. C recommends that you venture in, and ye shall not be disappointed.

Vegetarian and omnivore dishes share equal space on the large menu, and almost everything comes in meat/non-meat varieties. A "Chili Bird Melt" ($7.95), featuring smoked turkey, provolone, onion, tomato, and avocado, topped with chili, was Mr. C's favorite. Fruit and nut salad, loaded with apples, bananas, raisins, sunflower seeds, and cashews, all in a honey-sweetened yogurt dressing, makes a tempting light choice for $6.95. To please the die-hard meat and potato lovers, a six-ounce organic beef burger, with potato chips, is also $6.95.

Restaurant hours are Sunday through Thursday from 8 p.m. to 1 a.m., and Friday and Saturday from 7 p.m. to 2 a.m.

On the entertainment end, call ✆ (202) 667-4490 for the gig schedule.

Julia's Empanadas

- 2452 18th Street N.W., Washington, D.C.; ✆ (202) 328-6232

Tip-free

This storefront does most of its business as carryout, but they do have counters and one table if you just can't wait to dig in (empanadas are made to be held in one hand, though, so they're good for those of you who are into walking and eating). Some of these Salvadoran pies are baked and some are fried; and here at Julia's, all have a creative twist to them. Even the broccoli and cheese empanada is flavored with dill and nutmeg. Best of all, everything is priced under $3.

Try Chilean, Jamaican, or Colombian-style beef, spinach with pine nuts and three types of cheese; or saltena, with chicken, hard-boiled egg, potatoes, peas, onions, and black olives. Vegetarian empanadas are made with different combinations of ingredients each week; the mix during Mr. C's visit was butternut squash, carrots, peas, onions, and olives. You can even try a fruit empanada for dessert!

Julia's hours are Monday through Thursday from 11 a.m. to 10:30 p.m., Friday and Saturday from 11 a.m. to 4 a.m., and Sunday from 11 a.m. to 8 p.m.

Kramerbooks & Afterwords Cafe

- 1517 Connecticut Avenue N.W., Washington, D.C.; ✆ (202) 387-1462

- ✍ www.kramers.com

Cool and literary as it is, Afterwords Cafe is still a bit pricey; however, you can still stop by, soak up the scene, and actually find some good deals on drink and light bites. Between 4 p.m. and 7 p.m.,

---

MR. CHEAP'S PICKS

Dupont Circle

El Tamarindo—A hearty selection and incredible hours help put this place over the top.

Food for Thought at the Black Cat Club—Hey, here's a thought: a menu equally devoted to vegetarian and meat dishes, so herbivore and carnivore can coexist inexpensively.

Lauriol Plaza—One of Washington's best restaurants—and the prices meet Mr. C's rigorous standards for "high value."

---

and again from 11 p.m. to 1 a.m. during the week, you may partake in happy hours that include beer, wine, and mixed drinks for $3.85, as well as a selection of five delicious appetizers offered at $5 each. Choose from gourmet versions of old favorites—smoked salmon tortillas, Thai basil grilled shrimp, and chilled Asian spring rolls with julienne breast of chicken, just to name a few.

Lauriol Plaza

- 1835 l8th Street N.W., Washington, D.C.; ✆ (202) 387-0035

Before you read further, don't forget part of Mr. C's credo: A place need not be "cheap" to have high value and earn mention. So, although this restaurant outside of Dupont Circle goes a bit over Mr. C's thriftiness, it makes up the difference with fine food and an elegant atmosphere—at prices that are still reasonable for such a romantic setting. Fresh flowers, fine linens, large windows—small wonder it's one of the city's favorite restaurants over the past decade. The cuisine includes Mexican and South American specialties. An appetizer of shrimp sautéed in light garlic and sherry wine makes a fine start at $7.95. Or dive right into the tasty seafood like *camarones diablo*, jumbo shrimp seasoned with spices and Mexican butter, served on a sizzling platter with rice and vegetables ($14.95).

Sunday brunch makes a trip to this restaurant worthwhile. It's sure to win over any "tough crowd" with Huevos Rancheros (two fried eggs on crispy tortillas and side order of refried beans) for $6.50, or *bistec con huevos* (steak and eggs any style) for $7.95.

Another treat, *lomo saltado a la Peruana*, features sautéed strips of prime sirloin with fresh tomatoes, cilantro, sweet and jalapeno peppers, in a special Peruvian sauce ($13.95). If you'd like to save some money for wine, go with beef, chicken, or seafood enchiladas for a mere $8.95. And do finish up with a dish of flan ($4.95), the only dessert to have with Spanish food. And definitely try out their *cajeta* as well—it's made with ice cream rolled in coconut, chopped nuts, and topped with caramel.

MR. CHEAP'S PICKS

Adams Morgan

Adams Morgan Spaghetti Garden—Cheap and filling—this sure is Mr. C's kind of place! Here, you can treat yourself to large portions of pasta for around $7, including the house specials.

Florida Avenue Grill—Great Southern comfort food.

Julia's Empanadas—You've never had them like this before.

Lauriol Plaza's (sounds more like a hotel than a cozy restaurant, doesn't it?) hours are Monday through Thursday from 11 a.m. to 11 p.m., Friday and Saturday from 11 a.m. to midnight, and Sunday from 11:30 a.m. to 11p.m.

Meskerem

- 2434 18th Street N.W., Washington, D.C.; ✆ (202) 462-4100

This large restaurant certainly sports the most authentic atmosphere of the half-dozen Ethiopian restaurants in Adams Morgan. Patrons sit on low tables and stools, while cloth-draped tables are designed to hold large round trays of food served family-style. If you're with a group, order several dishes; they all come together on top of *injera*, the flat, tangy, soft Ethiopian bread. Extra *injera* pancakes come folded on a plate so you can eat the Ethiopian way, using the bread to pick up your food. (No utensils here.) All dishes run in the $8.95 to 12.95 range. Meskerem's hours are Monday through Sunday from noon to midnight.

Also very good, and located just across the street, is Fasikals, at 2447 18th Street N.W.; telephone, ✆ (202) 797-7673. It features sidewalk seating in fair weather and a wealth of Ethiopian specialty drinks and beers. An Ethiopian friend of Mr. C's gave the place high marks, so check them out too. Fasikal's hours are Monday through Sunday from noon to midnight.

Millie and Al's

- 2440 18th Street N.W., Washington, D.C.; ✆ (202) 387-8131

Keep your eyes peeled: The sign for this restaurant is up high, and the front is so nondescript that Mr. C walked right past it the first time.

The inside is just as dark, but despite its dive atmosphere, this place somehow manages to achieve a comfortably casual feel. The place is loud and busy; kids can be seen running around amongst the tables. A wide-screen television is on hand for sporting events.

The menu is chock full of burgers, subs, pizzas, and other good ol' bar food—you can get a juicy burger for under $5. Even so, M & A also features specials like lasagna and chicken cacciatore, served with "Chef's bread" on the side. The prices on these dinners are almost as small as the lounge itself—a wallet-pleasing $5 to $7. Good thing credit cards are accepted.

Hours are Monday through Sunday from 4 p.m. to 2 a.m.

Polly's Cafe

- 1342 U Street N.W., Washington, D.C.; ✆ (202) 265-8385

Polly's undoubtedly draws Washington's "social circuit" crowd. Of course, location, location, location is everything. This cozy bar/restaurant, down a few steps from the bustling and funky U Street, serves up salads, sandwiches, burgers, and more. In addition, creative specials of chicken, fish, and pastas vary; there's no freezer space, according to management, and so "Whatever we get in that morning, we serve it all that night!" On Mr. C's visit, that meant broiled mahi mahi with soy sauce and lime served with rice for $11.50.

Among the appetizers, homemade soups and chili run $4 per bowl; bruschetta with tomato and feta cheese, $4.50. A two-fisted hamburger, half a pound of pure ground beef, starts at just $4.75, with toppings an additional $1 each. For entrees, a 10-ounce steak, marinated and grilled, is $10,

served with a choice of vegetables; speaking of which, the heaping "Polly's Vegetable Plate" comes in at a mere $7.75. Wash your meal down with a variety of tap and bottled beers, or several different kinds of wine.

Weekend brunch gives you a choice of eggs, omelets, waffles, or French toast, for $7.25; that includes home fries, bacon or sausage, coffee or tea, and juice. Or, for $8, try their wonderful variations on eggs Benedict—with ham, avocado, spinach, or smoked salmon, all served with home fries, coffee or tea, and juice. Add a mimosa, screwdriver, or Bloody Mary for $2.75. Now that's a breakfast of champions. Polly's offers three specials daily. Whip out that mobile and call ahead for details.

Polly's is open Monday through Thursday from 6 p.m. to 1:30 a.m., Friday and Saturday from 10 a.m. to 2:30 a.m., and Sunday from 10 a.m. to 12:30 a.m.

Star of Siam

- 1136 19th Street N.W., Washington, D.C.; ✆ (202) 785-2839

For award-winning Thai food, nothing beats Star of Siam. The chefs will happily give any dish more kick—some spicier dishes can certainly bring tears to your eyes! Going the other way, a surprisingly mild curry is *gang gra-ree goong*, yellow curry with shrimp, coconut milk, and tomato, served with cucumber sauce ($10.95). *Ped num dang*, boneless duck with mixed vegetables, is also good for those faint of heart and weak of taste buds. The noodle dishes are wonderful, like Pad Thai with shrimp ($9.25). Noodles can still be quite fiery: *Ba mee Siam*, fried egg noodles with beef, pork, chicken, egg, and vegetable is served in a zippy Thai hot sauce for $9.25.

Star treatment is available Monday through Saturday from 11:30 a.m. to 11 p.m., and Sunday from 5 to 10 p.m.

Timberlake's

- 1726 Connecticut Avenue N.W., Washington, D.C.;
  ✆ (202) 483-2266

The atmosphere at Timberlake's is very different from most pubs—there are plants and lots of natural light in here. The pub fare, while familiar, has some interesting twists, too. Burgers range between $6.95 and include such toppings as provolone and mushroom, ham and Swiss, and chili con carne. All are served with your choice of fries or crudit (raw vegetables with dipping sauce). Healthy food at a bar? Believe it. Mr. C enjoyed the "1726 Club," loaded with turkey, bacon, and Swiss cheese, served with veggies and house dressing ($7.95). Same price for the cornmeal-battered fish and chips dinner.

Timberlake's happy hour starts at 3 p.m. and goes 'til 7 p.m.; along with drink specials, all appetizers are 25 percent off. These finger foods include onion strings, chili con queso, baked Brie, and other goodies.

Timberlake's is open until 2 a.m. Sundays through Thursdays and until 3 a.m. on Fridays and Saturdays.

GEORGETOWN

Including Glover Park

Austin Grill

- 2404 Wisconsin Avenue N.W., Washington, D.C.;
  ✆ (202) 337-8080
- 750 E Street N.W.; Washington, D.C.; ✆ (202) 393-3776
- 801 King St, Alexandria, VA; ✆ (703) 684-8969

Festive and casual, the Austin Grill serves up authentic Mexican food that puts fast-food versions to shame. Start with *chile con queso* ($4.95), or "East Austin Nachos" ($8.95), made with hot chili, grilled jalapenos, and Chihuahua cheese.

All your fave dishes can be found here. Try macho tacos—apparently they're quite the thing in Austin—made with eggs, chorizo, and cheese for $7.99. Mr. C especially liked the grilled beef and bean burritos ($10.95). Most dishes come with rice and a choice of toppings, including guacamole and *pico de gallo*. You can't go wrong with dishes like chili-and-garlic marinated pork chops, crabmeat quesadilla, or roasted poblanos and cilantro. Be sure to save some room for the Ibarra chocolate brownie.

For a unique culinary experience, try weekend brunch from 11 a.m. to 3 p.m. Enjoy Mexican breakfast treats like cornmeal pancakes with pecan butter, or migas—eggs scrambled with corn tortillas, peppers, tomato, and onion, served with rice, beans, flour tortillas, and cheese.

Hours are Sunday through Thursday from 11:30 a.m. to 11 p.m.; Saturday and Sunday from 11:30 a.m. to midnight.

Bistro Francais

- 3124 M Street N.W., Washington, D.C.; ✆ (202) 338-3830

Entering Bistro Francais is like stepping into a charming French cafe. The two dining rooms are large but not overly crowded; carved wooden partitions offer a degree of privacy, and add to the cozy feel of the place. Can Mr. C afford such continental style?

Admittedly, the prices here are not cheap; most entrees are $17.95 and higher. However, even devout Cheapsters can enjoy the lovely atmosphere and delicious French cuisine by taking advantage of the "Early Bird" and "Night Owl" specials. These specials include a glass of wine, soup du jour or appetizer, an entrée, and dessert for $18.95—the regular price of most entrees alone! Selections change daily; past choices have included seafood plates, steak tartare, french onion soup, lamb steaks, blackened mahi-mahi, duck with raspberries, bouillabaisse, and pork tenderloin. Desserts may offer kiwi, or pecan tarts, and pastry dough baked with custard and fruit inside. Stop by for a real treat, French style. The "Early Bird" is available between 5 p.m. and 7 p.m. and the "Night Owl" goes from 10:30 p.m. to 1 a.m.

Bistro Francais' hours are Sunday through Thursday from 11 a.m. to 3 a.m.; Friday and Saturday from 11:30 a.m. to 4 a.m.

Booeymonger

- 3265 Prospect Street N.W., Washington, D.C.; ✆ (202) 333-4810

- 5252 Wisconsin Avenue N.W., Washington, D.C.; ✆ (202) 686-5805

- 4600 East-West Highway, Bethesda, MD; ✆ (301) 718-9550

  Tip-free

  See the listing under *Restaurants—Upper Northwest*.
  Hours are Monday through Sunday from 7:30 a.m. to midnight.

MR. CHEAP'S PICKS

Georgetown

Bistro Francais—How can this upscale eatery make Mr. C's book? Before 7 p.m. and after 10:30 p.m., you can get a three-course continental dinner, including wine, for about $16.95. C'est magnifique!

Miss Saigon—This moderately priced Vietnamese fare tastes absolutely superb, and the price is right.

Zed's Ethiopian Cuisine—If you're already familiar with Ethiopian food, you'll love this place. And if you've never had this cheap and hearty fare, you'll love to discover this place.

Bread & Chocolate

- 2301 M Street N.W. Washington, D.C.; ✆ (202) 833-8360

  See the listing under *Restaurants—Upper Northwest*.

Burrito Brothers

- 1815 M Street N.W., Washington, D.C.; ✆ (202) 785-3309

- 1718 Connecticut Avenue, N.W.,Washington, D.C.; ✆ (202) 332-2308

- 205 Pennsylvania Avenue S.E.,Washington, D.C.; ✆ (202) 543-6835

  See the listing under *Restaurants—Capitol Hill*.

Chadwicks

- 3205 K Street N.W., Washington D.C.; ✆ (202) 362-8040

- 213 Strand Street, Alexandria, VA; ✆ (703) 836-4442

Chadwicks is a comfortable, neighborhood tavern. Even in trendy Georgetown, locals crowd the bar. And you'll find more than good spirits here—there's a complete menu for lunch or dinner.

Mr. C enjoyed a perfectly seasoned Chesapeake crab cake sandwich with onion rings ($8.95), while his dining buddy gave a "thumbs up" to the Southwest chicken club, complete with guacamole, bacon, fresh vegetable salsa, and fries ($7.95). Heartier dishes will leave you too full for dessert; try the vegetarian lasagna ($8.95) and grilled St. Louis BBQ ribs ($9.95), served with fries, snap bean succotash, and chopped vegetable slaw. If you do make it to a sweet ending, Chadwicks' mud pie ($4.95), made with coffee liqueur, is sinfully sublime.

Hours are Monday through Thursday from 11 a.m. to 1 a.m., Friday and Saturday from 11 a.m. to 2 a.m., and Sunday from 11 a.m. to 10 p.m.

Chipotle

• 1937 M Street, N.W., Washington, D.C.; ✆ (202) 466-4104

• ✐ www.chipotle.com

This stylish and fun establishment served stylish and fun Tex-Mex and at good prices. Try some of their delectable chunky guacamole ($1.25) along with freshly made tortilla chips, and wash it down with an ice-cold beer or margarita. Your can then get to the main courses, including burritos, tacos, and fajitas (ranging from $4.25 to $5.25), along with Chipotle's steaming cilantro and lime-flavored rice. Not too shabby. Chipotle is open 11 a.m. to 10 p.m. every day.

Clyde's of Georgetown

• 3236 M Street N.W., Washington D.C.; ✆ (202) 333-9180

• ✐ www.clydes.com

Georgetown ambiance while partaking of tasty gourmet eats at discounted prices. You may be surprised to find Clyde's in this book, since their entrees start at Mr. C's usual $10 limit. However, after a hard day at work, you can soak up some of that quaintness at Clyde's weeknights from 4 to 7 p.m. at a happy hour that features half-price specials on such delectable offerings as crab cakes, Caesar salad, and burgers!

If you can't make it to Clyde's for the "beat the rush" special, there are plenty of sandwiches, burgers, salads, and appetizers under $10. Hot crab and artichoke dip, served with French bread, is $6.50. This appetizer makes a light supper, or can be ordered with a bowl of soup of the day ($3.95), or house salad ($4.50), to make a more complete meal. Sandwiches, all served with fries, start at $5.50; try the grilled cheese with Muenster and American, melted on country-white bread. For larger appetites, the $7.95 "Washingtonian," hot roast beef with horseradish, cream cheese, and red onion on pumpernickel toast, fits the bill. The $7.75 bacon cheeseburger will also fill you up without emptying your wallet. During happy hour (4:30 to 7 p.m., weekdays), appetizers are half price.

Clyde's hours are Sunday through Thursday from 11:30 a.m. to midnight; Friday and Saturday from 9:30 a.m. to 1 a.m.

Enzio's Neapolitan Kitchen

• 2319 Wisconsin Avenue N.W.,Washington, D.C.; ✆ (202) 965-1337

Well, if you ask anyone working there, it's actually called "Enzio and Mama Marie's," 'cuz they both run the show. The show is small, actually—only eight glass-topped tables are comfortably set inside. It may be no frills, but the pasta is homemade (thanks, Mama!), the portions are big, and the prices are quite good.

If you've got a dining companion, start with hot antipasto for two ($12). Try not to fill up too much—spaghetti carbonara ($7.75) and linguine with white clam sauce ($7.50) is surely substantial enough to satisfy your stomach. A little high for Mr. C's budget was shrimp scampi al limone ($13.95) . . . but definitely worth it. The veal parmigiana ($10.95) was also noteworthy.

Enzio's (and Mama's) hours are Monday through Sunday from 11 a.m. to 11 p.m.

Faccia Luna Pizzeria

- 2400 Wisconsin Avenue N.W., Washington, D.C.;
  ✆ (202) 337-3132

- ✍ www.faccialuna.com

Casual yet trendy, Faccia Luna is a boisterous place serving brick-oven pizza, and great beers and wines, in an atmosphere highlighted by open kitchens, so you can watch pies going in and out of the fire.

This place, which came out of the collaboration between two Alpha Sigma Phi fraternity brothers at Penn State, Bill McFadden and Joe Corey, was the first in what is now a small chain of upscale pizza places.

The pizza, in traditional or white varieties, starts at just $6.50 for a 10-inch pie (a meal for one person, or an appetizer for two), all the way up to $11.50 for a 16-incher. A wide assortment of toppings, both standard and inventive, adds another $1.25 each. That white pizza features extra virgin olive oil, garlic, oregano, red pepper, and several cheeses. Heavenly.

Build your own calzone ($6.50) or stromboli ($6), each of which feature that same chewy pizza dough folded and stuffed with tomato sauce and different cheeses. Choose from two dozen fillings, at $1 each; these include chicken, potatoes, peppers, and more. A tasty sandwich choice is the char-broiled chicken breast ($6), boneless and basted in Dijon mustard, white wine vinaigrette, and served with walnut garlic dressing.

Faccia Luna has four beers on tap and over 30 different bottles; for dessert, check out the chocolate marquis, a shortcake filled with chocolate cream and topped with "chocoglaze" and whole pistachios ($4.50). This is to die for.

Hours are Sunday through Thursday from 11:30 a.m. to 11 p.m.; Saturday and Sunday from 11:30 p.m. to midnight.

Fettoosh

- 3277 M Street N.W., Washington, D.C.; ✆ (202) 342-1199

Fans of Middle Eastern fare should head to Fettoosh, where good value and a soothing atmosphere make the food seem even tastier. Light eaters should try the lentil soup ($3) and gyro sandwich ($5.50). Or, choose from the long list of veggie or meat appetizers and platters; most are between $5 and $6.50. Order a few of these to create a filling dinner with variety. Good bets include maqanik, Lebanese-style lamb sausages with lemon.

Most entrees are between $9.95 and $10.95. Mr. C recommends *shish tawook*, boneless chicken breast marinated in olive oil, lemon juice, and garlic; it's grilled with tomato, onion, and green peppers; and served with rice, salad, and pita bread. *Kussa mihshi* was also quite tasty and different—cored baby zucchini, stuffed with meat and rice, and cooked in tomato sauce.

Fettoosh is open Sunday through Thursday from 10 a.m. to 3 a.m.; Friday and Saturday from 10 a.m. to 5 a.m.

Garrett's

- 3125 M. Street N.W., Washington, D.C.; ✆ (202) 336-6122

Despite the pervasive railroad and rhino theme at Garrett's, the historical building in which the restaurant is housed was neither a depot nor a zoo. In fact, Thomas Sim Lee, friend of George Washington and governor of Maryland, built this corner house in 1794. There's no explanation given for the decor, but when the food is good and cheap, who cares about embellishment?

The downstairs is a comfortable pub, but venture upstairs to three cozy dining rooms, one of which is a glass-enclosed greenhouse-style sunroom. American favorites fill the menu, under such headings as "Main Tracks," "Side Tracks," and "The Bar Car." If you like, begin with "Stokers," a.k.a. appetizers. "Nachos Sierra" are blue corn chips loaded with two cheeses, beef chili, avocado relish, jalapenos, black olives, salsa, and sour cream, available in large ($4.50) and huge ($6.50) portions.

All burgers are half-pounders and come with house fries. Choose from unusual but tasty topping combinations, like bleu cheese and bacon; or mushrooms, Monterey jack cheese, and caramelized onions—burgers are between $6.50.

Dinners requiring utensils are interesting and delicious concoctions; salmon ($10.50), made with dill butter, served with rice and fresh veggies, was quite good. "Pasta Michelangelo" ($9.50) is a combination of chicken and fresh vegetables served over angel hair pasta with white wine garlic herb sauce. Dee-lish!

Finish up with something from the "End of the Line." You're sure to enjoy bourbon bread pudding and cream ($2.95), or a warm walnut brownie sundae, with vanilla ice cream and chocolate sauce ($3.95). Hours are Sunday through Thursday from 11 p.m. to 1:30 a.m.; Friday and Saturday from noon to 2:30 a.m.

The Georgetown Cafe

- 1623 Wisconsin Avenue N.W., Washington, D.C.; ✆ (202) 333-0215

Open 24 hours a day, this diner-style restaurant looks like it was decorated in the '70s, complete with red rug and wood paneling. The prices also seem stuck in a time warp; when Mr. C perused the menu, he found only one item over $10, and that was a 10-ounce rib eye steak, topped with sautéed onions and mushrooms, served with potatoes and vegetables ($13.95). Everything else is way below.

Breakfasts are served any hour of the day or night. Hot cakes or French toast are $3.95, two eggs any style are $2.95. Add a side order of home fries for $2.25, and you're set for the day. Sandwiches include chicken salad ($5.95) and crab cake ($6.50), all served with chips. There's also a selection of Middle Eastern dishes, including hummus ($5.95) and falafel platter ($7.95), which includes tahini salad, cheese, olives, and pita bread. Save room for dessert—they are just scrumptious! Have some chocolate mousse cake ($5.95), or deep dish apple pie ($3.75).

Martin's Tavern

- 1264 Wisconsin Avenue N.W., Washington, D.C.; ✆ (202) 333-7370

Since 1933, Martin's has been serving everyone from Presidents

Truman and Kennedy to "just plain G.I. Joes." The dark, cozy environment, complete with little candles on each table, definitely lends itself to unwinding with friends after a long day. The menu is small but covers the basic favorites, and adds a few unusual gourmet treats for variety. Appetizers include New England clam chowder ($3.95 for a cup and $4.95 for a bowl) and potato skins ($4.50). Sandwiches all come with fries, coleslaw, or homemade potato chips. Mr. C recommends the "Monte Cristo," ham, turkey, and cheese dipped in batter and grilled with apple butter for $7.25. Same price for hot pastrami and Swiss. Martin's specialties include Welsh rarebit ($8.25); and eggs Benedict, with a choice of ham, smoked salmon, or crab meat ($9.50 to $11.50).

Martin's hours are Sunday through Thursday from 8 a.m. to midnight; Friday and Saturday from 8 a.m. to 1 a.m.

Miss Saigon

- 3057 M Street N.W., Washington, D.C.; ✆ (202) 333-5545

Situated in an outdoor garden setting (and indoor garden atmosphere during the closer months!), at Miss Saigon, you get a lot of bang for the buck. This moderately priced fare tastes absolutely superb. Aside from the serene backdrop and affordable prices, there's another bonus—the wait staff service is cheerful, efficient, and helpful in explaining the Vietnamese cuisine featured on their menu.

Here you can order the following main entrees from anywhere between $10 to $15: skewers of marinated fish, beef and chicken cooked on the grill, juicy caramel pork, Yunnan ham, salads with a spicy bite, and stir-fries over thin

vermicelli noodles. The tangy side sauces are also fun to experiment with flavor-wise. The whole experience will surely make your taste buds sing—and beg for more!

Hours are Monday through Friday from 11:30 a.m. to 11 p.m.; Saturday and Sunday from noon to 11 p.m.

Mr. Smith's of Georgetown

- 3104 M Street N.W., Washington, D.C.; ✆ (202) 333-3104

- 8369 Leesburg Pike, Tysons Corner, VA; ✆ (703) 893-1204

- ✑ www.mrsmiths.com.

Mr. Smith came to Washington, bringing with him plenty of style and elegance with him. This comfy pub has several intimate dining rooms, leading to a larger garden room complete with glass roof, tile floor, and lots of plants. There's a working fireplace, and every night after 9 p.m. you'll be treated to live piano music.

In keeping with the atmosphere, the fine pub cuisine Mr. C and his companions sampled was a cut above the typical bar food. The appetizer sampler ($6.95), for example, came with old faves like potato skins, mozzarella sticks, and chicken fingers, but also included fresh mushroom and zucchini tempura. It was a meal in itself, and a great way to share the opening round.

One of Mr. C's buddies enjoyed a half-pound bacon cheeseburger ($5.95), served with hand-cut, homemade potato chips. There are 13 varieties of burger, most under $7. You could break the bank and order the $999 wineburger, which is accompanied by a bottle of vintage Chateau Lafite Rothschild; you'd think they'd throw in a few French fries for that price. It's not a very popular item, though definitely eye-catching. Mr. C's other pal gave two thumbs up to the spicy pecan-crusted chicken ($9.95), topped with a light cucumber sauce and served with rice pilaf and fresh zucchini.

Meanwhile, Mr. C uncharacteristically ordered one of the more expensive dishes, lobster fettuccini ($13.95). Lobster meat, in a light cream sauce, was mixed with fresh fettuccini and served with salad and garlic bread. Seafood-lovers who want an even better deal should stop by Monday nights after 5 p.m. for "All You Can Eat" fish and chips ($8.95).

A popular Georgetown hangout, Mr. Smith's features a happy hour on weeknights from 4 to 7 p.m. with half-price appetizers, $1.50 "rail" drinks, $1.50 for house wine, and $1 off draft beer. Same deal in the 'burbs. On Friday and Saturday nights a rock band takes the stage with no cover charge.

Mr. Smith's hours are Sunday through Thursday from noon to midnight, Fridays and Saturdays 11 a.m. to 1 a.m.

Old Glory All-American Bar-B-Que

- 3139 M Street N.W., Washington, D.C.; ✆ (202) 337-3406

This large, casual Georgetown pub features a long bar, a row of booths, several TVs—and, good as its name—a whole pitful of barbecued delights. Wash 'em all down with one of their star-spangled glory of beers on tap.

Smokehouse chili ($4.25) or "oak fired-up" chicken wings ($5.25) make for a fine start. Move on to one of the barbecue platters, all of which are smoked and cooked on an open pit—including a half-rack of pork spare ribs ($11.95); a sliced smokehouse combo of beef brisket, sliced pork, and corncob-smoked ham ($12.95);

and for you health nuts (should you venture into such a joint), there's even a pit-roasted garden vegetable platter ($8.25). All of these come with a choice of two sides, including barbecued red beans, potato salad, and creamed succotash.

You can also scarf up the half-pound burgers ($8.25); sandwiches, all served with fries, potato salad, or mustard slaw; and a half-dozen gooey desserts. Old Glory fires up the grill every day of the week.

Hours are Sunday through Thursday from 11:30 a.m. to 1:30 a.m.; Friday and Saturday from 11:30 a.m. to 2:30 a.m.

Rocklands

- 2418 Wisconsin Avenue N.W.; Washington, D.C.; ✆ (202) 333-2558

- ✐ www.rocklands.com

Stroll into Rocklands, inhale deeply, and let that smoky, barbecue-scented air waft over you. This is primarily a takeout place, but if you'd like to soak up more of that atmosphere, there is one large communal table with several seats.

The food more than lives up to first impressions. A whole barbecued chicken is $8.99; a half, $4.99; and a quarter, $3.99. Feed a small family or just yourself—this barbecue is so good that you may not want to share. You can also bring home some baby back ribs, in whole ($17.99) and half-rack ($8.99) sizes.

The sandwiches will definitely liven up your day. Barbecued pork and hot Italian sausage are both $3.95; pulled barbecued chicken is just a dollar more. Side dishes are just $1.25 and include potato salad, Southern-style mustard greens, and barbecued baked beans. Rocklands is smokin' round the clock.

Hours are Monday through Saturday from 11 a.m. to 10 p.m., and Sunday from 11 a.m. to 9 p.m.

Romeo's Pizzeria

- 2132-G Wisconsin Avenue, Washington, D.C.; ℅ (202) 337-1111

This Italian eatery offers a cross-section of standard fare ranging from pizza, salad, calzones, and stuffed pitas. The not-so-typical aspect of this establishment is the prices: A large gourmet pizza costs $7.99. Their lavash rolls come in a variety of flavors such as spinach, artichoke, feta with garlic sauce, and also chicken, portabella mushrooms, spicy red pepper sauce—for just $5.99 each. Friendly atmosphere, you'll want to linger.

Hours are Monday through Thursday from 11 a.m. to 3 a.m.; Friday and Saturday from 11 a.m. to 4 a.m.

Thomas Sweet

- 3214 P Street N.W., Washington, D.C.; ℅ (202) 337-0616

Located on the corner of Wisconsin Avenue, Thomas Sweet is your basic coffee shop, serving plenty of cheap and filling sandwiches. "Hoya" ($4.75), one of the vegetarian selections, is filled with fresh mozzarella, tomatoes, basil, and dressed with balsamic vinaigrette. "New York Avenue" ($5.50) has a little more kick, with roast beef, grilled onions and peppers, horseradish sauce, and melted Gruyere cheese.

Health concerns are addressed here, more than at most diners. Some sandwiches use low-salt ham or no-cholesterol mayonnaise and all are served with a side salad. Tip to Cheapsters: Pick up a "meal ticket" card, buy 10 sandwiches, and your next lunch is free.

Hours are Sunday through Thursday from 8 a.m. to 11 p.m., Fridays and Saturdays from 9 a.m. to 11 p.m.

Treats Bakery and Cafe

- 1754 H Street N.W., Washington, D.C.; ℅ (202) 659-0558

- 409 Third Street S.W., Washington, D.C.; ℅ (202) 488-2887

- 300 D Street SW #101, Washington, D.C.; ℅ (202) 659-0558

- 50 Massachusetts Avenue N.E., Washington, D.C.; ℅ (202) 898-2570

See the listing under *Restaurants—Downtown Area.*

Vietnam Georgetown Restaurant

- 2934 M Street N.W., Washington, D.C.; ℅ (202) 337-4536

At Vietnam Georgetown, you'll find a variety of tasty, low-priced Vietnamese dishes. The best deal is the "all you can eat" lunch buffet for $6.75. Choose from three entrees, plus an appetizer and rice. Selections change daily; you may get to choose from such dishes as summer rolls, cinnamon beef with orange, lemon chicken, and sweet-and-sour shrimp.

At dinner, the painted lamps give a cozy glow to the place. During the summer, you can also dine in their garden. Begin with crab meat and asparagus soup ($4.40 for small and $6.60 for large), then try one of many specialties—Vietnamese crepe ($11), with shrimp, pork, mushrooms, and bean sprouts tucked inside a large crispy shell, was Mr. C's favorite. Caramel pork with coconut milk ($11.28), served with steamed rice, should not be missed, either.

Hours are Monday through Sunday from noon to 11 p.m.

Zed's Ethiopian Cuisine

- 3318 M Street N.W., Washington, D.C.; ✆ (202) 333-4710

Zed's immodestly calls itself "indescribably delicious," and local reviewers seem to agree; it's been voted one of *Washingtonian's* "very best restaurants" for the past five years. If you've never tried Ethiopian fare, this is a fine place to take the plunge.

Start with *kaisa* ($5.25)—dried cottage cheese with purified butter, collard greens, and red-spiced pepper. Zed's specialty is vegetarian dishes: *kik alitcha*, yellow split peas puree with onions, green peppers, and garlic; and *miser watt,* red lentil puree in red pepper sauce, are exceptionally good. Each dish is $11.25. Carnivores have plenty of choices, too. Try *yebeg alitcha* ($13.50), spiced lamb in herb butter, or *awazei fitfit* ($13.50), injera bread soaked in red pepper sauce with beef; each is delicious and delicately prepared. Complete your dinner with *torta rustica,* layered sponge cake soaked with coffee. Heavenly!

Zed's hours are Monday through Sunday from 11 a.m. to 11 p.m.

UPPER NORTHWEST

Including Chevy Chase, Cleveland Park, Friendship Heights, Tenleytown, and Woodley Park

American City Diner

- 5532 Connecticut Avenue N.W., Washington, D.C.; ✆ (202) 244-1949

Bold statement made by this place: "Not just a restaurant but a way of life." Of course, being open 24 hours helps validate such a claim, as does its wealth of options for all three meals of the day. Then there's that throwback '50s diner feel, a welcome sight to Mr. C in one of the city's more upscale areas.

Breakfast is served round the clock—another good sign! Order up eggs, home fries, and toast for $4.95; ham steak or pork chops for $7.95. Omelets, in six different varieties, run $7 to $8. There's a plethora of sandwiches for under $8, including grilled chicken breast with cheese and bacon, and good ol' corned beef; the American City Burger, with all the fixin's, is a mere $6.50. Or check out one of their daily specials served from 11 a.m. all the way to 11 p.m. Previous specials include prime rib for $12.95, pork chops for $10, and fresh flounder for $10. Among the choices: "America's Favorite," nothing less than meatloaf, mashed potatoes and gravy, vegetables, and a roll and butter. A way of life? You betcha. Hours are 24/7.

MR. CHEAP'S PICKS

Chevy Chase

American City Diner—Blueplate specials in white-collar land. Breakfast served round the clock, too.

Armand's Chicago Pizzeria

- 4231 Wisconsin Avenue N.W., Washington, D.C.; ✆ (202) 686-9450

- 5000 Wisconsin Avenue N.W.,
  Washington, D.C.;
  ✆ (202) 363-5500

  And other suburban locations

  See the listing under *Restaurants—Capitol Hill.*

Babe's Billiard Cafe

- 4600 Wisconsin Avenue N.W.,
  Washington, D.C.;
  ✆ (202) 966-0082

For the most part, Babe's is a pool hall and a pub—but don't let that scare you diners away. Its full menu even includes late-night breakfast options, so come with friends, grab some grub, and spend a few hours on the tables (playing pool, that is).

Between midnight and 3 a.m. you can get all types of breakfast foods—eggs, omelets, the works. Otherwise, you have a good selection of pub favorites, from fried mozzarella ($5.95) and Buffalo wings ($7.95), to burgers ($6.95) and grilled chicken sandwiches ($7.95). All sandwiches come with chips, fries, or coleslaw.

For something more filling, try Babe's full rack of barbecue spare ribs ($12.95), served with fries and coleslaw), a half rack is $9.95. Homemade lasagna ($9.95 with salad), mussels and linguine ($9.95), and a 10-ounce T-bone steak with two vegetables ($10.95) are among the other choices.

D.C. night owls are going to love this: Hours are Monday through Sunday from 11 a.m. to 4 a.m.

The Booeymonger

- 5252 Wisconsin Avenue N.W.,
  Washington, D.C.;
  ✆ (202) 686-5805

- 3265 Prospect Street N.W.,
  Washington, D.C.;
  ✆ (202) 333-4810

MR. CHEAP'S PICKS

Friendship Heights

The Booeymonger—Cozy, casual deli, good for hanging out.

Greet the day with "Attila the Hun." No, not the notorious tyrant—the Booeymonger's breakfast sandwich with fried egg, hot pastrami, horseradish, and cream cheese served on a Kaiser roll ($5.75). Big eaters won't go hungry with the weekday breakfast special of two eggs, any style, with bacon, ham, or sausage, home fries, and toast or bagel for $3.75.

The lunch and dinner menu is mostly sandwiches, salads, and the like. "Pita Pan" ($4.95) probably won't be a children's hero—a whole wheat pita is stuffed with salad veggies, Muenster cheese, alfalfa sprouts, mushrooms, avocado, tomato, and house dressing. You'll be captivated by the "Patty Hearst" ($4.95) featuring turkey, bacon, melted provolone cheese, and Russian dressing served on an English muffin. Or, take "Manhattan" ($5.25) with grilled roast beef, fresh spinach. bacon, and cheddar served on French bread. Stop by and pick up breakfast, lunch, or dinner—this casual hangout is open daily.

Hours are Monday through Sunday from 7:30 a.m. to 8 p.m.

Bread & Chocolate

- 5542 Connecticut Avenue N.W.
  Washington, D.C.;
  ✆ (202) 966-7413

Bread & Chocolate doubles as a bakery and a restaurant. The seemingly basic menu of sandwiches and salads features gourmet touches and unusual twists, making these dishes out of the ordinary.

"Old-fashioned" chicken salad sandwiches are made with walnuts, grapes, and celery, mixed with lemon mayonnaise, and served on a croissant. Hardly old-fashioned, eh? Smokehouse turkey comes with bacon, raisin coleslaw, and Russian dressing, also on a croissant. Either is a bargain at $6.75. Non-meat eaters can enjoy a "Vegetarian Hye Roller" ($7.45), with fresh and sun-dried tomatoes, alfalfa sprouts, cucumber slices, and garlic and herb spread, all rolled together onto Armenian cracker bread.

Salads are anything but a bowl of lettuce. Mediterranean pasta salad ($6.75) is made with ziti, olives, red peppers, artichoke hearts, and cucumbers, tossed in a red wine vinegar, olive oil, and feta cheese dressing. How 'bout smoked salmon, shrimp, and pasta salad ($8.75) tossed in a light tarragon dressing? Mmmm!

Hours are Monday through Saturday from 7 a.m. to 7 p.m. and Sunday from 8 a.m. to 6 p.m.

Chadwicks

- 5247 Wisconsin Avenue N.W., Washington, D.C.;
  ℅ (202) 362-8040

See the listing under *Restaurants—Georgetown*.

MR. CHEAP'S PICKS

Cleveland Park

Ivy's Place—An inexpensive Thai restaurant adds Indonesian cuisine for something a little different.

Chicken Out Rotisserie

- 4866 Massachusetts Avenue N.W., Washington, D.C.;
  ℅ (202) 364-8646

This area chain almost makes fast food homey, with its clean and cheery blue-tiled locations. They serve up big sandwiches and big chicken dinners for the whole family. In fact, all of its menu selections are emphatically described as "big," so go—expect to eat hearty.

"Big Meal Deals" give you a main entree with two sides (potatoes, beans, various vegetables and salads, and more). Choose a whole chicken with white meat for $7.34 and a half size for $6.29. Whole chickens with dark meat are also available for $6.29 and half size for $5.24. Pretty big in terms of selection!

"Family Feasts" are another value option, meant for 4, 8, or 12 people. The small size gives you three side orders and four baguette rolls with a whole chicken for $15.99. Not a bad price for three, or even four really hungry people.

Hours are Monday through Sunday from 11 a.m. to 9:30 p.m.

Chipotle

- 2600 Connecticut Avenue, N.W., Washington, D.C.;
  ℅ (202) 299-9111;

- 4301 Wisconsin Avenue, N.W., Washington, D.C.;
  ℅ (202) 237-0602;

- 7600 Old Georgetown Road, Bethesda, MD;
  ℅ (301) 907-9077;

- ✑ www.chipotle.com

See the listing under *Restaurants—Dupont Circle*.

Colonel Brooks Tavern

- 901 Monroe Street N.E., Washington, D.C. ✆ (202) 529-4002

Extremely popular with students (and faculty) from nearby Catholic University, Colonel Brooks has long been a bright spot in this otherwise bland area, with a cozy tavern feel and relaxed, friendly wait staff.

Try one of a dozen sandwiches, huge and hearty: grilled marinated chicken with smoked bacon, jack cheese, and jalapeno mayo ($7.99, served with French fries) is just one excellent choice. "The Colonel's Favorite," a triple-decker of pastrami, turkey, cheese, and coleslaw, is the same price; a salmon filet handful ($8.99) also rates a look. Burgers run $5.75 to $6.95 and are similarly immense.

For dinner, Mr. C couldn't overlook the mixed grill of marinated shrimp, cumin sausage, and breast of chicken with roasted garlic and sweet peppers, served with potatoes and vegetable, all for $11.99. Not your humble scribe. Check out curried chicken or sugar-cured ham, both $10.99, or pasta Florentine ($11.99), served with a house salad. Most appetizers are reasonably priced, like a grilled vegetable enchilada for $4.99.

The tavern adds a quieter upstairs dining area to its main "Tap Room"; either option enables you to enjoy a variety of microbrews, three of which are new every month. Connoisseurs can sample a pint of beer for around $4.

The restaurant hours are Monday through Sunday from noon to 1 a.m.

El Tamarindo

- 7331 Georgia Avenue N.W., Washington, D.C.; ✆ (202) 291-0525

- 1785 Florida Avenue N.W., Washington, D.C.; ✆ (202) 328-3660

See the listing under *Restaurants—Dupont Circle.*

49 Twelve Thai Cuisine

- 4912 Wisconsin Avenue N.W., Washington, D.C.; ✆ (202) 966-4696

This restaurant's name does guarantee that you will find them on Wisconsin. Once you get there, start your meal with skewers of crispy shrimp wrapped with minced chicken, bean thread, and mushrooms, served with a spicy sweet-and-sour sauce. Or order the popular satay, marinated beef, pork, or chicken with peanut sauce. Both are a very reasonable $6.95.

Check out the curry dishes, which are especially good and can be made either mild or spicy. Mr. C enjoyed seafood in green curry sauce—shrimp, scallops, and squid combined with (you guessed it) green curry, coconut milk, bamboo shoots, and basil ($8.95). Another choice is duck with pineapple, smothered in wine sauce; also delicious, also $8.95—pretty much the highest price for entrees. A lighter meal may consist of pork salad, with fresh ginger and peanuts in a spicy lime dressing ($6.95); and vegetable lemon grass soup ($3.95). Hours are Monday through Sunday from 11:30 a.m. to 10 p.m.

Ivy's Place

- 3520 Connecticut Avenue N.W., Washington, D.C.; ✆ (202) 363-7802

Ivy's isn't exactly elegant, but don't judge this Indonesian and Thai cafe by its plain cover. The food is quite good, and the prices are even better. The most expensive items are the "deluxe satay" plates, which feature chicken, beef, or pork skewers served with rice for $10.95. Just about everything else is $7 to $8—appetizers and soups are even less ($3.35 to $4.50), so you can afford to try a few things.

Mr. C thought crab wonton soup and deep fried bean curd (only $1.50) were very tasty ways to start his dinner. It was difficult deciding between the Thai and Indonesian dishes, which were equally represented and remarkably compelling: Thai shrimp with cashews, chicken with garlic and sweet pepper, grilled spicy sweet fish, stir-fried pork with bean sprouts. Mr. C ultimately opted for Indonesian spicy beef cooked in coconut sauce; it was just heavenly. Stop by and see (and taste!) for yourself. Ivy's hours are Sunday through Thursday from 11 a.m. to 10 p.m.; Friday and Saturday from 11 a.m. to 11 p.m.

Thai Town

• 2655 Connecticut Avenue N.W., Washington, D.C.;
  ✆ (202) 667-5115

This restaurant is simple, elegant, and offers most of its entrees for under $10—a dining combination certain to get Mr. C out on the town. Sure, you'll find the standard Thai favorites on this menu, like pad Thai ($7.95), shrimp lemon grass soup ($3.95 per bowl), and various noodle and rice dishes ($7–$8). But don't shy away from the more unusual items, like crab meat sausages—bean curd crepes filled with chicken and crab meat and served with plum sauce ($5.50).

For something more substantial, try the duck with black bean sauce, homemade with ginger and onion, for $8.95. And be sure to save

room for dessert. The homemade ginger and coconut ice creams ($3) are really something special.

You can paint Thai Town red on a daily basis from 11 a.m. to midnight.

Toojay's

• 4620 Wisconsin Avenue N.W., Washington, D.C.;
  ✆ (202) 686-1989

This diner-style restaurant features a large menu, busting with old-world Jewish specialties—plus a few other things, for good measure. Appetizers include such delicacies as potato pancakes with sour cream and applesauce ($4.75 for three); *tabouleh* ($3.95) and stuffed cabbage ($4.50), any one of which should get your meal going on the right track. Then check out the salads—one of the more tempting combinations is tomato, basil, and linguine, with parmesan and brie cheeses, all mixed in a special house dressing ($7.25). Pasta salad, with albacore tuna, olives, and red and green peppers tossed in herb dressing; or Chinese chicken salad, flavored with a sesame soy dressing, both zing your taste buds for $7.95.

Next, live the "Sandwich Experience," as Toojay's calls it. All are served with coleslaw and include hot corned beef or pastrami, both on rye, for $7.50. A "turkey BLT" ($7.95) adds turkey and Russian dressing to the old favorite. Smoked salmon on a bagel with cream cheese and onion is just a dollar more. And last but not least, the sizable and tasty dinners include vegetable lasagna and homemade meatloaf with mashed potatoes (both $7.95). Mr. C especially liked that old favorite, cheese blintzes with fruit sauce and sour cream ($6.95 for three). Toojays' hours are Monday through Sunday from 8 a.m. to 10 p.m.

MARYLAND

Armand's Chicago Pizzeria

- 1909 Seminary Road, Silver Spring, MD; ✆ (301) 588-3400

- 190 Halpine Road, Rockville, MD; ✆ (301) 231-5000

- 18208 Contour Road, Gaithersburg, MD; ✆ (301) 990-2500

  And other suburban locations

- ✑ www.armandspizza.com

See the listing under *Restaurants—Capitol Hill.*

The Athenian Plaka

- 7833 Woodmont Road, Bethesda, MD; ✆ (301) 986-1337

Zeus must be smiling down on Athenian Plaka. This large, comfortable restaurant serves up delicious Greek favorites with old-world flair. Start with fresh mushroom caps stuffed with spinach and feta cheese ($4.25), or *imam baldi* ($5.25), chilled eggplant filled with tomato, onion, pine nuts, and raisins.

Entrees range between $9.95 and $18.95. If you've never had Greek food before, or if you'd like to try a variety of dishes, order *plakiotiki pikilia* for $13.95. This sampler platter includes *pastitsio* (ground beef, macaroni, and grated cheese, topped with bechamel sauce), *mousaka* (seasoned ground meat, fried eggplant, and cream sauce), spinach pie, grape leaves, sliced lamb, and rice pilaf. Another delicious choice, also $12.95, is *exohikon*, lamb sauteed in butter with artichokes, kalamata olives, and imported cheese, then baked in filo dough.

And don't forget the scrumptious desserts—one of Greece's lasting contributions to civilization. Baklava ($4.25), sweet walnut-filled filo pastry, and rizogalo ($3.25), traditional rice pudding, are just two of the mouthwatering treats.

The Athenian Plaka is open every day of the week from 11 a.m. to 10 p.m.

Austin Grill

- 7278 Woodmont Avenue Bethesda, MD; ✆ (301) 656-1366

- ✑ www.austingrill.com

See the listing under *Restaurants—Georgetown.*

Bombay Bistro

- 98 W. Montgomery Road, Rockville, MD; ✆ (301) 762-8798

- ✑ www.bombaybistro.com

If you're looking for an award-winning restaurant (including kudos from *Washingtonian* magazine and the *Washington Post*) that also offers great value, you can't do much better than this place! Check out the great luncheon buffet here, where you'll have a wide choice of savory Indian foods ranging from *tandoori* chicken to a variety of vegetarian dishes. The buffet is a mere $8.95 on weekends, and two bucks less during the week!

You can also sample a spicy lamb *vindaloo* and lamb *saag*, served with spinach, or lamb *biryani*, composed of meat chunks in saffron-enhanced basmati rice, with a sprinkling of raisins and carrots. Bombay also offers good vegetarian curries made from chickpeas, cauliflower, potatoes, and lentils.

You can also order off the menu, which features main courses priced from $5.95 to $11.95, or you can get a little more adventurous with some of the daily specials. How about tandoori salmon marinated with a special blend of spices, yogurt, and charcoal; or perhaps the shrimp and scallops tossed in a *masala* made of tomatoes, tamarind, coriander, and other spices? They're both $14.95.

Bombay Bistro is open for lunch from 11 a.m. to 2:30 p.m., and evenings from 5 to 9.30 p.m.

The Booeymonger

- 4600 East-West Highway, Bethesda, MD;
  ☎ (301) 718-9550

See the listing under *Restaurants—Upper Northwest.*

Bread & Chocolate

- 7704 Woodmont Avenue, Bethesda, MD;
  ☎ (301) 986-9008

See the listing under *Restaurants—Upper Northwest.*

Cameron's Seafood Market

- 4831 Bethesda Road, Bethesda, MD; ☎ (301) 951-1000

At this great little place, decorated with nautically themed murals, you can get very fresh seafood for remarkably low prices—usually under $10! Sure, the utensils are plastic, but who cares when the food is this good—and cheap!

The main menu focuses on broiled and fried fish platters, including salmon, swordfish, flounder, and tuna. You'll also enjoy their fried oysters and crab cakes, as well as the delicious shrimp and lobster salads.

Restaurant hours are 10 a.m. to 9:30 p.m. every day, except on weekends, when Cameron's serves until 10:30 p.m.

Chicken Out Rotisserie

- 11325 Seven Locks Road, Rockville, MD;
  ☎ (301) 299-8646

- 1560 Rockville Pike Rockville, MD; ☎ (301) 230-2020

- 10116 River Road, Potomac, MD; ☎ (301) 299-8585

- 15780 Shady Grove Road, Gaithersburg, MD;
  ☎ (301) 921-9119

- 31 Grand Corner Road, Gaithersburg, MD;
  ☎ (301) 948-6820

- 15952 Shady Grove Road, Gaithersburg, MD;
  ☎ (301) 907-8646

- 245 Kentlands Boulevard, Gaithersburg, MD;
  ☎ (301) 975-0100

  And other suburban locations

- ✐ www.chickenout.com

See the listing under *Restaurants—Upper Northwest.*

Chipotle

- 7600 Old Georgetown Road, Bethesda, MD;
  ☎ (301) 907-9077

- 7332 Baltimore Road, College Park, MD; 240-582-0015

- 2231 Crystal Drive, Crystal City, VA; ☎ (703) 920-8779

- 564 N. Frederick Road, Gaithersburg, MD;
  ☎ (240) 632-1228

- 11830 Rockville Pike, Rockville, MD; ☎ (301) 881-2600

- 1735 N. Lynn Street, Rosslyn, VA; ☎ (703) 294-6669

- ✐ www.chipotle.com

This stylish and fun establishment served stylish and fun Tex-Mex—and at good prices. Try some of their delectable chunky guacamole ($1.25) along with freshly made tortilla chips, and wash it down with an ice-cold beer or margarita. Your can then get to the main courses, including burritos, tacos, and fajitas (ranging from $4.25 to $5.25), along with Chipotle's steaming cilantro and lime-flavored rice. Not too shabby.

Chipotle is open 11 a.m. to 10 p.m. every day.

Cuban Corner

- 825 Hungerford Drive, Rockville, MD;
  ✆ (301) 279-0310

This authentic Cuban restaurant features delicious island food at totally reasonable prices, with most dishes priced under $10.

For an appetizer, try the Spanish sausage coated with melted cheese ($5.99), or perhaps the fried green plantains stuffed with ground beef ($3.59).

All entrées come with white rice and black beans, and are all priced around $10.99. These include *bistec empanizado*, a thin piece of steak that is seasoned, breaded, and deep-fried; rabbit fricassee, cooked in a tomato sauce and white wine and served with sliced potatoes; *masitas*, marinated and charred chunks of pork; *ropa vieja* (shredded flank steak), cooked with tomato sauce, wine, and spices; and *montuno Cubano*, pork stir-fried with onions, pimentos, and olives. If you're into succulent seafood, check out the red snapper (or shrimp) cooked with tomatoes, capers, and white wine—both priced at $13.99.

Popular lunchtime fare includes Cuban submarines stuffed with marinated roast pork, grilled Spanish sausage, just $6.69.

Cuban Corner is open Monday through Thursday from 11 a.m. to 9 p.m.; Friday and Saturday from 11 a.m. to 10 p.m.

Delhi Dhaba

- 7236 Woodmont Avenue, Bethesda, MD;
  ✆ (301) 718-0008

Combining a taste of India with cafeteria-style service, Delhi Dhaba is clean, neat, and wonderfully inexpensive. Tandoor cuisine is prepared in front of you on steam tables, a feast for both the visual and the olfactory senses; Mr. C believes that means the food looks and smells great.

Appetizers are tasty; Mr. C liked the vegetable samosas ($1.75), crisp turnovers filled with potatoes, green peas, and spices. Tandoori specialty meals, like chicken or lamb (each $5.95), are marinated in yogurt with herbs and then oven-cooked. Mr. C went with the day's special of a quarter Tandoori chicken, served with vegetables, for $5.95.

Go on Sundays for an all-you-can-eat brunch buffet ($7.95) from 11 a.m.to 3:30 p.m.

A "Best Bargain" winner in *Washingtonian* magazine, Delhi Dhaba is open from 11 a.m. to 10 p.m. Sunday through Thursday, and until 11 p.m. Fridays and Saturdays.

Everyday Gourmet

- 6923 Laurel Avenue, Takoma Park, MD; ✆ (301) 270-2270

The cheerful name alone catches the eye, and the food more than holds up its end of the bargain at this popular Takoma Park bakery-deli.

The bakery whips up breads, cakes, pies, and scones every day from scratch. Their unusual breakfast sandwiches are another good start to the day, served on a croissant. Try a Brie, ham, and egg concoction for $4.50; this is something you won't find at the golden arches.

Then there are the special gourmet sandwiches, all just $4.45. Ten luscious choices include "hamberry" (Bavarian ham smothered in spicy cranberry spread); plum turkey (smoked turkey with spicy damson plum spread); saga bleu turkey (with imported bleu cheese); and more.

There's also a fresh soup each day ($2.80), a selection of hot dishes (Mr. C loved the zesty Dijon meatloaf with rice, a trifling $4.89), plus pasta and chicken salads made daily. The only "everyday" thing about this place is the fact that you can eat here every day without getting bored . . . or going broke.

Hours are 7 a.m. to 8 p.m. seven days.

Hamburger Hamlet

- 10400 Old Georgetown Road, Bethesda, MD; ✆ (301) 897-5350

- 1601 Crystal Square Arcade, Crystal City, VA; ✆ (703) 413-0422

- 9811 Washingtonian Boulevard, Gaithersberg, MD; ✆ (301) 417-0773

- ✎ www.hamburgerhamlet.com

The name of this popular pub divulges its specialty, and in fact *Washingtonian* magazine has voted these the best hamburgers over 20 years running. Toppings include anything you could ever think to put on a burger, including jack cheese, Muenster cheese, bacon, barbecue sauce, Dijon mustard, onion, as well as more unusual toppings, like guacamole and grilled peppers and onions. Nevertheless, the prices are strictly plain Jane; most burgers are $6.95.

Other menu items are equally tasty. For appetizers, you can load up on scrumptious Zucchini Zircles for about $5, or French onion soup for as little as $4.50. The nachos come highly recommended, loaded with beans, cheddar, guacamole, sour cream, and chili. Baby cheeseburgers, hot dogs, chicken wings, and stuffed jalapeños are a few other scrumptious choices. "Chinese Chicken Salad" is loaded with shredded chicken breast, mandarin oranges, toasted almonds, crispy sesame wontons, and chopped scallions, and then topped with sesame-ginger dressing ($9.25). Or you could try a daily special, like beer batter fish and chips ($10.95). (Man, Mr. C is getting hungry just writing about this stuff!)

Between 3 and 7 p.m., Hamburger Hamlet has a happy hour (a happy four hours, actually) when all beer and "rail" drinks are $2.50 to $2.75. Hamburger Hamlet is open seven days for lunch and dinner, mainly between 11 a.m. and 10:30 p.m. Big groups and kids are welcome.

Hard Times Cafe

- 3028 Wilson Boulevard, Arlington, VA; ☎ (703) 528-2233

- 1404 King Street, Alexandria, VA; ☎ (703) 837-0050

- 4738 Cherry Hill Road, College Park, MD; ☎ (301) 474-8880

- 8865 Stanford Boulevard, Columbia, MD; (410) 312-0700

  And other suburban locations

- ✐ www.hardtimes.com

See the listing under *Restaurants—Virginia.*

La Madeleine

- 3000 M Street NW., Washington, D.C.; ☎ (202) 337-6974

- 11858 Rockville Pike, Rockville, MD; ☎ (301) 984-2270

- 6211 Columbia Crossing Drive, Columbia, MD;(410) 872-4900

- ✐ www.lamadeleine.com

Leave it to the French to find a classy way to do American fast food. These restaurants are cafeteria style, yet the atmosphere is anything but plebeian. The dining room is divided into small, cozy rooms, which are decorated variously with faux antiques, kitchen tools, French oil paintings, or functional fireplaces, perfect for those chilly winter nights. Once you've chosen a dining room and removed your tray, you'll think you're in France, or at least an upscale French restaurant. That's how simply elegant La Madeleine is.

The food is equally impressive. At breakfast, try the strawberries Romanoff, laced with homemade brandy sauce ($4.25), or a breakfast croissant ($5.49), filled with eggs, bacon, cheese, and tomatoes; both are superb. Later in the day, start with la Madeleine's classic French onion soup ($3.99), followed by your choice of entrees, which include Salmon en croûte (sautéed with mushrooms, green onions, and anise-flavored liqueur, in a puff pastry shell with beurre blanc sauce), Shrimp pastis (flambéed in pastis, giving the shrimp a delicate anise flavor, and finished with beurre blanc sauce), Beef en croûte (steak in a puff pastry, layered with mushroom duxelle and finished with a rich burgundy sauce), and several other delicious treats, as well as a range of creative pasta dishes. All of these gastronomical delights are priced between $9 and $12!

For dessert, the French pastries and cakes are again surprisingly good. It's difficult to choose between a variety of croissants, éclairs, and Napoleons, generally priced between $3 and $4.

La Madeleine is open Sunday through Thursday from 7 a.m. until 10 p.m. On Friday and Saturday they stay open until 11 p.m.

Matuba

- 4918 Cordell Avenue, Bethesda, MD; ☎ (301) 652-7449

If sushi is a delicacy that reels you in, you won't be disappointed here. Matuba's menu includes complete dinners or a la carte selections. Either way, prices are reasonable, which is rarely the case with this cuisine.

For example, a 10-piece sushi dinner runs a surprisingly modest $9.50; at lunch, it's just $6.50. A "super deluxe" meal for two gives you nine pieces of sushi, six maki rolls, and two cups of miso soup, all for $16. You can order rolls individually, but at $2.95–$3.95 each, you can see why the combo plates are such bargains. Other a la carte selections include over a dozen different kinds of fish, even sea urchin and octopus.

Or you can order more common entrees like shrimp and vegetable tempura ($9.50) or chicken teriyaki ($8.95), both served with soup or rice. Lunches generally run as much as $4 less, so show up from 11:30 a.m. to 2 p.m. Mondays through Saturdays to take advantage. Dinner is served until 10 p.m. on weeknights, until 10:30 p.m. on Friday and Saturday, and until 9:30 p.m. on Sunday.

Negril

- 2301 Georgia Avenue N.W., Washington, D.C.; ✆ (202) 332-3737

- 965 Thayer Avenue, Silver Spring, MD; ✆ (301) 585-3000

- 18509 N. Frederick Avenue, Gaithersburg, MD; ✆ (301) 926-7220

- 12116 Central Avenue, Mitchellsville, MD; ✆ (301) 249-9101

Ya mon! This restaurant brings a little of Jamaica's savory Caribbean cooking to the heart of the D.C. suburbs, and its delectable offerings are pleasing to your palette and easy on your wallet. Keeping with the funky, informal attitude of the islands, here you place your order and pick up your food at a counter, so there's no tipping.

So sit back, relax, and get into the Jamaican spirit. For appetizers, choose from a range of beef, mixed vegetables, or chicken and vegetable patties (a dough-wrapped Jamaican turnover, for just $1.35 each), or perhaps a jerk-chicken sandwich ($3.25), or some sweet, fried plantain ($2). Then move on to a selection of main courses, which includes a variety of spicy meat and seafood entrees, including curries made with chicken, vegetables, and shrimp,

ranging in price from $5.85 to $8.95.

Hey, do you ever get craving for a little goat meat? Well, don't knock it 'till you've tried it! Here you can check out the curried goat for $6.25, or some goat *roti* (goat morsels in a pancake-like dough) for $6.25.

If you like fish, you'll enjoy the whole red snapper, either steamed or deep-fried, and priced at $9.95, or the curried shrimp *roti*, where the featured creature is prepared with a blend of potatoes, onions, peppers and tomatoes, and embedded in a flaky pastry ($8.95). Vegetarians will appreciate the curried vegetables ($5.60), the vegetable lasagna ($5.20), or the vegetable stew ($5.75).

For dessert, check out the coconut custard or plantain tarts ($1.15) or banana cake ($1.25). Mmmm. Good stuff, mon.

Negril is open from Monday through Thursday from 11 a.m. to 8 p.m., and Friday and Saturday from 11 a.m. to 9 p.m.

Old Hickory Grille

- 15420 Old Columbia Pike, Burtonsville, MD; ✆ (301) 421-0204

- 6420 Freetown Road, Columbia, MD; ✆ (410) 531-0326

This is another of those Southern food joints, specializing in such tasty vittles that have been grilled and slathered with all manner of wickedly delicious sauces and preparations.

You and your loved one could probably share a big rack of ribs, which comes with coleslaw and barbecued beans. They're $13.50 for a half, $18.50 for a full, and $22.50 for a "monster." (Lordy!) You could also order up your own portion of the Smothered Chicken *poblano* with fries or grits

($12.95); the grilled boneless, center-cut pork chops with Cajun spices ($13.50); the hickory grilled meatloaf, served over redskin garlic mashed potatoes ($12.50); the pecan crusted catfish ($13.50); or one of the pastas ($8.95 to $14.95). You could also try one of their delicious barbeque or Cajun-style sandwiches, priced in the $6.95 to $7.95 range.

Heck, you could make a meal from one of the Hickory Grille's large appetizers: Try the fried calamari, Southern-fried oysters, or Cajun fried crawfish (all $7.95), or order up some Buffalo wings or a grilled stuffed Portobello mushroom cap for $6.95.

Eat before 4 p.m. and take advantage of OHG's daily lunch specials, featuring ribs, meatloaf, chicken, and a selection of sandwiches and salads priced between $4.95 and $6.95.

Good desserts include custard-style banana-chocolate bread pudding ($3.25), a chocolate-spiked pecan pie ($2.95), a fudge brownie with espresso-chocolate mousse, topped with fresh whipped cream ($3.95), and peach cobbler ($4.95).

Old Hickory Grille is open Monday and Tuesday from 11:30 a.m. to 8 p.m., Wednesday through Friday to 9 p.m., Saturday 9 a.m. to 9 p.m., and Sunday from 9 a.m. to 8 p.m.

Pho 75

- 1510 University Boulevard, E Hyattsville, MD;
  ✆ (301) 434-7844

- 771 Hungerford Drive, Rockville, MD;
  ✆ (301) 309-8873

This Vietnamese restaurant is much more typical of Indochinese eateries. The essence of a simple, no-frills soup house, Pho 75 serves up nothing but variations of beef noodle stews—over a dozen of 'em.

The menu is largely unintelligible to the average Westerner; show the least bit of puzzlement to your waiter, and he'll instantly steer you toward the selections that are safely free of ingredients like tripe and tendon. In any case, you'll wind up with a large ($5.50) or ultra-large ($6.75) bowl filled with sliced beef, broth, rice noodles, and scallions, plus a plate of fresh bean sprouts to add in.

Forget atmosphere; the Arlington branch, at least, is an open, cafeteria-style room with long, family-sized tables, and not much else. What you will get is a whole meal in a bowl—and a terrific bargain.

Open daily until 8 p.m.

Red Hot & Blue

- 677 Main Street, Laurel, MD;
  ✆ (301) 953-1943

- 16811 Crabbs Branch Way, Rockville, MD;
  ✆ (301) 948-7333

- 3350 Crain Highway, Waldorf, MD; ✆ (301) 705-7427

- ✑ www.redhotandblue.com

That's right, it's an old-fashioned Memphis pit barbeque, right here in the buttoned-down land of national politics. Tennessee congressman (and later governor) Don Sundquist, two of his former staff members, and a former network TV correspondent opened the first restaurant in Arlington back in 1988. Since then it's expanded all over the D.C. area, and ultimately to numerous locations around the country.

Named after the 1950s Memphis "Red Hot & Blue" radio show, which helped introduce the world to Elvis Presley, Jerry Lee Lewis, Johnny Cash, and others, RH&B employs hickory logs, low temperatures, and long cooking times to produce that authentic Memphis barbeque flavor.

This is a fun kind of place; its walls lined with autographed photos from both actual pols and fake ones. (It's up to you to decide which category Dan Quayle falls into). They declare their food "the best you'll ever have in a building that hasn't already been condemned." Rhythm and blues play good and loud on the speakers, including one outside the front door. On tap? Bud Lite, Michelob, and the house brand: Red, Hot & Blue Amber.

As for that food, Mr. C drooled over RH & B's hickory-flavored ribs—a rack is just $10.95 (or $18.95 for one big enough to feed two people). The sumptuous order comes with barbecued beans, coleslaw, and fresh-baked bread. Other platters, ranging from $7.95 to $13.95, include moist pork shoulder, beef brisket, and a half chicken, all with the same sides.

Just want a sandwich? No prob. How about pulled pork, beef brisket, chicken, or one of several great burgers, ranging in price from $5.25 to $6.75. All of these choices come with potato salad. Don't forget to save room for dessert, as $3.50 to $5 gets you an Oreo brownie sunday, pecan pie, or apple cobbler.

Open 11 a.m. to 10 p.m. Monday through Thursday, from 11 a.m. to 11 p.m. on Fridays, noon to 11 p.m. on Saturday, and noon to 9 p.m. on Sunday.

Ricky's Rice Bowl

- 532 N. Frederick Avenue, Gaithersburg, MD;
  ℅ (301) 963-BOWL (2695)

Ricky's is a casual, clean, and bright spot serving Asian food that will—sorry—bowl you over. In fact, these two locations charmingly adorn a monthly calendar of specials with the kind of bad puns ("Happy Holidays to all you really rice friends") that Mr. C so obviously adores. The food is fresh, made to order, and wonderfully inexpensive.

The bulk of the menu, true to its word, offers delicious meals-in-a bowl, like teriyaki chicken with a mild ginger garlic and soy sauce ($4.50 for regular, $6 for large); beef curry ($4.99); and teriyaki fish ($6.25), which is always fresh, or not served at all. Weekly specials feature things like "The Princess Michiko's Favorite Ginger-Lemon Chicken," and there's also a different special soup each week.

Quality meals at fast-food prices? Yes, it can be done.

Open seven days until 9:30 p.m. They close at 8 p.m. on Sunday.

Rio Grande Cafe

- 4919 Fairmont Avenue, Bethesda, MD;
  ℅ (301) 656-2981

Uncle Julio, and his wife, Aunt Maria, came up north from Texas after creating a popular eatery, Lucky Boy, in the 1950s. Now, in the Washington, D.C. area, their fame is growing, and they have three enormously successful restaurants in Maryland and Virginia. Delicious recipes, enormous portions, and reasonable prices are what you can expect to find, complimented by a lively, festive atmosphere.

There's often a wait for a table during peak hours, but never more than an hour, and you can spend the time enjoying the excellent chips, salsa, and big, frosty margaritas. (You can also check out the restaurant's tortilla-making machine. Yes, flour tortillas are made fresh on the premises and are great!)

Mr. C dares you to try and finish dinners like "Juanita's Platter" ($12.75), with two cheese enchiladas, beef taco, and a pork tamale, served with rice, black beans, and fresh flour tortillas. Enchilada and tacos ordered a la carte range in price from $3.75 to $4.25. Mr. C thought *camarones diablos* ($17.25), broiled jumbo shrimp served on a sizzling platter, was especially delicious.

The Rio Grande is open Sunday through Thursday from 11 a.m. to 10:30 p.m., and Friday and Saturday from 11 a.m. to 11:30 p.m.

Taliano's

- 7001 Carroll Avenue, Takoma Park, MD; ✆ (301) 270-5515

Pizza, pasta, calzones—oh my! That's what is spoken in this fun, way-casual place, where you can enjoy 12-inch pizzas from $7.75, and 16-inchers from $9.75. The best time to go? Monday, when those prices are cut in half after 5 p.m. Toppings remain $1.50 to $1.75 and include unique choices such as spinach and banana peppers.

Don't fancy a pizza? Then try a calzone, a mere $7.50, for top-notch choices like one with sausage, green pepper, and onion. Pasta options are simple and inexpensive. Spaghetti with meatballs ($7.25), fettuccini Alfredo ($5.50), vegetarian lasagna ($6.95) all come with side-order salad and garlic bread.

But wait, there's more: Over a dozen sandwiches, subs, and burgers in the $5 range; salads as low as $1.95; and desserts $2.25 for cheesecake and carrot cake. It's all in a lively atmosphere that somehow blends pizza parlor and funky restaurant. There's a full bar at Taliano's, and on occasion, live music.

Check them out from 11:30 a.m. to 10 p.m., seven days a week.

MR. CHEAP'S PICKS

Rockville

La Madeleine—Delicious French food and atmosphere at very reasonable prices.

Pho 75—Here you'll get a whole meal in a bowl—and a terrific bargain.

Taste of Saigon—Both traditional and adventurous recipes meet here, and the price is right.

Tastee Diner

- 7731 Woodmont Avenue, Bethesda, MD; ✆ (301) 652-3970

- 8601 Cameron Street, Silver Spring, MD; ✆ (301) 589-8171

- 118 Washington Boulevard, Laurel, MD; ✆ (301) 953-7567

If you're talking diners, Tastee is the genuine article. It's open 24 hours, has chrome glittering everywhere, and serves up lots of good, cheap food at a counter crowded with friendly folks.

Big on breakfast? Try diner staples like biscuits topped with sausage gravy, or creamed chipped beef, each $3.95. If that's a bit heavy in the early hours of the morning, perhaps blueberry hotcakes ($3.65) or two eggs and bacon ($2.90) would better ease you into the day. Youngsters, age 12 and under, can order a special of one hotcake, one egg, and one strip of bacon for just $1.65.

Later in the day, burgers ($2), tuna melts ($3.75), and an assortment of sandwiches is always a good bet. Dinners thrill the wallet: The menu's marquee item is a 16-ounce T-bone steak served with two vegetables—and it's only $8.95! Pork chops for $7.95, a steak sandwich meal with French fries and coleslaw for $4.50, a barbecue sandwich meal for a quarter more . . . you can't go wrong. Rest assured, they'll be Tastee.

Daily specials are also quite a deal, and come with two veggies and rolls. You may find a 16-ounce Porterhouse steak for just $6.95. Mr. C didn't even come close to finishing his macaroni and cheese platter for $3.75. Meatloaf and country-fried steak are also among the specialties. And how can you pass up dessert when a slice of homemade pie is $1.50? Add ice cream, and it's still just $1.95. And of course, these places never close. Go, now.

Taste of Saigon

- 410 Hungerford Drive, Rockville, MD;
  ℘ (301) 424-7222

- 8201 Greensboro Drive, McLean, VA;
  ℘ (703) 790-0700

Both traditional and adventurous recipes meet here, and the price is right. On the traditional side are the crispy whole fish, as well as the

curries, ranging from chicken to venison, made with coconut milk—all starting at about $8.50. Pudding desserts made with taro or black-eyed peas are worth a look.

If your hankering for something more elaborate, check out the mussels with black beans and fresh-ginger sauce (Mmmm!) for $8.95, or perhaps the Saigon black-pepper steak (marinated in lime juice and served with a fried egg) and black-pepper shrimp ($15.95). You can also sample some mouthwatering appetizers, including a salad of lobster and green papaya.

Taste of Saigon is open Monday through Thursday from 11 a.m. to 10 p.m., Friday and Saturday from 11 a.m. to 11 p.m., and Sunday from 11 a.m. to 9:30 p.m.

That's Amore

- 15201 Shady Grove Road, Rockville, MD;
  ℘ (301) 670-9666

- 10400 Little Patuxent Parkway, Columbia, MD;
  ℘ (410) 772-5900

- ✑ www.thatsamore.com

Here you'll witness servers bringing heaping platters of antipasto, pasta, and main courses, which can be served "solo" or "famiglia" (family style). Many of the single entrees run in the $11.95 to $13.95 range (fish and steak run up to $21.95), and include the usual (though beautifully prepared) southern Italian pasta specialties—ranging from penne with tomato sauce or oil and garlic, on up to treats such as the smoked salmon, peas, and tomatoes in a vodka-cream sauce. Also on the menu are such choices as whole roast chicken Vesuvio with roast potatoes, chicken cacciatore, and *giambotto*—made with spicy sausage, chicken, fried potatoes, and vegetables.

Appetizers include charred grilled whole calamari; clams with a garlic-and-tomato broth; and sautéed baby shrimp and cannelloni beans with red onion and crushed red pepper.

That's Amore is open Monday through Thursday from 11:30 a.m. to 10 p.m., Friday from 11:30 a.m. to 11 p.m., Saturday from 4 to 11 p.m., and Sunday from 4 to 9 p.m.

The Vegetable Garden

- 11618 Rockville Pike, Rockville, MD; ✆ (301) 468-9301

This bright, comfortable restaurant uses no MSG, no eggs, no dairy products, and little or no oil. Needless to say, the absence of any meat is not only healthy, but it keeps prices down as well.

Instead of meat, many entrees consist of relatively close facsimiles made with tofu, tempeh, and other substitutes. Spicy selections work well—for example, *kung pao* vegi-beef or vegi-chicken, or those flavored with lemon, curry, and cashews (all $8.99). Or, avoid the whole is-it-or-isn't-it issue with just plain vegetable dishes. Asparagus options ($7.95) abound, served with white or brown rice, and zesty eggplant meals can be had for the same price. Mixed rice and noodle platters are $7.99. You will be well satisfied here.

Until 4:30 p.m. daily, you can choose from nearly two dozen $5.99 to $8.99 lunch specials, including sweet-and-sour vegi-pork and vegetable tempura. These are served with brown rice and your choice of soup.

The Vegetable Garden is open from 11:30 a.m. to 10 p.m., seven days a week.

VIRGINIA

Akasaka

- 514 C South Van Dorn Street, Alexandria, VA; ✆ (703) 751-3133

If you're like The Cheapster, you probably get a craving for sushi at least once a week. Aficionados know that there's nothing quite so satisfying as a fresh, well prepared tuna roll or assortment of nigiri (pieces of fish on vinegar rice), spiced up with a little wasabi and washed down with a tall cool one. Well, if that pleases your palette, you're gonna love this humble but excellent high-value establishment. Located in a suburban shopping center, Akasaka will surprise you with its high-quality Japanese food and low prices.

The owner here brings in fresh fish whenever possible, eschewing the frozen stuff that some other sushi bars tend to use. We're talking fresh and beautifully presented! Nigiri ($3.75 for two pieces) may include tuna, yellowtail, sea-urchin roe, or fatty tuna or sweet shrimp in season. Sushi rolls ($4.25) are beautifully prepared and presented, using such ingredients as lettuce, radish, sprouts, and fish roe (in addition to the succulent pieces of fresh fish, of course). The regular sushi dinner (eight pieces) is just $13.95 and comes with miso soup, salad, and a fruit dessert.

Cooked dishes are also very good. The shrimp tempura ($13.95) is crisp and light, not greasy at all, and the teriyaki ($9.95) also please. Soba (noodle) dishes run around $10.95.

Akasaka is open Monday through Thursday from 11:30 a.m. to 2:30 p.m., and 5 to 10 p.m.; Friday from 11:30 a.m. to 2:30 p.m., and 5 to 10:30 p.m.; Saturday from noon to 10:30 p.m.; and Sunday from 4 to 9:30 p.m.

Armand's Chicago Pizzeria

- 2151 Arlington Boulevard, Arlington, VA;
  ✆ (703) 526-9800

- 4716 King Street, Alexandria, VA; ✆ (703) 578-3303

  And other suburban locations

- ✑ www.armandspizza.com

See the listing under *Restaurants—Capitol Hill.*

Atlacatl & Pupuseria

- 2602 Columbia Pike, Arlington, VA; ✆ (703) 920-3680

Here's one of Arlington's many fine spots for authentic Mexican cuisine. First of all, its extensive menu is noteworthy for appetizers that won't automatically add $4 to $5 to your bill: Several different kinds of tamales are $1.50 each, and a variety of *pupusas*, just $1.60. Can't beat that. Okay, I suppose some of you want to know what a pupusa is: It's a type of tortilla from El Salvador, spiced with cumin and chile.

Most entrees are in the $6 to $13.50 range. Beef or chicken fajitas are an amazing $9.95, have a mix of both for $10.95. Another great option is the "Burro Grande," packed with beef or chicken and veggies and served with Spanish rice and refried beans, a mere $6.50.

Owner-manager Salvador Mejia's culinary skills have been recognized over the years by a national association of chefs, confirming that this is a place well worth crossing the border for.

Atlacatl & Pupuseria is open Monday through Friday from 11 a.m. to 11 p.m., and Saturday and Sunday from 10 a.m. to midnight.

Austin Grill

- 801 King Street Alexandria, VA; ✆ (703) 684-8969

- 8430 Old Keene Mill Road Springfield, VA;
  ✆ (703) 644-3111

- ✑ www.austingrill.com

See the listing under *Restaurants—Georgetown.*

Bob and Edith's Diner

- 2310 Columbia Pike, Arlington, VA; ✆ (703) 920-6103

Bravo to Bob and Edith. Their simple, homey diner is open 24 hours a day, serving up basic omelets, sandwiches, burgers, and desserts. Two eggs and toast will set you back a mere $2.05; or, splurge for pecan waffles at $4.45.

At lunch, you can't go wrong with a patty melt and vegetable soup for $4.95; unless, of course, you can eat like a horse. In that case, Mr. C recommends a country-fried steak, with mashed potatoes, cooked vegetables, rolls and butter—all for $5.95. Good luck.

What? You've still got some room left over? Fill it with a slice of homemade peach pie for $2.25. A simple counter and booths, plus a jukebox loaded with country and rockabilly tunes, make up the rest of the scene. The hours? Have you forgotten already?

Bread & Chocolate

- 5189 Leesburg Pike, Falls Church, VA; ✆ (703) 379-8005

- 611 King Street, Alexandria, VA; ✆ (703) 548-0992

- 11920 Market Street, Reston, VA; ✆ (703) 467-0460

See the listing under *Restaurants—Upper Northwest.*

Bombay Bistro

- 3570 Chain Bridge Road, Fairfax, VA; ✆ (703) 359-5810

- ✍ www.bombaybistro.com

See the listing under *Restaurants—Maryland*.

Cafe Dalat

- 3143 Wilson Boulevard, Arlington, VA; ✆ (703) 276-0935

True Cheapsters know that Vietnamese cuisine rarely disappoints, either in value or quality. At Cafe Dalat, huge bowls of *pho*—Vietnamese noodle soup—are just $6.50, stocked with beef or chicken. Same price for Saigon beef stew, or shrimp with fine egg noodles; portions big enough for two are just $6.50.

House specialties include Vietnamese steak-thinly sliced beef, sautéed with garlic and onion, and served over lettuce and tomato ($10.95). One seafood choice features grilled shrimp, scallops, and crabmeat on skewers, with rice vermicelli noodles, and fresh greens; it's all served with rice paper for wrapping and dipping into a tangy peanut sauce, all for $10.95.

There are also a wide variety of Chinese-style entrees, most around $8.50, such as sautéed vegetables and bean curd, curried beef, and spicy pork on a bed of noodles.

Cafe Dalat is open from 11 a.m. to 9:30 p.m. every day.

Cafe Italia

- 519 23rd Street S., Arlington, VA; ✆ (703) 521-2565

- 10515 Main Street, Fairfax, VA; ✆ (703) 385-6767

A warm and cozy spot for a romantic lunch or dinner, Cafe

MR. CHEAP'S PICKS

Alexandria

Cajun Bangkok—Simply eat at this reasonably priced restaurant to be convinced that the idea of mixing Cajun and Thai was a brilliantly lucid inspiration!

King Street Blues—Texas-style roadhouse packed into three floors of fun.

Le Gaulois—The menu offers enough moderate entrees to make this a worthy splurge for the lunch crowd or for visitors on a touring budget.

Southside 815—This great find combines some fine American cooking with reasonable prices.

Italia offers a broad selection of pastas (natch), pizza, and seafood. Enjoy it all from an indoor patio at the front, or in the low-lit dining room, decorated with old-time musical instruments and unusual memorabilia along with letters of praise from politicians and other muckety-mucks. Go figure.

Or go eat, choosing from pasta options such as cannelloni ($10.95), crepes filled with veal and chicken in a white cream sauce, fettuccine Alfredo ($10.95), or the old standby of spaghetti ($9.95), all served with a salad. A variety of pizzas start from $9.95; splurge on pizza Camille ($11.95), with artichoke hearts, olives, pepperoni, eggplant, and more.

Go for lunch, served until 3:30 p.m. weekdays, and enjoy smaller portions of many of the same choices—for $3 to $5 less. Wash them down with a selection from the wine list, and finish up with one of several desserts, like Baba al Rhum: rum-soaked cakes with butter pecan ice cream and whipped cream ($3.50).

Hours at Cafe Italia are 11 a.m. to 10 p.m. On Sundays, they have a great brunch buffet for just $9.95.

Cafe Parisian Express

• 4320 Lee Hwy., Arlington, VA; ✆ (703) 525-3332

"French food with plastic forks" describes the experience here, as Cafe Parisian serves up the unlikely combination of gourmet meals in a fast-food setting. Meanwhile, the small tables and chairs are far more reminiscent of an American ice cream parlor than a romantic spot on the banks of the Seine. No matter; the cuisine is both tasty and cheap.

It's not often that Mr. C gets to describe food like this. Lunch and diner entrees, served from 11 a.m. to 9:30 p.m., include steak *au poivre* ($9.99) with peppers and vegetables; and Moroccan pasta with lamb, chicken, zucchini, carrots, rutabagas, and more ($9.75). The regular lunch menu, meanwhile, offers sandwiches such as tarragon chicken salad and tuna salad Provencal, each $5.50, and specialties like crepes with chicken in cream sauce ($5.99). Add a de rigueur bowl of onion soup ($3.50) and you've got a fine meal.

For breakfast (or anytime, really), have a chocolate croissant for $1.65; crepes with sugar, honey, or strawberry sauce are just $3.55, French toast $2.99, and quiche for $6.02, including taxes. Not to forget a cup of cafe au lait. Take your own tray from the counter to a booth or out to the small patio, and watch the world go by.

Cafe Parisian is open 9 a.m. to 9:30 p.m., Monday through Saturday, with breakfast served until 11 a.m. On Sunday the place is open for brunch from 9 a.m. to 3:30 p.m.

Cajun Bangkok

• 907 King Street, Alexandria, VA; ✆ (703) 836-0038

Is it a little strange to contemplate a combination of Louisiana and Thai food? When you think about it, not really. Both cuisines rely on a lot of seafood, and both employ an almost magical mix of hot spices. In fact, all you need to do is to simply eat at this reasonably priced restaurant to be convinced that mixing Cajun and Thai was in fact a brilliantly lucid inspiration!

This place has established itself as one of Old Town's most popular places. Here, the appetizers are mostly Thai and main courses mostly Cajun. Start out by sharing an appetizer of Crying Tiger, New York strip steak served with a hot lemongrass sauce ($5.95), or perhaps Meang Kham, which is crispy roasted coconut, fresh limes, ginger, red onion, dried shrimps, roasted peanuts, hot peppers and collard green leaves with sweet ginger sauce ($6.50). Awesome! You can also try the soup: Lemon Grass Shrimp ($3.50) or Bangkok She Crab ($3.50), and you won't be disappointed.

Then move on to the main courses: Cajun Chicken, a pan-fried chicken with tomato and scallion in spicy Cajun seasoning ($11.95); Roasted Pecan Catfish, pan-roasted filet of catfish in spiced pecan seasoning, topped with butterfly shrimp over lemon cream sauce ($12.95); Bourbon Shrimp, sautéed shrimp with mushroom, scallion in spicy seasoned dry bourbon sauce ($13.95); or any number of other mouthwatering entrees. You can also enjoy several Thai main course specialties, most of which range in price from $8.95 to $12.95.

It's truly hard to go wrong at this place. Here's to international cooking!

Enjoy the delectable offerings here Sunday through Thursday from 5 to 10 p.m., and Friday and Saturday until 11 p.m.

Calvert Grille

- 3106 Mt. Vernon Avenue, Alexandria, VA;
  ✆ (703) 836-8425

Look carefully on your way into Old Town for this place, hidden away in a plain-Jane shopping center, or you're sure to pass it by. Once inside, two large, casual rooms are still ordinary looking, but the down-home food surpasses the simple decor. There's also a full bar.

The lineup of house specialties includes fine grub like a 12-ounce NY strip steak ($9.95); four pieces of mouthwatering fried chicken ($7.95), and barbecued baby-back ribs ($13.95), all sure to send your blood pressure soaring. Blue-plate deals may consist of Salisbury steak ($8.95), or a salmon platter ($10.95). Dinners are served with two side orders or a fresh salad.

Lunch specials, usually a few dollars less, can offer anything from Maryland crab cakes to chicken fajitas. Hefty hamburgers start at $3.60; sandwiches include a smoked pork platter with fries and slaw for $4.95, and a marinated flank steak for the same price.

Good eatin'. And of course, Mr. C had to finish his meal with fresh key lime pie ($3.95), and was glad he did.

The Calvert is open Monday through Thursday from 11:30 a.m. to 10 p.m., from 11:30 a.m. to midnight, Saturday from 9:30 a.m. to 11 p.m., and Sunday from 9:30 to 9 p.m.

Casablanca

- 1504 King Street, Alexandria, VA; ✆ (703) 549-6464

- 🖳 www.moroccanrestaurant. com/

Like Humphrey Bogart, you may think you'll get trapped (as in tourist trap) by going to this Casablanca; but in fact, as several reviews in the window will attest, the food here is quite good, and you certainly get a lot for your money, since the show of live Moroccan music and belly dancing is included in the price. The atmosphere is authentic too, with large, plush pillows for you to sit on in your most princely manner.

A dinner/show package is $20 per person, covering a five-course meal. All dinners include appetizers, one or two entrees, homemade bread, and dessert. Start with your choice of Middle Eastern soups and salads; move on to main courses like chicken in a spicy *harrisa* sauce, lamb with honey and almonds, salmon with onions and raisins, couscous with vegetables, and plenty of others.

By far the best deal, though, comes early in the week. Dine on Monday, Tuesday, or Wednesday evenings, and you get the whole shebang—same full dinner and show—for just $9.95 a person, with a coupon that you can print out from Casablanca's Web site.

Casablanca is open for dinner from 5:30 to 11:30 p.m. nightly. The belly dancing begins at 8 p.m.! Reservations are recommended, certainly on weekends.

Chadwicks

• 203 Strand Street, Alexandria, VA; ℘ (703) 836-4442

See the listing under *Restaurants—Georgetown*.

Chicken Out Rotisserie

• 1443 Chain Bridge Road, McLean, VA; ℘ (703) 917-8646

• 4238 Wilson Boulevard, Arlington, VA; ℘ (703) 358-5678

• 1202 W Broad Street, Falls Church, VA; ℘ (703) 237-5444

• 2946 Chain Bridge Road, Oakton, VA; ℘ (703) 319-8646

• 701 S Washington Street, Alexandria, VA; ℘ (703) 684-9280

• 1042 Elden Street, Herndon, VA; ℘ (703) 481-8200

• 8426 Old Keene Mill Road, Springfield, VA; ℘ (703) 644-7771

• 21031 Triplesleven Road, Sterling, VA; ℘ (703) 406-9667

And other suburban locations

• ℘ www.chickenout.com

See the listing under *Restaurants—Upper Northwest*.

Chipotle

• 2231 Crystal Drive, Crystal City, VA; ℘ (703) 920-8779;

• 1735 N. Lynn Street, Rosslyn, VA; ℘ (703) 294-6669

• ℘ www.chipotle.com

See the listing under *Restaurants—Maryland*.

Coco's

• 3111 Columbia Pike, Arlington, VA; ℘ (703) 920-5450

For fine Italian food at one of Virginia's oldest restaurants, Coco's may be just your cup of tea. A dozen different spaghetti and linguine dishes run from $9.95 to $11.95—and that's before you even get to the house specialties of chicken, veal, and seafood. Dare Mr. C say it? He went cuckoo for Coco's.

He did so by starting with a terrific bowl of minestrone for $3.95, following this with an order of veal cacciatore ($15.95) sautéed with onions, green peppers, tomatoes, mushrooms, and red wine. Several different chicken choices start from $9.95, and the shrimp scampi over spaghetti ($15.95) looked spectacular as it went by.

Finish off with—what else?—cannoli and cappuccino. Coco's is open for lunch and dinner, from 11 a.m. to 11 p.m. seven days.

Cowboy Cafe

- 2421 Columbia Pike, Arlington, VA; ✆ (703) 486-3467

- 4792 Lee Hwy. Arlington, VA; ✆ (703) 243-8010

This place doesn't look like much from the outside, but when you walk in you notice a '57 Chevy sticking out of the wall—and, hey, you might as well be in "Dubya" country. Anyway, the Cowboy Cafe is a popular and rowdy entertainment spot, and a home to Texas feeding at its riproarin' best. Burgers, sandwiches, and choices "from the chuck wagon" fill a menu as simple as it is mouthwatering. Hearty half-pound burgers, all $6.50, are served with fries, coleslaw, or chips. Mr. C recommends the Cowboy's "Best Damn Burger," made with herbs and onions and topped with the cheese of your choice. Rolled sandwiches include the "Snakebite," with roast beef and horseradish, and the "Longhorn," with roast beef, two cheeses, onion, and barbecue sauce. You can also get "Road Kill Chicken," made up of a boneless chicken breast with creamy sauce served over fettuccini, for $8.50. Yee haw!

The spectacular burrito plate: three burritos (chicken, cheese, and chili) served with refried beans and Spanish rice is just $7.75. You can also chow on a $7 plate of goulash, pork chops, or meatloaf, as well as other daily specials—just strap on the feedbag!

Weekends feature hearty breakfasts served from 9 a.m. to 3 p.m.; Texas-style French toast is a good bet at just $2.95. Hitch your pony to this fun spot from 11 a.m. on weekdays, with food served until 11 p.m. Sundays through Thursdays, and to 1:30 a.m. on weekends.

Delhi Dhaba

- 2424 Wilson Boulevard, Arlington, VA; ✆ (703) 524-0008

See the listing under *Restaurants—Maryland.*

El Pollo Rico

- 2917 N. Washington Boulevard, Arlington, VA; ✆ (703) 522-3220

- 2541 Ennalls Road; Wheaton, MD; ✆ (301) 942-4419

Simplicity is a real virtue at these fast-food-style, family-owned Peruvian restaurants. Tasty, marinated chicken is all they serve here, grilled up before your very eyes. A quarter chicken, with French fries and coleslaw, costs a mere $3.61. A half-chicken plate is $6.16, and you can even have a whole bird for $11.61.

Whichever you choose, it's all dee-lish. Like the depth of the menu, El Pollo Rico is not much on atmosphere—unless you count the mouthwatering aroma that literally hangs in the air and hits you the moment you walk through the door. Now, who do you think "does chicken right"?

Hours are 11 a.m. to 10 p.m., seven days.

Faccia Luna Pizzeria

- 2909 Wilson Boulevard, Arlington, VA; ✆ (703) 276-3099

See the listing under *Restaurants—Georgetown.*

Five Guys

- 6541 Backlick Road, Springfield, VA; ✆ (703) 913-1337

- 4626 King Street, Alexandria, VA; ✆ (703) 671-1606

- 107 North Fayette Street Alexandria; ✆ (703) 549-7991

302   MR. CHEAP'S WASHINGTON D.C.

How many guys does it take to prepare a phenomenal burger? Five, or possibly more? Who's asking when the outcome is the best all-round burger in town—certainly not Mr. C!

The hamburgers are truly unsurpassable, especially for the price. A burger with the works (lettuce, tomato, onion, mayonnaise, mustard, ketchup, cheese, and bacon) will only set you back four bucks. The quality of the French fries matches the companion burger. Freshly prepared on a daily basis, these spuds cost only about $1 for the small size and $3 for the large. You can dust them off with Cajun spice seasonings or malt vinegar.

Five Guys will welcome you every day of the week from 11 a.m. to 10 p.m.

Generous George's Positive Pizza & Pasta Place

- 3006 Duke Street, Alexandria, VA; ✆ (703) 370-4303

There's a lot to be said for accuracy. And the name of this eatery could not be more precise, every last word of it. George offers a ton of food, with a menu centered around two fun favorites. Sure, you can get pasta, and you can get pizza, but have you ever had pasta on your pizza? Not just lightly arranged across it, like pepperoni slices, but literally an entire serving of noodles dumped on top of it. That's the gimmick, folks, and it packs 'em in like crazy.

But there's plenty of room. Two floors of bar and lounge rooms, kiddie rooms, and basement rec rooms are all done out in glorious pastel pink and green, like an episode of Miami Vice gone haywire. Plus wacky posters, old-time gas pumps, red fire engines—the kind we all rode in as kids—hanging

from the ceiling . . . they all add to the "positive" atmosphere that make GG's fun for baby boomers as well as baby-laden families.

And the food? It's a carb-loader's dream. A soft, doughy crust is the bed for a heap of linguine, fettuccini, or even lasagna. Inside may be sausage, chicken, shrimp, vegetables, you name it—a ton of options all range from $12.95 for individual-sized pies. Good luck finishing; take some home for lunch tomorrow instead.

There are also more "conventional" pizzas, priced at $9.95 for medium and $12.95 for large, topped with such items as ham and pineapple, chicken and salsa, pesto, and more. (Toppings are $1.50 each.) Plus, you'll find sandwiches and salads, though it's hard to imagine coming here and not getting a "pasta pie."

George's generosity extends to the drinks, which include some good beers; sodas come in two sizes, huge and huger. There's also a children's menu with half a dozen items all under $3.95. Needless to say, the place is ready for birthday parties (complete with balloons) and carryout orders.

Go ahead, pig out. Pound for pound—and you'll feel every one for hours—this has to be one of the best food values Mr. C has ever seen.

Generous George's is open Monday through Thursday from 11 a.m. to 10 p.m., Friday and Saturday from 11 a.m. to midnight, and Sunday from noon to 10 p.m.

Hamburger Hamlet

- 1601 Crystal Square Arcade, Crystal City, VA; ✆ (703) 413-0422

- ✐ www.hamburgerhamlet.com

See the listing under *Restaurants—Maryland*.

Hard Times Cafe

- 3028 Wilson Boulevard, Arlington, VA; ✆ (703) 528-2233

- 1404 King Street, Alexandria, VA; ✆ (703) 837-0050

- 6362 Springfield Plaza Springfield, VA; ✆ (703) 913-5600

- 428 Elden Street, Herndon, VA; ✆ (703) 318-8941

  And other suburban locations

- ✐ www.hardtimes.com

Chili, and more chili, is the rule at these popular suburban restaurant/bars. In fact, they offer four different kinds of chili, and merely for asking, they'll bring you a free "taster" plate of all four—Texas, meaty and basic; Cincinnati, sweeter and more tomatoey; a red bean chili; and a delicious vegetarian variety, spicy and made with cooked peanuts in place of beef.

Once you've chosen your stew, you're done, right? Wrong. Order a plate of it with beans for $4.95, over spaghetti for $5.25, or with both for $5.50. All of these come with homemade cornbread, by the way. Oh yes, and you can add various toppings, like shredded cheese, sour cream, and jalapeños. Whew! And you thought chili was just chili.

Of course, man (or woman) cannot live by chili alone. Hard Times also offers spicy chicken wings, plus a few burgers, sandwiches, and salads, all priced around $5. There's also a children's menu.

They'll enjoy washing this all down with a bottle of HT's own honey-tinged root beer ($3.95); you can choose from lots of great microbrews, like Pete's Wicked Ale, Telluride, and Sierra Nevada. All the while, country tunes from Elvis to Garth wail on the jukebox.

No wonder this place is consistently rated as one of the area's best bargain spots by readers of *Washingtonian* magazine.

Hard Times will welcome you Sunday through Thursday from 11 a.m. to 11 p.m. On Friday and Saturday they stay open until midnight.

Iota Restaurant & Bar

- 2832 Wilson Boulevard, Arlington, VA; ✆ (703) 522-8340

- ✐ www.iotaclubandcafe.com

Formerly a dilapidated old storefront, this place re-opened in mid-'94 as a hip lunch and night spot for the suburban crowd that longs for a bit of downtown atmosphere. The narrow, high-ceilinged space has been renovated to show exposed brick, wood rafters, local musicians, and lots of style.

The menu, still being played with, offers a little bit of everything trendy—soups and salads, sandwiches, and full meals—all priced fewer than nine bucks. You can go for a bowl of potato leek soup for about $4.75, or perhaps a blackened salmon ($9.75) or Caesar salad ($5.25 or $7.25).

The entrees are awesome and more reasonably priced than the soups or salads! Try a dinner of grilled salmon for $11.75 or a seared Ahi tuna plate for $14.75. Vegetarians will love roasted mushroom ravioli for $12.75. Daily specials run from $13.25 to $18.25. A few dessert items (chocolate truffle, $3.75) are not to be missed if you, like the always-fit Mr. C., can afford the calories.

The full bar is well stocked with microbrews and selected wines. The Iota complements these with live music and poetry most nights of the week. (See the listing under *Entertainment—Music.*)

Hours are from 11 a.m. to 2 a.m. every day, further making Iota a natural hangout.

Kabob Bazaar

- 3133 Wilson Boulevard, Arlington, VA; ✆ (703) 522-8999

"Have a taste of Persia," encourages Kabob Bazaar, which offers far more than a taste. The ornate interior is covered over by an elaborate canopy, making this place really stand out from other Middle Eastern eateries, with a more upscale atmosphere.

Tender lamb shish kabobs run just $7.75 with bread and rice. Beef kabobs are the same price, while the chicken version is a bit less. All are delicious. You can also opt for a vegetarian platter $5.75, with plenty of choices available. A number of side dishes can be had for under $2—the *torshi* is a good choice, with a mixture of vegetables marinated in vinegar and spices ($1.95). One variant, at the same price, features whole Italian eggplant.

As you might guess, homemade baklava ($2.35) is among the desserts served here, a rich and flavorful finish to any meal.

Explore the Bazaar from 11 a.m. to 10 p.m. Monday through Saturday, 11:30 a.m. to 9 p.m. Sundays.

King Street Blues

- 1648 Crystal Square Arcade, Arlington, VA; ✆ (703) 415-2583

- 112 N Saint Asaph Street, Alexandria, VA; ✆ (703) 836-8800

- 5810 Kingstowne Center, Alexandria, VA; ✆ (703) 313-0400

- ✐ www.kingstreetblues.net

All three floors of what must have once been a quiet, stately, respectable Old Town home have been totally revamped into the wildest little roadhouse in (or actually *not* in) Texas. Red neon in the windows, bright blue-and-white checked tablecloths, wacky papiermâché airplanes hanging from the ceiling, and rockabilly music keep this place jumping all day and night. Catch the autographed pix of Lyle Lovett and Jerry Jeff Walker by the door, too.

The menu is strictly casual; from country fried chicken or steak ($9.95) and pecan crusted farmraised catfish ($11.75,) to a blackened swordfish sandwich ($7.99) and a variety of po'boys ($7.95), served in a basket on fresh-baked sourdough bread with homemade potato chips and coleslaw. King Street also offers a one-pound rack of ribs (which they boast is the best in Virginia) for just $9.95.

If you can, go for the daily blueplate specials, served Monday through Thursday until 6 p.m., $5.95 gets you a different deal each day, like homemade meatloaf with garlic-mashed potatoes. Try that for lunch, and everyone back at the office will insist that you take the rest of the day off.

The bar, on the ground floor, is well stocked; the upper two floors are dining rooms. It's a rowdy, over-the-top kind of joint that's just plain fun.

King Street is open Monday through Saturday from 11:30 a.m. until 10 p.m., and on Sundays from 11:30 a.m. to 9 p.m.

La Madeleine

- 500 King Street, Alexandria, VA; ✆ (703) 739-2854

- 5861 Crossroads Center Way, Baileys Crossroads, VA; ✆ (703) 379-5551

- 1915 Chain Bridge Road,
  McLean, VA; ✆ (703) 827-8833

- 1833 Fountain Drive, Reston,
  VA; ✆ (703) 707-0704

- ✍ www.lamadeleine.com

See the listing under *Restaurants—Maryland.*

Le Gaulois

- 1106 King Street, Alexandria,
  VA; ✆ (703) 739-9494

Enter this handsome brick townhouse, and you'll be instantly transported to the French provinces. Two floors of elegant, country-style decor make this a rather ritzy stop for Mr. C. Can such a place be inexpensive? *Mais oui!*

Not entirely, mind you. Many items are fancy, and priced accordingly; but the menu offers enough moderate entrees to make this a worthy splurge for the lunch crowd or for visitors on a touring budget. Omelets are $8.75; seafood *crepes au gratin* are $12.50. Or, opt for *salade de poulet canard* (that's duck salad to the rest of us) for $7.25; other healthy choices from their "low-cal" section include things like veal scaloppini over spinach with vegetables ($18.25). Finish off with excellent coffee, and perhaps a creme caramel. Luscious desserts range between $4.25 and $7.25. Not exactly cheap, but good prices for such a romantic and classy restaurant.

Le Gaulois is open Monday through Thursday from 11:30 a.m. to 10:30 p.m., and Friday and Saturday from 11:30 a.m. to 11 p.m. Reservations are recommended.

Lite N' Fair

- 1018 King Street, Alexandria,
  VA; ✆ (703) 549-3717

Located in historic Old Town Alexandria, this place offers something no true cheapster can pass up: exotic food at carryout prices. Gourmet chef Ki Choi's elegant entrees include charbroiled mahi mahi with lemon butter for a mere $8.95, or an 8-ounce New York sirloin with sautéed mushrooms; tempura with hot sauce for $9.95. All entrees are served with vegetables plus rice or potato.

If your tastes are more basic, they've still got you covered. Turkey, cheese, and tomatoes on a croissant make for a light n' fair $4.95; Caesar or garden salads are just $2.14; a piping hot bowl of German potato soup is the same price. A dozen different desserts, including chocolate mousse and apple strudel, run around $3.95.

Lite N' Fair prepares party platters to go and offers complete catering; call for details.

Hours are 11 a.m. to 9 p.m. Monday through Thursday. On Friday and Saturday they're open 11 a.m. to 10 p.m., and they're closed on Sunday.

Little Viet Garden

- 3012 Wilson Boulevard,
  Arlington, VA;
  ✆ (703) 522-9686

This attractive little spot, regularly named one of *Washingtonian* magazine's best bargain restaurants, combines authentic Vietnamese cuisine, an outdoor cafe, and healthy and tasty food.

Many of the entrees come in comfortably under $10, but it's tough to pass up a house specialty like the Saigon combo platter ($12.95) with shrimp, scallops on a skewer, beef tenderloin slices, green peppers, onions, and tomatoes, all served over rice. You won't go wrong with spring rolls and lemongrass pork with vermicelli ($8.95) either, while more unusual options include caramel chicken with ginger and roasted quail with rice, each $8.95

Soups, never to be overlooked at Vietnamese restaurants, include an egg noodle variety with shrimp and pork ($3.25). Most dinner entrees are also available as lunch options, for around $2 less.

And speaking of lunch, it's served from 11 a.m. to 2:30 p.m. Monday through Friday. Dinner is served from 5 to 10 p.m. Weekend hours are noon to 10 p.m.

Matuba

- 2915 Columbia Pike, Arlington, VA; ✆ (703) 521-2811

See the listing under *Restaurants—Maryland.*

Mexicali Blues

- 2933 Wilson Boulevard, Arlington, VA; ✆ (703) 812-9352

This twentysomething hangout specializes in Mexican and Salvadoran specialties, served up good 'n cheap. The guacamole is chunky and piquant. The corn tamales are homemade and loaded with chicken and vegetables ($1.95). Tacos de camaron with delicate fried shrimp ($9.25) also satisfies, and the tortillas come with warm spicy salsa and that fresh "guac." Salvadoran-style marinated steak known as *carne asada* goes for $10.95, and you can also try the delicious fried yucca wedges covered in sour cream for $3.75.

Check out Sunday brunch, featuring *huevos rancheros, flautas* loaded with cheese and eggs, and chorizo or pork-and-cheese omelets.

Mexicali Blues is open every day from 11 a.m. to 10 p.m. Sunday brunch is served from 10:30 a.m. to 2 p.m.

Mr. Smith's

- 8369 Leesburg Pike, Tysons Corner, VA; ✆ (703) 893-1204

- ✑ www.mrsmiths.com

See the listing under *Restaurants—Georgetown.*

Murphy's Grand Irish Pub

- 713 King Street, Alexandria, VA; ✆ (703) 548-1717

- ✑ www.murphyspub.com

Murphy's packs its menu with standard pub fare, traditional Irish dinners, and a variety of seafood selections. The decor, with its handsome dark wood and a charming fireplace, completes the picture. Throw in some live music upstairs and you've got a pretty good idea why this place is frequently jammed.

Mr. C suggests you start with a pint of Harp lager with a snack of homemade onion rings or a mountain of Murphy's cottage fries, each $3.25. Wolf down one of 20 different sandwiches, most served with the aforementioned cottage fries: Hot corned beef ($5.95), several different chicken breast sandwiches ($5.50), or a Murphy's club sandwich ($5.95) are excellent choices.

Entrees are generally served with potato and vegetables. These include, naturally, corned beef and cabbage ($7.50); Irish meat and potato pie ($6.95); and Irish stew ($5.95). Seafood choices of fish and chips ($7.50), fresh clams, lightly fried ($8.95), and sea scallops over pasta with garlic bread ($9.95). All are fine choices. If you're not in an Irish mood, you can get fettuccine Alfredo or fettuccine tossed with olive oil, fresh basil, and tomatoes—each is $6.95.

Most nights Murphy's has live Irish music with no cover charge, and has wide selection of wine and Irish beer. The sum total of all this: A complete, cheap, evening of dining and entertainment!

Murphy's is open daily from 11 a.m. (10 a.m. on Sundays) into the wee hours.

Nam Viet

- 1127 N. Hudson Street, Arlington, VA; ✆ (703) 522-7110

- ✑ www.namviet1.com

Look carefully down a side street off of Wilson Boulevard for this restaurant, which offers a multitude of delicious entrees for all interests—and with a more user-friendly menu than that of many such places. Nearly as important, it's also Cheapster-friendly.

For an appetizer, a pair of shrimp and pork rolls is $3.45. Four different kinds of salad are $4.25 each; a good choice is the Nam Viet special of shrimp, chicken, and shredded vegetables mixed with a house dressing. Among soups, the tasty and interesting blend of crabmeat with asparagus earned Mr. C's attention—and a small serving runs just $2.45.

Moving to the entrees, grilled pork with thin rice noodles costs a mere $7.95. Another interesting choice, caramelized pork with black pepper, is $9.50. Or go for the delicious house special of beef wrapped with beans, vermicelli, mushrooms, cooking wine, and chopped onions ($8.95). Yummy.

There's also a raft of seafood options, most priced under $10, like a spicy sweet-and-sour shrimp soup mixed with vegetables ($9.75). The seafood combination is $12.95. Fried rice and vegetarian meals come in at $7.95 each. Some 15 chef's specialties include "orange pork chops, Saigon style," made with fresh orange slices ($8.50).

Nam Viet is open Sunday through Thursday from 10 a.m. to 10 p.m.; Friday and Saturday until 11 p.m.

Old Hickory Grille

- 7263 Arlington Boulevard, Falls Church, VA; ✆ (703) 207-8650

See the listing under *Restaurants—Maryland.*

Peking Gourmet Inn

- 6029 Leesburg Pike, Falls Church, VA; ✆ (703) 671-8088

- ✑ www.pekinggourmet.com

Mr. C doesn't always go out of his way to describe Chinese restaurants, which are plentiful and usually inexpensive; when he heard, though, that back in the late 1980s, the elder Mr. and Mrs. Bush used to sneak over here from across the river, he became mildly curious. Or is that hot-and-spicy curious?

Sure enough, your humble scribe found one of the tastiest, cheapest, and most wonderful meals he's had in many a city. Now, the specialty of the house is a $34 dish of Peking duck carved at your table; since he was dining without his own First Lady, Mr. C opted for something close: Peking Gourmet Chicken. What arrived shortly thereafter can only be described as ambrosial for any poultry lover. An entire small chicken is basted with a tasty special sauce, fried up crispy, chopped into sections, and served on a platter. Just pick it up with your fingers and enjoy; the Colonel never had it so good. Meanwhile, the whole deal, with rice, only cost a budget-balancing $9.45 at lunchtime. (At dinner, a similar dish called Peking Spring Chicken, considered an appetizer for two, costs $10.45).

Most other hefty lunch specials are priced under $10. A combination platter and an egg roll go for $6.95 and up. Dinner, alas, is a bit more expensive across the board, with most main selections ranging between $12 and $17. Still, the surroundings are ornate, and the quality and portions of food are well worth the splurge. Plus, you get the added excitement of wondering: Did they sit at our table? Was it this one over here, or maybe *this* one . . . ?

Peking Gourmet Inn is open Sunday through Thursday from 11 a.m. to 10:30 p.m., and Friday and Saturday from 11 a.m. to midnight.

Pho 75

- 1721 Wilson Boulevard, Arlington, VA; ✆ (703) 525-7355

- 3103 Graham Road, Falls Church, VA; ✆ (703) 204-1490

- 382 Elden Street, Herndon, VA; ✆ (703) 471-4145

See the listing under *Restaurants—Maryland.*

Red Hot & Blue

- 1600 Wilson Boulevard N., Arlington, VA; ✆ 703-243-1510

- 1701 Clarendon Boulevard, Arlington, VA; ✆ 703-276-8833

- 4150 Chain Bridge Road, Fairfax, VA; ✆ (703) 218-6989

- ✐ www.redhotandblue.com

See the listing under *Restaurants—Maryland.*

Rio Grande Cafe

- 4301 Fairfax Drive, Arlington, VA; ✆ (703) 528-3131

- 1827 Library Street, Reston, VA; ✆ (703) 904-0703

See the listing under *Restaurants—Maryland.*

Royal Restaurant

- 734 N. Saint Asaph Street, Alexandria, VA; ✆ (703) 548-1616

This popular restaurant has been king in Alexandria for almost a century. One side's a luncheonette with counters and booths, decorated with ceiling fans, an "oldies" jukebox, and nostalgic ads—which, come to think of it, may have been current when they were put up— while the other is a larger, more conventional dining room and lounge. Friendly coffee shop-type waitresses will call you "hon" while they keep your cuppa joe filled.

The Royal is most popular for its delicious breakfasts, served up on huge platters but very inexpensive. Two extra-large eggs with crisp bacon or country sausage are $4.89, served with toast and home fries or grits. Belgian waffles with bacon, sausage, or scrapple run $3.55; with Virginia ham, $6.67. And for a real deal, check out the "Royal Breakfast," offering two pancakes, two eggs, home fries, and a choice of bacon, sausage, or scrapple for $6.72. On Sundays, an all-out buffet brunch, served from 7 a.m. to 2 p.m., is priced at just $8.87.

For lunch, go with a hot open-face roast beef sandwich, served with mashed potatoes and gravy for $7.47. You'll pay a bit more for seafood, like scallops ($10.48), or salmon ($13.17); but these do come with a baked potato and a trip to the small but well-stocked salad bar. Daily lunch and dinner specials abound; Fridays feature karaoke and complimentary munchies. Basic beers, wines, and cocktails are also available.

Get the Royal treatment from 6 a.m. to 9:30 p.m. Mondays through Saturdays, and 7 a.m. to 2 p.m. on Sundays.

The Scoop Grill

• 110 King Street, Alexandria,
VA; ✆ (703) 549-4527

This popular spot near the waterfront just exudes good cheer, from
its old-timey ice cream parlor look
to its yesteryear prices. The fact
that you can scoop this place up for
breakfast, lunch, and dinner seven
days a week is an added bonus.

Those breakfasts include a $4.50
meal of two eggs, bacon, or sausage
with toast and home fries—along
with pancakes and the like. For
lunch or a quick supper, you'll
spend just $4.50 on a quarter-pound
cheeseburger, $5.50 on a steak and
cheese sub, or $4.50 on a smoked
turkey sandwich. A large chef's
salad is a healthy $4.95.

Oh, yeah—and then there's
homemade ice cream! According to
the manager, the Scoop makes over
200 flavors; at any one time there
are 32 different varieties available.

The Scoop is open from 10 a.m.
to 11 p.m. Mondays through Fridays, until midnight Saturdays, and
10 p.m. Sundays.

Southside 815

• 815 South Washington Street,
Alexandria, VA;
✆ (703) 836-6222

• ✑ www.southside815.com

Located in Old Town Alexandria,
this is a great restaurant (listed in
the *Washington Post's* top 15) that
combines some fine American
cooking with reasonable prices.

Early in the day, check out the
Boardinghouse Breadbasket, which
includes good biscuits, sweet-potato
biscuits, and cornbread for just
$1.95. Later on, you can scarf
down po'boy sandwiches ($7.50),
some tasty Chicken-fried steak
served with cream gravy, mashed
potatoes, and vegetables ($9.95), or
perhaps Charleston Chicken—

chicken breast, shrimp, kielbasa,
corn, and shallots, sautéed in a
sherry butter ($12.95). You can
also other such uniquely southern
specialties as chicken gumbo
($13.95), Low Country Shortcake—
roasted chicken, oysters, and
Mason-Dixon mashed potatoes, layered with cornbread, succotash, and
smothered with gravy ($13.95)—
and several other super specialties.
Almost unbelievable, ain't it? The
Cheapster is gaining weight (and
cholesterol) just thinking about this
stuff.

Southside is open Sunday
through Friday from 11:30 a.m. to
10:30 p.m.; Friday and Saturday
until 11 p.m.

Taste of Saigon

• 8201 Greensboro Drive,
McLean, VA;
✆ (703) 790-0700

See the listing under *Restaurants—Maryland.*

That's Amore

• 46300 Potomac Run Plaza, Sterling, VA; ✆ (703) 406-4900

• 150 Branch Road, Vienna, VA;
✆ (703) 281-7777

• ✑ www.thatsamore.com

See the listing under *Restaurants—Maryland.*

Whitey's

• 2761 Washington Boulevard,
Arlington, VA;
✆ (703) 525-9825

• 4399 Henninger Court, Chantilly, VA; ✆ (703) 968-0344

• ✑ www.whiteyseat.com

Head across the river to Whitey's,
and you'll think you've gone much
further—landing in some Texas
roadhouse. Everybody whoops and

hollers, knocking back beers, throwing a game of darts, shooting pool, and otherwise having a rip-roaring good time.

So, assuming you haven't come in here for a quiet, candlelight dinner, you can enjoy a wide range of inexpensive food and drink deals. Monday's mean "All You Can Eat" dinner specials, when $8.95 can get you broasted chicken—four pieces (a half chicken) served with potatoes, coleslaw, sour cream, hot rolls, and butter. You can enjoy a New York strip steak dinner, served with fresh rolls, butter, and your choice of two side dishes, for just $12.95.

The term "Happy Hour" is generously stretched at Whitey's, offering discounted drinks and a dollar off appetizers from 4 to 7 p.m. on weekdays, and noon to 4 p.m. on weekends. Monday night, meanwhile, is "Pitcher Night," with pitchers of Whitey's own draft beer for $5.50. If you prefer snootier brews, they also serve brands like Harp, Bass, Double Diamond, and others,

Through it all, classic rock tunes blare from the speakers, competing with sports games on numerous televisions around the two large rooms. Most nights also present music—anything from live bands to karaoke—from 9 p.m. to midnight, with "never a cover." How could Mr. C not like this joint?

The place opens up for breakfast, too, by the way. On any day you can get juice, two eggs any style, your choice of bacon or sausage, home fries, buttered toast and jelly for just $3.50, or omelets starting at $2.95.

Whitey's is open 9 a.m. on weekends and 8 a.m. on weekends, and it doesn't close 'til 1 or 2 a.m.

MR. CHEAP'S SUNDAY BRUNCH

Who doesn't love brunch? This longtime Sunday morning/afternoon activity is an institution in our nation's capital. It's certainly Mr. Cheap's all-time favorite weekend ritual. For one thing, brunch is more or less two, sometimes even three, gourmet meals rolled into one sitting: breakfast, lunch, and possibly dinner. So, if you have a belly with a sizable capacity, brunch could very well translate into automatic savings as it's one less meal to buy—at least, from Mr. C's perspective. Of course, the type of brunch you choose (a la carte vs. buffet) may determine the amount of food you're prepared to eat . . . and don't we agree it's important to get your money's worth?! Here are a few suggestions for getting started on the Sunday brunch circuit:

WASHINGTON

Georgia Brown's

• 950 15th Street N.W., Washington, D.C.; ✆ (202) 393-4499

Georgia Brown's, known for its refined soul food, offers an all-you-can-eat jazz brunch with a choice of either a buffet that is "breakfast driven," or pick from one of five main entrees that are "lunch driven." Either way, Mr. C highly recommends you try the crispy collard greens (traditional style also available), black-eye peas, fried chicken, grilled catfish, and Carolina gumbo. The $22.95 brunch special includes coffee, mimosas, and Bloody Mary's. Hours are on Sunday from 10:30 a.m. to 3 p.m.

Café Promenade at the Mayflower Hotel

- 1127 Connecticut Avenue N.W., Washington, D.C.; ✆ (202) 347-2233

Indulge in Café Promenade's brunch—it's flowing with unlimited champagne and a buffet featuring a soup bar, salad bar, fish bar, meat bar, dessert bar. You name it, they have got a "bar" for it. Live music plays throughout, well worth the $40 splurge. Brunch hours are from 11 a.m. to 3 p.m.

Cashion's Eat Place

- 1819 Columbia Road N.W., Washington, D.C.; ✆ (202) 797-1819

The trendy, sleek, and beautiful convene here at Cashion's Eat Place. The menu rotates on a regular basis and their brunch offers distinctive dishes such as grilled rainbow trout, fresh granola and yogurt, and French toast with candied apples. The menu is a la carte with prices ranging from $7 to $15. Open from 11:30 a.m. to 2:30 p.m.

Chadwick's

- 3205 K Street N.W., Washington, D.C.; ✆ (202) 333-2565

Chadwick's unlimited champagne brunch serves up eggs any style you can name: fried, scrambled, poached and . . . they have variations along the lines of "eggs Idaho" and "eggs Chesapeake." Egg-cellent deal at $10.95. Brunch hours are from 11 a.m. to 4 p.m.

Perry's

- 1811 Columbia Road N.W., Washington, D.C.; ✆ (202) 234-6218

Here's an unexpected twist: Perry's showcases a drag show at Sunday brunch. Nothing too over the top, mind you. The entertainment features four or five performers who lip sync and dance while you dine. The drag show starts at 11 a.m. and, unfortunately, it's not possible to make reservations ahead of time. For $22.95 (the show is included), you can at least count on brunch libation, coffee, and a full buffet with both breakfast and lunch fare. Don't miss out, the queens wear colorful boas and are on par with Dame Edna. Hours are from 10:30 a.m. to 2:30 p.m.

Tony Cheng's Mongolian Barbeque

- 619 H Street N.W., Washington, D.C.; ✆ (202) 842-8669

Looking for an alternative to typical brunch food? Then stop by Tony Cheng's Mongolian Barbeque to sample dim sum Chinese dumplings filled with a variety of delicious meats and veggies (pork, beef, chicken, mushrooms, beans, broccoli, etc.). Hours are from 11 a.m. to 3 p.m.

Gabriel's at Radisson Barcelo Hotel

- 2121 P Street N.W., Washington, D.C.; ✆ (202) 956-6690

Gabriel's brunch is nothing but amazing, period. While $26.75 sounds steep, you get all the coffee and champagne you could possibly want—along with the opportunity to fill your plate with roast suckling pig, and an array of food from their tapas, seafood, and dessert stations.

Mr. C vouches for the empanadas stuffed with plantains and other fillings. Brunch is served from 11 a.m. to 3 p.m.

MARYLAND

Louisiana Express Company

- 4921 Bethesda Avenue, Bethesda, MD;
  ✆ (301) 652-6945

Mr. C suggests that you get your taste buds jumpin' at Louisiana Express Company's brunch. Here, you can sample jambalaya, soft shell crabs, po'boy sandwiches, crawfish, and more. The a la carte menu ranges from $10 to $12, Brunch hours are from 10 a.m. to 2:30 p.m.

Normandie Farm

- 10701 Fall Road, Potomac, MD;
  ✆ (301) 983-8838

At Normandie Farm's Sunday brunch, a basket of hot, fluffy popovers fresh from the oven awaits. The brunch costs $22 per person and comes with coffee, mimosas, Bloody Mary's, smoked fish, oysters on the half shell, clams, fruit, cheese, and dessert— just to mention a few of the things you can come by here down on the farm. Hours are from 11 a.m. to 2 p.m.

VIRGINIA

Carlyle Grand Hotel

- 4000 28th Street, Shirlington, VA; ✆ (703) 931-0777

At Carlyle Grand's Sunday brunch ($10 to $15, a la carte) you can choose from a wide selection of New American cuisine including crab cakes hollandaise, ham and asparagus omelets, and hot beignets in lieu of bread. Mr. C promises that it won't disappoint. Brunch hours are from 10:30 a.m. to 2 p.m.

Heart in Hand

- 7145 Main Street, Clifton, VA;
  ✆ (703) 830-4111

Set in an historic farmhouse, the backdrop for this Sunday brunch ($5 to 13.95, a la carte) was a favorite of former first lady Nancy Reagan. Nestled in horse country, Heart in Hand offers hearty fare of quiche, pasta, soup, baskets of bread, and homemade desserts. Mr. C thinks that's something to write home about! Brunch hours are from 11:30 a.m. to 3 p.m.

Market Street Bar and Grill

- 1800 Presidents Street, Reston, VA; ✆ (703) 709-6262

Mr. C says if you're in the "market" for Sunday brunch, then come indulge at Market Street Bar and Grill for $18.95, which includes a glass of champagne. And for an additional $4 you're entitled to an unlimited supply of Bloody Mary's and mimosas. The range of unique items on this menu is astonishing. To name a few of the buffet selections: shrimp scampi, mushroom strudel, sauteed vegetables, lobster claw and grits, peel-and-eat shrimps, and a dessert bar. Mr. C heard something about a chocolate praline tort . . . Brunch hours are from 11:30 a.m. to 2:30 p.m.

Lodging

Mr. C finds it very difficult to fall asleep if he thinks he paid too much for his hotel room; he ends up counting dollars all night.

Luckily, Mr. C has found ways to navigate the tricky waters of the hotel biz to find rooms in Washington where you can stay for under $100 a night. In fact, some offer rooms for under $50 a night. He's also found a few that cost more than that but deliver good deals.

Remember though: hotel rates ebb and flow with the seasons. And don't forget that taxes are always going to be added on top of any quoted price. Be sure you understand other policies of the hotel, too: Do they charge extra for additional persons in the room? Do they charge extra for local calls and toll-free calls? (Mr. C heads for the pay phone in the lobby if they do.) Is free parking included?

When it comes time to *negotiate* for a room rate, always ask about discounts. I've never seen an instance where a hotel room ever has only one price. Take advantage of any discounts you can—including corporate, AAA, military personnel, American Association of Retired Persons, and others. Furthermore, if you're going to be in town long enough, ask about weekly rates.

Finally, the peripatetic Mr. C strongly recommends that you peruse lodgings on one or more of the travel-oriented Web sites, such as Orbitz.com or Travelocity.com. These companies usually have the best connections to discounted room rates, which can change minute to minute. They also offer frequent promotions that can save you even more money. Once you have their best rate, try calling the hotel directly to see if they have an even better deal; hotels pay commissions to travel agents and online sites and sometimes they retain their very best rates for those who call them directly.

HOTELS AND MOTELS

Allen Lee Hotel

- 2224 F Street N.W., Washington, D.C.; ☎ (202) 331-1224 or ☎ (800) 462-0186

- ✎ www.allenleehotel.com

If you're looking for a unique lodging experience, the Allen Lee may be for you. Be warned, though, this is no place for squares. There are 85 rooms laid out in a variety of shapes, including octagons, hexagons, and even pentagons (particularly appropriate for D.C.) Heck, the entire building is triangular.

This hotel is somewhat on the older side, and the furniture may be a bit worn. All rooms do have air conditioning, phone, and TV. The Allen Lee is located about three blocks south of the Foggy Bottom Metro, in a student neighborhood considered quite safe. Rates for a single, shared bath start at $45; it's $58 if you want a private bath. Doubles are $62 for a shared bath, $74 private. Rooms with two twin beds are available at the same price as doubles. Hopefully you and your travel partner can agree on the same lovely trapezoid.

Americana Hotel

- 1400 Jefferson Davis Highway, Arlington, VA; ☎ (703) 979-3772 or ☎ (800) 548-6261

- ✎ www.americanahotel.com

Nestled among the glittering (and high-priced) hotels of Crystal City, this older motel has somehow managed to co-exist. Recently renovated, the simple rooms are tastefully furnished and include nice, big new color televisions, mini-refrigerators, and air conditioning. Cable TV is included, a continental breakfast is provided

each morning in the lobby, and local telephone calls are just a dime. Remember when?

The Americana also offers a free shuttle service to nearby National Airport, and to shops and restaurants in the area too. It even goes to the Pentagon. Rooms are mostly $75 to $85 a night in the spring tourist season. Rates drop to about $60 a night during the winter.

Budget Motor Inn

- 1615 New York Avenue N.E., Washington, D.C.; ☎ (202) 529-3900

This is your basic motor lodge, plain and simple. A single room is $60 and a double room is $70. The amenities are few but the place is clean and the price is right. If you're looking for an un-fancy, inexpensive place to stay for a few nights, and you won't miss a pool or a workout area or an on-premises restaurant (hey, there are lots of great places to eat nearby), this just might be the spot for you.

The Carlyle Suites

- 1731 New Hampshire Avenue N.W., Washington, D.C.; ☎ (202) 234-3200 or ☎ (800) 964-5377

- ✎ www.carlylesuites.com

From the chic lobby to the comfortable, elegant suites upstairs, a classy, art deco style pervades the Carlyle Suites. In fact, the Carlyle is billed as "Washington's Art Deco Hotel." But don't be put off by the nickname or the luxurious looks. Prices here aren't fancy. The rack rate for a basic suite, complete with kitchenette, TV, and air conditioning, starts at $189 per night, and rooms can occasionally be had

for as little as $89. If you're
staying for several weeks or arrive
during off-peak season, even
better bargains sometimes can
be negotiated.

For your convenience, the Carlyle has coin-operated laundry
machines, and a turn-down service
for extra pampering. The Carlyle's
quiet neighborhood is lined mainly
with townhouses, and yet it's only
about two blocks away from
Dupont Circle. Affordable fine
dining is available right in the
hotel; the Neon Cafe serves up traditional American favorites with
artistic flair.

Days Inn

- 2700 New York Avenue N.E.,
  Washington, D.C.;
  ✆ (202) 832-5800

- ✍ www.daysinn.com

There are two Days Inns in D.C.
This one is less expensive, which,
of course, appeals to Mr. C.

That doesn't mean a room here
is cheap; the official rate is right at
Mr. C's limit. A single is $95.90
and a double is $99.90 per night.
While some rooms have coffee
makers, others do not. If you are a
business traveler, be advised that
the Internet connection you may
need is made by disconnecting the
phone in your room. You can get
an ironing board from the desk, if
you leave a $20 deposit.

Still, when you stay here, you
are staying at a brand-name hotel
but paying a downscale price.
There's a nice gift shop, and
Sammy's, a Chinese-American
restaurant, is on premises. You can
sign-up at the gift shop for a bus
tour of the city and catch the bus
right outside the front door. Good
service is standard at this national
chain, so that shouldn't be a
problem. And no other hotel of this
quality is priced this low.

Highlander

- 3336 Wilson Boulevard,
  Arlington, VA; ✆ (703) 524-
  4300 or ✆ (800) 786-4301

- ✍ www.highlandermotel.com

The Highlander is your standard-
issue economy motel, with plainly
decorated rooms and low prices.
However, its dark-brown carpeted
spaces are quite large, and each one
contains two double beds. The 46
rooms also feature other motel
basics, like air conditioning, TV
(with HBO), phone, and private
bath. Free parking and complimentary coffee and doughnuts make for
even more savings and convenience.

The Highlander is located about
two blocks away from the Virginia
Square Metro. The corridors are
located outside of the building,
which may not be comfortable for
everybody, although this is a fairly
residential area. The prices sure are
cozy: singles and doubles run
$74.95 during the warmer months,
down to as low as $64.95 during
the off-season. There is a $5 charge
for each person after the first two,
although children under 13 can stay
for free with their parents.

Hotel Harrington

- 436 11th Street N.W., Washington, D.C.; ✆ (202) 628-8140
  or ✆ (800) 424-8532

- ✍ www.hotel-harrington.com

Though it can be difficult to find
inexpensive hotels in the heart of
downtown, Mr. C found one. The
neighborhood has seen better
times, but Hotel Harrington is quite
nice inside. It's located just two
blocks away from the Metro Center
station and its rates are certainly
economical.

The building was constructed
around 1906, but renovations are
constantly going on. That doesn't

mean you'll be hearing hammering—ask for a rebate if you do. It *does* mean that you can request a recently renovated, freshly decorated room. These newly spruced-up rooms are lovely and bright and a bit larger than the old rooms. Some come with sofa beds. The older rooms, although somewhat cramped, are still convenient. They too have a phone, desk, and TV on hand. Refrigerators can be requested ahead of time, and there are coin-operated laundry facilities on the premises as well.

Families will find spacious accommodations here. The family suite is spread over two compact rooms, with a double bed in one and three twins in the other. There are two TVs, two full baths, two desks, and several chairs. Prices begin at $139 for these rooms, while singles are $85 and doubles are $99. Extended-stay arrangements feature lowered rates.

Howard Johnson's Express Hotel

- 600 New York Avenue N.E., Washington, D.C.; ✆ (202) 546-9200 or ✆ (800) 446-4656

- ✑ www.hojo.com

Mr. C is a no-frills kind of guy, so this joint is perfect for him—and there's plenty of "no" in the no-frills here: no restaurant, no workout area, no swimming pool, and no laundry facilities. You know, *no-frills!*

This 53-room facility is a clean, convenient place to stay if you're looking for a low-price, nice room and not much more. Prices vary according to time of year. In the spring, peak season and a time when rates are at their highest, a single room is $69.95 a night and a double is $79.95. There are no

family rooms, so this place is mostly for singles and couples who are budgeting. In other words, this is the spot for folks like The Cheapster, whose cheapnik thrills don't require . . . uh . . . frills.

The Bethesda Court Hotel

- 7740 Wisconsin Avenue, Bethesda, MD; ✆ (301) 656-2100 or ✆ (800) 874-0050

- ✑ www.tbchotels.com

This newly renovated 75-room hotel sits on the site of what used to be the Manor Inn, and though it's a bit pricey for a committed cheapster, it's a great place to stay nonetheless.

Rooms run from $119 to $179 a night depending on the time of year, but the charge always includes a continental breakfast and an English tea in the afternoon, and every room has an ironing board, blow-dryer, and coffee maker. There's no restaurant here, but there is a workout facility, and there's a coin-operated laundry on the premises as well. You want cheap, this is not the place, but you want shiny, new, and comfortable at a manageable price, come to the Bethesda.

State Plaza Hotel

- 2117 E Street N.W., Washington, D.C.; ✆ (202) 861-8200 or ✆ (800) 424-2859

- ✑ www.stateplaza.com

Roll out the red carpet: The State Plaza is among the ritziest of Mr. C's suggestions and thus a bit pricier, but you'll still save a bundle compared to other upscale hotels. Rooms are bright and spacious, with two queen-size beds, and a large, fully equipped kitchen. All your hotel basics are included, like daily maid service, air conditioning, TV, and phone. Extra perks include a free copy of the *Washington Post* at your door every morning.

A friendly staff goes out of its way to be helpful. Why, between the Garden Cafe bistro, coin-operated laundry, and exercise facilities on the premises, you'll never even have to leave!

Considering how much you get, the prices are quite reasonable. The basic stateroom suite is $165 for a single or double room. Ask about weekend and seasonal specials, and long-term stay discounts. The hotel is about four blocks away from the Foggy Bottom Metro station.

The Virginian

- 1500 Arlington Boulevard, Arlington, VA; ✆ (703) 522-9600 or ✆ (800) 275-2866

- ✑ www.virginiansuites.com

Conveniently located in Arlington, The Virginian claims to have "all the comforts of home at a very comfortable price"—and they manage to pull it off. Single rooms run as low as $109 on weekends and $129 on weekdays and doubles $129 on the weekend and $149 on weekdays. Monthly rates come even cheaper, and the amenities may have you thinking about staying that long.

Every room includes a fully equipped kitchen and cable TV with HBO. There's shuttle service to the Rosslyn Metro (barely a 10-minute walk away, in any case), as well as a coin-operated laundry, exercise facilities, sauna, and an outdoor swimming pool. That Metro stop is just across the river from downtown D.C. Call for advance reservations. Deals like this are snapped up fast, even in a 262-suite building.

ALTERNATIVE LODGING

Any Cheapster worth his discounted salt knows that you can usually find some great deals by straying from the mainstream, and lodgings are no exception. B&Bs, hostels, smaller independent inns—all offer a range of accommodations at reasonable prices.

Bed and Breakfast Accommodations, Ltd.

- P.O. Box 12011, Washington, D.C.; ✆ (202) 328-3510

- ✑ www.bedandbreakfastdc.com

Not a place to stay, but rather a reservation service, BBA can make arrangements for you in dozens of B & Bs around the area. And you may be surprised to discover the diversity of such lodgings. Sometimes it'll be a small private home, where you'll come down to breakfast each morning and compare sightseeing notes with a handful of

fellow tourists, other times an inn, with more rooms and amenities.

Off-season rates for rooms in some private homes range from $55 to $65 a day. Peak rates are still fine at $65 to $75. In general, inn rates fluctuate tremendously but are an average of $125 to $165 a day. The roster of options is always growing. When you call the agency, they'll describe each setting in detail, and make all the arrangements for you. You can also get the information on the Web site and see a picture of the inn or room as well. BBA is open Monday through Friday from 10 a.m. to 5 p.m.

The Bed and Breakfast League/Sweet Dreams and Toast

- P.O. Box 9490, Washington, D.C.; ✆ (202) 363 7767

Another good source for B & B info, and yes, that's their real name. Office hours are Monday through Thursday from 9 a.m. to 5 p.m., and Friday from 9 a.m. to 1 p.m.

Brickskeller Inn

- 1523 22nd Street N.W., Washington, D.C.; ✆ (202) 293-1885

- ✑ www.brickskeller.com

The Brickskeller has been family owned and operated since 1957, as has the famous cellar pub of the same name. (Hey, it's not bad to have an inn located directly above a bar that serves over 800 kinds of beer, as long as your room isn't *directly* above the bar.) During the spring, the rooms tend to get filled up, so make your plans to stay well in advance. Reservations can be made.

Renovations during 1995 left the small, European-style rooms carpeted and freshly painted. Large common rooms have televisions. Maids circulate daily. For security reasons, only guests are allowed upstairs—visitors will just have to be met in the pub. The Brickskeller is a few blocks west of the Dupont Circle Metro stop.

The following rates include taxes and are still remarkably low. Singles begin at $54; doubles, $73. All the rooms have shared baths. More economical weekly rates are also available. There are 40 rooms, so even without reservations (except during peak tourist season), you shouldn't be forced to sleep in the park.

The Embassy Inn

- 1627 16th Street N.W., Washington, D.C.; ✆ (202) 234-7800 or ✆ (800) 423-9111

- ✑ www.vacationspot.com

Affiliated with the nearby Windsor Inn (see the listing below), the 38-room Embassy Inn caters primarily to individual travelers and couples. The small rooms are beautifully decorated in a simple, Federalist style, and with only a double bed, sink, TV, bureau, and chair, there's little space for anything else. But c'mon, chances are you're going to be out all day and just need the room for sleeping, and the beds are quite comfy. Each room comes with a private bath, air conditioning, and phone.

Also for your convenience and comfort, complimentary continental breakfast and an evening glass of sherry (!) are available in the lobby. Single rooms range between $89 and $109, while doubles are $99 to $119. Rates go up during peak season.

Hosteling International/ American Youth Hostel

- 1009 11th Street N.W., Washington, D.C.; ✆ (202) 737-2333

- ✑ www.hiwashingtondc.org

As hostels go, this one offers more than most in the way of entertainment. Not only are movies shown nightly, but residents (many of whom are Cap Hill interns) organize frequent trips. With your hosteling companions, you may attend a piano concert at the National Gallery of Art, take a guided tour of the Pentagon, or participate in such seasonal activities as Alexandria's Scottish Christmas Walk. Other extras include laundry facilities, daily housekeeping service, air conditioning in every room, and a common kitchen.

Now, unless you are an intern and have made prior arrangements for a long-term stay, there is a 14-day limit per six-month period. The single-sex dorms have 8–12 bunks apiece. There are also five smaller "quad rooms," which hold just four people. You and three friends may qualify to stay in these more private dwellings.

The cost is a mere $26 per night for AYH members, and $29 for non-members. Quad rooms are semiprivate and run from $28 a night for members to $33 for non-members (with reservations.) The Metro Center station is just three blocks away. This place is so cheap that for the right sort of lodger it is invaluable.

Kalorama Guest House

- 1854-64 Mintwood Place N.W., Washington, D.C.; ✆ (202) 667-6369

- 2700 Cathedral Avenue N.W., Washington, D.C.; ✆ (202) 328-0960

- ✑ www.bestinns.net/usa/dc/kghkp.html

In the heart of trendy Adams Morgan, near the Woodley Park-Zoo Metro, you'll find this collection of Victorian brownstones turned into guesthouses. Kalorama is widely known among budget travelers for being spotless, cozy, and well appointed; all of the rooms are air conditioned (a blessing in summer) and lavishly furnished with antiques and turn-of-the-century decor.

Guests get a free continental breakfast and a glass of sherry or lemonade in the evening. Common facilities include living rooms with fireplaces, outdoor gardens and patios, laundry machines, and

public telephones with free local calling. The rooms themselves can be rather small, but when they start at $45 a night, with all those amenities, who's complaining? You can, of course, find larger rooms, including some with private bath, but even these start around just $70 a night. (Some parking is available, at a $7 fee.) Not bad at all.

Needless to say, at these rates, the Kalorama is frequently filled up. Mr. C does recommend calling as far in advance as you can.

Tabard Inn

- 1739 N Street N.W., Washington, D.C.; ✆ (202) 785-1277

- ✑ www.tabardinn.com

The Tabard Inn (Chaucer fans will immediately recognize the name) offers comfortable lodgings at reasonable rates. All of its rooms are furnished with air conditioning and a phone, but alas, no TV (hey, with so much to do in this town, who needs it?). A complimentary continental breakfast is available every morning in the lobby.

The inn is located on a quiet side street, about two blocks away from the Dupont Circle Metro. Prices remain fairly consistent throughout the year. With a shared bath, singles range from $77 to $105; doubles, $100 to $120. Private bath rates are quite a bit higher, but still worth a mention: Singles are between $105 and $165, and doubles are $125 to $180.

Thompson-Markward Hall

- 235 Second Street N.E., Washington, D.C.; ✆ (202) 546-3255

The Young Woman's Christian Home was established over a century ago to house and care for young women who came to live and work in Washington. This tradition continues in Thompson-Markward Hall, the "new facility," dedicated by Eleanor Roosevelt in 1933. TMH is a simple, elegant dormitory for women ages 18 to 34 who will be staying between two weeks and two years.

Don't be scared off by the rules, strictly enforced to insure the safety and well-being of the 120 residents. Men, for example, are only allowed in the public areas; no drugs or alcohol are permitted on the premises (smoking is allowed outside in the garden); and no electrical appliances can be used in the rooms—microwaves, refrigerators, and hot plates, that sort of thing. Not so bad.

One of the best features here is the TMH meal plan. Yes folks, included in the price of your room are breakfast and dinner Mondays through Saturdays, and brunch on Sundays. If you're running late at work or have an evening class, just let the front desk know by 4 p.m. and they'll even set aside a dinner for you, just like Mom would. Also for your convenience, a coin-op laundry is on the first floor and maids clean the rooms at least

twice each month. A piano is available for your entertainment in the beautiful, spacious common room and there is a TV in the basement.

Thompson-Markward is located in a safe area on Capitol Hill. Union Station is about three blocks away. The single rooms are small, but they are outfitted with air conditioning and a phone. Mr. C was told that $220 covers room and board for 10 days, $330 for 15 days, and $650 for a month. Call well ahead for reservations.

The Windsor Inn

- 1842 16th Street N.W., Washington, D.C.; ✆ (202) 667-0300 or ✆ (800) 423-9111

- ✐ www.vacationspot.com

Affiliated with the Embassy Inn (see above), located down the street, the Windsor Inn specializes in providing lodging for families or groups. Its 46 simply decorated rooms are compact, even the suites; but all come with a private bath, TV, air conditioning, and a phone. Some rooms have a refrigerator, too.

While somewhat spartan, the Windsor is pleasant and does have its fair share of perks. A daily housekeeping service keeps the entire place spotless, and a complimentary continental breakfast and evening glass of sherry ensure a relaxing start and finish to your day. Daily rates range between $79 and $99 for a single, $99 and $139 for a double, and $139 and $189 for a suite.

The Woodley Park Guest House

- 2647 Woodley Road, Washington, D.C.; ✆ (202) 667-0218

- ✐ www.woodleyparkguesthouse.com

If you are old enough to remember the '70s, and you have a taste for tacky, retro decorative motifs, then perhaps you will miss the former occupant of this site, the Connecticut-Woodley Guest House. The funky, Brady Bunch look of that now-departed establishment has been replaced by elegance and a cool, grown-up restraint. The result is a wonderful and surprisingly inexpensive place to stay while you're in D.C.

After extensive inside and outside renovation, this new hotel, renamed the Woodley Park, opened in September of 2001 with new policies: no TV or radio on the premises, no more than two people to a room, no children under 12 admitted, and no shag carpeting. The result is a premeditated quiet that will appeal to anyone who is past Brady watching age.

Whether you are in Washington to look for a house or apartment, or to attend a graduation, or simply to take in the sights, a few days here (two weeks is the maximum anyone may stay) will soothe the most agitated soul. There are, alas, just 16 rooms in the house, so make your plans early.

Room rates are soothing, too: Single rooms with shared bath are $50 a night, $90 to $130 with a private bath, and double rooms are $80 with shared bath and up to $160 with private bath. A continental "plus" breakfast (cereal, pastries, fruit, biscotti, etc.) comes with the room. Parking is in short supply and costs $10 a night, but the money you save on the rest of the deal makes up for that.

The neighborhood is very safe and the Metro is 300 feet from the hotel. You need to scratch your nostalgia itch? Catch the Bradys on cable. You need a good place to stay while in Washington? Try the Woodley Park.

YWCA

- 901 Rhode Island Avenue N.W., Washington, D.C.;
  ℰ (202) 667-9100

The YWCA is inexpensive, very secure, and its neighborhood is much improved. The renovations in the area make this a much nicer place to spend the night.

All of the rooms are singles, and only women are allowed to stay here. Frills are limited. Most lodgers share the dorm-style bathrooms. There's a common kitchen available, and laundry facilities, but no services. As for security, the doors are locked at midnight, so if you're going to be out later, you'll need to make arrangements with the house director. Buses stop right in front of the Y, and the Shaw-Howard University Metro stop is just a couple of blocks away.

For more privacy, the Y also offers efficiency apartments. Though more expensive, these rooms are larger and have private baths, stovetops, and other amenities.

Maybe the accommodations are not exactly deluxe; the low prices make these concessions worthwhile, and you can stay indefinitely. The rate is just $57 a night or $350 a month, $400 with half-bath. Efficiency apartments run from $450 to $590 a month.

Alphabetical Index

Subject Index

About the Author

Corey Sandler is the author of more than 150 books on consumer issues, travel, business, and computers. Among his bestsellers: the *Econoguide Travel Book* series (Globe Pequot Press), *Buy More Pay Less* (Prentice Hall Direct), and *Fix Your Own PC* (John Wiley). Sandler is a former correspondent for the Associated Press and a newsman for Gannett Newspapers. He was also editor-in-chief of *Digital News* and executive editor of *PC Magazine*.

THE *MR. CHEAP'S*® SERIES:

Today's consumers aren't cheap . . . but we all know the importance of a bargain—and the thrill of the hunt for getting quality at a good price. From neighborhood shops to outlet centers, from cheap bites to fancy dinners, from free activities to high quality lodging for a low price, *Mr. Cheap's*® offers all the information to find it and get it.

Also Available in the Series:

1-58062-692-0
$9.95

1-55850-556-3
$9.95

1-58062-374-3
$9.95

1-58062-271-2
$9.95

1-55850-388-9
$8.95

1-55850-445-1
$9.95